John Barleycorn
Must Pay

Paul A. LeBel

# John Barleycorn Must Pay

*Compensating the Victims of Drinking Drivers*

UNIVERSITY OF ILLINOIS PRESS
*Urbana and Chicago*

Library of Congress Cataloging-in-Publication Data

LeBel, Paul A., 1949-
    John Barleycorn must pay : compensating the victims of
drinking drivers / Paul A. LeBel.
        p.     cm.
    Includes index.
    ISBN 0-252-01792-7
    1. Liability for traffic accidents—United States.   2. Drunk
driving—United States.   3. Reparation—Unites States.   4. Victims
of crimes—Legal status, laws, etc.—United States.   I. Title.
KF1290.ABL38   1991
346.7303′22—dc20
[347.306322]                                              91-8268
                                                              CIP

*To Cindy and Lisa,*
*for being there*
*and*
*for being them.*

# Contents

# Preface

This study began in the summer of 1987 as a law review article, and it quickly grew beyond the limits that any law review editor could be expected to publish. As the project turned from a law review article into a book, the nature of the intended audience underwent a transformation as well. I have tried to strike a balance that serves readers who have formal legal training and readers who do not. The former will undoubtedly find some of the explanations of basic concepts too simple. While the book is addressed to a general readership of people who are concerned about the drinking-driver problem in contemporary society, I hope that it contains enough that is new and interesting to reward the attention of even the experts in tort law and accident compensation.

In part 1, I examine a number of the major options available under current tort law to shift drinking-driver accident losses from the injured party to either the drinking driver or some third party. I identify the principal shortcomings of each option, and I present a detailed overview of the policy considerations that underlie the adoption or the rejection of these various options. The remainder of the book then draws on part 1's critical examination of the existing legal landscape to determine what features ought to be present in an accident loss allocation scheme with a more ambitious and better integrated set of goals than those that are possible to achieve under the current system of tort law theories that are used to deal with drinking-driver traffic accidents.

Part 2 presents a fairly lengthy explanation of the economics of drinking-driver accident costs, beginning with the first principles of economic analysis of liability rules, proceeding through an application of those principles to the various options that were examined in part 1, and concluding with a justification for the move beyond the existing tort law options to a new administrative compensation system. In part 3, I identify the major issues surrounding the development of such a system. Among the topics I look at are the assignment of accident costs to particular actors and activities, the determination of appropriate levels of compensation for injury, the creation of an efficient administrative structure for processing claims for compensation, and the constraints on public policy reform that are posed by the need for obtaining legislative action in order to implement a reform proposal. I offer specific suggestions for each of those topics as part of my proposal for an Alcohol-Related Accident Victim Compensation Fund. Under the terms of this proposal, the most seriously injured victims of drinking-driver traffic accidents would have a major share of their otherwise uncompensated accident losses paid from a compensation fund that would be financed by a new tax imposed on the alcohol industry. Finally, in part 4, I address the policy rationales behind the proposal's provisions that are necessary to gain the support of legislators and the public. In chapter 15, I provide model legislation that could serve as a prototype for legislatures interested in creating such a fund and demonstrate how the compensation fund would operate.

I use both real and hypothetical cases in this book to illustrate my points about the inadequacy of the legal remedies that are currently available for victims of drinking-driver traffic accidents. The facts of the real cases are derived from the official reports of the judicial opinions cited in the notes and from the cited articles in legal periodicals. The hypothetical cases are purely my invention and have absolutely no reference to actual individuals or events.

# Acknowledgments

The outstanding research assistance provided during the summer of 1988 by John L. Ehrler, William and Mary law school class of 1990, made the prospect of expanding this work into a book much less forbidding than it otherwise would have been. The research that was performed by Mark Mullins, of the class of 1987, was valuable at the earliest stages of the project. Throughout the work on this book, the assistance of James Heller and the law library staff of William and Mary was superb. I am particularly appreciative of the efforts of Brenda Frank and Joan Pearlstein, who seemed to have material in my hands almost as soon as I thought about asking for it.

I am also grateful for the comments and insights of my present and former colleagues Trotter Hardy, Jerome Hoffman, Charles Koch, Elmer Schaefer, Elaine Shoben, Rodney Smolla, Michael Wells, and Martin Zelder, who read portions of the book in earlier drafts or commented on various ideas as they were being developed later on in the project. My interest in the subject was both sparked and sustained by the experience of teaching the first-year course in torts to four classes at the University of Alabama and seven classes at William and Mary. The contribution of those students to the development of my thinking about tort law is immense, particularly those at Alabama who were so generous, supportive, and encouraging in my first years of teaching.

Professor Jeffrey O'Connell read the entire manuscript and was extremely generous in providing encouragement and suggestions for improving the book. While not all of those suggestions were followed, the substance of the proposal that appears in this book nevertheless reflects the care with which a busy and prolific scholar was willing to read and comment on a lengthy manuscript. All of us who teach and write in the field of accident loss compensation are of course indebted to the work of Professor O'Connell, but I am particularly grateful for the support that he provided to me in the completion of this project.

The enthusiasm with which this book was received and the care with which it has been treated by the University of Illinois Press have been a source of great comfort. My special gratitude goes to Beth Bower, whose herculean efforts in editing the manuscript were enormously helpful in making this a much more readable book.

A number of people took considerable time and effort to provide me with information that was helpful in the latter stages of this project. James T. Wakefield, George Plunkett, and Lisa Lewis of the Virginia Department of Alcoholic Beverage Control provided useful information about the assessment and collection mechanisms for state excise taxes on alcohol. Philip C. Katz, of the Beer Institute, was generous in supplying copies of studies that had been submitted by that organization to the Surgeon General's Workshop on Drunk Driving. The public information departments of the Surgeon General's office, the National Highway Traffic Safety Administration, and the Centers for Disease Control routinely responded promptly and helpfully to requests for documents.

As work on this book was completed, the students of the William and Mary law school class of 1990 had just completed their legal education and were preparing to embark on careers that offer challenge and excitement. As my friend and former colleague at Alabama Charles Trost would say, they have a chance both to do good and to do well. The roll of that law school class at graduation was, however, two members short. In the summer before they were to begin their third year of law school, Laurie Patarini and Jonathan Hudson were involved in a collision with a drinking driver. Laurie was killed and Jon was seriously injured. The tragedy of this accident affected all of us at William and Mary who have been fortunate to be their teachers, fellow students, and friends. The memory of the loss that was suffered on that day will undoubtedly continue to inspire efforts to attack the needless waste caused by drinking and driving.

Work on this book was supported in part by summer research grants from the College of William and Mary Committee on Faculty Research and from the Law School Foundation of the Marshall-Wythe School of Law, College of William and Mary. A semester research leave from the college came at an opportune time, providing an interval from teaching and normal committee work for virtually undivided attention to the completion of the manuscript.

For the last eight years, I have been privileged to work in a professional environment that both encourages and supports scholarly efforts. For that I thank my colleagues at William and Mary, particularly those who participated in the faculty colloquium at which I was able to present some of the ideas in this book at a time when their constructive critique was extremely helpful. The quality of the working environment at William and Mary is especially attributable to the efforts of Timothy J. Sullivan, dean of the law school for the last six years, whose generosity, integrity, and decency have provided a model of principled and humane administration. Finally I would like to note that a university's commitment to serious scholarship and the highest quality education can benefit enormously from support by the individuals who hold the top administrative posts. Those of us who teach at the College of William and Mary are fortunate to have the benefit of the leadership of President Paul Verkuil and Provost Melvyn Schiavelli.

Even such a supportive professional environment as the one at William and Mary would have been substantially less than satisfactory had it not been for the love and, above all, the patience of the most special people in my life, my wife, Cindy, and my daughter, Lisa. By the time this book was nearing completion, they had become quite good at harmonizing their "Not as much as we do" reply to my recurrent whining about how much I wished the book was finished. A great deal more than just this book is dedicated to them.

John Barleycorn
Must Pay

# 1

## Perspectives on the Drinking-Driver Accident

A traffic accident involving a drinking driver can happen in less time than it takes to read about it. A serious accident of this sort happens in the United States on an average of every twenty minutes. Tens of thousands of people die each year in these accidents. Nearly half a million more suffer serious injuries.

These figures are just numbers to many of us, perhaps because we are confronted with so many other overwhelming numbers such as figures on drug use and poverty, defense spending, budget deficits, and savings and loan bailouts. Others of us know someone who has been involved in an accident of this sort, either a drinking driver or a victim. To bring home what all of this really means, it might be helpful to look behind the numbers and consider a hypothetical but typical accident.

*The Bloom family—Alan, Molly, Billy, and Sally—were on their way home after spending a late summer day at the beach. Alan was driving and Molly was riding in the front passenger seat. The children, Billy and Sally, were seated in the back of the car. Billy was staring out the window at the scenery on the right side, thinking whatever five-year-olds think on their way home from the beach. Eighteen-month-old Sally was asleep in her car seat. Molly was wondering whether they ought to stop at a drug store and pick up something to put on Sally's sunburned shoulders in case they were going to be as sore as they looked. This had been Sally's first time at the beach, and she had been a lot quicker to burn than Molly had expected.*

*The speed limit was fifty-five on this stretch of the road, but Alan was only doing a little under fifty. He seldom drove at fifty-five here because the road was only two lanes wide and had a lot of blind curves. The only traffic he could see was a truck coming toward him that was just appearing around a curve up ahead. That truck was about a hundred yards away when suddenly a car pulled out from behind it and occupied all of Alan's lane. Before Alan could apply the brakes or turn the steering wheel, the two cars collided.*

*Alan was killed instantly in the collision. Molly and both of the children suffered serious physical injuries — broken bones, internal injuries, and concussions. Billy was in a coma for a couple of weeks, and the latest medical prognosis is that he will have a permanent learning disability as a result of the head injury that he suffered. The force of the impact twisted the Bloom car into an almost unrecognizable shape. The car was so mangled that Sally was trapped in her car seat for nearly half an hour before the rescue squad and the paramedics could work their way into what had been the back seat. During much of that time, she was awake and screaming in pain and terror. In addition to the lingering effects of the physical injuries she suffered in the accident, Sally continues to have frightening nightmares, and she often becomes terrified while riding in a car.*

*Alan had made out a will leaving everything to Molly, but it may not be enough for the family to keep its old standard of living. The last time Molly had worked full-time was just before Billy was born, and she had just started putting in a regular volunteer shift at the local public library three mornings a week while Sally went to her play group. Now Molly would have to think seriously about finding a well-paying job and see about arranging extended day care for the children.*

*Life hadn't been perfect for the Blooms before the accident. They had certainly had their share of worries and frustrations. But this . . .*

*What really made Molly furious was what she learned from reading the police report on the accident. The driver of the car that hit the Blooms, Tommy Smith, had been only slightly injured in the crash. A police officer at the scene had said she thought it was a miracle that Smith had survived the accident, let alone that he had come through it virtually unharmed. One of the emergency medical teams that responded to the accident took Smith to the trauma center at the nearest hospital so that he could be examined for more serious injuries. As Smith had been helped from his car, a police officer had noticed that beer had spilled onto Smith's clothes, that his breath smelled of beer, and that both empty and unopened cans of beer were in the front of the car. Because of this evidence, the state trooper in charge of the accident investigation had ordered a blood alcohol test to be done on Smith when he arrived at the hospital. The test showed that the level of his blood alcohol concentration was nearly two times the legal standard that constituted driving while intoxicated in that state.*

*The driver of the truck that Smith had been following had stopped after the collision. He told the state troopers that he had seen Smith's car coming up behind him and that it had been trying to pass him for a couple of miles, even though the road was winding and was marked with a double yellow line down the center for that entire distance. The car had repeatedly been crossing the center line and pulling back and had also been weaving off onto the right shoulder of the highway. The truck driver said that there was nothing he could do when he saw the Bloom car approaching. He never would have thought that anyone would try to pass in a location like that.*

*John Barleycorn Must Pay* has a dual purpose. Roughly the first half of the book presents a critical analysis of the legal remedies that are currently available to compensate the victims of drinking-driver traffic accidents. The remainder of the book develops in considerable detail a reform measure that will have two beneficial effects: it will provide more complete compensation for the more seriously injured victims of drinking drivers, and it will cause the alcoholic beverage industry to absorb—and presumably pass on to consumers—a greater share of the accident costs that are attributable to its products than is currently the case under existing law.

The story of the Bloom family is fictional, but the facts it portrays are not unusual. Alcohol consumption plays a role in a substantial number of traffic accidents that result in serious personal injury or damage to property.[1] Recent figures indicate, for example, that as many as one-third of the drivers who are involved in fatal traffic accidents are drinking drivers.[2] Of the more than 46,000 people who were killed in traffic accidents in 1987, 40 percent of them died in crashes in which at least one of the individuals involved was intoxicated.[3] Whether one looks at the number of drinking drivers connected with fatal accidents or at the number of people who die in those accidents, it is clear that alcohol is involved in a significant proportion of the carnage that occurs on our highways.

A traffic accident in which someone is killed or seriously injured by an alcohol-impaired or intoxicated driver—a drinking driver[4]—touches many members of society in a number of different ways. The primary focus of this book is on what happens to the people who are injured in those accidents and to the survivors of those who die in them. Thus a major concern is how our legal system imposes liability for the losses suffered in drinking-driver traffic accidents and how it distributes the cost of those accidents. Drinking-driver accident costs are primarily distributed among the accident victims, the drinking drivers who cause the accidents, the third parties who are related in some way to the accidents, and members of society at large. The book ends with a specific proposal for a better way of allocating the costs of the most serious injuries suffered in these accidents. Along the way, some more general observations are made about the nature and the effectiveness of tort law in contemporary society—the body of law that is primarily concerned with the recovery of damages for harm caused by wrongful conduct.

Although drinking drivers sometimes cause death or serious injury to themselves, I have chosen to focus on the injuries they cause to others and the compensation problems that result. Studying how our society deals with the innocent victims of a widespread activity such as drinking and driving offers an insight into society's general practice regarding injury compensation and the potential for reform. In 1987 almost seven thousand of the people who were killed in alcohol-related traffic accidents were not themselves alcohol-impaired at the time.[5] The number of nondrinking victims who are injured but not killed in these accidents is difficult even to estimate, but it is surely many times the number of fatalities. Understanding the nature of the legal and public policy problems surrounding the plight of the victims of the drinking driver and then devising a solution require a detailed consideration of what our legal system and what we as a society currently do to soften the impact of the most harmful consequences of drinking-driver traffic accidents.

## Different Perspectives on a Social Problem

Both the legal consequences and the practical effects of a traffic accident in which a drinking driver causes death or serious injury to another person can be viewed from a number of different perspectives. The particular public policy concerns of tort lawyers and scholars will be better understood if their perspective is compared to some others.[6]

*The Perspective of the Victims and of Society.* Those who are most closely related to the victim of an alcohol-related traffic accident feel grief and outrage. Any serious accident is likely to produce loss and regret, but a drinking-driver accident provokes an additional element of personal and societal anger at the fact that unnecessary and unacceptable behavior has contributed to the injury and loss. The author of a recent newsmagazine article detects a similarity in the way the public's perception of both drunk driving and pollution has shifted. Both are "now seen as fundamentally disgraceful and bespeaking lack of character, as opposed to just mistakes."[7]

The concern and the outrage of those who are closest to the individual victims of drinking drivers have been an important impetus for institutional reform efforts. The last decade's growth in the size and influence of such groups as Mothers Against Drunk Driving (MADD) and Students Against Drunk Driving (SADD) may reflect the emergence of a more sustained community feeling that current attitudes toward drinking and driving, a social practice that is still fairly ubiquitous, are inadequate. This growth also indicates an increasing level of public frustration with weak and ineffective official actions to control and punish drinking and driving. Citizens' interest groups have often played a significant role in raising the public's awareness of the seriousness of the problem and in lobbying for new legislation such as laws that lower the standards for defining drinking-and-driving offenses and laws imposing more stringent sanctions on offenders. Citizens' groups have also been active in regularly monitoring courtrooms to see whether and how existing laws are being applied.[8]

During the early days of trench warfare in World War I, the British War Office referred to casualties from shellfire in relatively quiet sectors of the front as "normal wastage."[9] Today, when public attention is likely to skip around from topic to topic depending on what the most influential members of the news media decide is the crisis of the day, carefully focused and sustained efforts to keep the problems caused by drinking drivers near the forefront of public consciousness are needed if the victims of drinking-driver traffic accidents are not to be considered the "normal wastage" of our contemporary lifestyles, which so easily mix alcohol and automobiles.

*The Drinking Driver's Perspective.* Drinking drivers responsible for causing a traffic accident may well feel more remorse than their nondrinking counterparts because they must face the knowledge that their consumption of alcohol contributed to the accident. It is a common and natural reaction for people to inquire about whose fault was responsible for an accident, but this question is much easier to ask than it is to answer. Personal responsibility is a complex issue. It is not easy to reconstruct and evaluate actions that occurred in an instant of time or to identify and distinguish the multiple and overlapping causal precursors to an accident. The general difficulties of administering our automobile accident compensation system, which is based mainly on proving fault, have prompted a number of states to move to a no-fault system of automobile insurance.[10]

It is also human nature to try to blame others for the results of our own misbehavior. In the popular understanding, the term "accident" may subtly imply that an event was impossible to avoid or that we should not attach a great deal of blame to it. After an accident in which serious injuries have occurred, however, the natural inclination to deny that one was at fault may be much more difficult for a drinking driver to indulge in than a nondrinking driver who would have been better able to avoid the accident. The drinking driver may have an increased sense of responsibility and guilt. In fact, after one recent drinking-driver case was litigated, the intoxicated driver committed suicide.[11] Short of producing that extreme reaction, an alcohol-related accident may leave lasting psychological scars on the drinking driver, who has to live with the knowledge that purely self-indulgent behavior contributed to a disastrous result that may have been preventable.

However natural that reaction of guilt and regret might be, it is not the only attitude displayed by drinking drivers who cause serious harm. The frequency with which drivers charged with driving under the influence of alcohol (DUI) are discovered to be multiple offenders is disturbing, and it suggests that at least some percentage of the driving population is relatively indifferent to the consequences of drinking and driving. The United States Department of Justice reports that nearly half of the people who are jailed for driving while intoxicated (DWI) have had a previous DWI conviction.[12] Although the primary focus of this book is on accident victim compensation, the legal system would benefit from both a heightened enforcement of DWI laws and a more vigorous application of criminal penalties for their violation. Those options would seem to offer the best chance of changing the behavior of these repeat offenders, but, of all drivers, they are the least likely to be affected.[13] Better odds of affecting the behavior of drivers are likely to be had with educational efforts promoting the responsible use of alcohol.[14] These efforts may be made within the family and through churches and civic organizations, and obviously they can also be included in school-run substance abuse programs and in high-school driver training courses.[15]

The less cynical observers of popular culture might even expect some good to come from the "responsible use" advertising campaigns recently introduced by several beer producers, the segment of the alcohol industry that does the most advertising on television. This new campaign sometimes sends very mixed signals, however. Consider what message is actually being communicated by an ad such as the one featuring the canine party animal named Spuds McKenzie that knows "when to say when." Still, it does seem that the brewing industry is at least becoming sufficiently concerned about its public image and its potential legal responsibility that it is beginning to try to change its customers' behavior for the better and thus reduce the risk of harm to human life and property posed by the consumption of its products.

*The Criminal Prosecutor's Perspective.* When a drinking-driver traffic accident occurs, the local prosecutor must make a legally complex, politically sensitive, and often emotionally charged evaluation of the case.[16] The prosecutor has substantial discretion in deciding whether to file criminal charges against the driver and in choosing what offenses to charge. Given the many demands on a prosecutor's limited time and financial resources, the criminal enforcement process for drinking-and-driving offenses can be very different in practice from the way it would appear to work on the books.

The discrepancy between the way the law should work and the way it is actually applied is widened even more by the effects of other factors such as mandatory sanctions that must be imposed for particular intoxicated driving offenses[17] and statutory presumptions and per se offenses that come into play depending on the driver's blood alcohol concentration (BAC).[18] Typically a statute will provide that a BAC above a certain level constitutes a per se offense, subjecting the violator to criminal or administrative sanctions, while a BAC within a lower range will raise a presumption that the driver was operating a vehicle while under the influence of alcohol.[19] A growing number of states require a minimum stay in jail upon even a first-time conviction for drinking and driving. Prosecutors who think that such measures are too harsh or unfair or that they represent too great an intrusion into the exercise of prosecutorial discretion can be reluctant to charge a drinking driver with the highest offense that the facts of a case would seem to warrant.

An additional consideration is that in many jurisdictions the chief criminal prosecutor is an elected official. As a result, this official's decisions on whether to prosecute a drinking-driver case and what offenses to charge can be significantly affected by the publicity associated with the case. A lot of public attention is frequently directed at the more serious accidents, whether because of the gravity of the offense (for example, a drinking driver colliding with a school bus)[20] or because of the driver's public status (as in the case of a political figure or an entertainer). High-visibility cases can tie a prosecutor's hands when the pressure of public opinion affects prosecutorial decision making. Nevertheless, these cases also represent an opportunity to educate the public about the scope of the drinking-driver problem and about the range of legal sanctions that are available to deal with it effectively. A public prosecutor needs to be sensitive to that educational function and to be conscious of what signals the office is sending by the way in which prosecutorial discretion is being exercised.

*The Public Health and Safety Perspective.* Various federal and state public health and transportation safety authorities have an interest in either the health or safety dimensions of the drinking-and-driving problem. In the first instance, drinking-driver accidents must be accounted for in their statistical studies of the relationship between alcohol and accidents. The United States Public Health Service, for example, included the reduction of alcohol misuse as one of the goals of its "1990 Health Objectives" project.[21] Similarly, the National Highway Traffic Safety Administration collects information on drinking-driver accidents for its annual reports on causal factors in traffic accidents and injuries.[22]

Under the leadership of C. Everett Koop in the 1980s, the office of the Surgeon General of the United States became an effective platform for widespread efforts to educate the public about significant threats to health. Highly publicized campaigns of the Koop administration, such as the one that emphasized the relationship between sexual practices and the spread of AIDS and the one that drew attention to the addictive quality of nicotine, focused media attention on health problems in a way that tried to break through the barriers to a full comprehension of this information. These barriers have been created by public complacency about issues that do not appear in the minds of many people to affect them personally; by the reluctance of bureaucrats to raise potentially embarrassing or discomforting topics; and by the determined, and frequently successful, efforts of skilled industry lobbyists trying to deny the existence of a problem or to downplay its magnitude. In December 1988, Surgeon General Koop assembled public officials from federal and state agencies and private individuals in a three-day workshop devoted to the problem of drinking and driving.[23] The recommendations that were issued at the conclusion of that meeting attempted to map out a strategy for coming to grips with the drinking-driver problem, and some of that strategy is reflected in the reform proposal I offer in this book.

*The Tort Law Perspective.* Finally, and of primary concern, is the perspective of the traffic accident victim and that victim's personal injury lawyer. Of all the perspectives on this problem, theirs is the one most concerned with questions of compensation for injury. At the most practical level, the tort law perspective focuses on whether the losses incurred in drinking-driver traffic accidents can be shifted away from the victim to someone else, and if so, to whom they ought to be shifted. Injury compensation problems present courts and legislatures, as well as other public policymakers and scholars, with complex questions about how best to identify an optimal scheme of loss allocation, how to measure that scheme's risk reduction effects, and how to put the scheme into operation.

*John Barleycorn Must Pay* uses a tort law perspective to look at the problem of compensating the victims of drinking-driver accidents on a number of levels. At the most basic level lies information about current routes to compensation, including a critical analysis of the tort law remedies now in place. Then I identify a set of goals that are not now being achieved very effectively but might be if some reform efforts were undertaken. I propose the creation of an alcohol-related accident victim compensation fund that would be financed by a new tax on alcoholic beverages at the wholesale level of distribution. The development of the specific details of the compensation fund proposal can be viewed as an experimental yet highly practical exercise in public policy-making in an age that is marked by limited resources and a glut of demands for the attention of policymakers.

### The Search for Adequate Injury Compensation for the Victims of Drinking Drivers

From the tort lawyer's perspective, the current methods of allocating accident victim's losses caused by drinking drivers are considerably less than satisfactory. In part 1 of this book I take a close and critical look at the tort law remedies currently available to the victims, beginning with legal action to establish the driver's liability. In cases involving the most substantial losses, the drinking driver's financial ability to compensate the victim is apt to stop well short of the amount actually required. The most important factor behind this phenomenon is that the liability limits of the drinking driver's automobile insurance policy are often quickly exhausted by large recoveries of damages.[24]

This danger that policy limits will be exhausted is particularly likely when there are multiple victims of a single accident. Automobile insurance policies typically set total liability limits for each accident at somewhere in the range of two or three times the policy limits of liability to each injured person, for example, as a maximum of $10,000 of liability to any one person or $25,000 of total liability for any single accident. Even if there are only two or three victims with roughly equal injuries, there is a good chance that the insurance fund available will not be distributed equally among them.[25] The insurance fund may be exhausted by those claimants who are fortunate enough to be the first to obtain a tort judgment against the insured, or it may be exhausted by those who have the most advantageous bargaining position during settlement negotiations. For a number of reasons, then, the victim may face the prospect of a depleted insurance fund by the time a court judgment is obtained against the driver.

The undercompensation problem is aggravated by the fact that a significant proportion of the driver's other assets besides insurance may be protected, at least to some extent, from the enforcement of any tort judgment that might be obtained against the driver. Thus the single most reliable source of funds to compensate a victim is likely to be the driver's liability insurance, but, as we have seen, that insurance is both limited in amount and potentially subject to multiple claims that can leave the victim with only a fraction of the necessary compensation. The legal theories that can be used to establish an accident victim's right to recover damages from the drinking driver, along with the major practical obstacles to obtaining complete recovery via that route, are discussed in detail in chapter 2.

Tort lawyers whose clients are unable to satisfy a large judgment despite a court's decision that they are entitled to it will naturally try to solve this problem in precisely the same way they try to do so in other contexts: they will look for a more financially responsible party— a party with a "deep pocket"—from whom some of the damages can be collected. The notion has grown in recent years that an injured party who is looking for a defendant with a deep pocket is somehow acting in a disreputable manner. In fact, however, this notion is unfair: the accident victim is simply attempting to obtain compensation from a party with assets who has been judged liable to pay under the existing rules of tort law. Objections to deep-pocket recoveries are often really demands for a shift from a system that employs a joint and several liability rule to one that uses a proportional liability or equitable share rule.

Under the joint and several liability rule, any person who is legally responsible for causing an injury can be held liable for *all* of the damages awarded to compensate the victim regardless of whether other persons also contributed to the victim's injury. Under the proportional liability rule, the persons whose conduct combined to cause the victim's injury may only be held liable for a proportional share of the total damages based on their proportional share of the responsibility for the harm done. The deep-pocket phenomenon is more pronounced under a joint and several liability rule because the defendant can be held liable for all the harm suffered by an accident victim even though the defendant may have been only minimally responsible for the injury. The effect of a deep-pocket approach is lessened but not eliminated by a move to a proportional responsibility rule. Under that sort of rule, the injured victim is provided with an incentive to join as many defendants as possible in one lawsuit in the hope that the uncollectible portion of the damages awarded will be kept to a minimum.

The legal responsibility of a deep-pocket defendant can be established in two ways. One method is to find a way to impute the fault of the drinking driver to the deep-pocket defendant. The second way is to find some wrongful conduct on the part of the deep-pocket defendant that contributed to the accident and carries with it its own liability. Using the first method, the victim might try to prove that, at the time of the accident, the drinking driver was related to a third party in such a way that the driver's fault can be imputed to that party. For example, if the driver was acting within the scope of an employment relationship at the time that the accident occurred, the victim could try to impute the driver's fault to the driver's employer. Other possibilities are to use the common-law family purpose doctrine to impute the driver's fault to a member of the driver's family or to use an owner consent statute to impose responsibility for the driver's fault on the owner of the vehicle driven by the drinking driver (see chapter 3). These third parties who are held liable in these ways may be more financially able to compensate the victim than the driver is.

In the absence of any of the standard relationships that would support an imputation of the driver's fault to a third party, the accident victim can turn to the second method for extending liability and try to identify some wrongful conduct by a third party that contributed to the accident. Many states have passed "dram shop" statutes, which provide that a seller of alcohol may be liable for injuries that are caused by an intoxicated or underage purchaser. Tort lawyers are drawing on the model of legal responsibility provided by dram shop legislation to develop an analogous common-law liability that can be imposed on those who dispense alcohol, in either a commercial or a social setting, to an individual who subsequently causes harm to others while driving in an intoxicated or alcohol-impaired condition. The legal rules governing these possibilities for extending the scope of fault-based liability beyond the drinking driver and their policy implications are explored in the remaining chapters of part 1.

The principal thesis of this book is that a greater proportion of the accident costs associated with drinking and driving needs to be, and can be, imposed more directly on the alcohol industry.[26] The current practice of searching for a defendant with a deep pocket is at best only a partial solution to the problem of adequately and fairly compensating the victims of drinking drivers. Modern tort law has not adopted a comprehensive theory that supports complete compensation for accidental harm in the drinking-driver context. Rather, it does here what it has accurately been accused of doing in general, which is to tackle the problem on a piecemeal basis.[27] The various legal theories and tort remedies that have been patched together thus far to provide compensation for the victims of drinking-driver traffic accidents are only partially effective. In cases of catastrophic losses, the range of sources of compensation is frequently likely to be inadequate. Furthermore, the loss shifting that does occur is unlikely to have much of a financial impact on the firms that produce or distribute alcoholic beverages or distribute them at points in the chain of sale other than direct consumer sales. Contemporary products liability law provides a recent example of accident costs imposed on those levels of an industry that are remote from the ultimate purchaser. Unfortunately, that example is only of limited usefulness as a model for how to approach the victim compensation problem in the drinking-driver context.

## Alcohol as a Dangerous Product

The idea that it is appropriate to place accident costs on those who are responsible for manufacturing and distributing a product involved in an accident is not a new one. The last quarter-century has seen an explosion in the liability of product manufacturers and sellers for injuries suffered by product users and others affected by dangerous products. Underlying this explosion is the increasing acceptance of a variety of new legal theories and adaptations of old ones. These are the tools tort lawyers have used to promote the idea that manufacturers should be responsible for bearing at least some of the costs attributable to product-related injuries.

For a considerable period in the nineteenth and early twentieth centuries, Anglo-American tort law grudgingly recognized a limited form of product manufacturer's liability. That liability extended only to the person with whom the manufacturer was in privity of contract, usually the immediate purchaser of the product from the manufacturer.[28] Under this restrictive products liability rule, a manufacturer could effectively insulate itself from liability to injured consumers or users of its product simply by introducing intermediate sellers into the product's chain of distribution. Today, however, well-established theories of recovery are available in both tort and contract law to allow injured consumers to recover damages from product sellers with whom they have had no direct dealings.[29] Most courts today would also have no reluctance to extend the manufacturer's legal obligation beyond consumers or users of the product to include more remote victims, such as a pedestrian who is injured when struck by an automobile with a flawed steering mechanism.

Contemporary products liability law is of limited use, though, in helping to achieve better compensation for victims of alcohol-related traffic accidents. Today in the routine products liability context, the accident costs of victims can fairly readily be passed up a product's chain of distribution from retail sellers to distributors and manufacturers, either directly or through a series of indemnity or breach of warranty actions.[30] But contemporary tort law does not provide an effective mechanism for imposing the costs of drinking-driver accidents on the firms within the alcoholic beverage industry that are higher up on the chain of distribution and are not involved in dispensing alcoholic beverages for immediate consumption.

An alcoholic beverage is undoubtedly a product that is sold in normal commerce to people who are sometimes injured by its consumption and who occasionally injure other people after consuming it. This fact, at first glance, appears to be a natural basis for bringing alcohol-related accident losses within the scope of the developing law of products liability. However, it is usually not possible to classify alcohol as "defective" in the sense that is required for a products liability theory to apply.[31] A defective product is frequently defined as one that falls below the expectations that consumers have about the product.[32] For example, a car that runs into a brick wall because its steering mechanism fails presents a considerable surprise to its owner,[33] and such a car fails to meet the average purchaser's expectations about the car's safety.

When the unmet expectations rationale is applied in the alcoholic beverage context, the shortcomings of the products liability analogy readily become apparent. The dangerous characteristics of alcoholic beverages are not a surprise to the average person who purchases them, even if those characteristics might be unknown to the occasional consumer. Indeed, in the most influential statement of a rule in modern products liability law, which was set forth by the American Law Institute, the drafters used liquor as an example of what is ordinarily not meant by a defective product. This interpretation is found in the commentary explaining the institute's basic provision on the liability of sellers of defective products and runs as follows: "The article sold must be dangerous to an extent beyond that which would be contemplated by the ordinary consumer who purchases it, with the ordinary knowledge common to the community as to its characteristics.

*Good whiskey is not unreasonably dangerous merely because it will make some people drunk,* and is especially dangerous to alcoholics; but bad whiskey, containing a dangerous amount of fusel oil, is unreasonably dangerous."[34] In most instances, then, the general level of awareness of the risks associated with alcohol consumption will be sufficiently high to make it difficult to characterize an alcoholic beverage product as defective. The product is not dangerous to an extent beyond the expectations of the ordinary purchaser. What the consumer gets is precisely what the consumer expected to get.

Even if alcoholic beverages in general are not defective, some limited types of alcohol-related harm lend themselves more readily to an imposition of products liability, under what might be considered only a relatively minor extension of contemporary products liability theories. The first such extension requires a court to use a utilitarian balancing test as an alternative to the consumer expectations approach in characterizing a product as defective. Applying this test can produce different results in some cases. Some products whose risks are known to the ordinary consumer are nevertheless so dangerous that their risks outweigh their utility. Under the consumer expectations approach, that kind of product is not defective because consumers expect it to be just as dangerous as it actually is. Under a risk/utility analysis, however, the product's risks are balanced against its utility, regardless of consumer expectations. Thus a product that poses risks, even known risks, that are greater than its utility can nevertheless be characterized as defective.

Risk/utility analysis has emerged as the leading alternative doctrine for determining defectiveness in modern products liability law, either as a substitute for the consumer expectations test or, more commonly, as a supplement to that test. The appropriate risk/utility question for a products liability claim involving alcohol is whether the risks associated with the product are greater than the utility of the product. Still, even posing the defectiveness question in that form does not readily lead to a decision that alcoholic beverage products in general are defective. The alcoholic beverage product's ability to intoxicate the consumer is arguably one of the features that puts it in such widespread demand. The characteristic that makes the product risky is the same one that gives it its utility; thus in normal circumstances it would be difficult to obtain a legal decision holding that the risks outweigh the utility.

Nevertheless, there may be certain subdivisions of products within the alcohol industry that lend themselves to this approach. The idea is that the product has such a low utility that almost any risk would support a characterization of the product as defective. A claimant pursuing this theory of alcohol manufacturer liability could draw support from a recent decision of the highest state court in Maryland, which held the distributor of a "Saturday night special" handgun liable for injuries to the victim of a robbery and shooting in which the weapon was used.[35] Regardless of the utility of firearms and handguns, the court concluded, the type of weapon that was used in the robbery was of such poor quality and was sold at such a low price that its utility was virtually nonexistent. When that low utility is weighed against the risk posed to the potential victims of crimes committed by the users of this type of weapon, the Saturday night special can be characterized as defective. Following the implications of this decision, limited segments of the alcohol industry might be subjected to tort liability based on the needlessly dangerous nature of their products. The most likely candidate for the category "needlessly dangerous product" is the "fortified wine" manufactured by some of the largest firms and sold under brand names such as "Ripple" and "Thunderbird." The ability of alcoholic beverages to intoxicate may be what gives them their utility, but the risks to consumers of these sorts of beverages may be so great, given their poor quality and low cost, that their utility is negligible by comparison.

A second type of products liability theory has been used to try to impose liability on a member of the alcohol industry for making and selling a defective product. This theory alleges that legal relief should be available to an infant who suffers fetal injury as a result of alcohol consumption by its mother during her pregnancy. A case that was recently litigated in Seattle, *Thorp v. James B. Beam Distilling Co.*,[36] illustrates the nature of this sort of claim and indicates the formidable obstacles that make it highly unlikely that this theory will be used successfully on a widespread basis. The lawsuit was brought on behalf of Michael Thorp, who was a four-year-old child at the time of the trial. Michael's mother, Candace Thorp, was an alcoholic who drank a considerable amount of alcohol during her pregnancy. The complaint against the distiller of Jim Beam bourbon alleged that its bourbon was a defective product because it lacked adequate warnings about the risks associated with drinking alcohol during pregnancy.

The *Thorp* lawsuit drew on a well-established principle of modern products liability law. The failure to provide adequate instructions and warnings is generally recognized today as a standard basis for characterizing a product as defective.[37] The seller who puts a product on the market with inadequate information to the consumer is liable because of this defective marketing rather than because of an actual defect in the product's construction or design. The *Thorp* case reveals that, while the principle of liability for a failure to warn about product dangers is well-established, the application of that principle to a person injured as a result of alcohol consumption is considerably more problematic.

Following a three-week trial in the *Thorp* case, and after more than three days of deliberation, the jury returned a verdict that the defendant was not liable for Michael's birth defects connected to his Fetal Alcohol Syndrome. Product manufacturers have a number of standard responses to liability claims based on the inadequacy of consumer warnings for a product. Two of these defenses appear to be mutually exclusive: one asserts that "everyone knew about this risk," and the other argues that "no one could have known about this risk." Each of these assertions, if a jury believes it, can relieve the product manufacturer of liability for breach of an obligation to warn about the risk.

The "everyone knew about it" response, alleging that the risk was part of the common knowledge of the ordinary consumer,[38] flows logically from the consumer expectations premise of products liability. If a product poses risks that are within the body of common knowledge, then the product is not more unsafe than consumers expect it to be. It is, of course, a question of fact whether a particular risk really was part of the body of knowledge of the ordinary consumer.

One recent federal appellate court decision reversed a summary judgment a brewer had won against a plaintiff suffering from pancreatitis. The major factual issue was whether the risk of getting pancreatitis as a result of moderate consumption of beer was within the knowledge of the average consumer or of the actual consumer.[39] An intermediate appellate court in Texas recently reinstated a lawsuit raising even broader claims about liability for a failure to warn about the dangerous qualities of alcohol and a failure to provide instructions for its safe use.[40] In the *Thorp* case, the distiller's successful defense included evidence that the risks associated with drinking during pregnancy were generally well known by 1983, the year Candace Thorp became pregnant with Michael. In addition, the distiller presented evidence to prove that, even if the pregnancy-related risks of alcohol consumption were not part of the community's common knowledge in 1983, Candace Thorp learned of the risk of giving birth to a child with Fetal Alcohol Syndrome in a lecture she heard while attending an alcoholic treatment program in 1983.

In any lawsuit that claims a right to compensation for birth defects that occurred prior to the time that the medical and scientific communities were able to link alcohol consumption and fetal injury, the alcohol industry might be expected to follow the lead that was set by manufacturers in other product injury litigation contexts: to assert the defense that the risk was unknowable at the time of sale, and therefore no duty to warn can reasonably be imposed on the manufacturers of alcoholic beverages. Such an argument, which is often referred to as a state-of-the-art defense, has frequently been accepted by courts in other products liability contexts,[41] although there are occasional decisions to the contrary.[42] A related tactic, which was also employed by the defense lawyers in the *Thorp* case, is to introduce evidence questioning whether a causal link even exists between the victim's injuries and the allegedly defective product.

A consumer who sues one or more firms in the alcohol industry on a products liability claim for alcohol-related injuries thus faces an impressive series of obstacles to recovering compensation. The industry can claim it had no legal obligation to warn of the risks of injury, either because the risks were a matter of common knowledge or because they were scientifically and medically unknowable at the time that the product was put on the market. And even if a general duty to warn did exist, a defendant could deny liability in a particular instance by proving that the alcohol consumer who was injured was personally aware of the risks. Finally, the industry can attack the adequacy of the evidence used to prove the link between its products and the alcohol consumer's injuries that were alleged to have been caused by the consumption of alcohol.

As the *Thorp* case shows, the consumer expectations rationale for products liability contains within it the seeds of its own destruction. According to this approach, a product is defective when its dangerous characteristics come as a surprise to the average consumer. Because defeated or unsatisfied consumer expectations are the key to liability, the product manufacturer can escape liability by lowering consumer expectations of safety, thus making it impossible to characterize its product as defective. Of course, providing the consumer with too much information about product dangers could make it difficult to sell the product. Even so, just as the demand for a product can be relatively unaffected by changes in price, or price-inelastic, the demand can be risk-inelastic, that is, relatively unresponsive to the dangers the product poses to consumers and others. If demand for a particular product is relatively risk-inelastic, then, by providing warnings, its manufacturer could in effect insulate itself from defective products liability claims based on its defective marketing of products while only minimally affecting its sales.

Indeed, tobacco companies and cigarette manufacturers have insulated themselves from this sort of claim by providing more information about the risks of smoking on product packages and in product advertising. Courts have frequently held that the warnings that are required by federal law to be printed on cigarette packages preempt any state law claim based on a failure to provide information beyond those warnings.[43] Even if a tobacco products liability claim is allowed to proceed, the warnings can serve as evidence of lower consumer expectations of safety, thus making it less likely that the product will be found to be defective.

Alcoholic beverage companies may be similarly insulated by the new federally mandated warnings on its product containers. The Alcohol Beverage Labelling Act of 1988[44] established a new federal warning that went into effect in November 1989. The following statement must appear on containers of alcoholic beverages: GOVERNMENT WARNING: (1) ACCORDING TO THE SURGEON GENERAL, WOMEN SHOULD NOT DRINK ALCOHOLIC BEVERAGES DURING PREGNANCY BECAUSE OF THE RISKS OF BIRTH DEFECTS. (2) CONSUMPTION OF ALCOHOLIC BEVERAGES IMPAIRS YOUR ABILITY TO DRIVE A CAR OR OPERATE MACHINERY, AND MAY CAUSE HEALTH PROBLEMS.[45] Challenges to the alcohol industry's reliance on these warnings as a defense in products liability claims might be framed along the lines of the arguments that plaintiffs have used in cigarette cases. The principal argument is that, by the time the warnings appeared, the plaintiff was already addicted to the product, and thus the warnings were meaningless. Aside from this argument, however, if both the content of the warnings and the way they are communicated are found to be adequate, they may afford some protection. Because the warnings add to the general body of consumer knowledge about a product's risks, they can reduce the manufacturer's exposure to liability.

The insulation from liability that government-mandated warnings can afford manufacturers is not the only lesson that alcoholic beverage companies are likely to learn from the cigarette industry's experience in the products liability field. The level of resistance by tobacco companies to smokers' efforts to impose liability on them has been among the fiercest of any group of product manufacturers over the course of the last twenty-five years, a period when the scope of products liability in general has been expanding. The vigorous legal defenses and public relations and lobbying efforts mounted by tobacco companies against products liability claims over the last three decades have imposed substantial costs on smokers and their attorneys. When combined with the weaknesses in the substantive legal claims that are available to these consumers, it is clear that claimants face a pretty dismal prospect of success in litigation after incurring all that expense. The considerable difficulty that has been encountered in imposing liability on the cigarette industry suggests that anyone attempting to hold the alcohol industry liable as a matter of products liability law will similarly face a long and arduous struggle.

The possibility of treating alcohol as a defective product raises another concern that needs to be considered in the context of alcohol-related traffic accidents—the problem of the self-inflicted injury. The problem with asserting a products liability challenge against a need-lessly risky product such as fortified wine is that the most direct beneficiary of that type of claim is the alcohol consumer, not those whom the consumer may injure while alcohol-impaired. Policymakers and the public at large are likely to be resistant to the prospect of a person recovering damages for injuries that flow from the person's own choices. From the perspective of the tort lawyer attempting to apportion all or some of the costs of an accident victim's injuries to persons other than the drinking driver, the "uselessly dangerous products" approach simply does not go far enough to be of any use.

The *Thorp* case, however, comes closer to the case of the Bloom family hypothetical that began this book. The child who suffered from Fetal Alcohol Syndrome and the Bloom children were innocent vic-tims. Given the innocent status of the child injured in a traffic accident, it should be easier in a case involving child victims to overcome any argument by a liquor company that the alcohol consumer is being allowed to benefit in some untoward or illegitimate way from the decision to drink. Still, even in that case, it may be necessary to dispel the idea that a child is only a nominal party to the lawsuit and that any recovery of damages by the child really accrues to the benefit of the child's parent. If that parent is also a wrongdoer whose conduct contributed to the child's injury, then the reluctance to reward some-one for a self-inflicted injury may emerge once more. This problem of appearing to permit a recovery by someone other than an innocent victim needs to be directly confronted in the construction of any alternative compensation scheme to aid accident victims. Thus I have excluded claims by the drinking driver from the accident victim com-pensation fund I propose in this book (see chapter 14).

The failure of the child in the *Thorp* lawsuit to obtain a recovery from a member of the alcohol industry indicates the general difficulty of using existing products liability theories to shift the costs of drink-ing-driver accidents to firms within the alcohol industry. Except for the case in which alcoholic beverages are sold or served directly to a consumer (see chapters 4 and 6), the allocation of those accident costs under existing law is likely to exclude any parties involved in the manufacture, distribution, and sale of alcohol. As a result, the costs of injuries from drinking-driver traffic accidents are unlikely to be part of the business judgment calculation of alcohol manufacturers and distributors on the wholesale level (as opposed to firms that sell and serve beverages to the consumer). If, as I argue in part 2 of this book, those accident costs can properly be considered to be a legitimate part of the social cost of these firms' activities, a mechanism needs to be constructed that will shift the costs to these firms more effectively than tort law does.

## Beyond Traditional Tort Law

The substantial barriers that operate under contemporary tort law to prevent victims of drinking-driver traffic accidents from completely recovering their losses from the most appropriate parties liable for those losses can be frustrating. One reaction to this problem might be to advocate a combination of doctrinal change and a relaxed application of restrictive rules in order to expand the scope of tort liability and improve the level of victim compensation. That is, however, not the reaction that drives this book. Rather than encouraging courts to continue to tinker with the details of the tort recovery scheme as it is currently pieced together, I propose that the legal system needs to cross the boundaries of traditional tort theory and begin to explore the possibility of imposing at least some of these accident costs directly on firms in the alcohol industry.

In a significant sense, then, through this book I accept the challenge offered by Harvard Law School Professor Henry Steiner. In a thoughtful and provocative study of judicial decision making in contemporary tort law, Professor Steiner suggested that "[s]ome of the ideals shaping modern tort law could find . . . a fuller realization in [legislative] plans that are free of the boundaries set by traditional common-law thinking and free of the traditional constraints on what courts can achieve."[46] The alcohol-related accident victim compensation fund that I set out in detail in the second half of this book takes advantage of the freedoms that are obtained by moving beyond traditional tort law. By adopting this proposal rather than shaping an approach along the lines of existing tort law, a greater number of the deficiencies of the current scheme can be cured and a higher proportion of the benefits of an optimum allocation of accident losses can be obtained.[47]

For reasons that will be discussed in detail in chapter 14, the compensation fund system I propose operates, on the whole, as a complement to current tort law. It would not replace any of the existing tort actions and remedies that are available in any particular state. My proposal thus differs from more comprehensive "no-fault" systems that seek to move some or all of the accident injury compensation function out of the tort system. The Alcohol-Related Accident Victim Compensation Fund is a practicable and equitable complement to the current range of tort law options for providing more complete compensation to those who are seriously injured by drinking drivers. This fund will more fully accomplish the goal of reducing the substantial costs of the serious social problem of drinking and driving.

## NOTES

1. A recent collection of scholarly writing by distinguished specialists on a variety of aspects of the drinking-driver problem is found in M. LAURENCE, J. SNORTUM & F. ZIMRING, eds., SOCIAL CONTROL OF THE DRINKING DRIVER (1988). The individual contributions to this collection describe the nature of the problem and discuss different sorts of intervention to reduce its impact. Only a brief and fairly superficial survey of the tort law and insurance aspects of the problem is included.

2. The statistical description of the drinking-driver problem can be inexact due to differences in reporting requirements, legal standards, and the nature of the conduct or the physical effects being quantified. For a discussion of the difficulty of determining the magnitude of the drinking-driver traffic-accident problem, *see* Donelson, *The Alcohol-Crash Problem,* in LAURENCE et al., SOCIAL CONTROL, at 21-40.

The figure stated in the text was derived by comparing the number of licensed drivers who were involved in fatal accidents in 1986 (60,297) with the number of drinking drivers in those fatal accidents (20,659). *See* UNITED STATES STATISTICAL ABSTRACT 581 (1988) (Table 1001, Licensed Drivers, Fatal Motor-Vehicle Accidents, and Alcohol Involvement, by Age of Driver, 1986).

A summary of data on the connection between alcohol use and injury (and citations to the sources of the data) can be found in the introduction to the most comprehensive treatise for practicing lawyers on the tort liability considerations that are raised by the subject. See 1 J. MOSHER, LIQUOR LIABILITY LAW § 1.02 (1991). Individual states also attempt to compile and to collate statistics on alcohol-related accidents. See, e.g., Kelly v. Gwinnell, 96 N.J. 538, 545 n.3, 476 A.2d 1219, 1222 n.3 (1984) (state statistics for New Jersey on alcohol-related highway fatalities).

3. NATIONAL CENTER FOR STATISTICS & ANALYSIS, NATIONAL HIGHWAY TRAFFIC SAFETY ADMINISTRATION, 1987 FATALITY FACTS 2 (October 1988).

4. The terminology dealing with this subject can be confusing and po-

tentially misleading. *See A Note on Terminology,* in LAURENCE et al., SOCIAL CONTROL, at xvii. As used in this book, the terms "alcohol-impaired" and "intoxicated" will denote different levels of alcohol consumption, the former being inclusive of the latter. The two terms roughly correspond to the distinction that is made by the National Highway Traffic Safety Administration between "alcohol related/involved" and "drunk." The term "drunk" is used to refer to a level of alcohol consumption sufficient to classify a person as legally intoxicated under the state's laws governing driving while intoxicated. In most states, that is a blood alcohol concentration (BAC) of at least .10 per cent. The term "alcohol related/involved" covers incidents in which there was "a measurable or estimated blood alcohol concentration (BAC) of .01 percent or above." NATIONAL CENTER FOR STATISTICS & ANALYSIS, NATIONAL HIGHWAY TRAFFIC SAFETY ADMINISTRATION, DRUNK DRIVING FACTS 1 (August 1988).

The term "drinking driver" is used throughout this book as a nontechnical reference to a driver who has consumed any alcoholic beverage prior to an accident, at a time close enough to the occurrence of the accident and in an amount sufficient for the alcohol to have adversely affected the operation of the vehicle. It thus encompasses a broader pool of drivers than those who would be classified as legally intoxicated at the time of the accident.

5. NATIONAL CENTER FOR STATISTICS & ANALYSIS, 1987 FATALITY FACTS 2 (1988).

6. The most recent effort at providing a comprehensive examination of the drinking-driver problem from a sociological perspective is a frequently insightful book by New York University professor James B. Jacobs. J. JACOBS, DRUNK DRIVING: AN AMERICAN DILEMMA (1989). This book's treatment of the tort law and insurance system's handling of drinking-driver accidents, however, simply echoes the essay Jacobs contributed earlier to LAURENCE et al., SOCIAL CONTROL.

7. Easterbrook, *Cleaning Up,* NEWSWEEK, July 24, 1989, at 42. The similarity between the issues of pollution and drunk driving has also been noted by Professor Franklin Zimring in terms of the reciprocal effects of social attitudes and a government criminalization effort. Zimring, *Law, Society, and the Drinking Driver: Some Concluding Reflections,* in LAURENCE et al., SOCIAL CONTROL, at 382.

8. Professor Jacobs lists a variety of ways in which such groups can be significant in the drinking-driver reform arena. *See* JACOBS, DRUNK DRIVING, at 196-97.

9. W. MANCHESTER, THE LAST LION: WINSTON SPENCER CHURCHILL, VISIONS OF GLORY, 1874-1932, at 508 (1983).

10. *See generally* R. KEETON & J. O'CONNELL, BASIC PROTECTION FOR THE TRAFFIC VICTIM: A BLUEPRINT FOR REFORMING AUTOMOBILE INSURANCE 15-22 (1965). Keeton and O'Connell's work during the decade following the publication of that book was very influential in translating the theoretical justifications for no-fault insurance into a practical plan that could be implemented by a legislature. Professor O'Connell has continued the

search for no-fault alternatives to the tort system, proposing extensions of his original idea, which was first presented in the context of automobile accidents. *See, e.g.*, O'Connell, *Neo-No-Fault Remedies for Medical Injuries: Coordinated Statutory and Contractual Alternatives*, 49 LAW & CONTEMP. PROBS. 125 (1986); O'Connell, *Offers That Can't Be Refused: Foreclosure of Personal Injury Claims by Defendants' Prompt Tender of Claimants' Net Economic Losses*, 77 NW. U. L. REV. 589 (1983).

11. Lambert, *Tom on Torts*, 31 ATLA L. REP. 244 (1988), discussing Ely v. Murphy, 207 Conn. 88, 540 A.2d 54 (1988).

12. BUREAU OF JUSTICE STATISTICS, U.S. DEP'T OF JUSTICE, DRUNK DRIVING 4 (1988).

13. *See* Andenaes, *The Scandinavian Experience*, in LAURENCE et al., SOCIAL CONTROL, at 43; Ross, *Deterrence-based Policies in Britain, Canada, and Australia, id.* at 64. *See also* H. ROSS, DETERRING THE DRINKING DRIVER: LEGAL POLICY AND SOCIAL CONTROL (rev. ed. 1984).

14. Recent social science research on the behavioral factors that go into a decision to drink and drive is discussed in Smith & Remington, *The Epidemiology of Drinking and Driving: Results from the Behavioral Risk Factor Surveillance System, 1986*, 16 HEALTH EDUC. Q. 345 (1989); Vegega & Klitzner, *Drinking and Driving among Youth: A Study of Situational Risk Factors, id.* at 373; and Basch, DeCicco & Malfetti, *A Focus Group Study on Decision Processes of Young Drivers: Reasons That May Support a Decision to Drink and Drive, id.* at 389.

15. A review of educational efforts can be found in Mann, Vingilis & Stewart, *Programs to Change Individual Behavior: Education and Rehabilitation in the Prevention of Drinking and Driving*, in LAURENCE et al., SOCIAL CONTROL, at 248.

16. The results of a study of the prosecution process in one state, Vermont, are reported in J. LITTLE, ADMINISTRATION OF JUSTICE IN DRUNK DRIVING CASES (1975).

17. *See, e.g.*, NATIONAL INSTITUTE OF JUSTICE, JAILING DRUNK DRIVERS: IMPACT ON THE CRIMINAL JUSTICE SYSTEM (1985).

18. Summaries of state statutes on the subject are collected in AMERICAN INSURANCE ASSOCIATION, DIGEST OF STATE LAWS RELATING TO DRIVING UNDER THE INFLUENCE OF DRUGS OR ALCOHOL (1988).

19. The relationship between drinking and driving and the criminal justice system in the United States is considerably more complex than the text's statement about "typical" DWI legislation can convey. In large part because of the effectiveness of lobbying by anti–drunk-driving citizens' groups, legislators have frequently felt a need to appear responsive to this problem. As a result, states have adopted laws featuring numerous variations on the basic theme of criminal culpability for drinking and driving. The most recent comprehensive analysis of the conceptual and practical difficulties raised by this theme is found in JACOBS, DRUNK DRIVING, at 55-100.

20. In December 1989, a Kentucky jury convicted an intoxicated driver on multiple counts of a variety of offenses arising out of what was described

as the nation's worst drunk-driving accident. The driver collided with a church-owned school bus, killing twenty-seven of the bus occupants and injuring another twelve. *Jury Urges 16-Year Term in Bus Deaths,* Chicago Tribune, Dec. 23, 1989, at 3.

21. *See* PUBLIC HEALTH SERVICE, U.S. DEP'T OF HEALTH AND HUMAN SERVICES, THE 1990 HEALTH OBJECTIVES FOR THE NATION: A MIDCOURSE REVIEW (1986).

22. *See, e.g,* NATIONAL HIGHWAY TRAFFIC SAFETY ADMINISTRATION, U.S. DEP'T OF TRANSPORTATION, NATIONAL ACCIDENT SAMPLING SYSTEM 1984: A REPORT ON TRAFFIC ACCIDENTS AND INJURIES IN THE U.S. (1986)

23. U.S. DEP'T OF HEALTH AND HUMAN SERVICES, PROCEEDINGS OF THE SURGEON GENERAL'S WORKSHOP ON DRUNK DRIVING, DECEMBER 14-16, 1988 (1989).

24. The liability coverage of a standard automobile insurance policy creates two main obligations for the insurance company. One is to defend the insured against any legal claims asserted against the insured that arose as a result of the insured's conduct while driving the automobile. The other is to indemnify the insured for any liability that is established, that is, to be responsible for paying the monetary damages awarded to a victim in a legal judgment entered against the insured. The insurer's obligation to indemnify is limited to the amount specified in the insurance policy, and thus its size depends on the policyholder's selection of particular coverage limits and ability to pay for them.

25. A procedural device known as interpleader allows a party in the position of an insurance company facing competing claims whose total would exceed the amount of the policy to deposit the insurance fund with the court. *See* FED. R. CIV. P. 22. A court could use an interpleader proceeding to apportion the available funds among the multiple claimants so that each successful claimant receives at least some payment. This device does not, of course, increase the size of the fund out of which the proportional payments are made. The effect is to make a more equitable distribution of the existing pie rather than to increase the size of the pie.

26. This book will employ the term "alcohol industry" to describe firms engaged in the making and the distribution of alcohol prior to retail sale to the ultimate consumer. Included within the alcohol industry as so defined are distillers of "hard liquor," brewers of beer and other malt beverages, and wine makers. Also included are wholesale distributors of those beverages. Retail servers and sellers are excluded from this definition of the alcohol industry. They are treated instead as members of the distinct hospitality and retail beverage industries. This terminology is adopted from 2 MOSHER, LIQUOR LIABILITY LAW § 21.01[6]. The extent to which servers and retail sellers are currently held responsible for the losses of some alcohol-related accident victims and the manner in which they are held liable are described in chapters 4, 6, and 7.

27. *See* A. HUTCHINSON, DWELLING ON THE THRESHOLD: CRITICAL ES-

SAYS ON MODERN LEGAL THOUGHT 152 (1988): "The overwhelming characteristic of accident law is its piecemeal quality."

28. *See* Winterbottom v. Wright, 10 M. & W. 109, 152 Eng. Rep. 402 (Ex. 1842). For a somewhat wistful analysis of the privity requirement, *see* R. EPSTEIN, MODERN PRODUCTS LIABILITY LAW 9-24 (1980).

29. The breakdown of a privity-of-contract requirement for maintaining a product liability action can be seen in MacPherson v. Buick Motor Co., 217 N.Y. 382, 111 N.E. 1050 (1916) (negligence theory of liability), in RESTATEMENT (SECOND) OF TORTS § 402A (1965) (strict liability in tort theory), and in U.C.C. § 2-318 (1978) (Uniform Commercial Code breach-of-warranty theories of liability).

30. *See generally* M. SHAPO, THE LAW OF PRODUCTS LIABILITY, ch. 14 (2d ed. 1990).

31. *Id.,* ch. 8.

32. *Id.* at § 8.05; RESTATEMENT (SECOND) OF TORTS § 402A, Comment g (1965).

33. *See* Henningsen v. Bloomfield Motors, Inc., 32 N.J. 358, 161 A.2d 69 (1960).

34. RESTATEMENT (SECOND) OF TORTS § 402A, Comment i (1965) (emphasis added).

35. Kelley v. R.G. Industries, Inc., 304 Md. 124, 497 A.2d 1143 (1985). Other courts have refused to recognize the liability of manufacturers or distributors of firearms that perform as they were intended to perform, although limited liability has been imposed by statute in a few states. The cases are collected in J. HENDERSON & A. TWERSKI, PRODUCTS LIABILITY: PROBLEMS AND PROCESS 560 (1987). The statutes are cited at *id.,* 121 (1989 Supplement). *See also* Delahanty v. Hinckley, 900 F.2d 368 (D.C. Cir. 1990) (refusing to impose liability on the manufacturer of the handgun that was used in the assassination attempt on President Reagan, relying on a response to a question that was certified to the District of Columbia Court of Appeals).

36. No. C87-1527-R (D. Wash. 1989) (verdict rendered for defendant on May 18, 1989). The litigation is described in 17 PROD. SAFETY & LIAB. REP. (BNA) 381, 501 (1989).

37. *See* SHAPO, LAW OF PRODUCTS LIABILITY, ch. 19. *See also* J. CAMPBELL & R. EDWARDS, THE DUTY TO WARN AND THE DUTY TO INFORM: MARKETING DEFECTS IN STRICT PRODUCTS LIABILITY (1989).

38. *See, e.g.,* Jamieson v. Woodward & Lothrop, 247 F.2d 23 (D.C. Cir.), *cert. denied,* 355 U.S. 855 (1957) (no duty on manufacturer to warn of simple fact that a stretched elastic band will snap back when released).

39. Hon v. Stroh Brewery Co., 835 F.2d 510 (3rd Cir. 1987). The *Hon* case is analyzed in Comment, *In Support of Hon v. Stroh Brewery Co.: A Brewing Debate over Extending Liability to Manufacturers of Alcoholic Beverages,* 51 U. PITT. L. REV. 179 (1989).

40. McGuire v. Joseph E. Seagram & Sons, Inc., 790 S.W.2d 842 (Ct. App. Tex. 1990). The decision of the Court of Appeals was appealed to the

Supreme Court of Texas, which had not ruled on the case at the time of this book's writing.

41. *See, e.g,* Brown v. Superior Court, 44 Cal. 3d 1049, 751 P.2d 470, 245 Cal. Rptr. 412 (1988) (rejecting the assertion that a drug manufacturer should be strictly liable for failure to warn of the risks that were inherent in a drug if the manufacturer did not know and could not have known, given the state of the scientific knowledge available when the drug was distributed, about those risks).

42. One of the most significant decisions rejecting the state-of-the-art defense was Beshada v. Johns-Manville Products Corp., 90 N.J. 191, 447 A.2d 539 (1982). In that case, the Supreme Court of New Jersey held that imposing liability on a product manufacturer even when the dangers were unknowable at the time of manufacture would advance the risk-spreading, accident-avoidance, and administrative-efficiency goals associated with imposing strict liability on product sellers. Soon after, however, that same court allowed the state-of-the-art defense to be asserted in a products liability case involving prescription drugs, saying that *Beshada* should be restricted to the circumstances that were present in *Beshada*. Feldman v. Lederle Laboratories, 97 N.J. 429, 479 A.2d 374 (1984).

A federal district court has read the *Beshada* and *Feldman* decisions together as creating an exceptional prohibition on the use of the state-of-the-art defense by product manufacturers in asbestos cases such as *Beshada*. Gogol v. Johns-Manville Sales Corp., 595 F.Supp. 971 (D.N.J. 1984). However, an equally defensible reconciliation of the *Beshada* and *Feldman* decisions would be one that treats the *Feldman* case as carving out an exception for prescription drug cases, on the reasoning that the prospects of a manufacturer's liability for adverse side effects that are unknowable at the time of distribution would act as too substantial a disincentive toward the introduction of valuable new drugs. In other words, this alternative interpretation would put prescription drugs in a category of exceptional products liability cases in which the state-of-the-art defense *will* be recognized, rather than treating the asbestos cases as an aberrational category in which it will *not* be allowed.

43. *See, e.g.,* Cipollone v. Liggett Group, Inc., 893 F.2d 541 (3rd Cir. 1990), *cert. granted,* 111 S. Ct. 1386 (1991); Jacobson, *After Cipollone v. Liggett Group, Inc.: How Wide Will the Floodgates of Cigarette Litigation Open?,* 17 PROD. SAFETY & LIAB. REP. (BNA) 1154 (1989).

44. 27 U.S.C. § 213-219a. Regulations implementing the act were issued by the Bureau of Alcohol, Tobacco, and Firearms on February 16, 1989. Those regulations have been criticized, however, as being too lax. Kelly, *Warnings Required on Liquor,* Washington *Post,* November 13, 1989, at A11, col. 1.

45. 27 U.S.C. § 215.

46. H. STEINER, MORAL ARGUMENT AND SOCIAL VISION IN THE COURTS: A STUDY OF TORT ACCIDENT LAW 144 (1987).

47. This is, of course, not the first attempt to react to the limitations of

tort law by proposing an alternative compensation system. Typically, however, compensation systems are proposed in response to a perceived doctrinal inadequacy in the law of torts. A good illustration is the imaginative proposal for overcoming the restrictions that flow from traditional causation doctrines in toxic tort cases, in Harris, *Toxic Tort Litigation and the Causation Element: Is There Any Hope of Reconciliation?*, 40 S.W. L. J. 947 (1986). *See also* Merrill, *Compensation for Prescription Drug Injuries*, 59 VA. L. REV. 1, 87-120 (1973).

# PART ONE

---

## Current Channels to a Deep Pocket: The Search for Full Compensation in Drinking-Driver Tort Cases

Contemporary tort law offers a number of legal theories and litigation techniques for compensating the victims of drinking-driver traffic accidents. In part 1, I describe the ways that the various compensation options available under current tort law assign liability, or legal responsibility, for traffic accidents involving alcohol. I also address policy considerations that cut across the lines that separate the different theories of liability. On one level, each theory of compensation will be examined on its own terms to see whether it makes sense to impose liability in that way on the parties who come within the scope of the theory; on another level, each theory will be evaluated according to how effectively it meets the goal of fully and fairly compensating the victims of drinking-driver traffic accidents—in particular how well it is able to shift the costs of those accidents to those in the alcohol industry at the higher levels of the chain of distribution of alcoholic beverages.

A useful way to approach the question of how to shift the financial responsibility for the harm caused by a drinking driver away from the accident victim is to picture the search for compensation as proceeding outward through a series of concentric circles. At the center of the first circle is the drinking driver. As a potential defendant (the party from whom relief is sought) in a tort lawsuit, the drinking driver may offer the injured plaintiff (the party who is seeking relief) the litigation advantage of having acted in a way that displays a fairly high degree of personal fault. Thus it may be relatively easy to establish that defendant's liability, as a matter both of satisfying the substantive requirements of the governing legal theory and of appealing to the sympathies of the legal decision makers who have to resolve the dispute. Nevertheless, as discussed in chapter 2, it is frequently true that the level of financial responsibility of the drinking driver may be inadequate to satisfy a judgment or a series of judgments based on, and commensurate with, that demonstrable legal culpability.

In the next circle outward from the drinking driver are those parties who are not themselves at fault but to whom the driver's fault may be imputed. While the liability of these parties can often be established in a fairly routine or even mechanical fashion under standard tort doctrines, employing the vicarious liability doctrines and rules that are discussed in chapter 3, it may frequently be the case that the financial responsibility of those parties to whom liability can most easily be imputed is only marginally greater than that of the drinking driver. In any event, one can predict with some confidence that the greater the financial stake a vicarious-liability defendant has in resisting the imposition of this sort of liability, the more vigorous will be the attempt to establish that the drinking driver's fault should *not* be imputed to the defendant in the particular case.

Moving outward to the next order of liability, the search for more complete compensation encounters parties who are not subject to having the fault of the drinking driver imputed to them, but who may, either individually or in conjunction with other possible defendants, have assets that significantly improve the chances of providing fuller compensation to the accident victim. Because imputed fault under a vicarious liability theory is not necessarily available for use against the parties in these circles, the victim of a drinking-driver accident must find some basis on which these potential defendants can be held liable as a result of some fault of their own rather than merely relying on establishing the drinking driver's fault and assigning responsibility for its consequences to the defendants. Nevertheless, it must be noted that in any given instance there may very well be an overlap in the application of the imputed-fault and the independent-fault categories. A vehicle owner may, for example, be liable under an owner consent statute, in which the fault of the drinking driver is imputed to the owner, and under a negligent entrustment theory as well, which bases liability on the owner's own fault in letting an intoxicated person drive the owner's vehicle. Similarly, an employee's fault can be imputed to an employer in the case where an employee is served alcoholic beverages by an employer (under circumstances in which it was negligent for the employer to furnish the alcohol) and then becomes involved in a traffic accident while acting within the scope of employment. For purposes of maintaining the maximum degree of analytical clarity, however, these two different categories of liability of parties other than the drinking driver—one based on imputing fault to a party and the other requiring a characterization of that party's *own* conduct as culpable—will be kept separate.

Chapters 4, 6, and 7 provide a description and a critical analysis of each of the three principal methods of imposing liability by establishing a third party's fault in providing alcohol to a drinking driver. Chapter 4 introduces as the third order of tort liability the "dram shop" statutes that have been enacted in many states. These statutes create a form of civil liability for damages that can be imposed on commercial dispensers of alcohol in at least some circumstances. The term "dispenser" is used in this book to describe any person who furnishes alcohol to a person who is going to consume it either immediately or shortly after receiving it. In some circumstances, the furnishing will involve a sale of the alcohol, in which case the term "commercial dispenser" will be used. In other circumstances, there will be no sale, as in the case where the dispenser is a social host of the person to whom the alcohol is furnished. Occasionally, a distinction will need to be made between the service and the sale of alcoholic beverages. The term "service" means the furnishing of a drink for immediate consumption on the premises at which it is provided. The term "sale," when used to distinguish a sale of alcohol from the serving of alcohol in the sense given above, typically involves the furnishing of alcohol in a closed container to be consumed somewhere other than on the premises. The term "dispenser" includes both servers and sellers. If the difference between the two types of transactions is significant, the context in which the terms are used will indicate which is meant.

The most frequent case of dram shop liability occurs when a customer who is under the minimum drinking age or who is visibly intoxicated at the time of service causes injury to another person after being furnished with alcohol by the dispenser. In states in which dram shop legislation has not been enacted, or in situations in which dram shop statutory liability does not obtain, tort plaintiffs have often attempted to assert a common-law theory of recovery against a commercial dispenser based on principles analogous to those supporting liability under a dram shop act. That common-law liability of commercial dispensers of alcohol is discussed as the fourth order of tort liability in chapter 6.

Chapter 5 addresses the phenomenon of judicial reluctance to recognize a common-law claim for relief against a dispenser of alcohol. In that chapter I identify a series of arguments that could be made against a court's creation of a tort claim against alcoholic beverage dispensers and subject each argument to a critical analysis. These arguments are relevant not only to the common-law claim against the commercial dispenser discussed in chapter 6 but also to the tort claim against social dispensers of alcohol described in chapter 7 as occupying the fifth order of tort liability. The principles underlying the type of dispenser liability theory that is used to impose liability on commercial dispensers of alcohol have been extended in some states to include a person who, as a social host, serves alcohol to a guest who subsequently injures another person in an alcohol-related traffic accident. Chapter 7 looks at the particular issues that arise when dispenser liability is imposed on social hosts.

Part 1 concludes with a discussion of an issue that cuts across each of the three dispenser liability claims of chapters 4, 6, and 7. Whether it is created by legislation or as part of the development of the common law of a state, a dispenser liability claim involves the imposition of legal responsibility on a party who is almost always significantly less culpable than the drinking driver whose conduct directly caused the injury to the accident victim. In chapter 8, I confront the responsibility conundrum in dispenser liability cases and describe a theory of responsibility that can accommodate some of those claims more easily than courts appear to be able to do at present.

As the background to a reform effort, the legal landscape of tort law remedies for victims of drinking drivers is particularly diverse and is constantly developing along a variety of fronts. Part 1 attempts to capture both the diversity and the flux in the tort law treatment of drinking-driver accident victims through an orderly progression from the conceptually simplest to the more problematic theories of liability that are available in one form or another in many jurisdictions today.

Thus, in the chapters comprising part 1 of this book, I will examine each of the circles of potential liability under current tort law, focusing not only on the doctrinal possibilities of each for obtaining a recovery of damages but also on the barriers to recovery—legal, practical, and conceptual—that are likely to prevent tort actions of these types from fully compensating accident victims. It should be noted at the outset of this survey of tort remedies, however, that I do not purport to present in this book an exhaustive survey of all of the tort actions or other forms of loss shifting that are currently available to victims of drinking-driver accidents, nor do I try to identify and analyze each of the significant variations of the surveyed theories that have been adopted in different jurisdictions.[1] The purpose of this part of *John Barleycorn Must Pay* is to provide a sufficiently broad and critical look at contemporary tort law efforts to deal with the problem of accident costs caused by the drinking driver so that the reader can appreciate in a general way the manner in which the tort system in this country is currently set up to deal with the claims of victims of drinking drivers. Equipped with that appreciation, the reader can then use this survey to approach the subsequent discussion of the precise features that are desirable in an accident victim compensation system, features that are lacking in the current set of tort claims available to the seriously injured victim of the drinking driver. The details of the reform proposal I present at the end of this book can thus be evaluated in light of this understanding of the current legal regime and of the aims of the system that are not being accomplished as fully as they ought to be.

The tort liability theories that are surveyed in the next few chapters comprise the principal avenues of recovery that treat alcohol involvement in an accident as a factor that affects the presentation and the analysis of a claim for relief. These theories are, however, not the only roads to compensation available to a victim of a drinking-driver traffic accident. One method of obtaining compensation that needs to be considered by an injured victim is a products liability action that focuses not on the drinking driver but rather on the risks associated with the vehicles that were involved in the accident. Perhaps the most typical products liability claim in this context is one that identifies some feature of the passenger restraint system in the victim's own vehicle as defective. Examples would include door latches that disengage on impact, allowing the occupant to be ejected from the vehicle,[2] or lap belts in rear seats that cause serious abdominal injuries when the people wearing them are thrust forward by the impact.[3] Liability theories of this sort draw on what is now a well-established duty of vehicle manufacturers to design cars and trucks that are reasonably crashworthy.[4]

Crashworthiness products liability claims lie outside of the main focus of this book because they do not rely on any necessary relationship to the involvement of alcohol in the accident. Claims of that sort simply treat drinking-driver accidents as one subset of a larger class of traffic accidents in which vehicle design elements might pose a risk of injury to vehicle occupants. Tort lawyers could, however, creatively try to expand the reach of products liability claims so that the link between alcohol involvement and other types of vehicle defectiveness was more directly established. The two authors of an outstanding legal casebook on the subject of products liability have created a hypothetical case in which an automobile is alleged to be defective because it was not equipped with devices that would prevent it from being operated by a person who was intoxicated.[5] Included among the possible devices are ones that force the driver to pass a test as a prerequisite to starting the vehicle, such as a built-in breathalyzer test or some sort of mechanical or computer test of alertness or memory and coordination.[6] Of course, any plaintiff who would attempt to assert such a theory in the near future would face a daunting task in convincing a court that the devices are practicable, that they are both technologically and economically feasible, and that they could be sufficiently well engineered in order to eliminate "false positive" indications of intoxication that would prevent vehicle operation and perhaps thereby increase the risk of harm to vehicle operators in some circumstances.

Aside from this limited exception of a hypothetical design defect, though, the significant feature of products liability claims against vehicle manufacturers is that they treat the alcohol involvement as coincidental rather than essential to the accident injury. These claims are thus analogous to arguments that highway design changes are an appropriate focus in the effort to understand the nature of, and the solution to, the traffic-accident injury problem. While it is unarguably true that a variety of factors enter into a causal relationship with accident injuries, the focus of this book is primarily on the allocation of the costs of the injuries that are suffered in drinking-driver accidents. This focus requires a consideration of more than just the best way to reduce the frequency and the severity of accidents. The major concern instead is how to place the burden of accident losses in a way that fully compensates victims and also attaches injury costs where they belong—to the activities that have helped cause the accidents. Alcohol is a significant factor in causing injury that is too often overlooked as a result of the perspective that the legal system takes in assigning drinking-driver accident costs to appropriate activities.

## NOTES

1. For the reader who is seeking such a comprehensive survey, one of the best sources is the two-volume treatise by J. MOSHER, LIQUOR LIABILITY LAW.

2. Daly v. General Motors Corp., 20 Cal.3d 725, 575 P.2d 1162, 144 Cal. Rptr. 380 (1978).

3. An example of this type of claim outside of the drinking-driver setting is Garrett v. Ford Motor Co., 684 F. Supp. 407 (D. Md. 1987). The lawyers for the plaintiff in the *Garrett* case discuss what they see as the significance of the claim in Sakayan, Holtz & Kelley, *More Than A Case About a Car*, 25 TRIAL 34 (Feb. 1989).

4. *See, e.g.,* Dawson v. Chrysler Corp., 630 F.2d 950 (3d Cir. 1980), *cert. denied,* 450 U.S. 959 (1981); Larsen v. General Motors Corp., 391 F.2d 495 (8th Cir. 1968).

5. *See* J. HENDERSON & A. TWERSKI, PRODUCTS LIABILITY: PROBLEMS AND PROCESS 561-63 (1987).

6. A review of the technology for preventing drinking and driving can be found in Voas, *Emerging Technologies for Controlling the Drunk Driver,* in LAURENCE et al., SOCIAL CONTROL, at 321. An optimistic assessment of the prospects for a breath analysis interlock system is given in JACOBS, DRUNK DRIVING, at 170-71. *See also* Hinds, *Judges Turn to Ignition Locks to Ground Drunken Drivers,* New York Times, Dec. 24, 1988, § 1, at 48.

# 2

## The Tort Liability
## of the Drinking Driver

*More than six months have passed since the traffic accident in which Alan Bloom was killed and the other members of the Bloom family were seriously injured. Molly has begun to work part-time as a salesclerk in a local department store. The job could turn into a permanent full-time position, but Molly still faces an uncertain financial future. Her employer was recently acquired by another firm in a leveraged buy-out, and the new owner has sharply cut the employee benefit package in order to reduce its operating expenses.*

*As a part-time employee, Molly receives no health or life insurance contribution from her employer, and she would have to pay a substantial premium for coverage from a private insurance carrier. Alan's life insurance benefits have been paid to Molly in a lump sum, and she has invested that money in a very safe but relatively low-yield investment so that there will be money for the children's education in the future. The hospital and doctors' expenses for Molly and the children have been covered so far by the health insurance policy that was in effect at the time of the accident, but those policy benefits have nearly been exhausted. Molly is concerned about how she will afford the children's continuing medical care and the other services they will need as a result of the accident. These include Billy's special education needs and the psychological counseling that Sally is receiving. Molly is thankful that she and Alan had a mortgage life insurance policy in effect so that she doesn't have to make house payments each month, but she finds that the routine cost of maintaining the household takes up a large percentage of her current earnings.*

*One of Molly's friends was in a traffic accident about five years ago. He had sued the other driver, but the case had not gone to trial. Instead, the other driver's insurance company had settled for enough money to replace the friend's car, which had been totaled in the accident, and to cover his other losses. The friend gave Molly the name of the lawyer he had used, and Molly made an appointment with her to see if the lawyer thought that she had a promising lawsuit against the driver who had struck the Blooms' car.*

*The police report on the accident provided some personal information about*

*Tommy Smith, the other driver. Besides his name, this report indicated that his address was a post office box in a city about twenty miles away. The report also stated that Smith had told the investigating officer that he was a con-struction worker, but that he was currently unemployed. Smith had been driving without a license at the time of the accident. It had expired a couple of months earlier, but Smith insists that he had mailed in a renewal form and thought that he had received the currently valid license in the mail. In the state in which the accident occurred, however, a driver's license is not renewable by mail. Instead, a notice of renewal is mailed to each license holder no later than forty-five days prior to expiration, but that notice must be taken to an office of the Department of Motor Vehicles, where a license will be issued for the new term. After the accident, Smith was charged by the local prosecutor with involuntary manslaughter, driving while intoxicated, driving without a license, reckless driving, and failure to keep to the right of the center line of the highway. He was convicted of driving while intoxicated and sentenced to six months in the county jail. Smith had just begun serving that sentence when Molly went to see the lawyer.*

An injured person's lawsuit to recover monetary damages as compensation for the harm suffered as a result of an accident such as the one the Bloom family was involved in is governed by the law of torts. A tort is simply the technical legal term for a civil—as opposed to criminal—wrong for which some noncontractual legal remedy is recognized. The mastery of a few basic ideas, which together constitute the tort law primer that is presented in the first section of this chapter, will provide the foundation the reader needs in order to understand the legal positions of the plaintiff (the party who is seeking a legal remedy) and the defendant (the party from whom a legal remedy is being sought).

The law of torts traditionally has required a concurrence of two elements—wrongful conduct and causation—as a prerequisite to shifting the cost of an accident away from an injured person to someone else, who is made legally responsible for compensating the victim for that injury. Courts normally express the standard elements of a prima facie case for a tort claim as the breach of a legal duty that was owed to the injured party (the plaintiff) and a sufficiently close causal connection between the breach of that duty and the plaintiff's injury for the breach to be deemed the legal cause of the injury.[1] As will be seen in the discussion that follows, the need to establish these standard prerequisites of tort liability should not pose any substantial theoretical or evidentiary problems for the accident victim who is attempting to impose liability on the drinking driver.

## A Tort Law Primer—Duty and Causation

The initial element of a tort claim that a plaintiff is required to prove is that the accident involved a breach of a legal duty owed to the plaintiff. In the standard language used by courts to define breach of legal duty in accident cases, the defendant must exercise the same level of care that would be exercised by a reasonable person under similar circumstances in order to prevent harm from occurring to a person in the plaintiff's position. This rather vague legal standard can be broken down into a number of issues, beginning with the question of whether the plaintiff was a person to whom the defendant owed a duty of care. It should be easy for a plaintiff to establish that, as an automobile operator, a drinking driver owes a duty of reasonable care to all persons who are within the range of the destructive power of the vehicle.

Contemporary tort doctrine employs a basic foreseeability test to determine the scope of a defendant's legal duty. The test asks whether it was reasonably foreseeable that the defendant's conduct on this occasion posed a risk of harm to a person in the plaintiff's position.[2] This after-the-fact inquiry into foreseeability may seem conceptually confused in that the legal decision maker must look backward from an injury that we know *did* occur in order to determine whether an injury *could* have been expected to occur. In actual practice, however, the foreseeability test serves as a relatively simple device for initially identifying those classes of persons to whom a duty of care is owed. People who are using the highways are unquestionably among the class of foreseeable victims of a careless driver. Among the parties to whom a legal duty of care is owed are thus included drivers of other vehicles, passengers in those vehicles, as well as pedestrians and others who are close to the road. A small number of states have even expanded the scope of the driver's legal duty to include those who may be located outside the "zone of physical danger" from the automobile but who can nevertheless be expected to suffer emotional distress as a result of an injury to a person who is struck by the vehicle.[3]

Establishing that a plaintiff is a person to whom a drinking driver owes a duty of care is only the first step in establishing this element of a tort claim. An injured party must also prove that the defendant's conduct failed to fulfill that duty. If the drinking driver operates the vehicle in a manner that does not meet the minimum standard of reasonable care necessary to protect foreseeable victims from harm, then that driver has breached the legal duty owed to the injured plaintiff. The legal term used to describe the defendant's conduct in breaching that duty is "negligence."

Whether a defendant acted as a reasonable person under the circumstances is a question of fact to be decided by the jury in the typical negligence case. The plaintiff, of course, must first introduce sufficient evidence of the defendant's negligence. The judge in the case makes the legal determination of whether the plaintiff's evidence is sufficient. Thus the negligence standard is susceptible to at least some greater degree of specificity than its vague or open-ended formulation may otherwise indicate.

A useful way to conceptualize the negligence standard of reasonable care is to see it as a balancing test. The burden of taking measures to prevent an accident are weighed against the anticipated accident injury costs if those measures are not taken. If the expected accident costs are greater than the cost of prevention, then an actor is deemed to have acted negligently in failing to incur the prevention costs.[4] This conceptual image of negligence also provides a reasonably effective working definition of the various pockets of strict liability that are found in contemporary tort law. Liability is strict, in this sense of the term, when it is imposed without any requirement that a plaintiff prove that the cost of accident prevention was less than the anticipated accident injury costs.

Conduct that departs more substantially from the reasonable care standard may support an aggravated fault characterization, such as recklessness or willful and wanton misconduct. Recklessness can be defined as conduct that creates a substantially greater risk of physical harm to another than would be necessary to make the conduct negligent.[5] Against the background of the negligence standard described above, recklessness can be seen as conduct that poses a risk of harm that is very likely to occur versus merely foreseeable harm. In terms of balancing costs, negligence can be understood to exist whenever the anticipated injury costs outweigh, however slightly, the costs of preventing the accident. Recklessness exists when the anticipated injury costs so significantly outweigh the prevention costs that the balance is struck heavily in favor of the defendant's obligation to take the preventive measures. The distinction between the two fault standards of negligence and recklessness reflects an underlying belief that there is a qualitative difference in culpability between failing to exercise reasonable care to prevent injury and acting despite the knowledge that injury is very likely to result. Indeed, tort law now treats conduct that the actor *knows* is substantially certain to cause harm as constituting an intent to cause that harm.[6]

Establishing that a driver has breached a legal duty that was owed to the traffic accident victim is a necessary element of a prima facie case, but it is not by itself sufficient to make the driver liable. The injured plaintiff must also prove that the causation element of the tort claim has been satisfied, namely, that a legally sufficient causal connection exists between the drinking driver's wrongful conduct and the plaintiff's injury. Proving the causation element in a drinking-driver accident case is as unlikely to pose significant problems as proving the breach of a duty that is owed to the average accident victim.

Courts typically consider the causation element of a tort claim as proceeding on two related, but analytically and functionally distinct, levels of inquiry. The first level is presented as a matter of whether the defendant's wrongful conduct was a cause-in-fact of the plaintiff's injury. An affirmative answer to this question identifies the defendant as someone who can be held legally responsible for the harm suffered by the plaintiff. The second level of causal inquiry now comes into play, but the analysis focuses more on whether the defendant is a person who *should* be held liable for the plaintiff's injury. This analysis is commonly put in terms of whether the defendant's conduct was a proximate cause of the plaintiff's injury, and its major function is to provide an opportunity to determine whether there are policy considerations that make it unfair or unwise to hold the defendant responsible for the particular injury that happened to this plaintiff.

Traditional tort law thinking has routinely posed the preliminary cause-in-fact inquiry as a matter of whether the plaintiff would have been injured *but for* the wrongful conduct of the defendant. In the context of a drinking-driver traffic accident, under this traditional approach the question becomes whether the plaintiff would have been injured had the defendant's drinking and driving not occurred. The principal shortcoming of this sort of counterfactual inquiry—what would have happened if there had been no drinking driver—is that it may produce a misleading negative answer whenever a case involves multiple causal factors.

Suppose, for example, that a passenger in one vehicle is injured when the driver of her car negligently fails to signal for a left turn, and that car is struck from behind by another car whose driver has negligently failed to maintain a proper distance, pushing the first car into the path of an oncoming car driven negligently at a high rate of speed and without a proper lookout for hazards. When a variety of factors produce an injury, it can be difficult to identify any single factor under the traditional theory as one without which the plaintiff would not have been harmed. In reality, each of the factors contributed to the production of the injury to the passenger in the first car.

Today, however, even if traffic-accident plaintiffs may sometimes run into difficulty in obtaining an affirmative answer to the traditional question, the cause-in-fact element is unlikely to present much of a hurdle. The "but for" causation test in common law negligence actions is frequently replaced today by a significantly less demanding "substantial factor" test. The substantial factor test works particularly well in cases involving multiple causation, when the but for test would produce problematic results.[7] In the three-car collision example, the negligent conduct of each of the drivers would be found to be a substantial factor in producing the plaintiff's injury. Under the substantial factor test, even if the drinking driver's operation of a vehicle is not easily classified as a necessary cause or a sufficient cause of the accident in which the plaintiff was injured, causation can still be established as long as the defendant's conduct contributed in a meaningful way to the harm.

The second part of the causation element in contemporary tort law requires an injured party to go beyond proving that the defendant's conduct was a cause-in-fact of the harm and also establish that the defendant's conduct was a proximate cause of the injury. Using a literal meaning of the word "proximate" would restrict a defendant's liability to an injury that was the immediate or next result of the defendant's conduct. Under that approach, for example, a railroad would be liable for the destruction of a house that was set on fire by sparks that escaped from a negligently maintained locomotive, but the railroad would not be liable for the damage to other property to which the fire spread because that damage was remote rather than proximate.[8]

Today proximate cause analysis routinely begins with a foreseeability analysis, but one that differs slightly from the foreseeability inquiry used to determine the scope of the defendant's legal duty. There the question was whether the plaintiff was a reasonably foreseeable victim of the defendant's conduct. In the proximate cause analysis, the question shifts to whether the risk of harm from the defendant's conduct was foreseeable, focusing on a risk-specific foreseeability. An exceptionally instructive opinion, in a case called *Marshall v. Nugent*,[9] stated that the function of the proximate cause analysis is "to confine the liability of a negligent actor to those harmful consequences which result from the operation of the risk, or a risk, the foreseeability of which rendered the defendant's conduct negligent."[10] The opinion then went on to describe a variety of risks which are created by negligent driving . . . [including] injuries resulting from a direct collision between the carelessly driven car and another vehicle. . . . [Or] the plaintiff may fall and injure himself in frantically racing out of the way of the errant car. . . . Or the plaintiff may be knocked down and injured by a human stampede as the car rushes toward a crowded safety zone. . . . Or the plaintiff may faint from intense excitement stimulated by the near collision, and in falling sustain a fractured skull. . . . Or the plaintiff may suffer a miscarriage or other physical illness as a result of intense nervous shock incident to a hair-raising escape.[11]

In normal tort practice today, the risk-specific foreseeability analysis of the proximate cause element operates more as an inquiry into whether the relationship between the defendant's conduct and the plaintiff's injury is so unusual or so attenuated that liability ought not to be imposed. In one of the most influential dissenting opinions in United States tort law, Judge William S. Andrews of the Court of Appeals of New York described proximate cause analysis in a way that eschews "[a]ny philosophical doctrine of causation" in favor of "practical politics" and "our notions of public policy," in order to put into effect the idea that "because of convenience, of public policy, of a rough sense of justice, the law arbitrarily declines to trace a series of events beyond a certain point."[12] In a classic example of proximate cause analysis serving to limit the scope of liability, a driver negligently collides with an unmarked truck containing explosives. The collision causes the truck's cargo to explode, and a few blocks away, a nurse, startled by the sound of the explosion, drops a baby. The injury to the baby was a result of the negligence of the original driver, but for public policy reasons it should not be thought of as a proximate result. Under Judge Andrews's view of proximate cause, a decision to extend the liability of the negligent driver to cover that harm would go too far.[13]

When the role of the proximate cause doctrine is primarily to limit liability, then it is unlikely that the legal fact finders in a tort lawsuit against a drinking driver would very often be persuaded to place policy-based restrictions limiting the extent of the drinking driver's liability for the accident victim's injury. That conclusion is bolstered by a tendency in modern tort law to expand the scope of proximate cause determinations as the level of culpability of the defendant increases. If that trend is followed in drinking-driver accident cases, then the proximate cause element would be even easier for a plaintiff to establish in the aggravated-fault cases described in the discussion immediately below. In conclusion, then, as a matter of proving the elements of the plaintiff's prima facie case in tort law, the drinking driver is apparently a defendant whose liability to the accident victim should be fairly easy to establish.

As mentioned above in the description of the "breach of a legal duty" element of a tort claim, the fault of a drinking driver may have been at an aggravated level, making it possible to characterize the driver's conduct as recklessness, willful and wanton misconduct, or gross negligence. Although distinctions might be drawn among these three characterizations of aggravated fault, I use the term "recklessness" here in a way that includes the other terms, that is, simply to denote a level of fault that is more culpable than negligence but does not rise to the level of culpability that would be characterized as an intent to cause harm to the plaintiff. The important idea for purposes of this discussion is that a drinking driver's conduct at times may be found to display this higher culpability, which has been defined as acting while "knowing or having reason to know of facts which would lead a reasonable man to realize, not only that his conduct creates an unreasonable risk of physical harm to another, but also that such *risk is substantially greater* than that which is necessary to make his conduct negligent."[14]

In many cases, an aggravated fault characterization can be important to the plaintiff suing a drinking driver. A few states still retain automobile guest statutes that prohibit recovery by a "guest passenger"—that is, a passenger who has not paid for or provided any other consideration for the transportation—unless the passenger is able to prove that the driver's conduct meets the aggravated fault standard.[15] Under a statute of this sort, if the accident victim was a guest passenger in the driver's automobile, the victim would have to prove that the driver's conduct was more than just negligent.[16] Even if the plaintiff proves the higher level of fault, however, other barriers to recovery might exist. For example, the defendant might be able to raise a successful defense based on the plaintiff's conduct, such as contributory or comparative negligence[17] or assumption of risk.[18] The assertion of a defense of this sort might be based, for example, on the passenger's decision to accept a ride with an intoxicated driver, and it might turn on such issues as the reasonableness of accepting the ride and on the passenger's awareness of the driver's alcohol-impaired condition. Another sort of defense might be based on culpable conduct by the passenger such as furnishing alcoholic beverages to the drinking driver or encouraging the driver's consumption of alcohol. Nevertheless, if injured passengers are able to establish that the defendant's conduct met a higher level of fault, they do not have to worry about finding a way to get around the limitations imposed by the guest statute, such as establishing that the passenger had a status other than a guest.

The idea that a tort plaintiff's recovery can be reduced or barred because of the plaintiff's own conduct can play a role in any tort claim, not only one involving a guest passenger statue. The need to minimize the effect of that idea is a second reason why aggravated fault is an important issue. Plaintiffs who are able to characterize a defendant's conduct as more than just negligent can minimize the effect of their own culpable conduct. Historically, a plaintiff's recovery from a negligent defendant was totally barred if the plaintiff was negligent,[19] or if the plaintiff assumed the risk of being harmed by the defendant's negligence.[20] Today most states have replaced this type of a rule with a comparative negligence rule or a statute that reduces rather than bars a plaintiff's recovery according to the relative negligence of the parties.[21] The modern trend is to go even further and collapse the assumption of risk defense into the comparative negligence rule so that only unreasonable decisions to encounter a known risk will act to reduce a plaintiff's recovery.[22] The tort doctrines dealing with liability defenses based on a plaintiff's conduct can be seen to rest on a rough sense of proportionality: the general level of culpability of a plaintiff must reach the level of culpability of the defendant before the plaintiff's fault will constitute a defense.[23] That notion is what makes the aggravated fault issue so important in the tort claim against a drinking driver. If a drinking driver's conduct was reckless, then an injured plaintiff who was merely negligent should be able to recover regardless of the plaintiff's own fault.[24]

A third reason to try to characterize a drinking driver's conduct as more than negligent is to weaken any arguments the driver might have for recognizing public-policy restrictions or limitations on the extent of the driver's liability. Both the breach of duty and the proximate cause elements of a plaintiff's tort claim can be strengthened by proving a higher degree of fault on the part of the defendant. As the defendant's level of fault increases, these elements of a tort claim can expand to include a wider class of victims or a more attenuated chain of cause and effect as still being within the legal responsibility of the more culpable defendant.[25] As a practical matter, of course, a defendant whose conduct can be characterized as highly culpable will probably have much less of a chance to appear as a sympathetic figure to a jury. This disadvantage may also give a more highly culpable defendant an incentive to agree to settle a tort claim without litigation and on terms that are favorable to the plaintiff.

A final reason that establishing aggravated fault is important is the effect it can have on the nature of a plaintiff's recovery and the size of the monetary award. In addition to the compensatory damages the plaintiff normally recovers, a plaintiff who establishes a higher degree of fault on the part of the defendant may very well be able to obtain punitive damages.[26] Punitive damages are awarded over and above the amount needed to compensate victims for their actual losses in order both to punish the defendant and to deter this defendant and others from acting in the same way in the future. Lawsuits brought against drinking drivers who have injured other people would seem to be prime opportunities for invoking both the punitive and the deterrence functions of this type of award.

## Expanding the Liability of a Drinking Driver by Increasing the Effectiveness of Presumptions

However uncomplicated proving the drinking driver's breach of a legal duty may seem, this task could be made even easier if the standard common-law tort doctrine called negligence per se were applied more frequently. Courts in all states recognize the idea that, at least in some circumstances, proof of the defendant's violation of a statute is proof of the defendant's breach of the duty to exercise reasonable care.[27] Commonly referred to as the doctrine of negligence per se, this rule of decision treats a plaintiff's proof of the defendant's statutory violation as sufficient to establish that the violator acted in a negligent manner. The doctrine thus allows a plaintiff to bypass the requirement to prove what level of care a reasonable person in the defendant's position would have exercised under the circumstances and that the defendant's conduct in the accident fell below that standard of care. Underlying this doctrine is the notion that compliance with the statute is at least the minimum standard of care to which a reasonable person would adhere. The defendant's violation of the statute establishes, at least presumptively, a breach of the legal duty to exercise reasonable care. Negligence per se is typically invoked when a specific statutory command satisfies three prerequisites: first, the injured person is a member of a class of persons that the legislation is designed to protect; second, the injury is of a type that the statute is designed to prevent; and third, the statutory violation is causally linked to the injury.

A recent decision of the Supreme Court of Ohio, in *Gressman v. McClain,* approved the use in this fashion of a statute that prohibits serving alcohol to an intoxicated person.[28] A brief look at the *Gressman* decision will illustrate how the negligence per se doctrine operates. A woman who had been drinking at a golf course snack bar lost control of her car after leaving the golf course and killed four people. The accident victims had been in a car with which the drinking driver collided when she crossed the center line of the highway. At the time of the accident, an Ohio statute prohibited sales of beer and intoxicating liquor to an intoxicated person.[29] A lawsuit to recover damages for the wrongful death of the driver of the car that was struck by the snack bar patron included a claim alleging that the golf course was liable for the death of the victim. Well after the accident, the Ohio legislature enacted a dram shop statute that specified the liability of a commercial dispenser of alcohol in the precise circumstances of this case, that is, for injuries that occurred off the property on which the alcohol was served to the drinking driver.[30] At the time of the accident, however, no such express statutory authority existed establishing the golf course's civil liability to the accident victims of the drinking driver. Notwithstanding the lack of a direct statutory provision for the liability of the golf course in these circumstances, the Supreme Court of Ohio held that the golf course's failure to comply with the statutory prohibition on furnishing intoxicating beverages to an intoxicated person would constitute negligence per se. Therefore, the golf course could be held liable if the plaintiff was able to prove that the patron was served when she was intoxicated and then that she had caused the accident while intoxicated.[31]

The Ohio case demonstrates how a statutory violation can be employed to establish that a defendant's conduct was negligent. The doctrine of negligence per se, which allows statutes to be used in this way, has an obvious role to play in an accident victim's tort lawsuit against a drinking driver. For example, a tort plaintiff might draw on a statutory provision that makes the operation of a motor vehicle while under the influence of alcohol or other intoxicants a criminal offense.[32] A plaintiff who was able to use the doctrine would meet the evidentiary burden for establishing the breach of duty element of the tort claim against the drinking driver simply by proving the driver's intoxication level as established by a conviction (or its functional equivalent, such as a guilty plea) for violation of the statute.

The use of the negligence per se doctrine in this setting should comply with the first two of the three requirements that were described above. Someone who is injured in a traffic accident with a drinking driver is easily seen to be part of the class of people most directly intended to be protected by statutes outlawing driving while intoxicated or driving under the influence (DWI or DUI), and the personal injuries that are suffered in such accidents are certainly among the harms those statutes are intended to reduce or eliminate. Furthermore, the use of the evidence of the statutory violation in this way would appear to operate for the benefit of both the plaintiff and the judicial system as a whole. If a driver's statutory violation has been established in a criminal prosecution for driving while intoxicated, then the use of that conviction in the tort lawsuit by the accident victim can reduce the time and the effort needed to prove that the defendant failed to exercise sufficient care while intoxicated and operating a vehicle. Permitting the statutory violation to be treated as negligence per se can also reduce the risk of confusing the jury, a problem that often occurs in a more extended litigation of the legal and factual issues involved in proving a defendant's breach of duty.

The benefits of using a statutory violation as negligence per se in an accident case should, of course, be foregone if they would subject the defendant to a substantial risk of prejudice. In the case of a drinking-driver tort defendant, however, the benefits can be obtained without creating any significant risk of unfairness. A drinking driver who was convicted of a criminal offense, such as driving while intoxicated, should have had more than an ample incentive to resist the DWI conviction, given the legal penalties and the moral blame involved. In addition, because the DWI conviction was adjudicated in a criminal proceeding, the driver's guilt had to be proved beyond any reasonable doubt. The "beyond a reasonable doubt" standard of proof required in a criminal case is higher than what defendants face in the tort lawsuit, in which they can be found liable on the basis of a mere preponderance of the evidence. Therefore, the use of negligence per se in this instance would seem fair.

Nevertheless, courts adjudicating tort claims against drinking drivers more often than not display a reluctance to employ the statutory violation to show negligence per se. Their reluctance is principally based on doubts about the third prerequisite for establishing negligence per se, which requires that the plaintiff prove a causal connection between the violation of the statute and the harm to the plaintiff. Even though the defendant's conduct violated a criminal statute, courts in a number of states have ruled that it is still necessary for the plaintiff to prove independently of the statutory violation that the manner in which the defendant operated the vehicle fell below the tort standard of reasonable care.[33] The rationale the courts usually give for this ruling is that the doctrine of negligence per se requires proof that it was the statutory violation itself that caused the injury to the plaintiff. Proof that the driver was legally intoxicated at the time of an accident does not necessarily mean that the accident was caused by the intoxication. After all, according to this view, some intoxicated drivers may manage to operate their vehicles with a reasonable level of care, and some accidents involving intoxicated drivers might be caused by careless conduct that is separate from the intoxication. Because of those two possibilities, then, this restrictive view of the use of the negligence per se doctrine holds that a plaintiff should be required to prove that the accident was caused by some demonstrated act or omission that constitutes carelessness or negligence of the driver who was intoxicated, rather than simply relying on the fact of the statutory violation to establish the defendant's breach of the duty of reasonable care.

That restrictive view of the appropriate role for the doctrine of negligence per se could be replaced with a new one. Rather than continuing to require a plaintiff to offer this additional element of proof that an intoxicated driver actually failed to use reasonable care, a court could adopt a modified approach under which a driver who has been convicted of a statutory violation will be presumed to have breached a legal duty that was owed to the injured party. Indeed, the court could go further, giving an even stronger effect to proof of the conviction, by ruling that a driver's intoxication that was sufficient to support a conviction for violation of the statute will also be presumed to have played a causal role in the accident that injured the plaintiff.

A fairly strong case can be made for the recognition of the presumptions in these circumstances. Presumptions are appropriately invoked when a certain unproven state of affairs that is at issue in the lawsuit (such as a failure to exercise reasonable care) is sufficiently likely to coexist with another proven fact (such as a conviction for driving while intoxicated) that it is reasonable to accept the proven fact as proof that the unproven state of affairs actually existed as well. The appropriate question in this setting is whether drivers who have been convicted of violating a DWI or DUI statute after an accident (the proven fact) also have failed to exercise reasonable care to protect others from harm caused by the driving that led up to that accident (the fact in issue). Two critical factors provide considerable assurance that invoking the twin presumptions suggested here is justified. First, the plaintiff would be able to rely on the creation of the presumptions only upon proof of the defendant's criminal conviction, with all the safeguards that are part of a criminal proceeding. Second, the use of this presumption would be limited to traffic accident cases involving a defendant who has been convicted of a drinking-and-driving offense.

Some intoxicated drivers probably can be said to exercise reasonable care in the way they drive, but it is much more likely than not that the level of care they exercise falls below that of a reasonable person who is not driving while intoxicated. Similarly, some accidents involving intoxicated drivers probably do result solely from the operation of factors other than the driver's intoxication, such as a mechanical malfunction of the vehicle. But again, it is much more likely than not that the intoxicated state of a driver contributes, at least indirectly, to the occurrence of an accident in which that driver is involved.[34]

Presumptions do not have to be given such weight that they conclusively establish the elements that they are designed to prove.[35] A true presumption operates to create an inference that must be accepted unless the opposing party offers evidence to rebut the presumption. If the modification of the negligence per se rule that has just been described were to be adopted in tort cases concerning drinking-driver accidents, the drinking-driver defendant would have an opportunity to introduce evidence to rebut either or both of these twin presumptions of the lack of reasonable care and of the causal connection between the lack of care and the injury. However, if the defendant has no plausible rebutting evidence indicating that the court has before it one of those unusual cases in which an intoxicated driver was driving carefully or in which the intoxication played no substantial causal role in the accident, then a criminal conviction establishing that the defendant was intoxicated in violation of a state statute should compel the fact finder to conclude that the defendant was negligent and that the defendant's negligence was a legal cause of the plaintiff's injury.

Thus far this discussion has focused on a presumption of negligence. What of a criminal statute that characterizes the drinking driver's conduct as reckless? Recklessness in the tort context operates much differently than it does in the criminal context. The difference may be great enough, in terms of the meaning and the consequences attached to recklessness, that the better course of action would be to resist the temptation to presume, for example, that a defendant convicted of the criminal offense of reckless driving has also acted recklessly for purposes of a tort claim against that defendant. For levels of tort culpability greater than negligence, tort plaintiffs should be required to establish the fault of the defendant without the benefit of the enhanced presumptions that might be drawn from a drinking-and-driving conviction.

The modification of the negligence per se rules to create a more vigorous role for presumptions that has been outlined above is limited to a situation in which a tort defendant has previously been convicted of a statutory violation on an intoxicated driving offense for the accident that is also the basis of the tort claim. A more ambitious modification of these rules is possible: to allow the two presumptions in a negligence per se case—breach of a legal duty and causation—to be triggered by a plaintiff who introduces evidence that falls short of a driver's criminal conviction for DWI. Perhaps the most substantial expansion in the applicability of these presumptions would be obtained if courts were to use the National Highway Traffic Safety Administration's (NHTSA) three-part test for "alcohol involvement" in traffic accidents as the basis for the presumptions. NHTSA deems alcohol to have been involved in an accident anytime one of the following three criteria is satisfied: (1) a DWI or DUI citation is issued to a driver; (2) there is a test result of .01 percent blood alcohol concentration; or (3) there is a police statement alleging alcohol involvement.[36] Each of the three criteria raises different considerations as a basis for a presumption of negligence of a driver in an alcohol-related accident.

If the first criterion were employed, the presumption of negligence would be based on a police citation rather than the driver's criminal conviction. One's confidence in the ability of the police to identify intoxication accurately would have to be high enough that one could reasonably make the link between the issuance of a citation to a driver and that driver's negligence. When evaluating whether that degree of confidence is appropriate, it should be remembered that the negligence and causation presumptions would only come into play in a tort case after there has been a traffic accident involving the person who received the citation.

While the tort standard of proof is less stringent than that required to sustain a criminal conviction, it would seem that a citation alone is an insufficient basis for invoking the presumptions in the tort case against the driver who has been cited. A compromise use of the first NHTSA criterion for alcohol-involvement would be to allow a court to treat evidence of the defendant's post-accident citation for DWI as creating an inference rather than a presumption of negligence. The difference between an inference and a presumption turns on the strength of the logical and the legal connection between the proven fact and the unproven fact that is at issue in the case. While an unrebutted presumption requires that the fact finder *must* find that the unproven fact has been established, an inference simply *permits* the fact finder to conclude that the unproven fact has been established. Under the compromise just outlined, proof of a drinking driver's criminal conviction would require the fact finder to deem the defendant negligent in the absence of rebutting evidence. Proof of a defendant's citation for DWI would leave the question of the driver's negligence open. Even so, the reduced weight that would be given to the evidence of the defendant's DWI citation could be very helpful to a tort plaintiff. The permissible inference would at least allow the plaintiff to survive an attack on the legal sufficiency of the evidence of the citation in support of the contention that the defendant breached a duty of care that caused the injury to the plaintiff. While an unrebutted presumption assures a plaintiff of success in establishing the critical fact that is in issue, allowing an inference to be drawn from an evidentiary fact will at least give a tort plaintiff an opportunity to place the fact in issue and get to a jury.

The second and third NHTSA criteria emphasize the important distinction between alcohol *involvement* and legal *intoxication*. In many states, the legal intoxication limit based on blood alcohol concentration (.10 percent) is as much as ten times the NHTSA alcohol-involvement standard of .01 percent.[37] As for the third criterion, a police statement of alcohol involvement is obviously weaker proof than a DWI citation. One could argue in favor of basing the negligence and causation presumptions or inferences on these criteria as well. The stronger effect would depend on concluding that the alcohol-involvement criteria are a strong enough indication that a drinking driver's behavior is likely to have contributed to an accident that requiring the drinking driver to rebut a presumption of fault and a presumption of a causal role for that fault based on these criteria would not offend contemporary notions of fairness. As with the DWI citation criterion, evidence that either of these two criteria were satisfied could be treated as merely creating an inference that would operate to the plaintiff's advantage in meeting the "sufficiency of evidence" standard to get to a jury in the tort claim against the drinking driver.

A search for some lower standard of alcohol involvement seems to be particularly defensible in states where the legal intoxication limit set in the state DWI statute is too high. The Surgeon General's 1988 Workshop on Drunk Driving adopted this conclusion and recommended that over the next decade states should lower the level of blood alcohol concentration required for legal intoxication from the current widespread level of .10 percent to .04 percent and, for drivers under the age of twenty-one, any BAC level above .00 percent. That recommendation reflects the former surgeon general's conclusion that any drinking of alcohol has a negative impact on a driver's ability to operate an automobile safely.[38] Allowing some or all of the lower NHTSA standards of alcohol involvement, or a variant of those criteria, to help plaintiffs prove the breach of duty and causation elements of a tort claim against a drinking driver would be consistent with this view, and it would also reflect society's growing realization that a drinking driver, even if not legally intoxicated under existing laws, poses a risk that ought not to be tolerated.

## Legal and Practical Limitations on Recovery

A tort plaintiff faces two major obstacles to recovering full compensation. First, a defendant can defeat a plaintiff's case by establishing an affirmative defense, which is a legal limitation on recovery. Second, a plaintiff may win a court award of monetary damages against a defendant but be unable to collect all or some of the money from the defendant, which is a practical limitation on recovery.

In the context of the drinking-driver tort case, the defendant typically might turn to an affirmative defense based on the plaintiff's own negligence, proving that the plaintiff's negligence was one of the factors that caused the accident in which the plaintiff was injured. This defense is called an affirmative defense because the defendant bears the burden of proof on this matter. Its effect is to preclude or limit liability to the plaintiff in spite of the plaintiff's proof of a prima facie claim against the defendant, that is, proof of all the elements that are sufficient by themselves to allow the plaintiff to succeed. The basic issues are similar to those that lie at the heart of the plaintiff's prima facie case. Here the defendant must prove that the plaintiff failed to use reasonable care to prevent the injury that occurred to the plaintiff and, in addition, that the lack of care was a substantial factor in producing the plaintiff's injury. Historically, under the tort doctrine of contributory negligence, a plaintiff's negligence would completely bar recovery from a negligent defendant, regardless of how little a contribution the plaintiff's negligence made to the occurrence of the injury. Today most states have enacted some form of a comparative negligence defense, in which the plaintiff's recovery is reduced in proportion to the plaintiff's own negligence.

For the purposes of this look at the tort remedies that are available to an accident victim of a drinking driver, the most significant aspect of the affirmative defense based on the plaintiff's contributory or comparative negligence is that it operates independently of the alcohol-related feature of the drinking-driver accident. Any negligence on the part of a plaintiff can reduce the plaintiff's recovery from a drinking driver, and in some situations, a plaintiff's negligence can totally relieve a drinking driver of any legal obligation to compensate the plaintiff for the harm that was suffered in the accident.

Assuming that a tort plaintiff proves a prima facie case against a drinking-driver defendant and that the plaintiff is not met with an affirmative defense, the tort remedies that the plaintiff is entitled to recover as a matter of legal doctrine may nevertheless be limited as a practical matter. A plaintiff who wins a lawsuit against a drinking driver does not automatically receive any money from that driver. The court's award of monetary damages to the plaintiff has the legal effect of establishing that the defendant owes a debt to the plaintiff in the amount of the judgment entered by the court. Following a court's entry of a judgment in favor of the plaintiff, then, the winning plaintiff and the losing defendant assume the new legal relationship of judgment creditor and judgment debtor, respectively. The award of compensatory damages to the injured party—and punitive damages as well, if they constitute part of the award—is little more than an illusory benefit unless the successful tort plaintiff who becomes a judgment creditor of the drinking driver has some reasonable chance of collecting the money that is owed by that judgment debtor. A number of significant practical and legal factors can interfere with the plaintiff's ability to collect the monetary award from the defendant driver.

Typically, the primary source of funds for satisfying a tort judgment against a driver is the driver's liability insurance policy. For relatively minor accidents, that insurance coverage may be sufficient to pay all the claims that are made against the insured. As the seriousness of the accident increases, however, the ability to satisfy judgments out of the available liability insurance fund is likely to decrease. If the defendant driver has only the minimum liability coverage required by state law,[39] then the funds available will fall substantially short of the amount owed to the more seriously injured plaintiff. Even worse, the drinking driver may be uninsured. In this case, the plaintiff may be compensated by uninsured motorist coverage if that coverage was applicable to the case at hand. Furthermore, even if the drinking driver is insured, the defendant's liability insurer may deny its obligation to indemnify the defendant, arguing that driving while intoxicated transforms the accident into an uninsured event. An exclusion provision of this sort is written into many automobile rental agreements, and some no-fault insurance statutes authorize insurance companies to place such exclusions in the policies they write.[40]

If the successful tort plaintiff has been awarded punitive damages from the drinking driver, a different obstacle may arise. Approximately twenty-five states have adopted the position that insuring against liability for punitive damages is contrary to public policy.[41] Where a prohibition of that sort is in effect, the plaintiff cannot expect that an insurance fund will be available for paying the portion of the judgment that represents punitive damages. For those damages, the plaintiff will have to proceed against the driver's assets in order to satisfy the judgment.[42]

The chances of receiving the full compensation awarded in a large judgment may not be appreciably greater in the case of a plaintiff forced to go after the defendant's assets other than insurance. The most significant obstacle to recovery in this case is posed by state statutes that protect debtors by shielding some of their assets from the execution of judgments that have been entered against them. Although the nature and the extent of the protection varies from state to state, certain features are commonly found in these statutes. The debtor's house is likely to be protected by a homestead exemption,[43] and the debtor's personal property may be protected for much, if not most, of its value.[44] Even the defendant's employment income is likely to be protected from execution to a substantial degree.[45] The public policy rationale behind these exemptions is both clear and compelling: a careless act by the defendant ought not to reduce the defendant (and the defendant's family) to abject poverty. Nevertheless, it is just as clear that the exemptions can reduce or even eliminate the ability of a seriously injured accident victim to obtain complete compensation from the drinking driver who caused those injuries and has been held legally responsible for them.

When all of the legal and practical obstacles to satisfying a tort judgment that has been entered against a drinking driver are taken into account, the judgment creditor status that the successful plaintiff has managed to obtain can turn out to be substantially less attractive than it might have appeared to be on the day that a large jury verdict in the plaintiff's favor was announced. In fact, the obstacles outlined above are likely to prove so discouraging to any attorney whom a seriously injured plaintiff consults that the attorney would probably not consider a lawsuit solely against the drinking driver worth the time, expense, and effort required to obtain what may turn out to be a worthless judgment against the driver. The result, then, at this

first level of tort liability is that the most promising defendants—
from the standpoint of proving that the fault and causation elements
of a tort claim have been satisfied—are also the least promising in
terms of recovering any substantial sums of money that might be
awarded. This fact frequently leads the tort plaintiff's lawyer, as a
matter of course, to turn to the second order of tort liability to find
a more financially responsible defendant—a party to whom the fault
of the drinking driver can be imputed.

## NOTES

1. *See generally,* W. KEETON, D. DOBBS, R. KEETON & D. OWEN, PROSSER
AND KEETON ON TORTS (5th ed. 1984) (hereinafter cited as PROSSER &
KEETON, THE LAW OF TORTS); AMERICAN BAR ASSOCIATION, TOWARDS A
JURISPRUDENCE OF INJURY: THE CONTINUING CREATION OF A SYSTEM OF
SUBSTANTIVE JUSTICE IN AMERICAN TORT LAW (1984) (M. SHAPO, reporter).

2. *See, e.g.,* Palsgraf v. Long Island R.R. Co., 248 N.Y. 339, 162 N.E. 99
(1928).

3. *See, e.g.,* Dillon v. Legg, 68 Cal.2d 728, 441 P.2d 912, 69 Cal. Rptr.
72 (1968); Thing v. LaChusa, 48 Cal.3d 644, 771 P.2d 814, 257 Cal. Rptr.
865 (1989) (limiting recovery for damages for the emotional distress that is
suffered by bystanders to an accident to those plaintiffs who are closely
related to the accident victim who were located near the accident and directly
perceived the injury to the victim).

4. *See* United States v. Carroll Towing Co., 159 F.2d 169 (2d Cir. 1947);
Posner, *A Theory of Negligence,* 1 J. LEGAL STUD. 29 (1972).

5. *See* RESTATEMENT (SECOND) OF TORTS § 500 (1965).

6. *See* RESTATEMENT (SECOND) OF TORTS § 8A (1964).

7. *See* RESTATEMENT (SECOND) OF TORTS § 431-33 (1965); *see generally*
PROSSER & KEETON, LAW OF TORTS, at 265-69.

8. *See* Ryan v. New York Central R.R. Co., 35 N.Y. 210 (1866).

9. 222 F.2d 604 (1st Cir. 1955).

10. *Id.* at 610.

11. *Id.* at 610-11.

12. Palsgraf v. Long Island R.R. Co., 248 N.Y. 339, 351-53, 162 N.E.
99, 104 (1928) (Andrews, J. dissenting).

13. *Id.* at 353, 162 N.E. at 104.

14. RESTATEMENT (SECOND) OF TORTS § 500 (1965) (emphasis added).

15. *See, e.g.,* ALA. CODE § 32-1-2 (1986).

16. Under Nebraska's guest statute, however, the intoxication of the
driver is treated as an independent basis of liability to the guest. *See* NEB.
REV. STAT. § 39-6,191 (1986).

17. RESTATEMENT (SECOND) OF TORTS § 463 (1965).

18. *Id.* at § 496A.

19. Butterfield v. Forrester, 11 East 60, 103 Eng. Rep. 926 (K.B. 1809). *See generally* PROSSER & KEETON, LAW OF TORTS, at 451-62.

20. The history of the assumption of risk defense and the policy debate surrounding its retention and modification are discussed in Symposium, *Assumption of Risk*, 22 LA. L. REV. 1 (1961). *See also* PROSSER & KEETON, LAW OF TORTS, at 480-98.

21. *See* PROSSER & KEETON, LAW OF TORTS, at 468-79.

22. *See, e.g.*, Blackburn v. Dorta, 348 So.2d 287 (Fla. 1977); PROSSER & KEETON, LAW OF TORTS, at 495-98.

23. PROSSER & KEETON, LAW OF TORTS, at 462.

24. *See* RESTATEMENT (SECOND) OF TORTS § 503 (1965).

25. *See, e.g.*, Rowland v. Christian, 69 Cal.2d 108, 443 P.2d 561, 70 Cal. Rptr. 97 (1968) (scope of duty depends on a number of factors, including "the moral blame attached to the defendant's conduct").

26. *See generally* 1 L. SCHLUETER & K. REDDEN, PUNITIVE DAMAGES § 9.10(B)(1) (2d ed. 1989).

27. For a general discussion of the rules under which statutory violations may be considered negligence per se, see PROSSER & KEETON, LAW OF TORTS, at 220-33. *See also* C. MORRIS & C. MORRIS, JR., MORRIS ON TORTS 61-72 (2d ed. 1980); RESTATEMENT (SECOND) OF TORTS §§ 285-288C (1965).

28. Gressman v. McClain, 40 Ohio St.3d 359, 533 N.E.2d 732 (1988).

29. OHIO REV. CODE ANN. § 4301.22B (Page 1982).

30. OHIO REV. CODE ANN. § 4399.18 (Page 1989).

31. 40 Ohio St.3d at 362, 533 N.E.2d at 736.

32. *See, e.g.*, VA. CODE § 18.2-266 (1988). The relevant statutes of all of the states are summarized in AMERICAN INSURANCE ASSOCIATION, DIGEST OF STATE LAWS.

33. *See* 1 MOSHER, LIQUOR LIABILITY LAW § 1.05[2].

34. If a driver is intoxicated, the occurrence of an accident due to a factor other than the intoxication may still be indirectly affected by that intoxication. An intoxicated driver may, for example, be less likely to detect a mechanical problem at a time when the vehicle may safely be brought to a stop. Similarly, intoxication may interfere with a driver's reaction to a problem after it develops.

35. An exceptionally clear and insightful description of evidentiary sufficiency and weight can be found in Hoffman, *Alabama's Scintilla Rule*, 28 ALA. L. REV. 592, 593-602 (1977).

36. *See* NHTSA, 1984 REPORT ON TRAFFIC ACCIDENTS, at 9.

37. *See* AMERICAN INSURANCE ASSOCIATION, DIGEST OF STATE LAWS.

38. Koop, *Surgeon General's Workshop on Drunk Driving: Proceedings* (press release, May 31, 1989).

39. *See, e.g.*, VA. CODE § 46.1-1(8) (Supp. 1989).

40. *See, e.g.*, N. Y. INS. LAW § 5103(b)(2) (McKinney 1985) ("An insurer may exclude from coverage . . . a person who . . . [i]s injured as a result of operating a motor vehicle while in an intoxicated condition.").

41. *See generally* J. Morrison, THE INSURABILITY OF PUNITIVE DAMAGES: COMMENT AND JURISDICTIONAL ANALYSIS (2d ed. 1986).

42. *See* State Farm Mut. Aut. Ins. Co. v. Wilson, 782 P.2d 727 (Ariz. 1989) (the liability insurer of a drunk driver was not contractually obligated to pay punitive damages awarded against its insured; the court then held that the plaintiff's own automobile insurer was not required to pay an award of punitive damages under the underinsured motorist coverage provision of the plaintiff's policy).

43. *See, e.g.,* N.Y. CIV. PRAC. LAW § 5206 (McKinney 1978 & Supp. 1988).

44. *See, e.g.,* N.Y. CIV. PRAC. LAW § 5205 (McKinney 1978); VA. CODE § 34-26 (1984).

45. *See, e.g.,* FLA. STAT. ANN. § 222.11 (1989); VA. CODE § 34-29 (1984).

# 3

## Vicarious Liability for the Driver's Misconduct

*Molly Bloom's meeting with the lawyer who had previously represented her friend went very well. Based on what Molly told her about the accident and about its effects on her and the children, the lawyer was convinced that the tort law of her state would permit Molly and the children to recover a judgment for a substantial award of damages. The claim to recover the damages that represented the lost earnings of Molly's deceased husband—a wrongful death claim—was likely to produce well over a million dollars. In addition, there were substantial claims for damages to compensate for the physical injuries suffered by Molly and the children, and for the losses and expenses associated with Billy's long-term disability. The lawyer also thought it would be possible to succeed with claims for the emotional distress each of them suffered in being afraid for their own lives at the time of the accident and for being forced to view the death of Alan.*

*Although there was an excellent chance of establishing the Bloom family's right to a substantial amount of compensation, the lawyer's conclusions based on what she had learned about Tommy Smith, the drinking driver who had collided with the Blooms, were discouraging. Smith had been unemployed for nearly six months prior to the accident and was living in a spare bedroom in a house owned by Bill Green, who is his brother-in-law. The car that Smith was driving was owned by Green, who maintained only the minimum amount of liability insurance coverage required by state law. Green worked as a carpenter for the Acme Construction Company. Occasionally Smith would accompany Green on short trips in a company truck, and Green would drive by the house and pick him up. Smith would help Green load supplies into the truck and would sometimes ride to a construction site and help to unload the truck. An Acme foreman who supervised Green was aware that Smith helped out in this way from time to time, but Smith was never paid for this help by Acme or by Green.*

*At the time of the accident, Smith was driving to a neighboring town to pick up some special tools that Green needed the next Monday on a carpentry job. The tools were located at an Acme construction site in that town, and a crew was going to be working at that site throughout the entire weekend. As he was leaving work on Friday, Green had told his foreman that he and his wife were driving to that town on Saturday and that it would be no trouble at all for him to go by the site and pick up the tools. As it turned out, however, they never made the trip, and on Saturday evening Smith and Green agreed that Smith would take Green's car and pick up the tools on Sunday afternoon. It is unclear at this time whether Smith volunteered to make the trip or was asked to do so by Green. There had been no discussion of paying Smith for making the trip.*

A seriously injured accident victim who is faced with the prospect of going through the considerable time and expense of tort litigation against a drinking driver only to obtain what turns out to be an unenforceable judgment is likely to search for a more financially able party who can be held vicariously liable for the harm the driver caused. Vicarious liability is a form of legal responsibility for harm that has been caused by someone else.[1] Unlike the lawsuits that were discussed in chapter 2, in which the major focus was on establishing the wrongfulness of the conduct of the drinking driver, vicarious liability lawsuits require an understanding of the roles of three different persons: first, the plaintiff, who in this scenario is a victim of the drinking driver; second, the drinking driver, who may or may not be an actual party to the lawsuit; and third, a defendant other than the drinking driver, whom the plaintiff is trying to hold legally responsible for the injuries caused by the drinking driver. To avoid confusion in the discussion that follows, the defendant in the vicariously liability claim will be referred to as a "nondriving defendant."

In the context of the drinking-driver traffic accident, the vicarious liability claim depends not on a determination of the fault of the nondriving defendant but rather on the identification of a particular relationship between the nondriving defendant and the accident in which the plaintiff was injured. The two types of relationships that most frequently support vicarious liability are, first, those between the nondriving defendant and the drinking driver, and second, those between the nondriving defendant and the instrumentality of harm, which is the automobile that was being driven by the drinking driver. Before looking at those vicarious liability claims, however, I would like to use a third type of claim against a nondriving defendant to illustrate some of the fundamental principles of vicarious liability and also to explain how it is that a third party could be subject to legal responsibility for the harm caused by a drinking driver.

Consider the situation in which a police officer stops a car that is being driven by a drinking driver. For purposes of this analysis, it is irrelevant whether the stop was provoked by the officer's suspicion of alcohol-impaired driving or by some other factor unrelated to alcohol, such as a mechanical defect or a speed-limit violation. The critical point is that once the vehicle has been stopped, there is sufficient reason for the police officer to believe that the driver of the vehicle has been drinking. At the conclusion of the encounter, the police officer allows the drinking driver to proceed, and the driver is subsequently involved in an accident in which other people are injured. In looking for defendants to hold liable for their injuries, the victims of the drinking driver might focus on the police officer's failure to remove that driver from the road as a key element in the sequence of events that led up to the accident.[2] That failure could open the door to tort claims against two defendants other than the drinking driver — the police officer who stopped the vehicle and the governmental entity that employed the police officer.[3]

The claim asserted against the police officer would most likely be based on a negligence theory. The plaintiffs would contend that the standard of reasonable care demanded of a police officer under these circumstances required the officer to prevent the drinking driver from continuing to pose a risk of harm to other users of the highway. By allowing the driver to proceed, the police officer assumed at least some causal responsibility for the accident by reintroducing the risk of harm to others on the highway. If the standard of care that is required of police officers was breached on this occasion, then the police officer's conduct can be characterized as negligent, and that negligence can be causally linked to the ensuing accident and thus to the injuries the plaintiffs suffered.

Recognizing that a tort claim may be asserted against a police officer is still a far cry from establishing that the elements of that claim can be, or should be, satisfied in any particular case. Among the problematic issues that would have to be addressed are such matters as what constitutes sufficient reason to suspect the alcohol impairment of a driver, whether legal grounds for detention of a driver must exist before there can be liability to victims in subsequent accidents, what nonarrest alternatives to releasing a drinking driver are available, and how the police should be expected to cope with the tension between avoiding potential liability to accident victims and the administrative cost of detaining more drinking drivers. The extra demands imposed on the police force, whose time and energy are already overstretched, might justify a practice of favoring minimal intervention in marginal alcohol-involvement traffic stops.[4] I will not even attempt to answer those questions here. The hypothetical claim against the police officer is simply an introductory illustration of vicarious liability.

The remaining chapters of part 1 will focus on a fault-based theory of liability of people other than the drinking driver. The fault will involve serving or selling alcohol to the drinking driver, but even in cases in which the defendant's fault consists of something other than providing the alcohol to the drinking driver, such as the fault displayed by the police officer in this hypothetical case, the policy considerations are similar, and I will defer their discussion until later.

Let us return to the case in which a city or a county is sued because its police officer failed to keep a drinking driver from driving after stopping the driver. Under this form of vicarious liability, an employer is held legally responsible for the harm caused by the wrongful conduct of its employee. Liability of this sort depends on the plaintiff being able to establish two critical facts: first, that the harm to the plaintiff was caused by conduct for which the wrongful actor (here, the police officer) could be held liable, and second, that the relationship between the actor and the party being sued (here, the governmental entity) will support the imposition of vicarious liability on that party. Vicarious liability cases can be seen as involving a mix of strict liability and fault-based liability. The liability of a nondriving defendant who is being held vicariously liable is strict in the sense mentioned earlier—that is, the plaintiff need not prove that the nondriving defendant failed to take reasonable precautions for the protection of others. Nevertheless, the plaintiff still must prove the fault of the first party, the drinking driver, in order to hold the nondriving defendant vicariously liable.

The claim against the governmental entity employing the police officer is an example of an employment-based vicarious liability claim, but my primary focus in this chapter will be on claims based on a nondriving defendant's relationship with the drinking driver or with the driver's vehicle. I will not focus on more remote parties, such as law enforcement personnel, who, in one way or another, permitted the drinking driver to proceed.

### Vicarious Liability Based on a Relationship to the Drinking Driver

Two vicarious liability theories that are representative of the legal and practical considerations surrounding this second order of tort liability include the doctrine of respondeat superior and the theory of joint enterprise. The first theory is one of the more firmly established forms of vicarious liability in modern tort law. The Latin phrase *respondeat superior* means "let the master answer." According to this doctrine, an employer can be held liable for injuries caused by the negligence of an employee. The two main prerequisites are that the employee must have been a "servant" of the employer and must have been acting within the scope of employment at the time the plaintiff was injured.[5] Both of those prerequisites need some explanation.

Despite the archaic sound of the term, a "servant" in the respondeat superior setting includes many more employees than the butler and the maid. For vicarious liability purposes, calling an employee a servant simply requires that the employer have some control or right of control over the manner in which the employee carries out the functions of the job. An employee who is classifiable as a servant is distinguished from an "independent contractor." An employer is normally not vicariously liable for the negligent wrongdoing of an independent contractor. Most long-term employees are fairly routinely classified as servants.

The "scope of employment" requirement is similarly subject to misunderstanding without a further explanation of its meaning. A finding that an employee was acting within the scope of employment when the plaintiff was injured usually turns on two factors: either the employee was engaged in an activity that was directly related to the job, or else the employee's activity at the time of the accident was sufficiently closely related to the job that the activity was for the general benefit of the employer rather than exclusively for the personal gain of the employee.

At first glance, drinking and driving in general would appear to be an activity that lies outside the scope of employment so that the respondeat superior doctrine would not apply.[6] After all, one does not expect to find employers ordering employees to drink and drive as part of their job. Indeed, it is much more likely that an employer who has given any thought to the matter will have issued an order for employees not to drink and drive. In either case, employer vicarious liability would appear to be unavailable. There are, however, at least two fairly common situations in which a vicarious liability claim based on respondeat superior might apply to a drinking driver: the first situation involves an employee who drinks, and whose driving is job-related; the second involves an employee who drives, and whose drinking is job-related.[7]

The first category of cases includes those in which the drinking is not directly a part of the employee-driver's assigned task but in which no break occurs between the employee's drinking and the employee's job-related driving. Thus the drinking and driving occurred within the course of the employment and was not a "frolic and detour" of the employee. According to the law of agency, a frolic and detour is a purely private endeavor of the employee that provides no benefit to the employer.

The case of the "drunken sailor" on shore leave who causes damage on his way back to his ship is an example of vicarious liability under the doctrine of respondeat superior.[8] In the drinking-driver context, one could picture an analogous situation in which employees commonly consume alcohol during their lunch hour and then resume their employment, which involves driving. Or perhaps an employee consumes alcohol at a bar or restaurant operated by the employer. While these situations may lend themselves more appropriately to a claim based on a dram shop statute (see chapter 4) or a commercial-dispenser tort theory (see chapter 6), they also may provide an independent basis for imposing respondeat superior liability. For example, liability could be imposed on the owner of a bar or restaurant whose employee consumes alcohol while on the job and then becomes involved in an automobile accident that injures a third party.

In a case from Michigan called *King v. Partridge*,[9] both the employer and the employee were held liable under the Michigan dram shop act in a lawsuit that was brought by the victim of an accident caused by the employee. Attaching no consequence to the employer's contention that the employee had taken, rather than been furnished with, the alcohol she had consumed, the appellate court stated that the decision to impose liability on the employer for the harm that was caused by the employee's acts was "completely in accord with the responsibilities attaching to a master-servant relationship."[10] It is important to note that the employer's vicarious liability in this situation stems not from any finding of the employer's fault in failing to prevent the employee from drinking but rather from the employment relationship between the employer and the employee who caused the harm. The court concluded that the harm to the plaintiff flowed from acts performed by the employee while acting within the scope of that employment relationship.

A second category of cases in which the doctrine of respondeat superior might be used to establish an employer's vicarious liability for the harm caused by an employee who drinks and drives consists of those situations in which the drinking, if not the driving, is more directly related to the employment. Our business culture appears to encourage the consumption of alcohol as a natural part of making social and business contacts. An illustrative case would be the employer who expects an employee attending a convention to socialize with other convention delegates at cocktail parties and receptions.[11] Although the employer would probably not direct an employee to drink, just as the employer almost certainly would never tell the employee to drive after drinking, the fact that the socializing in which the drinking occurs furthers the business enterprise of the employer could support a claim of vicarious liability. The case of a sales representative who has a few drinks with clients and then injures someone in a traffic accident may also fall into this category of cases in which vicarious liability is imposed on the employer of the drinking driver.

Support for imposing vicarious liability under a respondeat superior theory in this sort of situation can be found in the decision of the Supreme Court of Washington in *Dickinson v. Edwards*.[12] Ersel Edwards drove the wrong way up a freeway ramp while he was intoxicated and struck a motorcycle that was being driven by William Dickinson. Edwards had become intoxicated at a banquet held by his employer, Kaiser Aluminum & Chemical Corporation. The accident occurred as Edwards was driving from the banquet to the plant where he worked the night shift. Among the tort claims asserted by Dickinson was a respondeat superior claim against Kaiser. Recovery under that theory was denied both by the trial court and by an intermediate appellate court, but the state supreme court reversed, holding that under some circumstances, an employer can be held liable for injuries that were caused by an employee who became intoxicated at an employer function and subsequently became involved in a drinking-driver traffic accident. The critical inquiry for the applicability of the respondeat superior theory, according to the state supreme court, was "whether the employee was within the scope of employment when he was drinking at the banquet. The initial focus would be on whether the banquet was a purely social function or sufficiently related to the employer's business to bring the employee's attendance within the scope of employment."[13] The court held that a jury would be able to find that Edwards was acting within the scope of his employment while he was at the banquet, based upon the cumulative effect of evidence that Kaiser deducted the cost of the banquet as a business expense, that the purpose of the function was to enhance employee relations, and that Kaiser encouraged and expected employees to attend.[14]

Again, as was true of the first category of these vicarious liability cases, the employer in the *Edwards* case was held vicariously liable because of the benefit the employee's drinking provided to the employment enterprise, rather than because of any personal fault on the part of the employer. Such fault on the part of the employer may very well exist in some cases, however, and a plaintiff injured by an employee's drinking and driving should not overlook this possibility. A nice illustration of that sort of fault-based claim is the case of an employer who hires a person known to have a pattern of alcohol problems and then assigns that person to a task that includes driving. If the employer's hiring or assignment of the employee can be characterized as negligence (recall chapter 2), then the employer's liability can be based directly on that negligence rather than on a vicarious liability theory.

Respondeat superior is a vicarious liability doctrine that holds an employer liable for the injuries that were caused by an employee who was acting within the scope of employment. "Joint enterprise" is the name that is commonly given to a vicarious liability theory that operates outside of the employment setting. It can be used to shift the losses from drinking-driver traffic accidents to nondriving defendants who have a temporary or shorter-lived relationship with the drinking driver. Joint enterprise liability typically requires a finding that there is an agreement among the members of a group, a common purpose and a common interest among the members, and an equal right to a voice in the direction of the enterprise.[15]

A recent decision of the Supreme Court of West Virginia, in a case called *Price v. Halstead*,[16] illustrates how this theory could be used to expand the scope of tort liability in drinking-driver cases. It also illustrates the reluctance of courts to stretch the theory. An automobile driven by Stephen Garretson collided with a truck in which Kenneth Wall was riding with his wife and their two minor children. During the course of the outing during which the accident occurred, Garretson had been both drinking and smoking marijuana. While attempting to pass a car, Garretson lost control of his vehicle and struck the Walls' truck. The collision killed Kenneth Wall and caused serious injuries to the family members who were passengers in his vehicle.[17]

Tort claims based on vicarious liability were brought against Larry Halstead, Bobby Gillenwater, and Timmy Clay, who were passengers in the Garretson car. The claims alleged that they should be held vicariously liable on a theory either of joint venture or joint enterprise. The actions against those passengers also included separate claims based on their direct negligence in failing to control Garretson, the driver, as well as in providing him with alcohol and drugs. The state supreme court upheld the liability of the passengers on that last claim, ruling that they could be liable for their own fault if the driver's alcohol- and drug-impaired condition was "substantially encouraged or assisted" by the passengers.[18] This theory of recovery is roughly analogous to social-host liability (see chapter 7). It is based on the fault of the passengers rather than on their vicarious liability for the fault of their driver. The focus here, however, is on the joint enterprise claim against the passengers that would hold them legally responsible for the harm that Garretson caused as part of that enterprise even if the passengers were not at fault.

The West Virginia state supreme court began its consideration of the vicarious liability of the drinking driver's passengers by drawing a distinction between a joint venture and a joint enterprise and then attaching different legal requirements to the two categories. The liability of the passengers on a joint venture theory in this case was rejected by the court on the ground that this theory was applicable only when the parties were engaged in a business enterprise carried out for profit.[19] Here the venture was purely social. The court did decide, however, that the passengers could be held vicariously liable under the joint enterprise theory even when there was only a non-business relationship between drivers and their passengers. While this decision demonstrates at least some measure of receptivity to the assertion of a vicarious liability claim in the drinking-driver context, it should be noted that some states take a more restrictive approach and apply the business-enterprise limitation to the joint enterprise theory as well. Thus in those states both the joint venture and the joint enterprise theories are equally unavailable when a social outing has led to a drinking-driver accident.

Persuading a court that a vicarious liability doctrine should be extended beyond the business enterprise setting may only be half the battle, however. Although the West Virginia supreme court in principle recognized a new possible vicarious liability claim in social joint enterprise cases in general, it did not allow the accident victims to succeed in their claim against the drinking driver's passengers in the *Price* case. The court stated that although the driver and the passengers were engaged in a common purpose, which it determined to be drinking and joy riding, that activity was not "the type of endeavor that would give rise to a joint enterprise."[20] According to the court, one "critical element" was not supported by the allegations in the plaintiffs' complaint—"the common right to control the vehicle on the part of its occupants."[21] Because this element was not satisfied in this case, the court upheld the trial court's dismissal of the plaintiffs' claim for relief based on a joint enterprise theory.[22]

The *Price* decision demonstrates a common problem that a plaintiff is likely to encounter in trying to use a joint enterprise theory in a routine automobile accident case. Even in a jurisdiction that follows the West Virginia approach and approves the more relaxed application of a joint enterprise theory to a purely social outing, the right-of-control element can act as a substantial barrier to recovery. Furthermore, in answering the question whether the passengers had an *opportunity* to exercise their right to control the vehicle in a responsible manner that reduced the risk of harm, the plaintiff is likely to have an even harder time making the necessary showing. Consider, for example, the situation in which all the occupants of a vehicle who are engaged in a joint enterprise have been drinking. While they may share a right to control the enterprise, it is unlikely that any one member of the group would be able to exercise control over the vehicle more responsibly than the others. The easiest case might be when one of the persons engaged in the joint enterprise is a passenger who owns the vehicle, and who could therefore base a right to control the vehicle on that ownership. In that sort of situation, however, the relationship to the vehicle will normally provide a sufficient basis for imputing liability to the owner under other theories described later in this chapter.

Each of the theories of vicarious liability that are based on a relationship between the nondriving defendant and the drinking driver has its own set of doctrinal hurdles that must be overcome before a plaintiff can make a successful use of the theory. A final factor that needs to be taken into consideration is the incentive for a tort plaintiff to expend the effort and incur the expense of getting over those hurdles. When this incentive factor comes into play, it is likely that the employment-based relationship offers greater promise as a means of providing substantial compensation for a seriously injured plaintiff.

　　Vicarious liability holds one person liable for the harm that is caused by another person. The legal concept of a "person" is broader than the term's ordinary meaning. If it was not, then the search for compensation would be limited to individual persons. The plaintiff would be left with simply aggregating the individual liabilities of the defendants. As individual persons, each of the nondriving defendants and drinking-driver defendants who made up the aggregate would be able to claim whatever legal limits on the enforcement of judgments against individual persons are available. Unless an individual defendant has substantial assets that are not protected from the execution of a judgment that has been awarded to the plaintiff, a seriously injured plaintiff suing only individual persons may well face the discouraging prospect of having to piece together a number of relatively small individual recoveries.

The legal definition of persons, however, includes "institutional persons." An institutional person is a fictional person that is nonetheless treated as a legal entity for many purposes. An institutional person can be held liable to a tort plaintiff, have a judgment entered against it, and be obligated to satisfy the judgment awarding monetary relief to the plaintiff. A common form of institutional person is a corporation, and it can be to a plaintiff's advantage to assert a claim against a corporate defendant. A corporation is likely to be insured, and it will usually rely on that insurance as the primary means of paying its judgment debts that are owed to injured parties. In addition, when the liability limits of the corporate insurance policy are exhausted, the general assets of the corporation are also available for satisfaction of the judgment.

To the extent that employers of drinking drivers are more likely to be institutional rather than individual persons, and to the extent that institutional persons are more likely than individuals to have sufficient assets out of which a substantial tort judgment can be satisfied, then a liability theory, such as respondeat superior, that opens up the possibility of imposing vicarious liability on institutional defendants can increase the chances of a plaintiff actually obtaining more complete compensation. It is important to recognize, however, that either or both of those conditions might be absent in a particular case. Individuals can operate businesses and employ others without forming a corporation, and corporations can be as bereft of assets as individuals. But as a general rule, seriously injured plaintiffs are in a better position to obtain substantial amounts of compensation if they can assert a claim against an institutional person rather than simply extend the scope of liability outward to include additional individuals.

### Vicarious Liability Based on a Relationship to the Vehicle Being Operated by the Drinking Driver

A second type of vicarious liability theory focuses primarily on the nondriving defendant's relationship to the vehicle that was operated by the drinking driver rather than on the defendant's relationship to the driver. Two fairly standard legal doctrines are used to impose this kind of vicarious liability: owner consent and family purpose. This type of vicarious liability is important because the owner of the vehicle is likely to have insurance coverage for the vehicle and may also have additional assets with which to satisfy a tort judgment. A good deal of overlap can exist between the types of vicarious liability theories that focus on the relationship to the driver and the types that focus on the relationship to the vehicle. The distinction is made here simply to illustrate the range of different theories that might be available to a seriously injured plaintiff who is looking for more complete compensation from a defendant other than the drinking driver.

Many state legislatures have enacted owner consent statutes,[23] which typically provide that the owner of a vehicle can be held liable for the harm caused by a driver who is operating the vehicle with the owner's consent. Determining whether the owner has actually given consent to the driver is often fairly straightforward, but in some cases the consent issue can present difficult questions of fact and policy. The more problematic cases include those in which consent is implicit rather than express and those in which the owner contends that the operation of the vehicle went beyond the scope of the permission that was granted. A not uncommon situation involves a vehicle that was driven by a companion of the person to whom the owner actually gave consent to operate the vehicle. That situation presents the question of whether the subpermittee (the companion) should be considered to have the owner's implicit consent and thus bring the owner within the scope of vicarious liability. While the answer varies depending on the facts of a particular case, one basic inquiry is useful in resolving this issue: were the risks that were posed by the person who was actually operating the vehicle of a different kind, or of a substantially different magnitude, than those that could be expected in cases in which the use of the vehicle was clearly permitted? If not, then the imposition of vicarious liability on the owner in this questionable permission case would be justifiable under the terms of the owner consent statute.

As is true of the vicarious liability cases that were discussed first in this chapter, liability under an owner consent statute is based on the existence of a relationship rather than on any personal fault on the part of the vehicle owner. An alternative theory of tort liability that *is* based on the fault of the owner is known as a "negligent entrustment" theory.[24] Liability under this theory is direct rather than vicarious because it is based on the negligent conduct of the owner in supplying the vehicle to the driver who caused the plaintiff's injury. A recent case in which an owner was found to be negligent in entrusting a vehicle to a drinking driver was *Jackson v. Price,* decided by the Supreme Court of South Carolina.[25] Jackson was killed when his truck was struck by a car that was driven by Price. One of the claims asserted in the tort lawsuit that was brought by Jackson's survivors alleged that Davis, who was the owner of the car that was being driven by Price, had been negligent in letting Price drive the car despite the fact that Davis knew that Price had consumed three beers within an hour and a half prior to the accident. The state supreme court held that evidence to that effect would be sufficient to support a verdict against Davis for negligent entrustment.[26]

In contrast to that fault-based theory of a vehicle owner's liability, negligence on the part of the owner is not a prerequisite to liability under the owner-consent statutes. The owner-consent sort of vicarious liability becomes important to a plaintiff in the case where the owner of a car has no reason to be aware that the car was being operated by a drinking driver. Liability in a case of that sort could be established solely on the basis of the nondriving defendant's ownership of the vehicle rather than because of any fault on the part of the owner in granting consent to the driver.

The other legal doctrine used to establish a vehicle owner's vicarious liability, which is somewhat narrower than liability under owner-consent legislation, is available under a common-law concept somewhat misleadingly named the "family purpose" doctrine.[27] Liability under this doctrine is usually imposed on an owner whose vehicle was driven by a member of the owner's immediate family or household. Despite the doctrine's name, it is the family *relationship*, rather than any explicit family *purpose* of the trip during which the accident occurred, that typically serves as the basis for the owner's liability. As is true of each of the other types of vicarious liability, the liability that is imposed under the family purpose doctrine does not rest on a finding that the owner was at fault in letting the family member drive the vehicle. In this type of situation, therefore, just as in the *Price* case above, an accident victim ought to explore an independent ground of liability: Was the owner at fault in entrusting the vehicle to a drinking driver? If so, then the owner's liability would be direct rather than vicarious.

A vehicle owner who is held vicariously liable under an owner-consent statute or the family purpose doctrine is not necessarily going to be better able to satisfy a substantial judgment than the driver. In fact, both the negligent driver and the vehicle owner who is held vicariously liable may be drawing on the same insurance coverage to compensate the plaintiff. Standard automobile insurance policies today contain an omnibus clause, which identifies any person who is driving the vehicle with the consent of the owner as a person who is insured under that policy. Thus an omnibus clause accomplishes through the insurance contract what the two vicarious liability doctrines just discussed accomplish: the victim of a drinking driver is given access to an insurance fund. The amount of the fund is limited by the insurance policy's liability limits, however, so a tort plaintiff may still face a shortfall.

Even if the vicariously liable defendant is able to compensate the victim fully, however, other problems remain. Adding defendants to lawsuits can increase the risks of confusion and error, and it is also likely to raise the expense of litigation. A tort plaintiff who pursues a vicarious liability theory introduces into the accident litigation peripheral questions focusing on such matters as whether the driver had the owner's permission to use the owner's vehicle or whether the driver was acting within the scope of employment at the time of the accident. In addition, to impose vicarious liability on an employer or a car owner, the plaintiff must also prove the underlying liability of the drinking driver and so is subject both to the expense involved and to the risk of not being able to persuade the jury of the driver's fault.

The prospects of recovering full compensation under the vicarious liability theories outlined in this chapter from nondriving defendants located on the second circle of tort liability can be as unpromising as those in the case of the direct liability of the drinking driver. This is particularly likely to be the case when the owner of the vehicle is an individual rather than an institutional person. Furthermore, even when a potential defendant with sufficient assets to satisfy a large judgment can be identified, that party may have a plausible basis—and more than an adequate incentive—for resisting the imposition of vicarious liability. All things considered, an injured party who extends the search for compensation to a deep-pocket defendant located on the second circle of tort liability may be only marginally better able to obtain full compensation than one who pursues a judgment against the drinking driver. For these reasons, tort lawyers who represent the more seriously injured victims of drinking drivers have frequently extended the search for a financially able defendant beyond those to whom the driver's fault might be imputed. With varying degrees of success, they have sought to impose legal responsibility on the parties who sold or served the alcoholic beverages to the drinking drivers at fault—the next order of tort liability.

## NOTES

1. *See generally* PROSSER & KEETON, LAW OF TORTS, at 499-501.

2. For competing views on the legitimacy of basing a tort claim on this sort of reasoning, *compare* Everton v. Willard, 468 So.2d 936 (Fla. 1985)

(rejecting government liability in this situation) *with* Irwin v. Town of Ware, 392 Mass. 745, 467 N.E.2d 1292 (1984) (recognizing liability for the breach of a duty that was owed to plaintiff by police officers who apprehended a drinking driver when the plaintiff was injured in an accident that occurred after the release of the driver by the officers). A general discussion of the cases on this kind of tort claim can be found in 1 MOSHER, LIQUOR LIABILITY LAW § 12.03[1].

3. The judicial resistance to recognizing tort claims of this sort is discussed in Note, *Insulating Negligent Police Behavior in Indiana: Why the Victims of a Drunk Driver Negligently Released by a Police Officer Have No Remedy*, 23 VAL. U. L. REV. 665 (1989).

4. *See* JACOBS, DRUNK DRIVING, at 110 (discussing the costs of police efforts to apprehend and process drinking drivers).

5. *See, e.g.,* W. SEAVEY, HANDBOOK OF THE LAW OF AGENCY, at 141-59 (1964); W. SELL, AGENCY, at 84-95 (1975).

6. The general topic of employer liability for harm caused by a drinking driver is discussed in Janes, *Employer Liability,* 1 MOSHER, LIQUOR LIABILITY LAW, ch. 17.

7. The Mosher treatise on liquor liability law also discusses the use of the respondeat superior doctrine (*id.* at 12.04[2][a]), but it does so mainly in the context of accidents following employer-sponsored parties at which employees consume alcohol beverages. For purposes of analytical clarity, this book will treat those cases as instances in which the liability of the employer is better viewed from the perspective of the employer as dispenser of alcohol, which is simply another version of the liability theory that is discussed in chapter 6. Accordingly, the discussion of this first category focuses on the situation in which the employer has not furnished the alcohol to the employee.

8. Ira S. Bushey & Sons, Inc. v. United States, 398 F.2d 167 (2d Cir. 1968).

9. 9 Mich. App. 540, 157 N.W.2d 417 (1968).

10. *Id.* at 543, 157 N.W.2d at 418.

11. Fruit v. Schreiner, 502 P.2d 133 (Alaska 1972), illustrates this fact pattern, although nothing in the reported decision of that case suggests that the convention delegate was intoxicated or had been drinking.

12. 105 Wash.2d 457, 716 P.2d 814 (1986).

13. *Id.* at 469, 716 P.2d at 820.

14. *Id.*

15. The elements of a joint enterprise are listed and discussed in RESTATEMENT (SECOND) OF TORTS § 491, Comment b (1965). *See generally* PROSSER & KEETON, LAW OF TORTS at 517-22.

16. 355 S.E.2d 380 (W.Va. 1987).

17. *Id.* at 383. The description of the facts of the case is taken from the report of the West Virginia supreme court decision and from Case Comment, *Price v. Halstead—Passengers Held Civilly Liable for Aiding and Abetting an Intoxicated Driver,* 90 W. VA. L. REV. 513 (1987).

18. *Id.* at 389. The merits of basing liability on this sort of theory are discussed in Note, *Torts: Price v. Halstead: Liability of a Guest Passenger for the Negligence of His Drunk Driver*, 42 OKLA. L. REV. 159 (1989).

19. *Id.* at 384.

20. *Id.* at 385.

21. *Id.* at 384.

22. *Id.* at 385.

23. *See generally* PROSSER & KEETON, LAW OF TORTS, at 527-28.

24. *See generally id.* at 523-24.

25. 288 S.C. 377, 342 S.E.2d 628 (1986).

26. *Id.* at 382, 342 S.E.2d at 631.

27. *See generally* PROSSER & KEETON, LAW OF TORTS, at 524-27.

# 4

## Liability of Alcohol Dispensers under Dram Shop Statutes

*The lawyer whom Molly Bloom consulted outlined for her the factors to consider in deciding whether to file a lawsuit. At the conclusion of their initial meeting, Molly entered into a contract in which the lawyer agreed to represent Molly and the children. The lawyer's regular fees were in the neighborhood of $150 per hour for office work, and she charged even higher fees for time spent in court. Molly could not afford to pay those fees as the lawyer's work was performed. If she were required to do so, she and her children would probably be denied any opportunity to obtain the legal relief to which they were entitled. To avoid that problem, the contract that Molly signed contained the "contingent fee" arrangement that is found in most attorney-client contracts regarding personal injury lawsuits. Under this arrangement, the attorney's fees would be paid as a percentage of any judgment or settlement that the attorney obtained for Molly and the children. If no recovery was obtained, then the attorney would receive no fees. Molly would have to pay for such items as court filing fees, but the attorney told Molly that her law firm could advance the money to cover those expenses as long as Molly understood that the payment of those costs would ultimately be her responsibility regardless of the outcome of the lawsuit.*

*The lawyer quickly completed her investigation of the circumstances sur-rounding the accident, including the identification of Bill Green as the owner of the car that had struck the Blooms. A tort claim that was brought only against Tommy Smith, the drinking driver, was unlikely to produce much in the way of a recovery. Smith had very few assets with which to satisfy a tort judgment. As a practical matter, the only available asset was the liability insurance coverage that Green carried on the vehicle that Smith was driving. By combining a claim against Green, as the owner of the car that Smith was driving, with an attempt to establish that Smith was acting within the scope of an informal ad hoc employment with the Acme Construction Company for the company's benefit, the lawyer could see a remote possibility of improving the Blooms' chances of receiving at least some greater measure of compensation than seemed to be possible in a lawsuit against only Tommy Smith.*

*A tort claim against Bill Green could open the way to otherwise unavailable assets from which to satisfy a judgment. Nevertheless, his liability insurance fund is already available to the plaintiffs through a claim against Smith, who would be treated as being insured under the policy's omnibus clause as long as Smith was driving the car with Green's consent. A claim alleging that Green was personally at fault in letting Smith drive when he knew or should have known that Smith would be drinking presents another possibility for the lawyer to pursue. In either event, however, recovering damages in a judgment against Green would be advantageous to the plaintiffs only to the extent that he had other assets besides the liability insurance policy funds out of which the judgment could be satisfied.*

*The vicarious liability claim against Green's employer presents a more difficult challenge for the Bloom family's lawyer. Although Smith was never formally employed by Acme Construction, the lawyer will attempt to persuade a court that he was at least a de facto employee of Green, and thus indirectly an employee of the company as well, while he was making the trip that was for the benefit of both the company and Green. The lawyer will attempt to bolster that argument by pointing to evidence that the company knew about and did not object to the previous instances on which Smith had performed work for the company. Still, the lawyer understands that this claim seeking to establish the vicarious liability of the construction company is tenuous at best.*

*Given the very high sum of damages which the Blooms could prove they were entitled to recover, their lawyer was determined to pursue any additional tort claim that might provide an alternative source of compensation. Further investigation revealed that on the day of the accident Smith had been drinking for most of the afternoon. He had begun his drinking by having a few beers at a tavern located a few blocks from where he was living. At this stage of the investigation, the lawyer does not know precisely how much alcohol Smith was served at the tavern. She has learned that Smith is considered a regular patron there. At the tavern, he had met a friend of his and had been invited over to the friend's house to watch a ball game on television. During the course of the game, each of the men apparently had another five or six beers, as well as some whiskey. Neither was able to state exactly how much alcohol had been consumed. The Bloom family's lawyer has scheduled an appointment with a toxicologist at the local medical school in order to find out if the amount of Smith's alcohol consumption can be determined from the results of the blood alcohol test that was performed after the accident.*

*When the ball game was over, Smith left on his trip to pick up the tools at the construction company site in the nearby town. As he pulled out of the driveway of the house where he had been drinking, the car he was driving struck the mailbox and knocked it over. Smith assured his host that he would come back the next day and repair it. The host accepted that promise and watched Smith drive away. Within five minutes after leaving the home of his host, the fatal collision with the Blooms' car took place.*

The tort actions surveyed thus far each involved a situation in which the influence of alcohol on the driver of a vehicle was alleged to have contributed to an accident in which the plaintiff was injured. In order to be compensated for those injuries, the plaintiff attempted to get a court to apply well-established general tort doctrines to a drinking-driver traffic accident. Liability for harm caused by negligent conduct has been the cornerstone of tort law in the United States at least since the middle of the nineteenth century; vicarious liability of principals for harm caused by their agents is another basic concept of the law of torts; and automobile owners have been held legally responsible for the damage associated with the operation of their vehicles for as long as automobiles have been common in our society. In that sense, then, the role of alcohol in the accident could be seen as merely an incidental factor in the doctrinally routine determination that an accident victim of a drinking driver is entitled to a legal remedy. Drinking and driving is simply one of a number of ways in which a driver may cause harm to another by tortious conduct. Similarly, harm that has been caused by a drinking driver with whom a defendant has a relationship is only one of many types of injury for which vicarious liability can be imposed.

One of the major ways by which the law of torts adapts to changing circumstances is through judicial interpretation. The fundamental tort concepts of fault and causation are sufficiently open-textured that new ways in which risks produce harm to others can be brought within the scope of the existing liability doctrines. Thus far, alcohol has been doctrinally incidental to the development or the application of a liability theory, but alcohol is at the heart of other liability theories that have been developed either by a legislature or a court.

The tort plaintiff who has been injured in a drinking-driver traffic accident, having failed to receive complete compensation either by proving the liability of the drinking driver or by using vicarious liability doctrines, may attempt to use one of the three additional major liability theories. The feature these theories have in common is that they can be used to shift accident costs from the accident victim either to an individual who sold or served alcoholic beverages to the drinking driver or to a business entity that did so. The oldest of the theories relies on dram shop legislation. Dram shop acts typically create a claim for relief against those who serve alcohol in a commercial setting to a person who then causes harm to others. Although automobiles are not specifically mentioned, the typical statutory language is obviously broad enough to cover harm caused through the operation of an automobile. In states that have not adopted dram shop legislation, a plaintiff may be able to persuade a court to use an equivalent common-law (that is, judge-made) theory of liability to impose liability on a commercial dispenser of alcohol (see chapter 6). The third dispenser liability theory, which may be available independently or in conjunction with either of the other two, extends the notion of dispenser liability beyond the commercial setting to a social host who serves alcohol to an intoxicated guest who is subsequently involved in a drinking-driver traffic accident (see chapter 7). The two nonstatutory liability theories rely on the recognition of a common-law claim for relief, and courts are frequently reluctant to adopt a theory of dispenser liability as a matter of the development of a state's common law of torts (see chapter 5).

Although the differences among these three dispenser liability theories are important, an understanding of their common features is useful in distinguishing them from the vicarious liability theories discussed in the preceding chapter. The most significant aspect of the liability that is imposed on parties who sell or serve alcoholic beverages to the person who drinks and drives is that it depends to a large extent on a finding of fault on the part of the dispenser of alcohol. In many of the cases in which a liability theory of this sort has been used successfully, the fault consists of serving alcohol to a person who is already intoxicated, whether or not the dispenser actually knows or should have known that the person will subsequently operate a motor vehicle. In other situations, the fault consists of serving alcohol to a person who is below the statutory minimum age for the purchase or consumption of alcohol. The common thread in both of these situations is that the dispensers gave alcohol to persons whom they should have recognized presented a foreseeable risk of acting unreasonably as a result of being furnished with alcohol by the dispenser.[1]

The fault-based nature of the tort liability that is imposed under these theories has both advantages and disadvantages for the seriously injured plaintiff who is seeking more complete compensation. Because the alcohol dispenser's conduct in this situation can be characterized as wrongful, a decision to impose some or all of the costs of the accident on the dispenser may seem to be roughly in keeping with a prevailing community sense of fairness that prefers to impose liability only when there is a fairly close link between a defendant's personal fault and that person's legal responsibility. However, proving that the defendant actually was at fault presents another hurdle that the tort plaintiffs must clear before they become entitled to a recovery from the commercial or social dispenser of alcohol. Each of the dispenser liability theories presents a fault element that, for reasons described below, may be particularly difficult for an injured party to prove to the satisfaction of a judicial fact finder. Furthermore, the causal connection between the dispenser's fault and the injury to the victim of the drinking driver may be difficult to establish. This factor requires not only a consideration of the legal doctrines of causation in fact and proximate causation but also an examination of the issue from the standpoint of popular notions of responsibility (explored more fully in chapter 8). A significant feature of these dispenser liability theories, then, along with the vicarious liability theories discussed thus far, is that they may actually turn out to provide less of an opportunity for channeling substantial compensation to the seriously injured victim of a drinking-driver accident than they initially appear to.

### *Common Restrictions on Dram Shop Liability: Plaintiffs, Defendants, and Damages*

The legislatures in nearly two-thirds of the states have created dram shop legislation, which provides a statutory right of action against a seller of alcoholic beverages when an intoxicated purchaser of those beverages causes harm as a result of the intoxication.[2] Both the specific terms and the judicial interpretation of these statutory provisions vary dramatically from state to state according to such variables as what persons may be entitled to recover in dram shop actions, the types of defendants who may be held liable, the nature or the amount of the recovery that may be obtained, and the circumstances under which dram shop liability may be imposed. It is probably safe to say that there are nearly as many different combinations of variables regarding liability under dram shop acts as there are states that have adopted these acts. Because of this diversity, the most useful way to convey both the strengths and the shortcomings of dram shop claims, short of a comprehensive analysis of each state's legislation, is to consider a representative sampling of the restrictions on recovery that a plaintiff asserting a dram shop claim for relief in a drinking-driver case can encounter.[3] A dram shop action can still fail to provide full compensation for the more seriously injured victims of drinking drivers.

One of the first questions confronting plaintiffs who attempt to sue dispensers of alcohol under a state's dram shop statute is whether the statute includes them within the class of persons who are entitled to recover. Lawyers who are considering filing a statutory claim often distinguish between two sorts of personal entitlement questions. In the context of a drinking-driver accident, the first is a question of legal standing: Does this particular person have the right to institute the claim against the commercial seller? In other words, has a proper plaintiff filed the lawsuit? The second question is how to identify the appropriate beneficiaries who are entitled to receive any monetary award that is recovered under a dram shop act claim, regardless of which particular party may have had legal standing to be a plaintiff in the action. In short, first a determination must be made that the person who brought the lawsuit had standing to sue under the dram shop statute, and, second, the lawyer must determine who is entitled to share in the proceeds of a successful dram shop claim.

The standing question by itself should not require any consideration of the merits of the claim for relief; it can normally be answered by looking at the terms of the dram shop statute. Many dram shop statutes provide a claim for "any person" who is injured as a result of a defendant's serving alcohol under the appropriate circumstances to trigger the statutory liability, although some statutes list specific classes of persons who may bring the action.[4] The right to recover the proceeds of a dram shop claim will typically correspond to the grant of standing in the simple dram shop action, but as the following discussion will reveal, a more complex fact pattern can sometimes raise rather tricky questions about how to resolve these entitlement issues.

In order to examine the ways in which the entitlement issues come up in a dram shop claim, consider first what is virtually the paradigm case in the context of the drinking-driver traffic accident. This least complicated claim under a dram shop act involves a drinking driver who collides with a vehicle operated by a plaintiff who has not been drinking and who is injured in the accident. That injured nondrinking driver then asserts a claim against the appropriate defendant who served alcohol to the drinking driver prior to the collision, alleging that the dispensing of alcohol to the driver was responsible for the plaintiff's injury. In this simple situation, the standing to sue for damages and the right to recover the proceeds of the successful dram shop action are both likely to be given to the nondrinking driver who was injured in the collision. The accident victim is both the proper plaintiff to bring the lawsuit and the person who receives the damages recovered in the lawsuit. The remedial purpose that is most reasonably attributable to the legislature in enacting the dram shop statute is undoubtedly fulfilled when the injured driver institutes the dram shop liability claim and recovers the damages that are awarded under the terms of the statute.

A particular drinking-driver traffic accident may not be quite as simple as the hypothetical just described, however. Many dram shop statutes either have been drafted or have been judicially interpreted in a way that precludes any recovery by persons who share responsibility for the intoxication that caused the accident. Two broadly defined groups of people are excluded: the intoxicated drivers themselves, the most obvious group, and persons who participated in the events leading up to the accident. Common sense tells us, after all, that the decision of a drinking driver to consume alcohol prior to driving is at least as much responsible for the accident as the conduct of the dram shop defendant who served the alcohol to that person. Indeed, many observers would unhesitatingly say that by far the greater measure of responsibility for intoxication lies with the drinking driver than with the commercial dispenser of alcohol. Excluding the intoxicated person from the category of those who can recover damages in a dram shop claim is thus consistent with the idea that plaintiffs should not be able to impose liability on others for injuries they caused to themselves, especially injuries for which the plaintiffs are personally most responsible.

The fault of the persons in the second group to be excluded from recovery is less obvious, and they are often more difficult to identify. These are injured persons who participated in the "drinking event" that resulted in the accident and who can be said to share some complicity in the intoxication of the driver because of that participation.[5] A good example is the passenger who rides with a drinking driver and is injured in an accident that occurs while the passenger and the driver are on a social outing in which both purchased and consumed alcohol. This was the fact pattern in *Price v. Halstead,* the case that was described in the last chapter's discussion of joint enterprise liability. The drinking driver involved in that case and his three passengers had all been consuming alcohol while they were driving around, and all the passengers were alleged to have contributed to or to have encouraged the driver's drinking. Had some of those passengers been injured in the accident and attempted to assert a dram shop action against one of the people who had sold alcohol to the group during their evening's outing, the dram shop statutes in many states would have barred their recovery on the ground of their complicity in the drinking event that led up to the accident. Some fine moral distinctions might be drawn based on the passenger's conduct, such as whether the passenger purchased alcohol for the driver or actively encouraged the driver's drinking or whether the passenger simply failed to discourage the drinking and driving. Nevertheless, a natural reaction to this sort of claim is that the passenger's own contribution to causing the accident was at least as great as, if not greater than, the fault of the dram shop defendant in serving the drinking driver. The legislative intent behind these exclusion provisions in a dram shop act is to limit a recovery of damages to those who are the "innocent" victims of a drinking driver. Accordingly, injured parties who helped produce the intoxication of the driver will be excluded from the scope of the remedy created by the dram shop legislation.

In terms of the illustrative cases just described, at least, it does not seem to matter whether the exclusion of those who participated in the drinking event is based on their lack of standing to bring a dram shop claim or on their lack of a right to recover damages under the claim. In both instances, however, the important further question of statutory interpretation is whether the dram shop act's exclusion operates only with respect to claims that have been brought by the participants themselves, or whether it also extends to those persons, such as family members, who would otherwise have derivative or secondary claims as a result of the excluded parties' injuries. Suppose, for example, that courts in the state in which a dram shop claim arose had previously recognized that a person who suffers serious emotional distress upon viewing an injury to an immediate family member is entitled to a legal remedy for this suffering. What are the rights of the family members of an injured passenger who has been barred from recovering damages under a dram shop statute for participating in the drinking event that led up to the accident?

The more restrictive approach would preclude the injured passenger's family members from maintaining a claim for the emotional distress they suffered. That approach might be defended on the basis that it would appear to enforce more completely the policy behind the dram shop legislation that bars recovery by those who have some complicity in producing the alcohol-related injury. That reasoning becomes more compelling to the extent that the injured passenger might be an indirect beneficiary of a family member's recovery of damages for emotional distress. In contrast, this restrictive application of the exclusion policy can also be seen as a harsh punitive measure that sweeps too broadly by including the innocent family members of the excluded party who suffer derivative or secondary losses. The restrictive approach seems especially harsh in the case of the participating passenger who dies in the accident. In this case recovery by a family member poses no risk of a back-door evasion of the intent of the legislation to prevent the person who shared responsibility for the driver's intoxication from benefiting from the dram shop claim.

Cases involving a deceased accident victim present a specific category of derivative claims that raises another major potential complication in resolving the entitlement issues of standing to sue and the right to recover the proceeds of a dram shop action. Every state has enacted legislation providing for tort liability on the part of those whose wrongful conduct causes the death of another person.[6] These wrongful death statutes typically contain explicit provisions designating the party who may bring the wrongful death action and the persons to whom the proceeds of a successful lawsuit are to be distributed. The problem is that the dram shop act and the wrongful death statute often identify different people. The personal representative of the decedent[7] is the party who is most frequently granted standing to bring a wrongful death action, and most wrongful death statutes direct that damages be distributed to a specific class of the decedent's survivors, who are often those who would inherit under the intestate succession provisions of the state statutes.[8]

To appreciate the precise nature of the potential issues raised by these complications, consider another hypothetical accident. A drinking driver and a passenger who is a participant in the drinking event are in a collision with a car that has two occupants. One of those occupants is killed, and the other is seriously injured. Assume further that the passenger in the car of the drinking driver is also killed in the accident. What starts out as a simple question of referring to statutory language to determine who can sue and who receives the benefits of a successful dram shop claim now looks significantly more complex.

Among the questions that a lawyer would have to answer are these: Can the drinking driver maintain a dram shop claim? Can a survivor of the deceased passenger/participant bring a dram shop claim? If there is a dram shop statutory exclusion of participants in the drinking event, would a wrongful death action on behalf of the passenger/participant's survivors be affected by the exclusion that is contained in the dram shop statute? Is the claim for damages for the death of the deceased occupant of the other car governed by the dram shop statute, with whatever restrictions on recovery may be contained in that statute, or is it instead governed by the wrongful death statute, which may involve a different measure of damages being distributed to a different class of persons?

There is nothing that is conceptually all that difficult about any one of these questions by itself. The point is not that they are incapable of being answered,[9] but rather that the application of even relatively simple statutory provisions in a dram shop act to the facts of a particular case may involve layers of complexity that need to be peeled away one at a time in order to produce a coherent scheme of rights and liabilities. Furthermore, simply arriving at definitive answers to the individual questions may not be a satisfactory way of proceeding. A demand for consistency in the policy aims involved and in the underlying principles of the various statutory provisions that might come into play ought to serve as a further constraint on the decisions that courts reach in these factually more complicated situations.[10]

After deciding that a person is legally entitled to bring a dram shop action, the next question that must be answered for a plaintiff considering a claim under a dram shop statute concerns the identification of the party or parties from whom recovery can be sought.[11] As with the entitlement issue just discussed, this question can be best understood by starting with the simplest situation and progressing to more complicated fact patterns.

The paradigm dram shop act defendant is a bar with a license or a permit to sell liquor at which the drinking driver has purchased and consumed alcoholic beverages.[12] The combination of those three factors—license or permit, sale of alcohol, consumption on the premises—presents the strongest case for bringing a particular defendant within the reach of the dram shop act. As a licensee or permittee, the defendant is already subject to an extensive set of regulations governing the manner in which it conducts its business, and it should possess the professional expertise to assure that the regulations are followed. As a seller of alcoholic beverages, the defendant has a customer base over which the cost of dram shop act liability can be spread. With the consumption of the alcohol occurring on the premises, the defendant ought to be put on notice that its dispensing of the alcohol under circumstances that violate the regulations under which it operates creates at least the potential of a risk of harm to the customer or to other people whom the customer may encounter upon leaving the bar.

As the number of these factors present in any given situation is reduced, the argument for bringing a defendant into the dram shop case is weakened, and the chances of finding that the defendant has escaped the net cast by the dram shop statute are correspondingly greater. A substantial number of dram shop statutes, either explicitly or through judicial interpretation, restrict their coverage to defendants who are licensed to sell alcoholic beverages. This restriction should not insulate from potential liability someone who is required by law to have a license but does not happen to have a currently valid license in effect at the time of the incident that forms the basis of the lawsuit. To hold otherwise would be to place a premium on a failure to comply with a licensing requirement. Limiting dram shop act liability to licensed sellers of alcoholic beverages, however, will preclude the success of a dram shop action asserted against a social dispenser of alcohol or against a person who may make an occasional sale of alcohol as something other than part of a normal business operation.

A careful examination of the transaction between a dram shop act defendant and a particular drinking driver may disclose additional facts that restrict the application of a dram shop statute in a particular case. If there has been a gift rather than a sale, for example, then a defendant may fall outside the scope of the dram shop act in some states. If the sale of an alcoholic beverage is made on a different occasion from the consumption of that beverage, that too may result in the dram shop act defendant not being subject to liability under the act, particularly if the sale was made to an adult.

Both the statutory language and the judicial experience in the application of the dram shop statutes are sufficiently diverse that generalizations about how these acts operate have to be made with considerable hesitation. The central point is that substantially fewer than all of the various parties who furnished a driver with alcoholic beverages are likely to be subject to a claim for damages under a dram shop statute.

Assuming that a proper plaintiff has established that an appropriate defendant is liable under a dram shop statute, an accident victim may face still another obstacle to full compensation. An additional question that needs to be asked is whether there is a limit on the amount of that dram shop act liability. An initial distinction needs to be made between statutes that contain express limitations on liability depending on the type of injury and those that refer generally to liability for any injury suffered as a result of a defendant's conduct that falls within the scope of the act. Even within the latter class of "any injury" statutes that provide for apparently unlimited liability, judicial interpretations can incorporate into the application of the dram shop act a set of restrictions that makes liability under the act correspond to the liability that defendants face under the general principles of tort law that obtain in that jurisdiction.

The dram shop legislation in a few states explicitly places a cap on the amount of damages that can be awarded to a plaintiff with a successful dram shop claim.[13] The strongest rationale that can be offered for caps on damages in dram shop cases, as in other tort cases in general, is likely to revolve around issues of the availability and the affordability of liability insurance.[14] Another rationale might be based on the issue of fault: while the dram shop violation by the dispenser of alcohol is at least partially responsible for the plaintiff's injury, the major share of blame properly lies with the drinking driver. Accordingly, the liability of the dram shop defendant could be capped at some reduced amount that reflects the relatively reduced significance of that defendant's fault. Still another rationale for limiting the amount of recovery under a dram shop act compares this legislation to other statutes that have created a new statutory remedy. This new remedy might have no counterpart at common law, or it may open up a more expansive scope of recovery in cases where a common-law remedy was subject to defenses that were difficult for a tort plaintiff to overcome. Workers' compensation laws, for example, typically provide a lower level of compensation to a claimant in return for the availability of a surer and speedier award of compensation than could be obtained in a tort claim. Although recovery under a dram shop claim may not be sure or speedy, a cap on damages may reflect a sense that, through this new remedy, an accident victim is being given a fairly substantial potential benefit. The plaintiff now has access to a new source of compensation, the dispenser of alcoholic beverages, that is probably better able to pay damages than the drinking driver who actually caused the plaintiff's injuries. A limitation on what damages a plaintiff is able to recover can be viewed as justifiable legislative balancing act through which an accident victim receives a benefit that was not available at common law. In fact, a particular dram shop act may create a form of strict liability for the commercial dispenser of alcohol, in which case this trade-off rationale for a cap on damages is even more compelling.[15]

A dram shop statute that contains no explicit restrictions on the amount of damages that can be awarded to a successful plaintiff is nevertheless subject to judicial interpretation. A court may introduce restrictions on the types of harm for which damages can be awarded. The most common type of judicial interpretation is to read the term "injury" as being equivalent to the harm that is compensable under the general rules of a state's tort law. If, for example, the recovery for the wrongful death of a person is limited to the economic loss that the death causes to the immediate survivors of the decedent, then a plaintiff who is suing under a dram shop act because of the death of a relative who was killed by a drinking driver is unlikely to be able to obtain a greater recovery than that afforded under the state wrongful death statute. Similarly, a plaintiff cannot use a dram shop claim to recover damages for an injury if liability for such an injury has not previously been recognized under a state's tort law; for example, imposing liability on a defendant for the emotional distress the plaintiff suffered by witnessing the serious injury of an immediate relative in an accident even though the plaintiff was not actually within the accident's zone of danger. As a general proposition, then, an accident victim will not be permitted to enjoy a substantially more advantageous legal position simply because of the fortuity that an alcohol dispenser wrongfully served alcohol to the driver who caused the accident. Instead, a more appropriate role for a dram shop statute is to help an accident victim obtain full compensation for those losses that are part of the existing tort law regime.

The limitation on an accident victim's recovery that undoubtedly has the greatest significance in dram shop act claims, as it does in almost all other tort actions, is the refusal to allow any explicit award of damages that would reimburse the successful plaintiff for the attorney's fees and litigation expenses that were incurred in obtaining the compensation. Absent any specific statutory authority for such an award, plaintiffs in this country are expected to finance the lawsuit either out of the damages awarded in the suit or out of other assets that are available to them. The adverse effect of this "American rule" regarding attorney's fees and litigation expenses may be mitigated in part by the fact that a plaintiff who loses a lawsuit is not obligated to pay the defendant's attorney's fees and litigation expenses. Nevertheless, the result can be that an accident victim who has ostensibly been awarded a judgment that provides for a complete recovery for the injuries suffered can end up with a substantially inadequate net recovery after paying these fees and expenses. When the legal remedies that are available to an accident victim produce a recovery that is, on its face, less than the amount that would provide full compensation, the impact of the American rule for attorneys' fees can be even more significant.

## A Preliminary Look at the Responsibility and Culpability of Alcohol Dispensers

Assuming that the proper parties have been joined in a dram shop action, a critical question is whether a sufficient basis exists for imposing dram shop liability on the defendant. In most instances, the dram shop statute will require the defendant to have acted in a way that can be characterized as culpable.[16] The two types of conduct that are most relevant here are serving alcohol to someone who is already intoxicated and serving alcohol to a minor.

The culpable conduct that makes a defendant liable under a dram shop act is not necessarily related to the risks posed by drinking and driving. Most states treat the conduct of serving either a minor or a person who is already intoxicated as illegal under state liquor control laws regardless of whether this conduct subsequently injures a third party. Selling alcohol to a seventeen-year-old, for example, can subject a commercial dispenser to criminal liability and administrative penalties regardless of whether that sale led to a traffic accident. Another point is that traffic accidents caused by drinking drivers are not the only sources of injuries for which a dram shop defendant might be liable. The injuries that are suffered by a victim of an assault by an intoxicated patron can fall squarely within the scope of liability that is imposed on alcohol dispensers under a dram shop statute.[17] In states with "habitual drunkard" or "habitual alcoholic" provisions prohibiting the furnishing of alcohol to persons so designated, dram shop liability might also be imposed for economic loss to the family of a person who was served in violation of the law by a dram shop act defendant.[18]

An alcohol dispenser's liability under a dram shop act for engaging in conduct that is additionally prohibited by other laws has two major effects. Civil liability under a dram shop act both reinforces liquor control laws and provides a remedy to the victims injured by the alcohol dispensers' culpable conduct. A person who illegally serves a drinking driver faces the prospect of being held liable for monetary damages to an injured party in addition to paying whatever criminal or administrative penalties apply. But that deterrence of criminal conduct is only part of the rationale for creating a dram shop act. That result, after all, could be achieved simply by raising the fines that are imposed on the violator and by increasing detection and enforcement efforts. The civil liability imposed on dispensers of alcohol under a typical dram shop statute if, for example, an illegally served minor subsequently injures someone underscores the fundamentally remedial nature of the dram shop statute. In the same way, although liquor control laws prohibit serving alcohol to an adult customer of a bar when the customer is already intoxicated, it is only when the patron injures someone that the dram shop act liability becomes an important addition to the remedial scheme that is available to the victims of that intoxicated person. And again, it is in that way that the prospect of civil liability for the consequences of the illegal serving of the alcohol become more significant to the violator. Both of these functions of dram shop legislation—sanction and remedy—are important components in the construction of any supplement or alternative to the existing panoply of legal solutions to the problem of fully compensating the accident victims of drinking drivers.

Although the scope of dram shop act liability is sufficiently broad to cover a wide range of injuries, the primary concern here, of course, is its impact on the ability of victims of drinking-driver traffic accidents to obtain compensation for their injuries. The best way to begin to understand the complexity of the culpable-conduct element of dram shop act liability in this context is to draw an initial distinction between two types of culpability. The first type involves culpability in producing the intoxication of the person who causes the injuries to the accident victim, while the second is a matter of a more direct culpability in producing the injuries themselves. The illustrations that follow draw useful distinctions among cases involving high culpability, low culpability, and no culpability.

The dram shop act cases in which dispenser liability is easiest to justify involve the dual culpability of the defendant. In these cases of "high culpability," the link between the prohibited sale and the intoxication of the driver is fairly easy to establish, as long as the dram shop act defendant sold or served to the consumer alcoholic beverages that intoxicated the consumer. What identifies a case of high culpability, however, is that a connection can be made not only between the defendant's sale of the alcohol to the driver and the driver's intoxication, but also between the sale and the traffic accident in which the plaintiff was injured. In other words, the high culpability case is one in which a plausible link between the defendant's unlawful sale or service to the driver and the defendant's responsibility for the accident can be established.

From the standpoint of establishing the high culpability of the defendant, consider this relatively uncomplicated dram shop case. A minor drives up to a convenience store twice during an evening and purchases a six-pack of beer from the same clerk on each visit. To strengthen the facts of the case, assume further that, on the second visit to the store, the clerk who makes the sale is able to smell beer on the breath of the purchaser, that the purchaser slurs his words and has difficulty counting his money to pay for the beer, and that the purchaser is holding car keys in his hand. After a traffic accident in which the purchaser collides with another car and injures its occupants, a blood alcohol test reveals that the purchaser was intoxicated at the time of the accident. An evaluation of the conduct of the convenience store employee would support the conclusion that the employee either knew or should have known that the alcohol sale to this purchaser increased the risk of harm to other people who would be on the highway at the same time as the purchaser. That same conclusion might be reached in a case in which a bartender serves a visibly intoxicated regular patron who became intoxicated at the bar and who the bartender knows will drive home after leaving the bar. In each of these two examples of high culpability, the legally prohibited (and thus culpable) conduct involving the defendant's sale of alcoholic beverages to a minor or to an intoxicated person has been enhanced by the defendant's culpability in contributing to a known risk to those who are exposed to the drinking purchaser's subsequent driving.

More complicated than these high culpability cases, and arguably less easily justified in terms of the defendant's culpability, are cases in which it would not appear that the seller should have been aware that the sale increased the risk of an alcohol-related traffic accident. Many dram shop statutes are written and interpreted in a manner that imposes liability even without the additional type of culpability found in the high culpability case. In the case of a sale of alcohol to a minor, for example, as long as the minor became intoxicated as a result of consuming that alcohol and the subsequent accident can be attributed to the intoxication, a sufficient showing of culpability for purposes of dram shop liability will have been made. These sorts of cases can be referred to as "low culpability" cases.

Consider, for example, the convenience store employee who sells a six-pack of beer to a minor who walks to and from the store in order to make the purchase, but who then drives a car while drinking the beer. The clerk is undoubtedly culpable in selling the beer to a minor, but the link between the sale and the accident is less direct than it was in the earlier variation of this example. Similarly, consider the bartender who serves an intoxicated patron only after being assured that the patron will not attempt to drive, but the patron then does drive after leaving the bar and is involved in a traffic accident. An argument could be made on behalf of the dram shop act defendants in these two low culpability cases that the injuries suffered in the alcohol-related traffic accidents are outside the scope of the risks that the defendants could have been expected to foresee in connection with the prohibited sales. Under standard tort law doctrines, that argument would be made under the label of proximate cause—it is

unfair to impose liability on a defendant for harm that is dispropor-
tionate to the risk that made the defendant's conduct culpable. The
specific risks that were posed by the sales were related to the customers
themselves. As long as there was no reason for the defendants to
know that the customers were going to drink and drive, then the risks
associated with their driving could be considered separate from the
risks associated with their drinking. A court that refused to accept
that argument in a dram shop case would arguably be introducing a
type of liability that is more strict than fault-based liability and that
extends the scope of legal responsibility for the defendant's conduct
beyond what is currently the custom under the proximate cause doctrines of negligence law.

The third type of culpability left to explore is a more extreme
imposition of liability under a dram shop act. In both the high and
the low culpability cases, courts ought to be receptive to evidence
that there was no culpability at all regarding the defendant's prohibited sale of alcohol. Examples would include selling alcohol to a minor
who has produced convincing proof of majority and also serving
alcohol to a person who displays no visible signs of intoxication. There
is, however, a category of dram shop statutes that are interpreted in
a way that imposes strict liability on the defendant regardless of the
lack of culpability in the sale.[19] For statutes of this sort, the absence
of any culpability on the part of the person who makes a prohibited
sale of alcohol is irrelevant to that person's liability to accident victims
under the dram shop act. The mere fact that the consumer of the
alcohol was a minor or actually was intoxicated at the time of the sale
is sufficient to trigger the seller's liability under a dram shop statute
of this type. It is in these sorts of cases that the combination of a
strict liability regarding the sale and an attenuated connection between
the sale by the dram shop defendant and the accident involving the
consumer can produce the greatest difficulty in justifying the imposition of liability on the seller for the accident victim's injuries.

As one moves down the scale from high to low to no culpability,
the argument that it is unfair to hold the defendant liable increases
in strength. One of the cornerstones of modern tort law is the idea
that liability attaches to conduct when a reasonable person exercising
foresight for the protection of others would have acted differently.[20]
In the high culpability case, a reasonable person would foresee both
the legally prohibited nature of the sale and the risk of the purchaser's
intoxication leading to a traffic accident. With this sort of case, society's
demand that the sale must not be made seems to be appropriately
reinforced by a requirement that the seller must pay for the adverse

consequences that result if that demand is ignored. In the no-culpability case, in which the reasonable seller had no way of knowing the sale was legally prohibited, even taking into account the professional expertise that ought to be required of the seller, many, but not all, of the states that have dram shop statutes would refuse to impose liability on the seller. That still leaves the category of low culpability cases. In these dram shop cases, the fairness argument on behalf of the defendant is less than compelling to many courts deciding claims brought by accident victims of drinking drivers. A decision to impose liability on a dram shop act defendant in these cases would be supported by the following policy consideration: the social practice of drinking and driving is sufficiently ubiquitous, especially in the case of minors and those who are already intoxicated,[21] that a person who is at fault in making a prohibited sale of alcohol in either of these situations, will not be allowed to argue that the risks posed by the drinking driver's conduct while intoxicated are outside the scope of the foreseeable risk that made the seller's conduct culpable. The underlying principle of proximate cause as a limitation of liability to foreseeable risks could thus be accepted in the low culpability case, but found not to be applicable.

Establishing the element of culpability in a dram shop claim is as crucial to a plaintiff's success as proving an entitlement to recover damages and the inclusion of the defendant within the scope of the statute. At least in those jurisdictions that insist on a finding of either high or low culpability, the difficulty of proving this element means that some injuries traceable to the commercial dispensing of alcohol to drinking drivers will lie beyond the reach of the legislative remedy provided in the dram shop acts. If a state has not adopted a strict-liability interpretation of its dram shop act, a claim will not succeed unless the dispenser defendant's conduct displayed at least some level of culpability.

This survey of the major issues that can arise when the victim of a drinking driver attempts to recover damages in dram shop act litigation does not purport to do justice to the complexity and variety of the practices found among the thirty-five or so states with dram shop acts. Instead, the objective has been much more limited: to illustrate some of the principal obstacles that a plaintiff who pursues a dram shop claim must overcome. Any precise assessment of the compensatory effectiveness of a dram shop claim depends on the specifics of the state statute involved, how it has been interpreted, and the particular facts of a case. Even when this additional channel to compensation is available to victims, a substantial number of them will be unable to prove liability, and thus this statutory remedy will fail to have any financial impact on the firms and the individuals who occupy the lowest levels of the alcoholic beverage distribution chain, at the "front line" where alcohol is dispensed to the person who actually consumes it.

## NOTES

1. *See* Rappaport v. Nichols, 31 N.J. 188, 156 A.2d 1 (1959).

2. The statutory provisions are identified in 1 MOSHER, LIQUOR LIABILITY LAW § 1.51.

3. The discussion in this section of chapter 4 draws heavily on the compilation of dram shop statutes and their analysis in the Mosher treatise on liquor liability law, chapters 2 through 7.

4. *See generally id.*, ch. 3.

5. *Id.* at § 3.04.

6. *See generally* S. SPEISER, RECOVERY FOR WRONGFUL DEATH (2d ed. 1975).

7. If the decedent left a will, then the personal representative of the decedent is the executor or executrix who was named in the will. If the decedent died without leaving a will (that is, died intestate), then the personal representative will be the person named by a probate court to serve as the administrator of the decedent's estate.

8. Typically intestate succession will proceed through categories of relatives expanding outward from the decedent. The initial preference would be for the proceeds to go to a surviving spouse, or if there is none, to the surviving children, or if there are none, to surviving parents, and so on, until some relative is identified as the appropriate recipient of the assets in the estate of the decedent.

9. *See* SPEISER, WRONGFUL DEATH § 1.16 (collection of annotations of cases on the relationship between wrongful death statutes and dram shop statutes).

10. The strongest argument for consistency is found in the jurisprudential writing of Ronald Dworkin. *See, e.g.,* R. DWORKIN, LAW'S EMPIRE (1986).

11. *See generally* 1 MOSHER, LIQUOR LIABILITY LAW, ch. 4.

12. If the dram shop act defendant is the business entity at which the drinking driver was furnished alcohol, then that entity must be shown to be vicariously liable for the wrongful conduct of its employees who actually served the customer. In that situation, the standard tort principles of vicarious liability (discussed in chapter 3) would be applied. For the sake of simplicity, references in the text will be made to the dram shop act defendant without distinguishing the individual employee from the employer.

13. The Illinois dram shop act, for example, currently contains a limit of $30,000 by any plaintiff for personal injury and property damage, and

$40,000 by a survivor for loss of the means of support caused by the death of a person. ILL. ANN. STAT. ch. 43, § 135 (Smith-Hurd Supp. 1990). New Mexico's Alcohol Licensees Liability Act limits dram shop liability for dispensing alcohol to someone who was known to be intoxicated to $50,000 for injuries that were caused to any one person, $100,000 for injuries to two or more people, and $20,000 for property damage. N.M. STAT. ANN. § 41-11-1(I) (1989). Under the Maine Liquor Liability Act, recovery of damages for losses other than compensation for medical care expenses is limited to $250,000. ME. REV. STAT. ANN. tit. 28-A, § 2509 (1988).

14. *See* 2 MOSHER, LIQUOR LIABILITY LAW, at App. B, pp. 36-37.

15. *See id.*, at App. B, p. 37.

16. *See generally* Clune, *Dram Shop Statutes: Acts Giving Rise to Liability,* in 1 MOSHER, LIQUOR LIABILITY LAW, ch. 5.

17. *See, e.g.*, Ward v. Rhodes, Hammonds, & Beck, Inc., 511 So.2d 159 (Ala. 1987).

18. *See, e.g.*, COLO. REV. STAT. § 13-21-103 (1987); FLA. STAT. ANN. § 768-125 (West 1986) (sale or furnishing of alcoholic beverages to a person who is "habitually addicted").

19. *See* 1 MOSHER, LIQUOR LIABILITY LAW § 5.03[2].

20. One of the best statements of this idea is found in an opinion of the Judicial Committee of the Privy Council of the United Kingdom, in Overseas Tankship (U. K.) Ltd. v. Morts Dock & Eng. Co., Ltd., 1961 A.C. 388 (P.C.).

21. Support for this conclusion could be found in Fell & Nash, *The Nature of the Alcohol Problem in U.S. Fatal Crashes,* 16 HEALTH ED. Q. 335 (1989), reporting the disproportionately high representation of young drivers and problem drinkers in fatal accidents involving drinking drivers.

# 5

## Resistance to Common-Law Liability of Alcohol Dispensers

The preceding chapter introduced the notion that someone who sells or serves alcohol to a drinking driver may be held liable for the injuries that are suffered by the accident victims of that driver. But what of cases that fall outside a particular dram shop act, and what of states where a dram shop act is not available? Should a court recognize a common-law theory of liability for an alcohol dispenser in these two situations?

Courts have done just that in cases involving both commercial dispensers and social hosts (see chapters 6 and 7). Nevertheless, courts are considerably reluctant to extend dispenser liability beyond the scope of its legislative enactment. In this chapter I take a critical look at a number of rationales for not recognizing a common-law dispenser claim for relief.

Many of these rationales were set forth by the Supreme Court of Wisconsin in a case called *Sorensen v. Jarvis*.[1] After surveying its prior opinions on the question of common-law liability, the court stated that those earlier decisions had relied on six "public policy bases" to uphold a rule that did not permit an accident victim to assert a common-law tort claim against a dispenser of alcohol.[2] Although the claim in the *Sorensen* case was asserted against a commercial dispenser, the rationales for nonliability that the court identified generally apply equally as well (or as poorly) to noncommercial or social host cases. They can be roughly summarized as follows:

1. "Leave social problems to the legislature." This rationale asks which branch of government—the judiciary or the legislature—is most competent to tackle complicated social problems.[3]

2. "Don't blame the liquor industry." This rationale opposes placing accident costs on an actor far removed from the accident itself,

such as a social host or a commercial entity whose employee dispensed alcohol to a drinking driver.[4]

3. "Duck the hard cases." This rationale suggests that the complexity of the decision making that a court would face in adjudicating dispenser liability claims is so great that these claims ought not to be recognized.[5]

4. The "slippery slope" argument views the prospect of virtually unlimited liability in other future cases as a reason for refusing to recognize liability in the case actually before the court.[6]

5. The "administrative burden" rationale questions the wisdom of spending limited judicial resources on the additional cases that would arise were a new liability theory to be recognized.[7]

6. "Don't let the drinking driver off the hook." According to this argument, holding someone other than the drinking driver liable for causing the accident would reduce the power of existing legal and social sanctions to deter drinking and driving.[8]

Collectively and individually, these six arguments present a fairly substantial hurdle for the lawyer attempting to get a court to recognize for the first time the right of victims of drinking-driver traffic accidents to bring a common-law tort claim against a dispenser of alcohol. Although the Supreme Court of Wisconsin ultimately found these arguments against dispenser liability to be unpersuasive, they could certainly be used in general by lawyers, judges, and policymakers to shield commercial or social dispensers from liability (and indeed, by extension, *any* parties other than the intoxicated driver). In fact, not long after the Supreme Court of Wisconsin adopted a prospective rule of tort liability of commercial dispensers in the *Sorensen* case, the Wisconsin state legislature enacted a statute that essentially restricted alcohol dispenser liability to a situation in which a commercial dispenser knew or should have known that alcoholic beverages were being furnished to an underage person.[9] Accordingly, the six arguments against dispenser liability need to be examined with some care.

## Leave Social Problems to the Legislature

> "[T]he problem of intoxication was a social, not a legal, problem and, hence, was a matter to be dealt with by the legislature."[10]

The view one adopts of the proper allocation of authority between legislatures and courts necessarily influences the attitude one displays toward the assertion of a previously unrecognized theory of tort liability, particularly when the new theory is likely to have a fairly significant impact both on the legal rights and duties of people and on the behavior of individuals and institutions affected by the change in the law. Courts have sometimes drawn an unsophisticated distinction between the types of problems wrapped up in the litigation bringing new theories of liability before them and then used the characterization of the issue before the court in a particular case to resolve the question of the respective institutional competence of courts and legislatures to deal with the issue. The underlying premise of this approach is that "social problems" should be relegated to the legislature, while "legal problems" are deemed to be appropriately within the province of the courts. Once this premise is accepted, the classification of a particular issue as presenting one or the other type of problem appears to produce a conclusion through deductive reasoning about whether a court should act or instead defer to the legislature.

Such a method of dealing with institutional competence questions is a substitute for careful decision making rather than an exercise in responsible allocation of decision-making responsibility between different branches of government. The initial difficulty comes in the identification of what is before the court. The court in *Sorensen* referred to the "problem of intoxication." A more narrowly defined statement of the "problem" before the court could easily be offered. Describing the case as one that presented the "problem of compensating accident victims" may produce a characterization that is different from the one that is reached in the quoted language.

Even assuming that the definition of the problem before a court could be stated in a relatively precise or noncontroversial manner, this method of deciding institutional competence questions is objectionable as a matter of principle. "Problems" cannot so easily be classified as social or legal. The line between the two is at least difficult to draw and is largely meaningless as well. The notion that courts somehow overstep the bounds of their authority when they venture into making decisions that have social implications reflects a fundamental misunderstanding of the relationship between law and society. Law is a social phenomenon. Indeed, one of the best measures of the quality and the character of a society is its law. There are, however, situations in which judicial deference to a legislature can legitimately be supported by arguments that display a firmer grasp of the nature of the underlying issue that is really before a court when it is confronted with an institutional competence argument against the recognition of a new theory of tort liability. Looking at the extent to which those situations are actually encountered in claims involving a commercial dispenser of alcohol provides an opportunity to identify and evaluate those arguments.

A useful starting point for arriving at an understanding of the "leave the problem to the legislature" argument in the drinking-driver accident setting is a realization of the way in which the argument actually misrepresents the dynamics of the situation in which a court finds itself. To the extent that the tort liability of a dispenser of alcohol relies on the application of the ordinary principles of the law of negligence, the argument really seeks to remove from the judicial arena a question that falls into a conceptual category of questions that are already there. The law of negligence, in which actors who injure others as a result of conduct that falls below a standard of reasonable care are liable for the harm that is caused to the victims of that conduct, is a creature of the common law. Courts created the doctrine of liability for negligence, and over the years, courts have routinely considered themselves to be the appropriate authority for determining whether liability ought to be extended to previously unrecognized classes of actors, categories of conduct, and types of injuries.[11] The same can be said for almost all of modern tort law. Against that background of pervasive judicial responsibility for both the creation and the modification of the rules of tort liability, an argument that invokes the institutional competence of the legislature to determine whether liability ought to be imposed on dispensers of alcohol suggests that there is something about the liability question in the drinking-driver context that distinguishes it from other situations in which courts routinely resolve the issue of whether established principles of tort law are properly susceptible to extension into new settings.

An explanation for a deferential attitude of courts in this particular setting could be built on the fact that the dispensing of alcohol is already a matter that is subject to a considerable degree of legislative activity. Licenses are required to operate an establishment that serves alcohol; statutes and regulations govern many of the conditions of sale; and both federal and state excise taxes are levied on the product. Given that there is already a high level of existing legislative involvement in the commercial distribution of alcohol, the question of whether a dispenser of alcohol should be held liable to the victims of drinking-driver accidents might be viewed by a court more as if it were an adjunct to a fairly comprehensive scheme of regulation that is already largely in place, rather than as if it were primarily a matter of extending general principles of tort law so that they operate in a setting in which they had not yet been applied.

The "deference to the legislature" rationale for not recognizing a new theory of tort liability can have varying degrees of strength depending on the sequence of judicial and legislative actions that preceded the case in which the liability issue is presented. A fairly compelling argument that courts ought not to recognize a common-law liability for dispensers of alcohol can be constructed in the situation in which the legislature has specifically addressed some aspects of the dispenser-liability question. Given that legislative involvement, the argument could be made that the existing legislation has preempted the field of dispenser liability so that a court has no authority to recognize a tort claim beyond the liability that has been created or ratified by the legislation.

A 1987 case decided by the Supreme Court of Iowa, *Fuhrman v. Total Petroleum, Inc.*, illustrates the preemption doctrine in the context of a claim against a commercial dispenser of alcohol.[12] The plaintiffs were injured when a car crossed the center line of the road on which they were traveling and struck their car. The driver of the car that hit the plaintiffs was seventeen years old and had been drinking beer that had been sold to her by the defendant convenience store. That sale of beer to a minor violated a state statute that prohibited the sale, gift, or other supplying of alcoholic beverages to persons who were under the legal age.[13] Dram shop legislation was in effect in Iowa, but it was limited in scope. Iowa's dram shop act provided that the liability of a licensed seller of alcoholic beverages was limited to the situation in which the person to whom the defendant sold or served the alcohol was already intoxicated at the time or the case in which the defendant's sale brought the person to the point of intoxication.[14] The defendant's illegal sale to the minor in the *Fuhrman* case did not fall within the scope of the act because the minor had purchased the beer and then had taken it away from the convenience store to a park where she consumed it.[15] Refusing to recognize a common-law right of recovery in this situation, the Iowa supreme court relied on the legislative history of the dram shop act as indicating "that the legislature preempted the field of dram shop torts."[16]

Such a decision in favor of preemption rests on the conclusion that the legislature has already extended liability as far as it wants liability to be imposed. Any change in the scope of liability should therefore be made by the legislature. The Iowa court found further support for this view in the legislature's recent reaction to the court's earlier extension of dispenser liability to victims of drinking drivers in 1985 in *Clark v. Mincks*.[17] In that case the Iowa supreme court had recognized the common-law liability of the social hosts of intoxicated drivers because of another provision of the state Alcoholic Beverage Control Act, which prohibited selling, dispensing, or giving alcoholic beverages to an intoxicated person.[18] In the very next legislative session, that statutory provision was amended to rule out the imposition of any civil liability for drinking-driver traffic accidents flowing from a violation of the statute.[19] As if to make sure that there could be absolutely no doubt about the legislature's disapproval of the action that the court had taken in the *Mincks* case, the statutory amendment included an unusually pointed statement that "this subsection shall be interpreted so that the holding of Clark v. Mincks . . . is abrogated."[20]

The Iowa experience that has been recounted so far would appear to stand for a fairly straightforward proposition. If a legislature has enacted a dispenser liability statute, the field of dispenser liability has been preempted by the legislature. As in many other areas of the law, however, things are rarely as straightforward as they may appear to be. It is, after all, the job of the courts to decide whether legislative preemption has occurred, and judicial resolution of that issue can be a controversial matter. The decision of the Iowa supreme court in the *Fuhrman* case was as close as it could be, with five members of the court joining in the majority decision in favor of legislative preemption and four justices dissenting. Such a sharp division may indicate at the very least that an issue is highly controversial. It may indicate as well that the court might be receptive to subsequent attempts to recast an issue in order to sway individual members of the court.

Just such an opportunity was presented to the Supreme Court of Iowa not long after the *Fuhrman* case was decided. In what must be seen as a fairly astonishing move in light of the legislative pronouncement that specifically rejected the social host liability that was created by the court in the *Mincks* case, the Iowa supreme court again recognized a common-law right of action against the social hosts of an allegedly intoxicated driver, this time in the case of *Bauer v. Dann*.[21] The court based the theory of tort recovery against the social hosts in *Bauer* on the fact that the defendants who had served alcohol to the driver had violated the Alcoholic Beverage Control Act's prohibition against serving alcohol to a person under legal age[22]—the same violation the court had refused to use as a basis for liability in the *Fuhrman* case. The court purported to be able to reconcile its decision in *Bauer v. Dann* both with the *Fuhrman* decision and with the earlier legislative abrogation of the *Mincks* decision. *Fuhrman* was distinguished as being a commercial dispenser case, and thus the court apparently limited the scope of the legislative preemption argument to the type of alcohol dispensers, that is, commercial dispensers, who were specifically covered by the state's dram shop act. The subsequent legislative abrogation of the common-law liability of social hosts that had been recognized in the *Mincks* case was similarly distinguished on the ground that it applied to a different section of the Alcoholic Beverage Control Act, the one that dealt with service to an intoxicated person, rather than the section relied on in *Bauer,* which prohibited the service of alcohol to an underage drinker.

This history might very well give the casual observer reason to pause and consider what sort of game playing is going on. A fairly plausible explanation might run as follows: Tort liability for any alcohol dispenser who lies outside the scope of the state dram shop act had not been recognized by the courts of Iowa. When such a common-law liability of a dispenser was recognized in a social host case, the legislature quickly and quite pointedly intervened to reject it. Now the court has relied on technical, if not specious, distinctions in order to evade the clear expression of a legislative intent to limit the liability of alcoholic beverage dispensers only to those people and those acts expressly within the reach of the Iowa dram shop act.

Although that explanation of the controversy over the last several years between the legislature and the courts over dispenser liability has considerable merit, a different explanation will help to put into a somewhat clearer perspective what is at stake in the controversy revolving around the issue of legislative preemption as it applies to dispensers of alcohol. First, it is the business of the court to say what the common law is. Should the legislature wish to impose its will concerning the nature and the extent of alcohol dispensers' liability to drinking-driver accident victims, it must do so with precision. Until such time as the legislature removes from the courts the authority to recognize liability under generally accepted notions of common-law tort liability, such decisions will continue to be made in accordance with what the court deems to be the public policy considerations that currently obtain. If the court is convinced that imposing tort liability on a social host for serving alcohol to a minor is a good idea, and the legislature has left a gap, even if only temporarily, so that the court may recognize such a theory without directly contravening a statutory directive, then the court is free to fill in that gap.

This recounting of the Iowa controversy over the dispenser liability issue also sheds some light on the dynamics of the debate over the relative competence of the courts versus the legislature. In a situation like the one in Iowa, the state legislature is being put into the role of a branch of government that is following behind the court and undoing what the court has done. Those against imposing liability on alcohol dispensers are thus in the position of having to overcome whatever inertia is associated with the legislative process, although admittedly the promptness of the reaction to the *Mincks* decision suggests that the inertia may not be all that strong. Furthermore, political considerations come into play that frequently influence how comfortable a legislature will be in returning to the issue of dispenser liability. The opponents of dispenser liability can be characterized either as protectors of the average homeowners who serve alcohol to their guests or as advocates of stripping away an important opportunity for compensation that the court has created for the accident victims of drinking drivers. A legislature may be willing to confront the court on occasion but be unwilling to do so too often. While it is true that not every state with a dram shop statute can be expected to match Iowa's experience, the Iowa example does suggest that the success of the legislative-preemption argument may depend as much on the strength of the public policy factors involved in dispenser liability as it does on the strength of the abstract rationale of leaving the problem to the legislature.

A court does not necessarily have to interpret the legislature's choice to enact dram shop legislation as closing the door on finding a common-law liability of dispensers. A court might instead take a legislative creation of a new basis of liability and extend, rather than limit, its reach by applying it to cases that arose prior to the enactment of the statute. In *Gressman v. McClain*,[23] (used in chapter 2 to illustrate the negligence per se doctrine) the Supreme Court of Ohio was presented with an opportunity to do just that. Recall that Holly Pasch was served a minimum of three or four drinks at a golf course snack bar one afternoon in 1979. After driving away from the golf course, she lost control of her car and collided with another vehicle. Both drivers and all of the passengers were killed. In 1986 the Ohio legislature enacted a dram shop statute that imposed liability on commercial dispensers of alcohol, using language that almost precisely described the facts leading up to the Pasch accident. The relevant statutory provision imposed liability on a commercial dispenser of alcohol for injuries that were caused by an intoxicated patron after the patron left the dispenser's premises.[24] The problem was that the legislature, in keeping with the common practice of having new legislative duties or penalties operate only prospectively, gave this provision of the new dram shop statute an effective date of July 21, 1986.[25] Even though the Pasch accident had occurred nearly seven years before this date, the Ohio supreme court recognized a common-law claim for relief against the snack bar, characterizing the 1986 statute as "clearly set[ting] forth the *preexisting* public policy on this issue."[26] Although the court in the *Gressman* decision admitted that the dram shop legislation created a new right of recovery for the victims of drinking drivers, it asserted that it was merely making the same public policy determination that the legislature had made; that rationale was just as accessible and compelling to the courts as it was to the legislature. As long as the court is comfortable with imposing liability retroactively in this fashion, there is no reason why it should ignore the policy considerations that motivated the legislature to enact the dram shop act. Furthermore, in this situation, in which the act of selling or serving alcohol was clearly prohibited at the time the dispenser acted, a court may very well consider itself particularly justified in adding civil liability for damages to the foreseeable victims of that unlawful conduct to the existing range of legal sanctions that the defendant faced at the time the defendant acted.

It is at least possible for a court to discern a legislature's intent when that legislature has spoken. A legislature's rejection of a judicial decision adopting dispenser liability can indicate general hostility to such a claim, while legislative adoption of a dram shop act imposing liability might indicate the legislative acceptance of a general policy in favor of such liability. In contrast to these situations is one in which a court must consider a dispenser liability claim against a background of legislative silence. In this case, deferring to the legislature could involve trying to read into the legislative inaction an implicit decision that liability ought not to be imposed on dispensers. In the absence of any evidence in a state's legislative history to support this conclusion, one could also point to the widespread adoption of dram shop legislation. The fact that an increasing number of states have recognized some form or another of common-law dispenser liability, at least for commercial dispensers, suggests that a legislature's inaction on this score was deliberate. In a sense, then, the remaining dozen or so states that have not jumped on a bandwagon might well be viewed as having chosen not to be on the bandwagon, while such a conclusion is less plausible when only a few states have taken a particular step.

The "leave the problem to the legislature" rationale in the context of alcohol-dispenser liability has considerable support in a number of states. A recent decision of the Supreme Court of Virginia, for example, demonstrates the reluctance that courts sometimes display to adopt a claim for relief that so closely resembles the liability that legislatures have imposed in other states. In *Williamson v. Old Brogue, Inc.*,[27] a state trial court dismissed a tort action that had been brought against the owner of a pub called The Old Brogue. Ethel Loredo was alleged to have been drinking at the pub for as long as four hours. When she left the pub, she was involved in a collision with a car driven by Howard Williamson. Williamson had reached an out-of-court settlement with Loredo and then had pursued a commercial dispenser common-law liability claim against the corporation that owned the pub.[28] In upholding the trial court's judgment dismissing the claim against the pub, the Virginia supreme court expressed an unwillingness to undertake the complex balancing of the "many competing economic, societal, and policy considerations" that were involved in the change from a rule of nonliability of dispensers, believing that "legislative procedures and safeguards are particularly appropriate to the task of fashioning" a new rule, if one were to be adopted.[29]

It is doubtful that the task of balancing competing considerations that was avoided by the court in *Williamson* is at all significantly different from the routine sort of balancing of competing interests that a court faces in many other instances in which it is presented with novel tort questions. However, the fact that a legislature has failed to enact a piece of legislation that has been fairly widely adopted in other states over a long period of time may be thought to have at least some minimal weight as an indication that the political climate in a state does not favor the substance of that legislation. A court looking at that history may be more sensitive to the political ramifications of a decision to impose liability on dispensers of alcohol and thus may be more reluctant to get too far ahead of the local political curve on the issue of dispenser liability.

The weaknesses of the argument that courts should defer to a silent legislature on the issue of dispenser liability can be identified by considering both the difficulty of drawing plausible inferences from legislative inaction and the balkanization of tort principles that begins to occur when courts carve out certain forms of tort liability as lying beyond the institutional competence of the judiciary. Legislative inaction may be due to a variety of reasons and pressures. Attributing to the legislature a conscious choice to reject liability, should it be imposed by a court, is no more justifiable than assuming that the same decision would be reached in the future when the social and political environment may be significantly different. Furthermore, deciding that alcohol dispensers are not liable for negligent conduct contributes to a generally undesirable fragmentation of standard tort principles. Instead of viewing negligent conduct as presumptively calling for the attachment of liability under a conceptually coherent approach, courts that operated under this ostensibly deferential view would tend to depict the body of negligence law as a collection of separate duty rules that have been developed independently in specific contexts. Once such a fragmented view of the scope of the principle of liability for harm caused by negligence has taken hold, a shift in the dynamics of common-law tort development could follow. After a shift of that sort, the proof that a defendant's exercise of reasonable care would successfully have avoided the harm that was inflicted on the plaintiff could be seen as an insufficient indication that liability ought to be imposed. Instead, the practical burden that would be placed on a proponent of a new instance of tort liability would require the plaintiff to overcome a judicial inertia that favored a no-duty or a limited duty rule of liability in the absence of legislative action that imposed liability.

Deference to the legislature as a rationale for dispenser nonliability is particularly objectionable as a matter of principle in cases of legislative silence, for it introduces an other-directedness into the judicial inquiry that is fundamentally misguided. The question that a court has to answer when it is faced with a novel claim asserting a theory of dispenser liability is not what the legislature intended; nor is it what the legislature might have intended had it intended anything at all; nor is it what the legislature would intend if someday it were to intend something about the issue. To the extent that a search for legislative intent can be a meaningful exercise, that search should not ask any of those questions. Instead, it should place the following demand on courts: Within the constraints that are set by constitutional authority and restrictions on institutional power, the language of the statutes that are currently in force is to be applied to the resolution of issues that the statutes govern. Courts are not to construct contradictory or evasive interpretations that the courts or the litigants would prefer the legislature to have enacted. Once that duty to follow the mandate of existing statutes is satisfied, however, then the proper question for the court to ask is what should the court do with the claim. To insist on anything more than an application of the statutes that legislatures have actually enacted is to invite a court to engage in an illusory exercise in determining the intent of an institution composed of many members, none of whose individual states of mind is particularly significant.[30] The proper question as it is set out above invites a court instead to undertake an exercise in public policy-making that is legitimately within the province of the judiciary.

Posing the question that is before the court in the terms that have been used here does not suggest that the result of this policy-making must necessarily, or even presumptively, be a decision in favor of imposing liability on a dispenser of alcoholic beverages. Indeed, a court may sometimes properly decide to defer to the legislature as the more appropriate institution to adopt a new form of liability. If, for example, a recognition of a particular claim for relief represents a radical departure from common expectations about the extent of a person's legal or moral responsibility or from apparently widespread contemporary notions of fairness, then a court might decide that the step toward expanded liability is one that should be taken by the more politically accountable and more popularly responsive branch of government. What is important to recognize, however, is that this decision is itself a public policy decision that is reached as a result of the careful consideration of the issue of institutional competence in the dispenser liability setting. It is not a technique for evading a consideration of the public policy implications of the issue.

## Don't Blame the Liquor Industry

> "[T]o hold a purveyor of spirits liable would be to impose liability upon a liquor industry that was declared to be legitimate and respectable."[31]

The second of the rationales for not imposing liability on alcohol dispensers rests on the idea that the liquor industry ought not to be blamed for traffic-accident injuries caused by drinking drivers. The rationale's underlying premise is equally applicable to commercial dispensers and social hosts, and admittedly it has a certain intuitive and superficial appeal: under this view, it was not the alcohol industry that injured or killed the accident victim, it was the drinking driver. The National Rifle Association's slogan of a few years ago, "guns don't kill people, people kill people," taps into the same vein of popular opinion, which argues that the greatest share of blame for an injury should be assigned to the person who directly caused it.

The rationale "don't blame the industry" can be attacked on a number of different grounds. In the first place, it misconceives the nature of the tort liability imposed on the dispenser of alcohol. This liability is not dependent on an industry-wide condemnation unrelated to actual fault; rather, it rests on a specific finding that on a particular occasion a server of alcohol acted wrongly in serving alcohol to a person who subsequently injured the accident victim as a result of the alcohol consumption. In other words, the blame is actually attached to the individual seller or server whose conduct was at fault, not to the alcohol industry as a whole.

The more significant flaw in the argument "don't blame the industry" is that it treats as equivalent two ideas that modern tort law has successfully managed to separate. Raising the issue of the legitimacy and respectability of the liquor industry confuses the concept of moral culpability with the concept of legal liability. The legitimacy and respectability of an industry may very well count as important considerations against attaching moral blame to a member of that industry, but, as the modern tort system's attachment of strict liability to useful but dangerous activities indicates,[32] those considerations do not by themselves preclude the imposition of legal liability for the harm that is associated with that industry.

Both the case authority and the scholarship of tort law in the last three decades indicate the emergence of a trend that views moral culpability as functioning more in the nature of a sufficient, but not a necessary condition, of tort liability. Conversely, an absence of moral blame for accidents associated with a very risky but socially useful activity is not a legitimate reason for refusing to impose liability for those accidents on those who engage in the activity.[33] It is appropriate to demand that these sorts of risky activities pay their own way, in the sense of being able to hold those who engage in the activity legally responsible for the harm caused by the activity (see part 2).

To the extent that the "don't blame the industry" rationale tries to equate either personal or institutional blamelessness with a per se rule of nonliability, the rationale should not be given a great deal of weight. There is, however, a sense in which this rationale does capture a significant objection to the imposition of tort liability on a dispenser of alcohol. The thrust of the argument may be shifted from "don't blame us for what the drinking driver did" to "don't blame us for what we failed to do." In other words, one should not be held responsible for harm caused by one's failure to control the actions of another person. That argument, premised on a general popular belief along those lines, is more deeply rooted in tort law and theory, and it merits careful scrutiny. The argument is equally applicable to social and commercial dispensers of alcohol and applies to both statutory liability under a dram shop act and common-law liability under a judicially created rule (chapter 8 will cover the responsibility conundrum in more depth).

## Duck Cases That Are Too Hard to Decide

"[T]he chain between breach of duty and the injury will rarely be clear and, thus 'hard' cases would be the rule."[34]

The third rationale for nonliability that was identified in the *Sorensen* opinion focuses on the difficulty of adjudicating a dispenser liability claim. The underlying premise of this rationale is that a court should not adopt a liability theory that creates the responsibility to decide hard cases, especially because courts have limited time, energy, resources, and authority. When faced with an opportunity to recognize a new tort claim against dispensers of alcohol, a court might decide that the resolution of these claims would impose too heavy a demand on courts and these claims would be too hard for courts to decide.

Two types of hard case arguments might be invoked. The first argument asserts that the complexity of deciding hard cases may call into question the ability of the courts to dispose of the cases. It therefore invokes an appeal to courts to avoid difficult issues. The second argument looks at the likelihood of a negative public reaction to the court's recognition of this new tort liability. This second argument is especially sensitive to the risk of a court jeopardizing its authority by reaching a decision that lacks a firm grounding in popular sentiment, thus suggesting that the court would be engaged in a fairly questionable enterprise if it were to impose liability. It is these two types of hard case arguments—one focusing on the case that is hard to decide and the other on the case that is hard to sell—that need further exploration.

The difficulty that a court faces in adjudicating a dispenser liability claim ought not to be taken lightly. Dispenser liability requires a finding that the defendant was at fault in selling or serving alcohol to the person who then caused the accident in which the plaintiff was injured. The court must be able to satisfy itself that the conduct of the dispenser on this occasion was actually below the standard of care that would be exercised under those circumstances by a reasonable person in the defendant's position. To reach this finding a court must arrive at satisfactory answers to two questions: (1) what was the appropriate standard of care that was demanded of the defendant, and (2) did the defendant fail to meet the standard of care on this occasion?

In a case against a commercial dispenser, the plaintiff can establish the nature of the standard of care that was required of the defendant by introducing testimony about prevailing practices in the alcohol industry regarding the commercial service and retail sale of alcoholic beverages. The plaintiff must address both the prevailing practices in general and within the specific locality where the accident took place. Important evidence on this issue would address such matters as whether employees who serve alcohol were trained to recognize when a customer is intoxicated, what steps were taken to determine whether the customer was under the legal drinking age, and whether the customer was encouraged to accept an alternative to driving while intoxicated. Variations in the standard of care may need to be made depending on the size of an establishment, its clientele, its resources, and its location. Those variations make the court's task in setting the standard of care more difficult. In the case of a social host, the standard of care must be established without the benefit of being able to hold the defendant to a standard based on the prevailing professional practice.

When the issue turns from asking what the standard of care is to asking whether the defendant in this particular instance acted with reasonable care, the inquiry becomes much more narrowly focused. The inquiry as to reasonable care presents potentially serious difficulties of proof regarding the ability of witnesses to recall past events and the credibility of their testimony. While it is, of course, true that virtually any tort litigation features those same difficulties, the commercial-dispenser tort claim may be troubled by them to an unusually high degree. Many of the litigated issues that arise in tort cases in general focus on incidents that are out of the ordinary, and thus are likely to be remembered by witnesses. While a witness's perception of the details of an event can certainly be distorted by the event's emotional impact, it is also true that a dramatic event stands out from everyday life. Witnesses are more likely to be able to recall a dramatic event and recount its details later in court. The critical issue regarding fault in the typical commercial dispenser tort claim, however, is not the conduct surrounding some dramatic event, such as an automobile accident, but a routine business transaction. The dispenser's selling or serving of alcohol on a particular occasion might not stand out at all in the memory of either the actual server or seller or even in the minds of other witnesses of the transaction.

The difficulty of reconstructing the events of a sale or service of alcohol to someone who is subsequently involved in a traffic accident is not limited to the context of a common-law claim against a commercial dispenser of alcohol. Claims that are brought under dram shop acts also frequently involve the same issue of proof. Many state legislatures have recognized the problem in this context and have attempted to accommodate the conflicting interests of the injured party and the dispenser. In these states the injured party bringing the dram shop claim is often required to give notice of the claim to the defendant within a shorter period of time than that allowed for the actual filing of the lawsuit.[35] With earlier notice, the defendant can begin an investigation at a time when it may be easier to locate potential witnesses whose memories of the challenged sale or service underlying the claim may be fresher than they would be a year or two later.

The reasoning in support of these notice provisions for dram shop claims is particularly compelling in situations in which the time and place of the seller's or server's alleged misconduct is different from the time and place of the actual injury. A commercial dispenser may have no reason to learn of an accident involving one of its customers or to associate an account of an accident with its sale or service of alcohol to a customer. Social hosts, on the other hand, are more likely to become aware of accidents in which their guests are involved, particularly when the host-guest relationship is more long-term than the bar-customer relationship. Under the circumstances of a commercial dispenser case, then, reasonably prompt notice to the dram shop defendant can increase the defendant's chances to investigate the case and prepare a defense. In the case of a common-law claim, however, a commercial dispenser defendant may not receive notice of its potential liability until the date for filing the lawsuit allowed by the statute of limitations. This could be as along as one or two years after the date of the defendant's alleged misconduct.

In chapter 2, I suggested that the courts could give an enhanced role to presumptions in order to simplify the litigation of tort claims against drinking drivers. Specifically, the courts could allow proof of a driver's criminal conviction for driving while intoxicated at the time of an accident to raise a rebuttable presumption that the driver failed to operate the vehicle in accordance with the standard of reasonable care and that the failure played a causal role in the accident in which the plaintiff was injured. Given the driver's criminal conviction for one kind of fault, it is reasonable to assume the driver's fault for imposing tort liability as well.

Could the same presumptions be used to establish the liability of commercial dispensers and social hosts and thus simplify these "hard cases"? A consideration of the fault element that lies at the heart of the tort claim against an alcohol dispenser reveals that the answer is no. For dispenser liability to be established, the least amount of fault that ought to be required is sale or service of alcohol under circumstances that a commercial dispenser is reasonably likely to understand will constitute a violation of the alcoholic beverage control laws, such as serving someone who is already intoxicated, or under circumstances that a commercial dispenser or a social host should know will create an unreasonable risk of harm to the drinking driver or to others. Those instances of wrongful conduct may well be insufficiently correlated with test results measuring blood alcohol concentration or with the drinking driver's criminal conviction for driving while intoxicated for presumptions based on proof of these facts to apply here. The appropriate question to ask is whether, given the later BAC reading of the driver who caused the accident, it is likely that the dispenser's conduct was at fault in the sense required in a dispenser liability claim. If the link cannot be reliably made as a general proposition, then the presumption should not be invoked, and the plaintiff should have to introduce independently credible evidence that the dispenser's conduct actually did fall below the relevant standard of care.

Courts are regularly faced with the prospect of having to adjudicate factually and legally complex claims. The complexity of alcohol-dispenser liability litigation may not itself be a sufficient reason for a court to refuse to recognize a common-law claim for relief, but a court at least needs to consider carefully whether the degree of complexity that is involved substantially interferes with the fact finder's ability to render judgments that are based on a reliable decision-making process. If doubts along these lines are added to an underlying lack of comfort with the nature of the liability that is being imposed on an alcohol dispenser, then the scale may tip against recognition of the claim.

Difficult decision-making tasks raise "hard to decide" concerns about the justifiability of the resources that a court must use in order to arrive at a decision in individual cases. The other hard case argument, which revolves around the "hard to sell" idea, draws into question the legitimacy of the decision that a certain type of conduct should expose an actor to tort liability. Legal rules operate with the least amount of disruptive social friction when they are either derived from or correspond to popular notions of what is right and wrong.[36] Tort law standards of liability tend to be stated in very generalized terms, with the negligence standard most often phrased as a defendant's failure to exercise the level of reasonable care that was required under the circumstances. Such open-ended or content-free standards can be made more concrete through application in one of two ways.

Either a court can turn over to a jury the specific issue of whether this defendant acted as a reasonable person, or a court can attempt to narrow the scope of the standard by refusing to allow a claim to proceed when it is based on a particular allegation of how the defendant acted. The choice between those two options frequently appears in the form of a procedural ruling on the question of whether the plaintiff has stated a legally sufficient claim for relief, but there is really more that is substantive rather than procedural in that ruling. Either option that a court selects—to turn the matter over to a jury or to dismiss for failure to state a claim upon which relief can be granted—engages the court in the substantive rule-making task of recognizing a cause of action or refusing to do so. As an intermediate position in the development of a common-law claim, a court might decide that a plaintiff's claim can survive a challenge on legal sufficiency grounds only when certain preconditions are satisfied, thus giving at least some more specific content to the general standard of reasonable conduct.

In the context of drinking-driver traffic accidents, a judicial decision to let a dispenser common-law liability claim go to a jury reflects a willingness to allow a jury to decide whether the dispenser acted unreasonably and should bear legal responsibility for the plaintiff's injuries. Even if the court were to restrict the availability of the common-law claim to particular circumstances, such as the service of alcohol to someone a reasonable dispenser would have realized posed a risk to others because of the consumer's level of intoxication, the court that initially recognizes this claim for relief would be opening the door to a new sort of tort liability in accident cases. Before taking this innovative step, a court ought to consider whether the new claim for relief departs so much from a conventional understanding of responsibility that recognizing it will produce negative results. For example, the legislature might act in rejection of the court's ruling, as described in the previous discussion of preemption. This turn of events can put a court into an adversarial relationship with the legislature, with potentially disturbing implications for other issues. Of equal concern, but usually less dramatically visible, is the risk of lowering the general level of public acquiescence in the decisions of the judicial system as a whole because of the public's dissatisfaction with a particular decision. Again, as is true of the legislative rejection of a specific common-law rule, the greatest concern in the long term may be with damage to the institutional position of the judicial system rather than the outcome of the particular issue of dispenser liability. In chapter 8, which deals with the responsibility conundrum in dispenser liability cases, I explore the extent to which a common-law rule imposing liability on alcohol dispensers might represent just this kind of departure from community experience and expectations, and I propose ways in which this difficulty might be avoided.

## Don't Start Down a Slippery Slope

> "[O]nce a negligence basis for liability is accepted, there could be no logical point to cut off risk of responsibility, *i.e.*, if a negligent vendor for profit is liable, why not a negligent social host."[37]

As judges decide the specific cases that are presented to them, they construct a body of common-law decisions about tort liability. Fundamental notions of justice demand that like cases should be decided alike and that inconsistent and contradictory decisions are to be avoided. A slippery slope argument of the sort presented above in the quotation from the *Sorenson* opinion is normally offered as a reason for a court not to break with the past for fear that, having taken the first innovative step, it will subsequently find itself necessarily taking additional steps that will produce undesirable consequences.[38] In the context of drinking-driver traffic accidents, a common slippery slope argument would urge a court to resist recognizing a theory of commercial dispenser liability in order to avoid expanding liability to cover other parties who are even more remotely connected to the accident under circumstances involving even less fault. The momentum with which a court slides down the slippery slope would be increased to the extent that the dispenser liability rule that is proposed or adopted in a landmark decision is grounded on a legal principle that encompasses a wider variety of circumstances than those that are presented in that initial case.

The functional distinction between rules and principles is best described in the early work of the legal philosopher Ronald Dworkin.[39] Rules govern the disposition of the cases to which they apply in an all-or-nothing fashion, while principles supply reasons in support of a result rather than dictating a result. Rules thus either apply or do not apply, while principles may conflict and compete in a particular case, in which case they need to be weighed to determine which is stronger in those circumstances. The basic elements of the rule/ principle distinction can be adopted for purposes of this discussion without any necessary commitment to the jurisprudential conclusions that Professor Dworkin reaches about the competence or legitimacy of particular types of judicial decision making.

In a common-law legal system, the principles on which judicial decisions in individual cases are based are as frequently developed by inductive reasoning and reasoning by analogy from the body of decisions in a number of cases as they are articulated in some authoritative or canonical form in any particular one of those cases. And yet it is not inaccurate for practitioners and interpreters of the common law routinely to assert that courts decide only the cases before them, so that a decision in one case does not necessarily tie the hands of a court that is presented at a later date with a dispute that arises from a different fact pattern. In contemporary American law there is a tension between the precedential effect of the implicit principles upon which decisions may be grounded and the binding force exerted by a case's *ratio decidendi* that is more limited in scope but more compelling in power than the underlying principles that might be used to explain or justify the decision.

For purposes of understanding the slippery slope rationale for not adopting a common-law rule that imposes tort liability on commercial dispensers of alcohol, that tension can be depicted in the following hypothetical example. A judge who decides to adopt a rule in favor of liability might write an opinion explaining that the rule is being announced in a case of a specific sort, that is, a case in which a defendant has served alcohol to a visibly intoxicated patron of the defendant's bar, for example, or a case in which a defendant has sold alcohol to someone whom a reasonable person in the business of selling alcoholic beverages would have adequate reason to suspect was a minor. Because that is the particular fact pattern that is presented by the case in which the court announces its new liability rule, this first judge could state that the rule is limited to the facts of this particular case. The question of whether a dispenser liability claim under another fact pattern that is similar but not identical to this one would be subject to the same rule of liability can legitimately by postponed until the court has before it a case that actually presents that different fact pattern.

A colleague of this first judge could use two different types of slippery slope reasoning to justify a decision not to adopt a rule imposing liability on a commercial dispenser. The first, which can be called the immature version of slippery slope argumentation, says that, once having decided that *anyone* is liable for serving alcohol to a driver who then injures another person, the court cannot (or cannot easily) determine the extent of the scope of that rule of liability. In other words, once having started down the path of liability for dispensing alcohol, the court will find it difficult to halt the extension of that liability until, finally, liability is imposed on all alcohol dispensers in all circumstances. A second type of slippery slope argument is more sophisticated than the immature version, which arguably gives too much weight to the difficulty of drawing distinctions between different fact patterns. This more sophisticated version of the argument would pay greater attention to the legal principle upon which the dispenser liability rule was grounded in the first case than to the specific rule the court adopted in that case. A judge who employs this more sophisticated type of slippery slope reasoning would understand that any future decisions that attempted to distinguish the case in which liability was imposed must demonstrate a consistency in the application of that principle. This second judge, when confronted with the first claim seeking dispenser liability, could then refuse to recognize dispenser liability based on skepticism about the ability of any court to make such a principled distinction in the future.

These two types of slippery slope arguments place different demands on judges, who arguably find themselves poised at the top of the slope of unending or unlimited dispenser liability to victims of drinking drivers. The immature version of the argument seems to call for a nonliability decision unless the court is prepared to accept universal dispenser liability. The more sophisticated version would instead suggest that an initial decision to impose liability on a dispenser of alcohol ought to be grounded on a legal principle that is sufficiently clear that it can provide guidance for the disposition of later cases that pose related but nevertheless distinct fact patterns.

Not much attention needs to be given to the immature version of the slippery slope argument. Much of the strength of the common-law method of decision making comes precisely from the opportunity that it affords courts to operate on a case-by-case basis, evaluating both the logic and the consequences of previous decisions and then considering whether the next step down a particular slope is warranted. It is precisely this difference between judges and legislators with regard to their ability to postpone decisions until more is known about how a rule will actually work that undercuts the force of the immature slippery slope argument. Legislators have at least some obligation to anticipate exceptional situations that will arise in the application of the rules that they promulgate and to arrive at a statement of some predetermined disposition of those situations. Judges, on the other hand, can adopt a posture of waiting to see how a particular decision works out in practice before deciding how far down a slope it is wise to go. The institutional differences between these two branches of government thus make it easier, rather than more difficult, for courts to take tentative initial steps in a new direction while still allowing for an evaluation of the consequences of those steps before making a wholesale commitment to proceeding in that direction.

The more sophisticated slippery slope argument requires a more careful consideration, but it too can be found to be deficient as a reason for rejecting a rule that extends tort liability beyond a drinking driver and parties who are vicariously liable for the driver's conduct. One response to the argument would simply treat the binding force of the principle underlying the new rule in the same manner that the rule itself was treated in the response to the immature slippery slope argument that was just sketched out. Just as a court need only commit itself to the precise contours of the rule as it was announced in a particular case, so too a court need only make a limited commitment to a particular principle as a basis for the initial decision that a court starts down a new path. In subsequent cases, while a court may not properly ignore the principle, the weight that is given to the principle can be substantially reduced should it appear to be producing unwanted effects.

That response may suffice in those situations in which judges cannot be expected to have enough of a grasp of the future implications of a new rule of liability for them to be able to announce a relatively narrowly articulated principle on which future decisions can draw. A better response, however, acknowledges that the more sophisticated slippery slope argument has at least some merit, and it would insist, where at all possible, that a court articulate a principle in the initial decision that identifies a principled basis for arriving at an understanding of the scope of the new theory of liability and the implications of recognizing this new claim for relief. Part of the problem with common-law commercial dispenser claims has been that the principles courts have offered in support of imposing liability have generally failed to perform that function. The broadest of principles that might be offered to support dispenser liability would state that a person who furnishes another person with the means by which the latter can cause harm to a third party is responsible for that harm. Following this principle, one can imagine (and lawyers have attempted to assert them) tort claims against those who sell gasoline to drinking drivers. It is possible to engage in even further attempts at *reductio ad absurdum* and contemplate claims being asserted against the state agency that issues a driver's license to a person who is known to have an alcohol abuse problem.

The appropriate way to reduce the persuasiveness of slippery slope arguments of that sort is, of course, to narrow the statement of the principle that underlies the adoption of commercial dispenser liability. Most of the dispenser liability theories of action that have been recognized so far rest on a finding that the dispenser must have sold or served alcohol to someone whom a reasonable person would recognize is either a minor or an intoxicated person. The underlying legal principle can now be narrowed to responsibility for the wrongful dispensing of the intoxicating agent to a person who is legally ineligible to consume it. Even that statement, however, arguably fails to reduce the scope of the principle appropriately.

Consider just one set of contrasting fact patterns, which will provide an illustrative situation. Suppose that a patron of the defendant's bar comes into the establishment, tosses his car keys onto the bar, and vociferously orders "a shot and a beer." Easily detecting that the patron is inebriated, the defendant refuses to serve him any alcohol. The patron then picks up his keys, drives away from the bar, and collides with a car that is being driven by the plaintiff. The liability of the defendant in that situation cannot rest on a dispenser liability claim, because the defendant neither sold nor served alcohol to the driver. Now, change the fact pattern only slightly. Instead of being refused service initially, the patron, who is actually just as inebriated this time, is allowed to purchase one beer. Before the patron can finish drinking the beer, however, the defendant becomes aware of the patron's intoxicated state and tells him that he cannot be served. The patron immediately declares his indignation at being subjected to such inhospitable and insulting treatment, leaves his unfinished beer on the bar, and drives away from the bar into the same collision previously described. Here, a dispenser liability claim against the defendant arguably stands on a stronger footing, because there was a sale of alcohol to a driver who was intoxicated. And yet one can question whether there is any significant difference between the role of the defendant in the production of the harm to the third party in these two fact patterns. Without a further narrowing of the principle upon which dispenser liability rests, a decision in favor of liability in the second hypothetical would appear to rest on a fairly trivial distinction from a nonliability decision in the first hypothetical.

The question that needs to be asked is whether a more precise articulation of a principle supporting dispenser liability is possible. If the answer is yes, then some of the slippery slope argument's fear about the future course of litigation against alcohol dispensers and other nondriving defendants can be alleviated. In chapter 8, where the issue of dispenser responsibility is addressed in detail, a narrower principle will be suggested, but only at the expense of excluding some situations in which dispenser liability can now be imposed under the broader standards currently in place in many states.

## Don't Overburden the Courts

"[T]his new rule of liability would create additional burdens on the courts."[40]

The rationales for a nonliability rule that have been examined in the last two sections of this chapter are built on concerns about the complexity of the decision-making task that dispenser liability claims would place before the courts, the legitimacy of the liability rule that the courts are being asked to adopt, and the pressure to extend even further the precedential effect of decisions that recognize a theory of tort liability that covers new situations or new classes of actors. The argument that is considered in this section, that recognizing the li ability of alcohol dispensers will overburden the courts, can be seen initially as involving a conceptually simpler matter of considering the mere number of cases that a court will have to adjudicate. According to this rationale, recognizing a common-law claim by victims of drinking drivers against dispensers of alcohol would open the floodgates for a volume of tort cases that will inundate the judicial system. As with the other rationales that have been analyzed, the occasion for making the "overburdening of the courts" argument is not limited to drinking-driver cases. In evaluating the force of the argument, then, it is helpful to consider both the general nature of this rationale and its particular application to the alcohol dispenser liability question.

The most superficial response to this argument against liability is to say that courts are in the business of deciding cases and, absent any special considerations regarding the nature of the claim that is being recognized, the increase in the volume of cases that may be filed is not a sufficient reason for refusing to recognize a claim. If justice to accident victims demands that a particular legal remedy or a specific theory of tort liability should be available, a concern about the increased workload for the courts ought not to outweigh the requirements of justice.

When the liability question is put in the form of a policy choice between the demands of satisfying justice and limiting the workload of the courts, the balance is admittedly tipped fairly decisively against the "overburdening of the courts" rationale for nonliability. The relationship between these two factors is, however, somewhat more complex than this simple phrasing of the question indicates. The quality of the justice that is administered by the courts is in part a product of the strain that the judicial workload puts on the system. Furthermore, it is an insufficient answer to say that society should simply devote more resources to the judicial system by creating more judgeships and by increasing facilities and support staff. If there is one lesson in public policy-making that should have been learned from the experience of the last decade, it is the reluctance of government at many levels to respond to social problems by infusing new finances rather than by shifting and spreading limited funds among a variety of demonstrated needs that may be equally compelling. Therefore, expecting that the total amount of resources that would be spent on the judiciary will expand substantially to meet any significant rise in the judicial workload would appear to be unrealistic in a time of significant budgetary constraints on government.

Even within the judicial system itself, a flood of new tort claims may produce a specific problem in the political climate in which we find ourselves at the beginning of the 1990s. The majority of trial courts that adjudicate tort cases in this country are courts of general jurisdiction, which hear both civil and criminal cases. When the total caseload of a court system increases, however, it is generally not the case that the reallocation of existing resources is evenly distributed between the civil and criminal sides of a court's docket. Criminal cases must be processed with greater dispatch than civil cases because of the pressure of meeting the speedy trial guarantees of the federal and the state constitutions. A major increase in the criminal caseload can therefore be expected to add to the delay in the disposition of cases on the civil dockets of a court system. Given the increasing attention to the drug problem in this country and the call for a greater commitment to criminal prosecution of both those who sell and those who use illegal drugs, one can predict that any sizeable increase that occurs in the number of tort claims that are adjudicated would be likely to correspond to a simultaneous decrease in the total amount of the judicial system's time and money available for the adjudication of civil cases.

The discussion of the "overburdening the courts" rationale has focused so far on general questions about the demands on judicial resources, suggesting that there is a relationship between the workload of a court and the quality of the justice it is able to administer. The specific effects that are likely to follow the recognition of a common-law claim against a dispenser of alcohol are an important part of the cost-benefit calculation of whether to recognize the claim. That calculation requires a consideration of a number of factors, the most important of which are the size of the increase in litigation that will follow and the social good that is expected to result. Estimates of these matters are necessarily inexact and lie in the province of social scientists rather than legal scholars,[41] but a few general observations can be offered with some degree of confidence.

In the first place, a realistic evaluation of the "overburdening of the courts" argument needs to include an appreciation of the pattern of litigation that exists in our society. Only a tiny fraction of the potential legal claims that arise in everyday occurrences result in the filing of lawsuits, and of those cases that proceed as far as the filing of a complaint against a defendant, only a small percentage go to trial. The vast bulk of the disputes that arise in our society are resolved without recourse to the legal system, except to the (not insignificant) extent that the legal system provides a background set of expectations about rights and responsibilities within which informal dispute resolution can take place. In a situation in which the formal dispute resolution mechanisms of the legal system have been invoked, the dynamics of the system produce a momentum that favors settlement rather than costly and protracted litigation. The recognition of a new tort claim for relief is therefore unlikely to produce a caseload increase that includes anywhere near every instance of conduct in which the new claim could possibly be asserted.

In the case of the alcohol dispenser liability claim, a factor that tends to produce a greater skepticism about the size of the additional caseload that is likely to result is the claim's role in expanding the range of defendants who might be liable to compensate an accident victim for injuries for which other legal remedies are already currently available. The recognition of a common-law claim for dispenser liability is not a situation in which a new type of injury is being recognized as now suitable for legal relief. Instead, the chances that an accident victim might be able to obtain a more complete recovery are being increased by an extension of legal responsibility to a class of parties who have previously been treated as being outside the scope of tort liability. When that is the case, an increase in the frequency of litigation is likely only in those situations in which the financial resources of the new class of defendants attract plaintiffs whose existing claims are practically infeasible. Thus some of the dispenser liability claims might overlap with lawsuits against other defendants that are already allowed by the legal system. While the complications that are associated with adding any new claim in general, and the dispenser liability claim in particular, ought not to be a matter to which the proponents of a new claim are indifferent, the nature of this sort of tort claim does suggest that the caseload increase will be further mitigated by the fact that other types of claims are already available. Claims against alcohol dispensers are likely to generate new litigation only in those situations in which no tort claims would be filed against any potential defendant in the absence of this new theory of liability.

Finally, the benefit to society needs to be factored into the evaluation of the "overburdening of the courts" rationale. In the context of the dispenser liability claim, two considerations are particularly relevant: the effect of this new form of liability on the frequency of drinking-driver accidents and its potential to help accident victims achieve better compensation. First, if the tort liability that is recognized in the commercial dispenser or social host claim provides an added deterrence to drinking and driving, then in the long run one can expect that the number of drinking-driver traffic-accident cases will decrease. Even if there is an increase in the frequency of tort litigation in the short run, adjudicating those dispenser liability cases might be worth the effort in order to obtain an additional instrument for controlling this social problem. Chapters 6 and 7, which focus on each of the two types of dispenser liability claims that might be recognized, will outline how these claims might influence people's behavior and affect the level of drinking and driving.

Second, to the extent that the seriously undercompensated accident victims of drinking drivers are made more financially secure by the addition of dispenser liability tort claims to the legal remedies already available to them, then the demands those victims place on other parts of the complex scheme of government and private social programs that make up the "safety net" of our society might be reduced. Increases in the costs of administering a particular legal remedy might therefore be offset by corresponding decreases in the costs of other means of protecting injured individuals from financial destitution. I take up these questions of cost allocation and of balancing different social programs in detail in part 2, which considers the economics of allocating the costs of drinking-driver accidents, and in part 3, where I propose a better system of handling the losses that are suffered by victims of drinking-driver traffic accidents.

## *Don't Let the Drinking Driver off the Hook*

"[A]llowing a vendor to be liable would erode the responsibility heretofore placed upon the drinker and would thus diminish a sense of responsibility for one's own conduct."[42]

Many of the nonliability arguments discussed above were able to be expressed in at least two versions, the more sophisticated of which was entitled to be given at least some weight. That is not as true of the final rationale, which is by far the weakest of the reasons for limiting liability to the drinking driver. This simplistic argument invokes the notion that imposing liability on a dispenser of alcohol will operate unfairly to benefit the drinking driver who has actually injured the plaintiff. Under this view, if any party other than a drinking driver can be held liable, then the full force of the legal system's response to the driver's conduct will be diverted. In other words, it will reduce the disincentive to drink and drive. Thus the off-the-hook argument contains a subtext that says that expanding the scope of tort liability to include alcohol dispensers (and potentially other non-driving defendants as well) may increase the number of drinking-driver traffic accidents.

The underlying assumption of the off-the-hook argument presents a fairly implausible assessment of the consequences of expanding liability on the behavior of a drinking driver. While it is true that a commercial dispenser of alcohol is likely to offer a deeper pocket from which to seek compensation, the victim's ability to pursue a tort action against the alcohol dispenser does not in any way preclude bringing a concurrent action against the drinking driver. The dispenser of alcohol is someone who can be held liable along with, not instead of, the drinking driver. As chapter 2 has pointed out, the decision about whether a seriously injured accident victim should sue the drinking driver is likely to turn mainly on a consideration of whether the driver has sufficient assets out of which a large tort judgment can be satisfied. If the drinking driver is the sole party who can be held legally responsible for the harm to the accident victim, one might expect to see at least some drivers not sued at all. However, if dispenser liability is added to the range of tort claims that the more seriously injured accident victim may pursue, the result might be that drinking drivers are sued even in those marginal cases. In some states, dram shop legislation requires that a drinking driver must be named and retained as a defendant in any action against a dram shop defendant.[43] Such a required joinder of the drinking driver would not necessarily be made part of a common-law tort claim against an alcohol dispenser. Nevertheless, even if the drinking driver has no reasonable chance of being able to satisfy a large tort judgment, sound litigation strategy might dictate that the drinking driver be joined anyway. In some instances, the reciprocal allegations of fault that multiple defendants might make about each other's conduct could be helpful to a tort plaintiff who has to prove that each defendant was at fault. The drinking driver may also be induced to settle for a relatively insignificant share of the plaintiff's total damages, such as the amount of the driver's liability insurance policy limits, but the amount that is received in that settlement could be used to subsidize some of the expense of establishing the tort liability of other more financially responsible defendants.

Suppose, however, that there is some merit to the argument that expanding the range of parties who can be liable will reduce the number of lawsuits filed against the drinking drivers. The question that remains is whether that result will have the further effect of reducing the disincentive to drink and drive and thus produce an increase in the number of accidents. It seems highly implausible to suggest that expanding liability to other defendants would significantly lessen the deterrent effect that the legal system has on drinking and driving. After all, drinking drivers who conclude that they face a reduced prospect of civil liability being imposed on them personally for the injuries they cause will still face the threat of criminal prosecution. They will suffer emotional trauma in connection with the accident and their role in causing it, and they will have to live with whatever social opprobrium they receive as a result of their conduct. In those circumstances, the argument that the drinking driver has been let off the hook as a result of a legal rule that imposes tort liability on someone other than the driver appears to lack much of a convincing basis in reality.

Even though the off-the-hook rationale for alcohol dispenser nonliability lacks much force, it does introduce an important concept—the relationship between legal rules and behavior. While it makes little sense to argue that holding a nondriving defendant liable will increase the number of drinking-driver traffic accidents because drivers will be more inclined to drink, the converse of that argument raises a question that needs to be considered carefully. Can legal responsibility for the harms that are caused by another person's conduct result in a lowering of the frequency of that conduct? In other words, is it possible to affect behavior positively with legal rules that impose accident costs on parties other than the person who directly causes the accident? Those questions lie at the heart of a good deal of contemporary tort scholarship, and they must be answered satisfactorily if any major reform effort involving how accident losses are spread is to be successful. In the next two chapters I discuss the effects that dispenser liability could have on the number of drinking driver accidents. The general question of how to allocate accident costs appropriately is explored fully in part 2, with a specific discussion of the economic analysis of various tort rules, including those that impose liability on dispensers of alcohol, in chapter 10.

## NOTES

1. 119 Wis.2d 627, 350 N.W.2d 108 (1984).

2. *Id.* at 642, 350 N.W.2d at 116.

3. *Id.* ("the problem of intoxication was a social, not a legal, problem and, hence, was a matter to be dealt with by the legislature").

4. *Id.* ("to hold a purveyor of spirits liable would be to impose liability upon a liquor industry that was declared to be legitimate and respectable").

5. *Id.* ("the chain between breach of duty and the injury will rarely be clear and, thus, 'hard' cases would be the rule").

6. *Id.* ("once a negligence basis for liability is accepted, there could be no logical point to cut off the risk of responsibility, *i.e.*, if a negligent vendor for profit is liable, why not a negligent social host").

7. *Id.* ("this new rule of liability would create additional burdens on the courts").

8. *Id.* ("allowing a vendor to be liable would erode the responsibility heretofore placed upon the drinker and would thus diminish a sense of responsibility for one's own conduct").

9. WIS. STAT. ANN. § 125.035 (1989).

10. Sorensen v. Jarvis, 119 Wis.2d at 642, 350 N.W.2d at 116.

11. There is a nice statement of this view in Ontiveros v. Borak, 136 Ariz. 500, 667 P.2d 200 (1983), a case in which the Supreme Court of Arizona recognized a common-law tort claim against commercial dispensers of alcohol.

12. 398 N.W.2d 807 (Iowa 1987). The decision is analyzed in Case Note, *Dram Shop Act,* 37 DRAKE L. J. 537 (1988).

13. IOWA CODE ANN. § 123.47 (West 1987).

14. *Id.* at § 123.92 (West Supp. 1990).

15. 398 N.W.2d at 809.

16. *Id.*

17. 364 N.W.2d 226 (Iowa 1985).

18. IOWA CODE ANN. § 123.49 (West 1987).

19. *Id.* at § 123.49(1)(a).

20. *Id.* at § 123.49(1)(b).

21. 428 N.W.2d 658 (Iowa 1988).

22. *Id.* at 659. A judgment in favor of the social hosts was affirmed by the Supreme Court of Iowa in Bauer v. Cole, 467 N.W.2d 221 (1991), on the ground that the hosts were not negligent.

23. 40 Ohio St.3d 359, 533 N.E.2d 732 (1988).

24. *See id.* at 362, 533 N.E.2d at 736.

25. *Id.*

26. *Id.* (emphasis added).

27. 232 Va. 350, 350 S.E.2d 621 (1986).

28. *Id.* at 352, 350 S.E.2d at 623.

29. *Id.* at 354, 350 S.E.2d at 624.

30. One of the more insightful writers on the question of legislative intent is Ronald Dworkin. *See* R. DWORKIN, A MATTER OF PRINCIPLE 316-31 (1985); R. DWORKIN, LAW'S EMPIRE 313-54 (1986).

31. Sorensen v. Jarvis, 119 Wis.2d at 642, 350 N.W.2d at 116.

32. *See generally* RESTATEMENT (SECOND) OF TORTS § 519-520 (1977).

33. *See generally* Priest, *The Invention of Enterprise Liability: A Critical History of the Intellectual Foundations of Modern Tort Law,* 14 J. LEGAL STUD. 461 (1985).

34. Sorensen v. Jarvis, 119 Wis.2d at 642, 350 N.W.2d at 116.

35. *See, e.g.,* MINN. STAT. ANN. § 340A.802 (West Supp. 1990) (written notice must be given to the defendant within 120 days of the claimant hiring an attorney).

36. *Compare* Pokora v. Wabash Ry. Co., 292 U.S. 98 (1934) *with* B. & O. R. Co. v. Goodman, 275 U.S. 66 (1927) (adopting, then rejecting, a judicially created rule of specific conduct that is required by a truck driver when crossing railroad tracks with obstructed view).

37. Sorensen v. Jarvis, 119 Wis.2d at 642, 350 N.W.2d at 116.

38. For a sophisticated jurisprudential analysis of slippery slope thinking, see Schauer, *Slippery Slopes,* 99 HARV. L. REV. 361 (1985).

39. *See generally* R. DWORKIN, TAKING RIGHTS SERIOUSLY 22-130 (1978).

40. Sorensen v. Jarvis, 119 Wis.2d at 642, 350 N.W.2d at 116.

41. Some of the best work in this country on the question of judicial caseload has been done by Richard Roper, a political scientist on the staff of the National Center for State Courts. *See, e.g.,* NAT'L CENTER FOR ST. CTS., STATE COURT CASELOAD STATISTICS: ANNUAL REPORT 1985 (1987); *idem,* STATE COURT CASELOAD STATISTICS: ANNUAL REPORT 1984 (1986).

42. Sorensen v. Jarvis, 119 Wis.2d at 642, 350 N.W.2d at 116.

43. Michigan's dram shop statute, for example, requires that the drinking driver must be named as a defendant along with the dram shop defendant and must be retained in the lawsuit until the claim against the dram shop defendant has been concluded. MICH. COMP. LAWS ANN. § 436.22(6) (West Supp. 1989).

# 6

## Common-Law Liability of the Commercial Dispenser

Establishing the third order of tort liability—that of a dispenser of alcohol under the statutorily created theory of liability that was described in chapter 4—depends in the first instance on the availability of dram shop legislation providing a claim for relief from that dispenser. As has been demonstrated in the last two chapters, in some cases the liability of a commercial dispenser depends on whether the courts recognize a common-law doctrine of tort liability for the server or seller who dispenses alcohol to a drinking driver. In the first case, a plaintiff may be injured in a state that has no dram shop legislation. Second, a plaintiff may be injured in a state that does have a dram shop act, but the effective date of the act is later than the date of the accident. Third, the dram shop act may have been in force when the accident occurred, but the specific situation that is before the court does not come within the scope of the liability defined in the dram shop statute (see chapter 4). In each of these three situations, then, a court will have to decide whether to create a common-law right for a drinking-driver traffic-accident victim to recover from a defendant who sold alcoholic beverages to the driver who subsequently caused the accident in which the victim was injured.

The doctrinal tools that would permit the construction of an affirmative answer to that question are easily located in the standard doctrines of contemporary tort law. The doctrine of negligence per se offers a way to incorporate into a negligence case against the dispenser conduct that constitutes a statutory violation, such as making a prohibited sale of alcohol. Some selectivity would have to be exercised in deciding which statutory violations should be treated as negligence per se, but the prerequisites outlined in chapter 2's description of this doctrine are adequate to perform this screening function. In sum, they require that the prohibition on the sale or the service of alcohol to the customer who subsequently causes a drinking-driver accident must be found by a court to be designed in general to protect a class of persons such as the plaintiff from the general type of harm that occurred in this case and that this harm was caused by the statutory violation.

The causation element may be the most difficult prerequisite for a plaintiff to establish persuasively. A court may be unwilling to find that there is a sufficiently strong causal connection between the plaintiff's injuries and the sale or service of alcohol that was prohibited by statute or administrative regulation. However, even if a court were to take a more restrictive approach to the use of the negligence per se doctrine in determining the tort liability of servers and sellers of alcohol, the elements of a standard negligence case—breach of a legal duty and causation—should be provable in at least some of the more frequently encountered situations involving a commercial dispenser of alcoholic beverages. All a tort plaintiff would have to establish is that under the circumstances a person in the defendant's position was required to exercise more care for the protection of those who are in the position of the plaintiff than the defendant used on the occasion in question, and that the defendant's failure to use reasonable care in the dispensing of alcohol made a substantial causal contribution, along with the drinking driver's conduct, to the production of the plaintiff's injuries.

The question of whether to recognize a common-law right of action against a commercial dispenser is affected by more than just the issue of whether the elements of a negligence claim against the dispenser can be assembled. Other important issues call into question the scope of judicial competence and authority to recognize a new claim in light of whatever legislative actions may have preceded the presentation of the dispenser liability question to the courts. Moreover, even if a court should decide that it is authorized to recognize an action against a commercial server of alcohol, that court must further decide whether the public policy considerations in favor of imposing such liability are sufficiently compelling. The common-law liability question thus comes down to two important considerations—judicial authority and public policy—in addition to the doctrinal acceptability or adaptability of standard negligence theory.

In the preceding chapter, I analyzed six rationales for not recognizing a common-law tort theory of liability of commercial dispensers of alcohol. These were drawn from a 1984 decision by the Supreme Court of Wisconsin in a case called *Sorensen v. Jarvis*.[1] The court found those six rationales for not imposing liability, even taken together, to be unpersuasive, and it recognized a theory of commercial dispenser liability. This case nicely illustrates both the institutional competence question and the public policy considerations that can affect the recognition of a drinking-driver accident victim's claim for relief from a commercial dispenser of alcohol.

While Ronald Jarvis was driving a car while intoxicated, he failed to stop at a stop sign. The car collided with the Sorensen vehicle in the intersection, killing both of the adult occupants, James and Sarah Sorensen, and injuring their two children, Zachary and Sarah. Scott Ferraro, who was a passenger in Jarvis's car, was also injured in the accident. A lawsuit on behalf of the Sorensen children was brought against Jarvis, the drinking driver. In addition, a claim was filed on behalf of the children against Robert Tonar, a liquor dealer who had sold Jarvis two bottles of liquor during the course of the evening on which the accident occurred. Those sales had been made at two different times during the evening, and Jarvis, the purchaser, was only seventeen years old at the time.[2]

In addition to the Sorensen children's claims against Tonar, a lawsuit was also filed by Ferraro, the passenger in Jarvis's car, against Jarvis and the liquor dealer. As was mentioned in chapter 4, most dram shop acts bar a passenger who had some complicity in the driver's intoxication from filing a claim against the dealer under the act. Two other important issues are, first, whether the state has a law that requires a driver to have acted with a higher level of culpability than negligence in order to be held liable to the nonpaying "guest" passenger, and second, whether the passenger's own conduct in riding with the drinking driver demonstrated either contributory negligence or an assumption of the risk of harm from the driver's alcohol-impaired operation of the car. Neither of those issues is relevant to the claims that were asserted by the Sorensen children, who are easily characterized as innocent victims.

The tort claims against Tonar, the liquor dealer, were dismissed by the trial court, on the ground that they failed to state a claim upon which relief could be granted. An attack on that ground (which is the modern procedural counterpart of a common-law pleading demurrer) calls for a court to evaluate the legal sufficiency of the plaintiff's claim. A motion to dismiss for failure to state a claim is one of the foremost procedural devices by which a tort defendant can question whether a particular theory of recovery has been, or will be, accepted in a jurisdiction. A ruling such as that made by the trial court in *Sorensen* in dismissing the dispenser liability claims serves as a judicial declaration that the plaintiff's theory of liability is not one for which the court finds a basis in the law of that jurisdiction. The trial court's dismissal in the *Sorensen* case was reversed by the state supreme court, which held that a cause of action for common-law negligence against the alcohol vendor would be recognized in the state of Wisconsin.

Addressing the issue of judicial authority, or institutional competence, first in its opinion in the *Sorensen* case, the Wisconsin supreme court noted that it was not writing on a clean slate. Previous decisions of that court had rejected the theory that a dispenser of alcohol was liable to the victims of a drinking driver who had been furnished alcohol by a person in the defendant's position. The court concluded that a failure to recognize a theory of recovery in the past should not end the inquiry, however. A decision that was reached in the past may have been responsive to considerations that no longer obtain, and a court ought to be receptive, as the *Sorensen* opinion reveals the state supreme court to have been, to arguments that demonstrate a need to reexamine prior decisions in light of contemporary conditions and needs.[3]

After reviewing the fairly complicated string of prior decisions and deciding that neither legislative enactments nor judicial precedent denied the court the authority to recognize a tort claim against the liquor dealer who sold the alcohol to the drinking driver, the court turned to the question of whether it *should* recognize such a claim. That led the Wisconsin supreme court to engage in a careful consideration of the nature of the policy factors, and the potential for conflicts among those factors, that had led the court in its previous decisions to withhold the recognition of such a claim for relief (recall the discussion in chapter 5, which concluded that in general the rationales for not recognizing dispenser liability were considerably less than compelling). Concluding that the balance of the relevant policy considerations favored the recognition of a theory of recovery in this situation presented in *Sorensen*, the supreme court decided to recognize the victim's claim against the commercial dispenser.

In recognizing a common-law tort claim against a commercial dispenser of alcohol, the court in *Sorensen* set out a list of the elements that most courts that have adopted this theory of liability would require a plaintiff to prove in order to be successful in asserting such a claim. First, the conduct of the alcohol dispenser who is sued by the plaintiff must be negligent. In a case such as *Sorensen,* in which the dispenser's conduct was also in violation of the state statute that prohibited a sale of alcohol to a minor, the court was willing to allow the tort plaintiff to invoke the doctrine of negligence per se. However, just as the plaintiff was allowed to use the statutory violation to establish that the dispenser's conduct was below a reasonable standard of care, the defendant would be allowed to raise the defenses that were available to a seller of alcohol under the relevant provisions of the state statutes.[4] The result of the combined uses of the statutory prohibition on sale to minors is in effect a presumption that a sale to a minor is negligent, with the seller given an opportunity to prove that the seller had no actual or constructive notice that the purchaser was in fact a minor.

If a court refuses to allow a plaintiff to use the negligence per se doctrine to establish that the alcohol dispenser acted negligently, then the plaintiff must offer evidence that the dispenser's conduct failed to meet the standard of reasonable care that was required under the circumstances. Although making this showing may be more difficult than merely relying on the statutory violation to prove negligence, it is not impossible. The most important investigatory task for a plaintiff who is attempting to establish negligence on the part of an alcohol dispenser is to determine precisely what occurred in the sale or service of alcohol to the drinking driver. The most persuasive evidence would undoubtedly be eyewitness testimony. Testimony that the customer appeared to be intoxicated or that the customer appeared to be underage would help to establish that it was unreasonable for the defendant to serve the customer. In the absence of direct eyewitness testimony, a plaintiff may be able to prove that the defendant's conduct was negligent by introducing evidence of the pattern of behavior that is customarily followed by the defendant. If, for example, the defendant routinely fails to check the identification of customers of questionable majority, then the jury might be asked to infer that this failure occurred as well at the time of the incident in question. Similarly, if the defendant regularly operates a promotional event such as a "happy hour," in which customers are encouraged to consume a great deal of alcohol in a short period of time, then the jury might infer that, as a result, the defendant made little effort or had little ability to identify any customers who had become visibly intoxicated and therefore should not have been served. Evidence about the defendant's pattern of behavior can support the conclusion that the pattern was followed on the occasion on which the drinking driver was served.

The second element of a common-law tort claim against a commercial dispenser of alcohol that was recognized by the court in *Sorensen* is a causal relationship between the sale and the plaintiff's injury. The *Sorensen* opinion followed the trend of modern tort law by requiring only that the plaintiff must prove that "the sale of the alcoholic beverage was a *substantial factor* in causing the injuries" to the plaintiff.[5] The court described a three-step causal chain that must be established if a plaintiff is to succeed in proving causation. A plaintiff must prove, first, that the driver consumed alcohol that was sold by the defendant; second, that the alcohol consumption made the driver intoxicated or impaired the driver's ability to drive; and third, that the impairment that was caused by the consumption of the alcohol was a cause of the accident in which the plaintiff was injured.[6]

There are two major justifications for imposing tort liability on commercial dispensers for the injuries their customers cause in drinking-driver traffic accidents. First, imposing liability on commercial dispensers increases the chance that seriously injured accident victims will be able to obtain more complete compensation. Second, it may lead commercial dispensers to take action to reduce the risk that their customers will cause accidents.

A commercial dispenser is typically better able to compensate an accident victim than the drinking driver who caused the accident. First, the commercial dispenser frequently has an opportunity to purchase insurance coverage that is specifically written to indemnify the policyholder for the costs of tort liability to victims of drinking-driver customers. Unlike the drinking driver, whose liability insurance is written to cover a broad range of conduct that might cause an accident for which the driver is held liable, the commercial dispenser of alcohol should be able to obtain a policy that is tailored to the risk that is posed by the dispenser's customers. Perhaps just as important, given the behavioral consequences of a liability rule that will be discussed below, the premium for the policy that the dispenser purchases may be set in a way that reflects the particular loss experience of the dispenser and the risk-reduction techniques the dispenser employs.

The second difference between a commercial dispenser and a drinking driver lies in the fact that the dispenser is operating a business. Thus the dispenser is able to spread the costs of tort liability, as reflected in the price of the dispenser's liability insurance, across a broad customer base. The liability of the dispenser to accident victims of drinking-driver customers thus becomes simply one of the costs of doing business.

The commercial dispenser is thus more likely to be able to insure against, and to satisfy, a substantial tort judgment than other potential tort defendants who may be more closely related to the drinking-driver accident. An additional benefit of adopting a commercial dispenser liability rule is that it may lead commercial dispensers to operate

their businesses differently in order to lower the risk posed by drinking
drivers. The most important changes are likely to involve serving
practices and transportation policies.

Serving practices may be changed so that there is less likelihood
that underage or intoxicated customers escape detection and continue
to be served. There are two sources of pressure for a dispenser to
adopt safer serving practices. First, the insurer writing the dispenser's
liability insurance policy may offer incentives to change the way that
alcohol is sold or served to customers.[7] Second, a handful of states
have enacted legislation that provides dispensers with a defense based
on its serving practices: "responsible" practices indicate that the dispenser has acted with reasonable care. Legislation of this sort can
provide a useful measure of predictability both to the commercial
dispensers themselves and to their insurers, who must make actuarial
decisions with regard to the liability exposure they face.

Some of these statutory provisions are little more than restatements
of a negligence standard. Michigan, for example, provides that a
defendant may introduce evidence that responsible business practices
were being followed at the time of the incident in question, but those
practices are simply defined as "those business policies, procedures,
and actions which an ordinarily prudent person would follow in the
circumstances."[8] Other states have adopted statutory provisions that
are more specific. The relevant provision in New Hampshire, for
example, begins with the general statement that is found in the Michigan statute but supplements it with six more statutory subsections
that expand on the definition of responsible business practices in both
a negative and a positive fashion.[9] These practices include comprehensive employee training to develop knowledge and skills regarding
responsible service and the handling of intoxicated persons.[10] Also
specified as responsible practices are those that encourage persons not
to become intoxicated, that promote nonalcoholic beverages and food,
and that promote alternatives to driving while intoxicated.[11]

This last example touches on transportation policies—the second
area of business operation a commercial dispenser of alcohol may try
to change in order to reduce the risk of drinking-driver accidents.
Serving practices only indirectly help to prevent drinking-driver accidents. Commercial dispenser practices that directly tackle the driving
side of the problem could produce a greater benefit in the form of
fewer drinking drivers on the road. Simple steps could be effective
in this regard. First, they could adopt policies that encourage a group
of patrons to have a designated driver, who will avoid alcohol consumption in order to provide the group with safe transportation.

Second, after a customer has consumed alcohol and is thought to pose a risk on the highway, dispensers could intervene in order to discourage the drinker from driving. Probably the most effective intervention would be a policy of paying for the alternative transportation that the customer is encouraged to use. The cost of that transportation would be treated as another cost of doing business, and it would pay dividends in the form of reduced exposure to liability to victims of the customer who drinks and drives.

The efforts to reduce the frequency of drinking drivers who are served alcohol by commercial dispensers may be undertaken even without the adoption of a rule that imposes tort liability on those dispensers for the injuries suffered by the victims of drinking drivers. As social consciousness about the seriousness and the preventability of drinking and driving increases, a sense of good citizenship and a desire for favorable publicity may lead a dispenser to take steps to reduce the risk that its customers pose as drinking drivers. The advantage of a rule of tort liability, however, is that it transforms the incentive for dispensers to take such efforts from altruism to rational business judgment. Commercial dispensers have a natural incentive to sell as much alcohol as possible. A tort rule that opens up the possibility that they will be held liable to victims of drinking-driver accidents caused by their customers serves to counteract the commercial incentive to sell alcohol without regard to the consequences of those sales. A rational commercial dispenser who is faced with such potential tort liability would balance the incentive to sell against the incentive to reduce the risk of such liability.

It is precisely this sort of accident cost internalization that will be explored in detail in part 2 of this book, and it will provide the key to a better way of compensating the victims of drinking-driver accidents. The commercial dispenser tort liability claim is a good example of a situation in which forcing the dispenser to internalize the costs of some drinking-driver accidents can produce the dual benefit of providing more complete compensation to the more seriously injured victims of drinking drivers and creating a greater incentive for dispensers to reduce the risk that their customers will cause drinking-driver accidents.

## NOTES

1. 119 Wis.2d 627, 350 N.W.2d 108 (1984). The state legislature subsequently limited the scope of dispenser liability. Wis. Stat. Ann. § 125.035 (1989).

2. *Id.* at 630, 350 N.W.2d at 110.

3. *See id.* at 632-40, 350 N.W.2d at 111-15.

4. *Id.* at 645, 350 N.W.2d at 117.

5. *Id.* at 645, 350 N.W.2d at 117-118 (emphasis added). The substantial factor test of causation is explained in the "Tort Law Primer" of chapter 2.

6. *Id.* at 645, 350 N.W.2d at 117.

7. *See generally* 2 MOSHER, LIQUOR LIABILITY LAW § 21.04.

8. MICH. COMP. LAWS ANN. § 436.22h (West Supp. 1990).

9. N.H. REV. STAT. ANN. § 507-F:6 (Supp. 1989).

10. *Id.* at § 507-F:6 (III).

11. *Id.* at § 507-F:6 (V).

# 7

## Liability of the Social Dispenser of Alcohol

A statutory or a common-law action against the commercial dispenser of alcohol might seem attractive as a means of allowing accident victims to obtain greater compensation than that available from the drinking driver, but this type of claim is of no avail when the dispenser is a social host. Some drinking drivers who cause traffic accidents become intoxicated or alcohol-impaired as a result of being served alcoholic beverages on a social occasion rather than in a commercial transaction.[1] Tort lawyers attempting to obtain adequate compensation for more seriously injured victims have experienced varying degrees of success in convincing courts to extend the theory of dispenser liability to allow a claim for relief against the social host of the drinking driver.[2] The distinctions between commercial and social dispensers of alcohol, however, are arguably much more significant than the surface similarities between them. Accordingly, while the social host theory of tort liability has received a certain level of acceptance in the judicial arena, sound policy considerations suggest that much more careful scrutiny ought to be given to the wisdom of adopting this claim for relief.

Indeed, one of the more striking phenomena in the last two decades has been the proclivity of state legislatures to respond fairly promptly when state supreme courts recognize social host liability and then to reject or sharply restrict this common-law development. The Oregon state supreme court was the first to recognize a social host liability claim. In response, the Oregon legislature enacted a statute that limited the scope of the common-law claim. Although plaintiffs in civil cases normally are allowed to prove the elements of their cases by a preponderance of the evidence, the Oregon statute required plaintiffs to prove by clear and convincing evidence that alcoholic beverages were served by the social host to someone who was visibly intoxicated.[3] At least the Oregon legislature did not abolish this new common-law claim altogether.

The Iowa legislature's response to judicial lawmaking was even stronger. In Iowa, the state supreme court's adoption of a social host liability rule was followed by the legislature's rejection of the basic idea of social host liability.[4] Arizona is another state in which a court's adoption of dispenser liability, in *Ontiveros v. Borak*,[5] was followed by a legislative rejection of social host liability.[6] Interestingly, even though the court in the *Ontiveros* case had recognized a common-law claim against a commercial dispenser, the subsequent statutory measure was addressed to social host liability. In effect, then, the Arizona legislature was announcing its determination that the scope of the dispenser liability theory the court had recognized ought not to be extended to new classes of defendants. This pronounced trend of legislative hostility to a tort liability rule that has achieved considerable judicial acceptance indicates that in the future courts need to weigh the policy implications of the social host liability rule before they rule on its adoption.

### The Common-Law Claim against a Social Host

A theory of social host liability based on basic common-law negligence principles appears to have originated in a 1971 decision of the Supreme Court of Oregon.[7] The Alpha Tau Omega fraternity chapter at the University of Oregon had rented a recreational facility located ten miles away from the university for a party attended by fraternity members and their guests. Members of the fraternity, some of whom were minors at the time, attended the party and consumed alcoholic beverages. One fraternity member, David Blair, who was also a minor, attended the party and allegedly drank "a large quantity of beer or other alcoholic beverages."[8] Blair then drove the plaintiff, Jane Wiener, and a number of other guests of the fraternity away from the party. During that trip, Blair collided with a building, and the plaintiff was injured in the accident. Tort claims were asserted by Wiener against a number of parties who were connected with the fraternity social event, including the fraternity chapter itself, the owners of the facility that had been rented to the fraternity, and an individual member of the fraternity who had actually purchased the alcohol for the party.

The trial court dismissed all of the plaintiff's claims, but the Oregon supreme court reversed with regard to the claim against the fraternity. The court held as follows: "The fraternity status as host and its direct involvement in serving the liquor to Blair are sufficient to raise the duty . . . to refuse to serve alcohol to a guest when it would be unreasonable under the circumstances to permit him to drink. The allegations that Blair was a minor and that the fraternity ought to have known that he would be driving after the party adequately charge the existence of circumstances from which a jury might conclude that the fraternity's behavior was in fact unreasonable."[9] It is interesting to note that the court recognized a rule that would allow liability to be imposed on the fraternity on the basis of a common-law negligence claim alone, regardless of any statutory violation that might have been involved in the events that led up to the accident.

The court found first that neither the fraternity nor any other defendant involved in the case was liable under the state's dram shop act, which limited the class of plaintiffs who could make use of the act to the spouse, the parents, and the children of the person who was served by the defendant.[10] The court then turned to the violation of the state statute that prohibited the furnishing of alcohol to any person under the age of twenty-one. Refusing to treat the violation of that statute as negligence per se, the court concluded that the purpose of the alcoholic beverage control provision on underage drinkers was to protect the minors themselves, and not to protect third persons who were injured by intoxicated minors. The decision to allow the plaintiff to proceed with her tort claim thus rested squarely on an assessment that the fraternity's conduct could be found to have created an unreasonable risk of harm to foreseeable accident victims of the person to whom alcohol had been served on a social occasion when the defendant was aware that the person who was served would be driving afterward.

The defendant in this original social host liability case was an organization rather than an individual. What of the average person who regularly or occasionally serves alcohol to guests? A relatively recent decision of the Supreme Court of New Jersey presented the social host issue in terms of an individual's liability and thus provides a better occasion to weigh the pros and cons of this theory of tort liability. In the incident that was the basis for the decision in the case of *Kelly v. Gwinnell,*[11] Marie Kelly was injured in a head-on collision with a car that was driven by Donald Gwinnell, who was a drinking driver. Kelly sued Gwinnell, Gwinnell's employer,[12] and Joseph and Catherine Zak, who were the social hosts of Gwinnell. Gwinnell had consumed a considerable amount of liquor at the Zaks' home.[13] The plaintiff had initially sued only Gwinnell and his employer. These original two defendants instituted a third-party claim against the Zaks, as the social hosts of Gwinnell, alleging that the original defendants should be entitled to receive some contribution from the Zaks if the defendants were found to be liable to Kelly. Kelly then amended her complaint so that she could add a claim of her own alleging that, as social hosts, the Zaks were liable to her for the injuries that she had suffered in the accident with Gwinnell.

The precise amount of alcohol that Gwinnell had consumed was the subject of some dispute in the litigation. Gwinnell's blood alcohol concentration after the accident was nearly three times higher than the statutory level necessary to establish that a person was driving under the influence of alcohol under the applicable New Jersey statute. While Gwinnell claimed that he had consumed only two or three drinks, an expert witness for the plaintiff testified that the measure of his blood alcohol concentration was consistent with a much higher level of consumption. The expert also testified that given such a high level of alcohol in his blood, Gwinnell must have displayed evidence of intoxication while he was at the Zaks' home.

Kelly's claim against the Zaks was disposed of in the trial court by a summary judgment in favor of the defendants, and that dismissal was subsequently affirmed upon review by an intermediate state appellate court.[14] Reversing the lower court's decision, however, the Supreme Court of New Jersey held that a common-law claim could be asserted by the victim of a drinking-driver traffic accident against a social host "who serves liquor to an adult social guest, *knowing both* that the guest is intoxicated *and* will thereafter be operating a motor vehicle."[15] Following the court's recognition of social host liability, the New Jersey legislature restricted the scope of the common-law liability.[16] While that legislation means that the result that was reached in the precise fact pattern of *Kelly v. Gwinnell* would no longer be possible unless the plaintiff were able to satisfy the requirements of the new statute, the court's opinion nevertheless provides a very useful introduction to the underlying policy considerations that apply to social host tort liability to the accident victims of a guest who becomes a drinking driver.

In recognizing this claim in *Kelly v. Gwinnell,* the New Jersey court somewhat inconsistently sought to portray its decision as both a rather modest extension of the existing complex of tort duties and a significant step in the right direction toward a responsible social treatment of the drinking-driver problem. The court's explanation was heavily weighted toward what the court described as a fairness rationale. Under that rationale the court was convinced that the accident costs that were incurred by innocent victims of drinking drivers should not be allowed to remain on those victims. The court was thus concerned that the injured parties in accidents of this sort should be able to receive adequate compensation for their injuries. That rationale by itself, though, does not speak to the question of why a social host is someone who should be liable in the first instance to those accident victims. The further decision that the court made, which was to shift those accident costs to the social host of the drinking driver, rested on a combination of rationales regarding remedial effectiveness and accident deterrence.

The thrust of the first rationale the court relied on in *Kelly v. Gwinnell* should by now be familiar to the reader. The tort system operates through a combination of legal rights and remedies. In the context of drinking-driver accidents, under fundamental tort law the innocent victim has the right to be compensated for the harm caused by the driver's wrongful conduct. As we have seen, that right currently receives substantially less than full enforcement from the range of remedies that are legally available to the plaintiff and practically obtainable from the drinking driver and from parties who are vicariously liable for the driver's misconduct. While it may be something of an exaggeration to say that a right without a remedy is worthless, it is at least accurate to say that a right to be free from harm becomes less meaningful to the extent that the right-holder lacks any effective means of preventing the occurrence of the harm and is also deprived of a meaningful opportunity to receive full compensation for the harm that is suffered.

Commercial dispenser liability under a dram shop act or under a common-law theory of recovery provides a further opportunity for more complete compensation for the seriously injured victim of a drinking-driver accident, but the ability to obtain a legal remedy from a commercial dispenser depends on a number of factors that are completely beyond the control of the accident victim. Most basic, of course, is the fortuity of the drinking driver having consumed alcohol in a setting in which the prerequisites for commercial dispenser liability will have been satisfied. Even if there has been a commercial transaction involving a sale of alcohol under circumstances in which imposing responsibility on the dispenser would seem appropriate, an accident victim can encounter a myriad of obstacles. These may have been erected either by the legislature in drafting the particulars of dram shop legislation or by the courts in refusing to fashion a common-law remedy at all or fashioning it in a restrictive manner that excludes the instant case from the scope of recovery that is permitted from a commercial dispenser. As a result of these factors, an entire class of drinking-driver traffic accidents may present no occasion for providing effective remedial measures for the most seriously injured victims.

Social host liability would open a new avenue to obtaining a tort remedy for those people who are injured by drinking drivers whose consumption of alcohol precludes the application of commercial dispenser liability.

Full and fair compensation of innocent victims is a worthwhile goal for a court to pursue when deciding whether to impose tort liability on social hosts, but the New Jersey court in *Kelly v. Gwinnell* rested its decision on another factor: deterring some of the wrongful conduct that contributes to the occurrence of drinking-driver traffic accidents. Under this deterrence rationale, a social host who faces the prospect of tort liability to the victims of guests who drink and drive may exercise greater control over the circumstances in which alcohol is furnished to guests. If guests are given less opportunity to drink before they drive away from a social occasion, then the number of alcohol-related traffic accidents might decrease.

In assessing the strength of this deterrence argument, it is important to understand the limited nature of the claims that can be legitimately made about deterrence. No reasonable person would assert that the prospect of an expanded tort liability could eliminate the problem of accident-related injuries. Human nature is such that most people who face the prospect of tort liability for causing harm to others will convince themselves that they will not actually cause the harm.

Considering the victim compensation problem at the heart of this book, that is not a wholly unrealistic conviction. Drinking and driving is a sufficiently common practice that on many occasions it produces no adverse consequences. Estimates of the ratio of the number of drunken driving arrests to the number of actual incidents run as high as 1 in 2,000.[17] Accordingly, adding civil liability of various parties to the existing criminal and social penalties for drinking and driving will have only a marginal deterrent effect.

That, however, is precisely the point: the effects that legal rules have on behavior occur at the margins.[18] Some people who otherwise might engage in an activity *are* likely to be deterred from doing so when the potential cost to them rises above the level that they are willing to incur. It is, of course, extremely difficult to identify individual instances of this and then determine what factor actually tipped the scale against that conduct. What is possible, however, is to identify the incidence of drinking-driver traffic accidents that occur *in spite of* the panoply of legal rules and other social constraints on drinking and driving.

Social host liability shifts the focus from the marginal drinking driver to parties who are located on a different margin. A court that adopts a theory of social host liability could see itself as shifting accident losses to a category of parties who had previously treated their furnishing of alcohol to guests as essentially free of accident costs to them. Nevertheless, although at least some accidents will be prevented as a result of social hosts choosing to exercise more restraint in dispensing alcohol to their guests, it is undoubtedly true that many hosts will take the same "it won't happen to me" attitude that drinking drivers often do. Even if hosts do change their behavior, it is probably also true that some guests will find a way to supplement what their host serves them, perhaps by drinking more before an event or by bringing and consuming their own alcohol. Furthermore, on some occasions, social host liability will actually increase the risk of alcohol-impaired driving. Consider, for example, the guest who knows that his host will provide him with only two beers. That guest might decide to have a beer or two before arriving, to bring along a six-pack and go to his car during the social occasion to gulp down his own beer, and then to drink the remainder of his beer while driving away from the event.

All of the above points may very well be legitimate indications that the liability of a new class of persons can have a variety of effects. The various hypotheticals demonstrate the complexity of the relationship between legal rules and human behavior. If the unrealistically strong claim were being made that social host liability would eliminate drinking-driver traffic accidents involving guests, then it would be substantially weakened by these hypotheticals. Again, however, it is crucial to understand that the appropriate focus is on the margins of the drinking-driver accident problem. As long as a court has reason to believe that *some* behavior will be changed for the better by the rule it is considering, and that whatever added deterrence that results will be "salutary," as the court in *Kelly v. Gwinnell* concluded,[19] then the fact that the decision will also help meet the goal of full compensation for victims provides a fairly compelling basis for adopting the rule.

Will the margins of behavior likely to be affected by a social host liability rule be large enough to lessen the drinking-driver problem significantly or to lessen the plight of the seriously injured and undercompensated accident victim? The fact remains that courts in many jurisdictions have refused to adopt a tort liability rule that imposes the costs of drinking-driver traffic accidents on the social hosts of drinking drivers. The arguments in favor of social host liability were of considerable merit but ultimately less than compelling for many courts, including, for example, the Supreme Court of Florida in a case called *Bankston v. Brennan*.[20] Many of the rationales for the non-liability of an alcohol dispenser in general (recall chapter 5) can surface when a court initially faces the question whether to adopt a common-law rule of social host liability.

The Florida case arose out of an accident in which an automobile in which the Bankston family was riding was struck by a car driven by a defendant named Brian Brennan. Brennan was a minor who had been served alcoholic beverages at a party hosted by the other defendants, who were named Ladika.[21] Acknowledging that social host liability "may be socially desirable" and that the court had the power to create a common-law cause of action imposing such liability, the Florida court nevertheless refused to do so. Given the fact that the state legislature had narrowed the scope of a common-law rule of tort liability of commercial dispensers of alcohol, the court concluded that "the more prudent course [was] . . . to defer to the legislative branch." The court's rationale was based on the institutional superiority of the legislature for undertaking "the task of listing and defining a new cause of action which could grow from a fact nucleus formed from any combination of numerous permutations of the fact situation before" the court.[22]

The deference to the legislature that was displayed by the Florida court in *Bankston* is distinguishable from, and arguably somewhat more justifiable than, the judicial inaction that was displayed by the Virginia supreme court in the *Williamson* case that was discussed in chapter 5. The Florida court's deference was based on very recent action by the Florida legislature. Unlike the legislative silence that confronted the Virginia court in *Williamson,* specific legislative action preceded the decision by the Florida court: following a judicial recognition of a common-law action against a commercial dispenser,[23] the legislature enacted a statute that placed restrictions on a vendor's liability.[24] Thus the Florida court had to address a legislative rejection of much of the scope of the only dispenser liability rule that the court had previously adopted. Otherwise the task that the court deferred to the legislature was precisely the sort of process that lends itself well to common-law adjudication.

An interesting concurring opinion in the *Bankston* case raised a symmetry rationale for the rejection of social host liability, stating that "we cannot find social hosts more liable than the legislature has determined vendors should be."[25] That rationale may have some surface appeal, but it is flawed. The resolution of each tort liability question depends on a consideration of a multitude of factors, some of which may be unique to a particular situation. While categorization is a useful intellectual technique for handling similar situations, lumping too broad a spectrum of cases into the same category deprives the courts and the litigants of the opportunity for the development of a set of rules that are tailored to heighten an appreciation of the full diversity of cases that might be presented. In a consideration of a social host liability theory, the factors that might have led the legislature to a conclusion that commercial dispenser liability is not in accord with sound social policy are not necessarily going to be the same factors that govern the disposition of the social host liability issue. Furthermore, the factors that are common to both situations do not necessarily point to the same result.

## The Critical Differences between Social and Commercial Dispensers

A natural way for a court to approach the issue of whether to recognize social host liability is to focus initially on the analogous claims that can be asserted against commercial dispensers of alcoholic beverages. Social host liability and commercial dispenser liability are both supported by a deterrence rationale, in that they both raise the potential cost of serving alcohol to social guests and to commercial patrons who are subsequently involved in drinking-driver traffic accidents. To the extent that the deterrent effect actually is felt by the dispensers, who then change their behavior and thereby reduce the consumption of alcohol by drivers, these forms of liability can reduce the frequency of drinking-driver traffic accidents. Furthermore, the availability of tort claims against both types of dispensers can increase the chances that a seriously injured accident victim can patch together a set of tort law recoveries that will adequately compensate the victim's injuries. Thus both types of dispenser liability serve to increase the effectiveness of the remedy that the tort system makes available to a person who has a legal right to be free from injury caused by drinking drivers.

The differences between the two types of dispensers are so significant, however, that they cast doubt on the argument that the policy bases for imposing commercial dispenser liability should be used to adopt social host tort liability. Even if these differences do not necessarily lead to a conclusion that liability should not be imposed on social hosts, they may at least reveal that even the extension of the search for compensation out to parties who are located on this fifth order of tort liability can still leave a substantial number of accident victims without a realistic prospect of obtaining complete compensation.

One major way in which social hosts and commercial dispensers differ concerns their comparative ability to pay court-awarded damages to the victims of drinking-driver accidents. As an ongoing business enterprise, a bar or a restaurant has both special insurance coverage for these additional liability costs and a customer base over which to spread the additional cost of this insurance. Adopting a rule of commercial dispenser tort liability, therefore, simply increases the cost of doing business.

Social hosts, on the other hand, are unlikely to be able to spread their liability costs in this regard very far beyond whatever liability coverage is provided by their homeowners' insurance, if the acts covered by the policy include entertaining guests. Social hosts who are renters, however, may be less likely to have adequate liability insurance coverage in this context. Social hosts who do own their homes may on occasion entertain at another site, which may take them out of the scope of their homeowners' insurance policy. Finally, their policy may cover only injuries that occur on the policyholder's property, not those that occur elsewhere as a result of what the policyholder does on that property.

Parties who are involved in the litigation of a social host claim may thus encounter the problem of trying to bring the event that gives rise to the host's tort liability within the scope of coverage of whatever insurance is available to the host. In fact, there may be no insurance at all on which the social host can draw. If that is the case, then the victim compensation problem is as troublesome in this instance as it is with regard to other alternative defendants. To the extent that social hosts are unable to pay tort damages the full compensation rationale for adopting social host liability is weaker than it is in the case of commercial dispensers. At the very least, it needs to be understood that, as a practical matter in a given case, the seriously injured victim of a drinking-driver traffic accident may not be appreciably better compensated than if social host liability were not recognized.

Another significant way in which social hosts differ from commercial dispensers of alcohol concerns the extent to which a realistic fault element can be built into the tort claim that is made available to victims of drinking drivers. The general notion of responsibility is discussed in detail in the next chapter, but a few preliminary points can be made about the fault issue in social host liability cases and the questions it raises. The first question is what effect a fault standard will have on the initial recognition of a tort claim against social hosts.

If such a tort claim is adopted, a second question is whether the culpability element that is built into the claim will so substantially limit its applicability that seriously injured plaintiffs are left with little more in the way of potential recovery than they had before the recognition of social host liability. The two inquiries, then, deal first with whether and how to adopt social host liability and then with what impact such adoption is likely to have on the central problem of this book, which is the compensation of victims of drinking-driver traffic accidents.

The furnishing of alcohol to an underage drinker or to someone who is already intoxicated is a *wrongful* act on the part of the social host defendant. In the social host setting, the two major indicia of wrongfulness—minority and intoxication—provide just as useful a set of prerequisites to liability as they do in the commercial-dispenser cases. A court that considered a social host who displayed that kind of fault to have acted in a way that is insufficiently culpable for liability to be imposed on the host may consider that a more appropriate way to attach liability to the conduct of the host would be to restrict liability to the host who displays fault that consists of producing the intoxication of the defendant. The more problematic culpability elements of the social host case involve a type of fault that consists of an awareness of the alcohol-impaired condition of the driver/guest and a failure to take reasonable measures to reduce or eliminate the risk that is posed by that driver to others. It is with respect to this latter fault assessment that the differences between commercial dispensers and social hosts can be most relevant.

The most difficult problem in constructing a social host theory of liability (and in litigating social host claims) is the variety of ways in which social hosts can make alcohol available to their guests. At one end of the spectrum is the fact situation in *Kelly v. Gwinnell* that was discussed earlier. In that case, one guest was being served by the two hosts in their home. The hosts had ample opportunity not only to observe the condition of the guest throughout the social occasion but also to be aware that the guest would be driving afterward. At the other end of the spectrum lies the social occasion, such as a wedding reception, that involve multiple invitations and an open bar. In those circumstances, the opportunity for the host to know either the condition or the transportation plans of any particular guest is correspondingly diminished as the length of the guest list grows.

The fault analysis that ought to be made of the conduct of the hosts in these cases does not precisely parallel the spectrum of behavior just described. In other words, it is not necessarily the case that a host's fault is greater in the case of one guest attending a social occasion than it is in the case of mass attendance. Each calls for an evaluation of what it was reasonable for a person in the position of the host in those circumstances to know and to appreciate about the risks that serving alcohol to guests posed. The strength of the demands on the behavior of hosts may vary with the different levels of sophistication and training that people are likely to have. Social hosts may be less adept at discerning the more subtle signs of the alcohol impairment than commercial dispensers are. Again, that does not necessarily lead to the conclusion that no liability should be imposed on the social hosts. The appropriate conclusion under a specific set of circumstances may be, for example, that a social host who is unlikely to be able to observe and to evaluate the condition of a large number of guests has an obligation not to allow guests the sort of unlimited consumption by a self-service open bar, for example, but to use trained professionals to distribute the alcohol to the guests. The lesson to be learned from considering the fault element of a dispenser liability case in the social setting, as opposed to the commercial setting, is that the analysis in the social host setting is often going to be more complex and to turn on a careful consideration of more variables than in the standard dram shop or common-law commercial dispenser case.

A reasonably well-publicized decision to recognize a tort claim that permits the imposition of social host liability is likely to produce more of an impact on behavior than is the case with a decision to recognize commercial dispenser liability. Recognizing commercial dispenser liability may have as its most immediate and most directly identifiable effect an increase in the price of the alcoholic beverages served by those exposed to this new liability. Imposing social host liability, on the other hand, may produce at least some marked change in the extent to which the dispensing of alcohol is controlled, in the way alcohol is served, and in the amount of alcohol made available to drinkers in noncommercial settings. These benefits are particularly likely when the imposition of social host liability coincides with a campaign to raise public consciousness of the risks of drinking and driving in general. Recognizing the tort liability of a social host to victims of drinking-driver guests may result in a greater restriction on the flow of alcohol than imposing liability on a commercial dispenser because in the commercial setting the potential for liability is already viewed as a cost of doing business.

## NOTES

1. Social scientists have estimated that about one-half of drinking-driver incidents are preceded by drinking in a commercial dispenser establishment.

*See* O'Donnell, *Research on Drinking Locations of Alcohol-Impaired Drivers: Implications for Prevention Policies,* 6 J. PUB. HEALTH POL'Y 510 (1985). The remaining 50 percent of such incidents would therefore be divided between cases in which alcohol has been purchased separately from the drinking-and-driving episode and cases in which drivers drink alcohol acquired in something other than a commercial transaction.

2. The relatively recent trend toward imposing tort liability on social dispensers of alcohol for the harm caused by guests who drink and then drive is surveyed and analyzed in a large body of legal scholarship. The cases in which social host liability has been adopted have generated a good deal of student commentary in the law reviews. Two such efforts of particular merit are Special Project, *Social Host Liability for the Negligent Acts of Intoxicated Guests,* 70 CORNELL L. REV. 1058 (1985), and Note, *Social Host Liability for Guests Who Drink and Drive: A Closer Look at the Benefits and the Burdens,* 27 WM. & MARY L. REV. 583 (1986). Current information about the status of social host liability can be found in the annually updated summary of state statutory provisions and case law in 2 MOSHER, LIQUOR LIABILITY LAW, at App. A.

3. ORE. REV. STAT. ANN. § 30.950 (1988) ("No . . . social host is liable for damages . . . caused by intoxicated . . . guests off the . . . social host's premises unless . . . [the] guest was visibly intoxicated . . . and . . . [t]he plaintiff proves by clear and convincing evidence that the . . . guest was served alcoholic beverages while visibly intoxicated."). *See also* CALIF. BUS. & PROF. CODE § 25602 (West 1985) (1978 amendment to the Alcohol Beverage Regulatory Provisions expressly abrogated three judicial decisions that treated the serving of alcoholic beverages as a proximate cause of the injuries that were inflicted on others by intoxicated driver); *id.* at § 25602.1 (West Supp. 1990) (allowing dram shop action for serving to an "obviously intoxicated" minor); and CAL. CIV. CODE § 1714(c) (West 1985).

4. The Iowa experience was described in the first section of chapter 5 to illustrate the legislative preemption argument as a reason for a court to refuse to recognize a common-law claim that imposes tort liability on alcohol dispensers.

5. 136 Ariz. 500, 667 P.2d 200 (1983).

6. ARIZ. REV. STAT. ANN. § 4-301 (West 1989).

7. Wiener v. Gamma Phi Chapter of Alpha Tau Omega Fraternity, 258 Or. 632, 485 P.2d 18 (1971).

8. *Id.* at 637, 485 P.2d at 20.

9. *Id.* at 643, 485 P.2d at 23.

10. *Id.* at 639, 485 P.2d at 21, n.2.

11. 96 N.J. 538, 476 A.2d 1219 (1984).

12. Although the court's opinion does not reveal the basis for the claim that was asserted against the driver's employer, it is interesting to note that Zak and Gwinnell were both employees of the same employer. That coworker relationship between the guest and the host raises some complex possibilities. An injured party might claim that the driving by Gwinnell was within the

scope of Gwinnell's employment. The plaintiff might also claim that the serving of alcohol to Gwinnell was within the scope of Zak's employment, or that the consumption of alcohol by Gwinnell was within the scope of employment of both Gwinnell and Zak. To review some of the potential claims based on the vicarious liability of employers, see chapter 3, which also discusses the conceptual hurdles that would have to be overcome by a plaintiff who wished to assert such a claim.

13. *See* 96 N.J. at 541, 476 A.2d at 1220.

14. That decision is reported at 190 N.J. Super. 320, 463 A.2d 387 (1983).

15. 96 N.J. at 548, 476 A.2d at 1224 (emphasis added).

16. N.J. STAT. ANN. § 2A:15-5.5 to -5.8 (West Supp. 1990).

17. *See* Snortum, *Deterrence of Alcohol-impaired Driving: An Effect in Search of a Cause,* in LAURENCE et al., SOCIAL CONTROL, at 199.

18. *See* JACOBS, DRUNK DRIVING, at 105 (the "realistic goal is marginal decreases" in drunk driving).

19. 96 N.J. at 555, 476 A.2d at 1226.

20. 507 So.2d 1385 (Fla. 1987).

21. *Id.* at 1386.

22. *Id.* at 1387.

23. The discussion of the prior decisions and their relationship to the state legislature's treatment of dispenser liability is found in the *Bankston* opinion, 507 So.2d at 1386.

24. FLA. STAT. ANN. § 768.125 (West 1986) (limiting tort liability of alcohol dispensers for injuries to third parties to cases in which the defendant willfully and unlawfully sold or furnished alcohol to a minor or knowingly served a person "habitually addicted to the use of . . . alcoholic beverages").

25. 507 So.2d at 1388 (Barkett, J., specially concurring).

# 8

## The Responsibility Conundrum in Dispenser Liability Claims

Liability under the statutory and common-law commercial dispenser claims, as well as in the case of the social host claim, proceeds from the premise that someone other than the drinking driver is capable of being held legally responsible for the result of the drinking driver's conduct. Furthermore, unlike the vicarious liability claims that were discussed in chapter 3, these dispenser liability claims depend on a characterization of the nondriving defendant's conduct as being at fault. The justification for that premise and the implications of the fault characterization that underlies dispenser liability need to be examined with some care.

The most serious of the legal doctrinal obstacles to the imposition of dispenser liability is the idea that the responsibility for the harm that is caused by a drinking driver is attributable only to the consumption of alcohol by the driver, and not at all to the dispensing of alcohol by the person who sold or served it to the driver. In the language in which courts frequently dispose of such claims, that idea is expressed by saying that the proximate cause of the accident was the consumption of the alcohol by the drinking driver, and not the furnishing of the alcohol by the dispenser.[1] Two lines of reasoning underlie the conclusion that responsibility rests exclusively with the consumer rather than being shared between the drinking driver and the dispenser. The first is a matter of causal reductionism, and it can be dealt with fairly easily. The second involves an attempt to ground legal rules in conventional morality and in generally accepted notions of sound public policy. It is in regard to this latter aspect that the responsibility inquiry potentially poses the greatest hurdle for advocates of dispenser liability to overcome. It is this aspect as well, however, that lends itself to a doctrinal modification of the extent of dispenser liability that could bring it more closely into line with a community sense of values about the appropriate way to assign responsibility for the acts of another person.

The simplest, if not simplistic, argument against dispenser responsibility for the harm that is caused by a drinking driver rests on an assumption that responsibility is a singular attribute that can be assigned to no more than one actor. Legal doctrine captures this reductionist view when courts speak of something as *the* proximate cause of a result. As was described in the tort law primer of chapter 2, however, contemporary tort law routinely recognizes that more than one act or omission can play a significant causal role in producing a particular result, and courts today understand that legal responsibility can legitimately be assigned to more than one of those acts or omissions. A pluralistic view of responsibility would thus replace the previous proximate cause statement with a recognition that neither the consumption nor the dispensing of alcohol was *the* proximate cause of the drinking-driver accident. Instead, it would be accurate to say that each was *a* proximate cause.

Even if one is inclined to adopt a pluralistic view of responsibility, however, situations can arise in which one causal factor is so dwarfed in significance by a subsequent event that a court would properly be reluctant to assign legal responsibility to the former factor. In the normal litigation of tort cases, this situation is frequently encountered when the negligent act of one defendant is followed by the criminal act of another person. The question that is then presented to a court is whether the subsequent criminal act should operate to cut off the legal responsibility of the negligent actor. Holding that, in the language of proximate cause, the subsequent criminal act "supersedes" the negligence of the first actor, many courts do regularly relieve the negligent actor of responsibility. The better reasoned of the superseding-cause decisions, however, take a closer look at precisely what it was that made the first act negligent. If the unreasonable risk that was created by the negligent conduct of the first actor was the risk that someone else's subsequent criminal conduct could produce harm to the plaintiff, then it makes little sense to relieve the negligent actor of liability when precisely that risk was realized.

The "superseding cause" notion has obvious application to the drinking-driver accident setting. It is frequently true that someone else's criminal conduct (driving while intoxicated or driving under the influence of alcohol) intervenes between the defendant's dispensing of the alcohol to the drinking driver and the occurrence of the accident in which the plaintiff is injured. Nevertheless, it is also just as true that one of the reasons why the dispenser's conduct is thought to be at fault in the first place is that it creates the risk that the person to whom the alcohol is being dispensed poses a risk of causing harm to others. In those circumstances, then, the risk that the alcohol consumer will drink and drive is one of the aspects of the alcohol dispenser's conduct that properly subjects it to a fault characterization. Treating the subsequent misconduct of the drinking driver as a superseding cause would therefore undercut rather than support the fault characterization of the dispenser's conduct.

The more compelling line of reasoning that calls into question whether furnishing alcohol to a drinking driver who causes a traffic accident should be treated as a basis of tort liability concentrates more on the policy considerations involved than a mechanical search for a dominant causal factor. In order to understand the force of this objection and to begin to construct an alternative theory of dispenser liability, it will be helpful to capture the essence of the earlier examinations of what it means to be at fault in dispenser liability cases. Recall from chapter 4 that to hold a dispenser liable almost all dram shop statutes require some sort of finding of culpability on the part of the person who serves or sells the alcohol to the consumer who subsequently injures the plaintiff. For the sake of convenience, the parties who occupy the relevant roles in these cases will be referred to in the following discussion as simply the driver, the dispenser, and the victim.

The first kind of fault that is relevant to the responsibility question in this context is fault with respect to the driver's alcohol consumption. In the dram shop case, that culpability inquiry usually translates into the question whether the dispenser knew or had reason to know that the sale to the driver was prohibited, either because of the age of the driver or because the driver was already intoxicated. A second type of fault relates to the dispenser's awareness of the risk that the driver poses to third parties. The issue of whether that second kind of fault exists translates into the question whether the dispenser knew or should have known that the driver would operate a motor vehicle while in an alcohol-impaired condition.

To fully appreciate the responsibility problem in dispenser liability cases, it is necessary to expand the range of fault beyond those two types of culpability, which for purposes of this discussion can be labeled "fault in dispensing" and "fault in awareness of the risk to others." The first of the new culpability inquiries introduces a factor that is in fact used by some courts in applying the dram shop acts of their states. Rather than asking only whether the dispenser was at fault in making a prohibited sale, this stronger culpability inquiry asks whether the dispenser was at fault in producing the intoxication of the driver. The difference between these two kinds of culpability is easily seen by considering a couple of the hypotheticals that were used in an earlier chapter involving the bar patron who comes into the bar and is already inebriated.

One of the variations of the hypothetical has the driver being served a beer, but consuming only a portion of it before the dispenser realizes the condition of the patron and informs him that he can no longer be served. The patron then drives away and collides with a car in which the victim is riding. Was the dispenser at fault? It is true that the service of the beer to the driver was prohibited by the alcoholic beverage control laws, and as long as a reasonable person in the defendant's position should have recognized the condition of the patron at the time of service, then the dispenser's conduct would be characterized as "fault in dispensing" the alcohol. The point of the hypothetical, however, is to demonstrate that the culpability of the dispenser in furnishing alcohol to the driver does not also involve causing the driver to be intoxicated. While one can imagine situations in which a very small addition to the alcoholic beverage intake of the driver is sufficient to produce just the degree of impairment of driving ability that is responsible for the subsequent traffic accident of that driver, this hypothetical is assumed not to present one of those unlikely situations. The driver was no more alcohol-impaired upon leaving the dispenser's bar than he was when he entered. Thus, while the dispenser's conduct may have displayed "fault in dispensing" the alcohol to someone who was intoxicated, the dispenser was not at fault with respect to producing the driver's intoxication or alcohol impairment.

In the second variation of this hypothetical, the driver enters the bar in an inebriated condition and tosses his car keys onto the bar. When he leaves the bar, he picks up his keys. Those facts should be sufficient to establish that a reasonable person in the dispenser's position should know that the driver posed a risk of harm to others. This second type of fault is connected with the driver's act of driving. If the driver was too inebriated to be served alcohol by the defendant, then it is probably also safe to conclude that he was too inebriated to operate a motor vehicle. Therefore, it does seem possible to attribute to the dispenser in this hypothetical two of the three kinds of fault so far identified. The question that needs to be pursued is whether these two types of fault, "fault in dispensing" and "fault in the awareness of the risk to others," should be sufficient to establish the responsibility of the dispenser for the injuries that are suffered by the victim of the drinking driver.

The most satisfactory affirmative answer to the responsibility question requires that yet a fourth type of fault should be added to the consideration — fault in the failure to control the drinking driver. The best way to illustrate this additional kind of culpability is to examine the facts of a case that was decided by the Texas courts nearly ten years ago.[2] Robert Matheson worked for the Otis Engineering Corporation. On the day in question, Matheson was observed by his fellow employees to be drinking on the job and on his dinner break. Noticing his alcohol-impaired condition, these other employees informed their supervisor that Matheson did not appear to be able safely to operate the machinery with which he was working. The supervisor then talked to Matheson after his break and advised him to go home. He did ask Matheson whether he thought he could make it home and was told that he could. Three miles from the plant, Matheson was in an accident in which the wives of the two plaintiffs were killed. The plaintiffs sued Otis Engineering for the wrongful death of their wives.

The first thing to notice about this claim against Otis Engineering is what it does *not* involve. The accident did not occur in the course of Matheson's employment,[3] so this was not a case in which the employer could be held vicariously liable under the doctrine of respondeat superior for the harm caused by the employee. Second, the alcohol consumed by Matheson was not furnished to him by his employer, so this is not a case in which dispenser liability can be asserted, either on the basis of a dram shop act or a common-law claim of commercial-dispenser liability or social host liability. What is present in the case against Otis Engineering Company is simply the employer's awareness of the alcohol-impaired condition of the employee. The question that was thus presented to the courts was whether Otis Engineering owed a legal duty to the victims of Matheson's accident, so that a finding that there had been a breach of that duty on this occasion could result in Otis being held liable for the deaths that occurred in the Matheson accident.

The Supreme Court of Texas held that Otis Engineering did have a duty to the victims of Matheson's drinking-driver accident. The court did caution, however, that a duty imposed on Otis Engineering "would not be based on the *mere knowledge* of Matheson's intoxication, but would be based on additional factors."[4] "[W]hen, because of an employee's incapacity, an employer exercises *control* over the employee, the employer has a duty to take such action as a reasonably prudent employer under the same or similar circumstances would take to prevent the employee from causing an unreasonable risk of harm to others."[5] Whether Otis actually had failed to exercise reasonable care under these circumstances would be a question for a jury to decide. The *Otis Engineering* decision does, however, list some of the factors that the appellate court thought were relevant to the jury's resolution of that issue, including "the availability of the nurses' aid station, a possible phone call to Mrs. Matheson, having another employee drive Matheson home, dismissing Matheson early rather than terminating his employment, and the foreseeable consequences of Matheson's driving upon a public street in his stuporous condition."[6]

The Texas supreme court's statement of the legal standard that should be applied to the conduct of Otis Engineering thus introduces the fourth type of fault that is relevant to the responsibility question, which is a culpability with respect to the failure to exercise control of the drinking driver. The significance of the *Otis Engineering* decision is its recognition of a tort liability that is based on the concurrence of two types of fault that do not involve either furnishing alcohol to the driver or causing the driver's intoxication. If Otis Engineering was to be held liable to Matheson's accident victims, it would be because of its awareness of the risk that Matheson posed to others and its failure to take reasonable measures to control Matheson in order to reduce that risk.

Now, consider the effect that the introduction of this final kind of culpability could have on the tort claim against the alcohol dispenser in the hypothetical in which the inebriated patron picks up his keys and leaves the defendant's bar after consuming only a small amount of alcohol. The additional inquiry into whether there was fault in a failure to control the driver would ask whether this dispenser acted as a reasonably prudent person would have acted under those circumstances to prevent the driver from operating a motor vehicle in his condition. For example, would it be reasonable for the dispenser to take the keys of the driver and request that he use some alternative form of transportation? Could a call be made to the home of the customer in order to locate someone who could take charge of the customer's transportation? Would arranging for a taxi keep the driver off the road? There may, of course, be some speculation about whether any or all of these steps would have been effective in a particular instance, but in the absence of any such simple attempt to reduce the risk of harm that is associated with the driver's condition, can the dispenser's conduct really be considered reasonable under the circumstances?

If the experience in other sorts of settings in which the defendant's conduct allegedly displayed an unreasonable failure to control is instructive,[7] then the specter of the dispenser's potential liability for false arrest or false imprisonment of the driver will be one of the first considerations that is raised to refute the suggestion that a dispenser has some legal duty to intervene and exercise some control over the conduct of the drinking driver.[8] To lay this specter to rest, the tort liability of the dispenser for false imprisonment of the driver could be modified by requiring that the driver first prove that the dispenser's exercise of control was unreasonable. In this way, then, as long as the dispenser's prevention of the drinking driver from operating his vehicle was a reasonable effort to reduce the risk that the driver posed to others, then the tort liability of the dispenser for any detention of the driver would be precluded.

An even more effective solution might be legislation that creates a legal privilege for the person who has a reasonable basis to conclude that a drinking driver poses a risk of harm to others and intervenes in order to reduce or eliminate that risk. Legislation along those lines would have to be written in such a way as to assure that excessive measures against suspected drinking drivers are not encouraged, but that is a relatively minor problem that could be solved by careful drafting. The New Hampshire dram shop act contains a comparable provision recognizing a privilege to use reasonable force to detain an intoxicated person who is attempting to operate a motor vehicle for a reasonable period of time that is necessary to summon police officers.[9] Furthermore, there is already an analogous body of legislation and judicial interpretation that recognizes the legal privilege of a merchant to use reasonable means to detain a suspected shoplifter.[10] By examining the language of those statutes and both the judicial and the practical experience in determining whether the defendant had such a privilege and whether the defendant's conduct on a particular condition remained within the bounds of the privilege, legislators could fairly easily construct an adequate legal protection for the person who responsibly intervenes in order to reduce the risk posed by a drinking driver.

The reasonableness and the effectiveness of efforts that might have been used but were not taken to control the drinking driver are admittedly not easy questions to answer, but from the perspective of the responsibility issue in dispenser liability cases, they are the right questions to ask. When the control issue is extended from the non-dispenser situation that was presented to the Texas courts in the *Otis Engineering* case to the dispenser liability claim that is the subject of the last chapters of part 1 of this book, more light is shed on the issue of the dispenser's responsibility in the context of the drinking-driver accident.

With four different fault options now in hand, one can begin to see the shape of an operating principle for dispenser liability that could be brought more closely in line with popular notions of responsibility than is otherwise likely to be the case with some of the rules that have been adopted by courts and legislatures. For purposes of analyzing how these different types of fault can be fit together, each of the first two that were described can be labeled as a variety of a "weak" fault, while the latter two can be called versions of a "strong" fault. Those designations roughly correspond to the degree of involvement of the nondriving defendant in the production of the injury to the victim of the drinking-driver traffic accident.

In addition to being labeled strong or weak, the nondriving defendant's culpability can be categorized according to whether the culpable conduct is primarily connected to the driver's drinking activity (Type I conduct) or the driver's driving activity (Type II conduct). The four categories of culpability that are produced by combining these two methods of distinguishing fault are displayed in figure 8-1. The two weak kinds of culpability are fault in dispensing alcohol, which will be designated as Weak I, and fault with respect to awareness of the risk the drinking driver poses to others, which will be designated as Weak II. As a result of the expansion of the culpability inquiry in this chapter, it should be clear that there now needs to be added to this taxonomy two strong types of fault: fault in producing the intoxication of the driver, designated as Strong I, and fault in failing

Figure 8-1
A Taxonomy of Culpability

|  | Conduct that Affects Drinking (Type I) | Conduct that Affects Driving (Type II) |
|---|---|---|
| Strong Fault Level | Producing intoxication | Failing to control driver |
| Weak Fault Level | Fault in dispensing | Awareness of risk posed by driver |

to use reasonable measures to control the alcohol-impaired driver, which will be referred to as Strong II.

A sound working principle regarding the defendant's responsibility can be constructed from this taxonomy: liability should not be imposed in the absence of a showing of a strong fault, but it is properly imposed when a person displays a form of strong fault in addition to some other form of fault. A combination of a weak fault (either Weak I—wrongful dispensing of alcohol, or Weak II—awareness of risk) with a strong fault (either Strong I—producing intoxication, or Strong II—failure to control) would also be sufficient for liability to be imposed on the dispenser. In a situation in which one of the strong types of fault is coupled with a weak kind of fault, a defendant will have had an opportunity to affect in a direct and effective manner one of the two elements that make up the drinking driver's activity. Liability of a defendant under those circumstances should find a fairly solid footing in notions of the responsibility that people owe to protect others from harm.

The Texas court's imposition of liability on Otis Engineering for the harm its drinking-driver employee caused is consistent with this working principle. The lesson that can be derived from that case is that a combination of a weak fault (Weak II—awareness of the risk that was posed by the driver's condition) and a strong fault (Strong II—failure to use reasonable means to prevent the driver from exposing others to a risk of harm) is sufficient to serve as a basis for holding a nondriving defendant liable to the victim of a drinking-driver accident. A similar result should be reached in a case that focuses on culpability in the dispensing of alcohol.

The working principle described here has as much significance in its negative aspect as it does in its positive, or liability-supporting, feature. In no event, under this principle, should the two weak kinds of fault be sufficient, either individually or in combination with each other, to impose liability. Alcohol dispenser tort liability that is structured in accordance with this principle would encompass a smaller group of cases than the group currently brought within the scope of liability under the dram shop act or common-law liability theories that prevail in many states. The principle presented here is based on the notion that the least amount of responsibility for harm to a victim of a drinking-driver accident that would support tort liability to that victim requires the defendant's conduct to have been linked to the drinking driver's conduct as directly as it is in one of the strong types of fault.

A further question that arises from this culpability taxonomy is whether one of the strong types of fault by itself should be treated as a sufficient basis for the imposition of liability. My preferred answer would be no. Although each of the strong types of fault is fairly highly culpable conduct, tort liability ought to be restricted to situations in which some additional indicia of responsibility are present in the form of at least one of the other categories of fault. A defendant who produces the intoxication of a guest, for example, has acted wrongfully, but unless the defendant has also been at fault in some other way, holding the defendant liable to accident victims of the guest would impose a disproportionately high price on the defendant for that conduct. Before liability should be imposed on the defendant in this situation, a plaintiff should have to prove some additional type of culpable conduct—that the service to the guest was wrongful in itself or that the defendant should have been aware of the risk that the guest posed to others. I would, however, allow a plaintiff to use a combination of strong types of fault to satisfy the responsibility element of a claim against an alcohol dispenser. Proof that the defendant produced the driver's intoxication would be sufficient to meet the working principle of responsibility when it was combined with proof that the defendant failed to take some reasonable measure to reduce or eliminate the risk of harm that the guest posed to others.

As described earlier, the working principle of responsibility I have sketched here would result in fewer instances of liability than existing tort rules do. In some situations, however, the principle could make it easier to conclude that a nondriving defendant does have a sufficient measure of responsibility for the harm to the victim to be held liable for that harm. For example, recall the hypothetical fact pattern in chapter 3 in which a police officer stops but does not detain a drinking driver. The officer's fault here consists of the Weak II and the Strong II varieties, assuming that the necessary factual predicate has been established. It is plausible to imagine that a reasonable police officer would be aware that a drinking driver who was stopped posed a risk of harm to others and that the officer could take some reasonable steps to reduce the accident risk that the driver poses. When depicted in this way, it is clear that the issue of the police officer's liability to the accident victim of the drinking driver falls within the same liability model that was presented in the *Otis Engineering* case. A court that insisted on something more than a combination of these two types of fault in the conduct of the officer would be reserving an imposition of tort liability for situations presenting an even higher level of responsibility that what I have suggested would be sufficient.

As I mentioned in chapter 3, there may very well be policy considerations that suggest caution in imposing liability on police officers in circumstances such as these. In cases where policy concerns demand a "responsibility plus" scenario, a specific relationship with either the drinking driver or the victim would be the most likely candidate for an additional element to require before tort liability can be imposed.[11] The operating principle that I have derived from the four-part culpability scheme introduced here should, however, make it clear that a court that decides to reject the imposition of liability in this situation is doing so in spite of a reasonable basis for concluding that the police officer is minimally responsible for the harm that is caused by the drinking driver. A nonliability decision may nonetheless be justifiable, but such a decision would have to be justified on the basis of a rationale other than the responsibility principle offered here.

This new responsibility principle provides a more satisfactory basis of deciding some of the problematic dispenser liability cases and hypotheticals that have been raised in the last few chapters. While the effect of adopting this new principle will frequently be to reduce the scope of dispenser liability, that is not invariably going to be the case. Consider, for example, the hypotheticals that were used earlier to examine the imposition of dispenser liability. The two examples involved, first, the inebriated patron who was denied service altogether, and second, the similarly inebriated patron who consumed a small amount of the dispenser's alcohol. The imposition of liability on the dispenser in the second of those hypotheticals could be explained on the basis of the Weak I type of fault in dispensing alcohol and the Strong II type of fault in failing to exercise some control over the driver if it was reasonable to do so. By contrast, the first version of the hypothetical would clearly not be an appropriate instance for the imposition of liability under any of the prevailing theories because no alcohol was dispensed and thus neither Weak I fault nor Strong I fault apply. Under the expanded culpability inquiry introduced here, however, tort liability could be imposed on the dispenser in this hypothetical if the dispenser's conduct displayed both the Weak II type of fault (awareness of the risk to others) and the Strong II type of fault (failure to use reasonable means to control the driver).

The legal responsibility of alcohol dispensers under the scheme that has been sketched out here arguably now starts to look much more like a meaningful notion of responsibility that could be grounded in conventional morality. One who has an ability to prevent harm to others by taking reasonable measures to control another person is responsible for the harm to those others just as much as the person who wrongfully provides the alcoholic beverages that intoxicate the driver when that person was aware of the risk that the driver's condition posed to others.

This enhanced concept of responsibility serves not only to sort out the commercial dispenser claims discussed in this chapter but to provide a basis for determining the appropriate limits of social host liability. Take, for example, the situation that was presented to the New Jersey court in *Kelly v. Gwinnell*,[12] the social host liability case that was discussed extensively in chapter 7. The conduct of the social hosts in that case could be found at least to have consisted of the Weak I type of fault, in that alcohol was served to a guest who was intoxicated, and the Weak II type of fault, in that the hosts should have realized the risk that their guest's condition posed to others. Under the new principle proposed in this chapter, a showing of fault that went no further than this would be insufficient to impose liability on the social hosts. Instead, the plaintiff would have to prove additionally either that the hosts served the alcohol that made the guest intoxicated or that the hosts failed to take reasonable steps to keep the highly intoxicated guest from driving. Given the court's description of the events that led up to the accident, the latter showing would not seem to be terribly difficult for a plaintiff to prove.

Another feature of the operating principle of responsibility is that it offers courts, such as the New Jersey court in the *Kelly* case, a way to draw lines in future cases. The court carefully noted that the liability rule it was adopting in *Kelly* arose from a situation in which a visibly intoxicated guest was directly served by hosts who knew that the guest would soon drive home.[13] The court specifically stated that the new rule did not cover a number of other situations that the court was likely to face in the future, such as guests serving each other, many guests at a party, a busy host who has many other responsibilities, or a host who is intoxicated. The responsibility principle set forth in this chapter could provide a court with a method of resolving the fault element in many varieties of social host cases on grounds that can be applied consistently and coherently.

Before leaving the general topic of dispenser liability, a number of situations should be considered that do not fall neatly into any of the alcohol dispenser categories that have been surveyed up until now. Consider first, a defendant's purchase of alcohol for someone else who is legally prohibited from making the purchase; second, consider a defendant's participation with the drinking driver in both the drinking and the driving that precede an accident; and third, consider the sale and the service of alcohol by a defendant as an incidental part of another business in which the defendant is primarily engaged. Each of these three situations represents a distinct category of fault on which the defendant's liability to accident victims might be imposed, and each calls as well for at least a passing consideration of the special factors that come into play.

Recall that in the typical dram shop act or common-law dispenser liability case, the appropriate defendant is a commercial dispenser who makes a wrongful sale of alcohol, usually either to a minor or to someone who is already intoxicated. The typical social host liability case involves a guest who consumes alcohol at a social function that was hosted by the defendant. In the case of a driver who either cannot purchase alcohol directly or has had someone else purchase it, the most likely scenario involves a drinking driver who was a minor and a defendant to whom that minor gave the money to buy the alcohol. The defendant in such a case has not really sold the alcohol to the driver, except in the rather strained sense of a two-part sales transaction, the first sale being from the commercial seller to the defendant and the second "sale" being from the defendant to the driver. Nor is there really a social host/guest relationship between the defendant and the driver. While it is true that the defendant is in a sense furnishing alcohol to the driver, the driver is the one who is paying for it. If anything is actually being "given" to the driver, it is the value of the defendant's legal ability to purchase alcohol, and not the alcohol itself. Because the defendant is merely serving as a conduit in this case, it would be difficult to explain a decision to impose liability using the precise terms that supported liability in the paradigm commercial-dispenser or social host cases.

The responsibility scheme that has been introduced in this chapter can assist in the analysis of the liability of the conduit defendant. Fault of the Weak I variety should be fairly easy to establish. At the very least, a defendant who is asked to make a purchase for someone else should be put on reasonable notice that there is reason to suspect that the other person is under some legal disability that prevents that person from making a direct purchase. That state of affairs should be enough to establish, absent evidence to the contrary, that the furnishing of the alcohol to the driver was a wrongful act by the defendant. Weak II-type fault, an awareness of the alcohol-impaired condition of the driver, may be less frequently encountered in this situation, particularly if the typical fact pattern involves a purchase of the alcohol by the defendant at some time prior to the actual consumption of the alcohol by the driver for whom the purchase was made. However, under the responsibility scheme that has been outlined here, as long as the injured plaintiff could establish either of the two strong varieties of fault along with the first of the weak types of fault, a prima facie case of responsibility has been made.

Accordingly, if the defendant was at fault in producing the intoxication of the driver, or if the defendant could have controlled the driver's risky conduct but failed to do so, then the defendant could be held liable to the victims of the drinking driver. Whether either of those two types of fault could be established might well depend on how strictly a court were to insist on a close connection between the defendant's role as a conduit of alcohol to the driver and the driver's drinking and driving. Arguably, however, that is precisely where the focus ought to be in a determination of a tort liability to the victims of a drinking driver that is based on the fault of someone besides the driver. The significant analytical point in favor of the responsibility scheme that has been developed here is not how those questions would be answered on any given occasion but rather that there is a conceptual structure that allows the cases that lie outside the normal dispenser liability scenarios to be analyzed in a consistent and coherent fashion.

The second type of hybrid alcohol-dispenser situation frequently overlaps with the case of the conduit defendant. It also presents a situation in which the defendant and the drinking driver are joint participants in a venture that involves drinking and driving. It can be difficult to impose vicarious liability on the nondriving defendant in this case, and the nondriving defendant is usually precluded on grounds of complicity from recovering under a dram shop act that might otherwise be applicable to the case. By now, it should be possible to see that an appropriate way to approach this situation would be to view it as a hybrid commercial dispenser/social host case. One could determine the extent to which that defendant's conduct satisfies the requirements of the operating principle set forth above regarding weak and strong faults. Instead of asking whether the nondriving defendant had a right to control the drinking driver's operation of the vehicle in which the defendant was riding, which is one of the key inquiries in a vicarious liability analysis, the defendant's liability should instead be evaluated in light of the question of whether there were reasonable steps that the defendant should have taken to control the driver in order to reduce the accident risk that the drinking driver posed to others. Perhaps the most likely scenario in which that question would be answered affirmatively is one in which the nondriving defendant has not been drinking, or at least has not been drinking to the point of being significantly alcohol-impaired. Letting the intoxicated companion drive under those circumstances may be just the kind of conduct that would qualify as Strong II fault, thereby opening the door to an imposition of liability when the defendant was also at fault either in furnishing the driver with alcohol or in being aware that the driver's condition created a risk of harm to others.

A third situation that sometimes may not fit neatly into either a commercial dispenser or a social host category is when a defendant who is engaged in a business other than the sale or service of alcohol furnishes alcohol to a person as an incident to the defendant's business. Typical examples are an airline's sale or complimentary service of alcohol to its passengers[14] or a hotel's complimentary cocktail policy for its guests. It is important to note that each of these alcohol-dispensing situations can (and probably frequently does occur) under circumstances that are completely removed from the context of contributing to the risk of a drinking-driver accident. The airline passenger who is served alcohol beverages during the flight may take a cab to her destination, and the hotel guest may use the complimentary alcoholic beverages as a way to unwind before retiring to his room. The critical factor in determining the defendant's liability to victims of drinking-driver accidents in each of these cases should be the extent to which the defendant knew or should have known that the person to whom it was serving or selling alcohol would later be posing a risk to others by driving in an alcohol-impaired condition.

Again, the significant point is that the responsibility analysis introduces a framework within which these incidental sale and service cases can be adjudicated. In many respects, determining fault in any given case will parallel the analysis of responsibility in the social host setting. In this situation as well, for example, a defendant ought not to be allowed to offer as a complete defense its assertion that it had no reason to suspect that a particular passenger or guest would drive after being served alcohol by the defendant if the practice of driving following these occasions is so widespread that a reasonable person would be aware of the risk and would at least take some precaution to reduce the risk posed by the driver to others.

## NOTES

1. California has adopted this view by statute. *See* CAL. BUS. & PROF. CODE § 25602 (West 1985) and CAL. CIV. CODE § 1714(b) (West 1985). However, the legislature subsequently relaxed its view of proximate cause with respect to the dispensing of alcohol to obviously intoxicated minors. CAL. BUS. & PROF. CODE § 25602.1 (West Supp. 1990).

2. Otis Eng'g Corp. v. Clark, 668 S.W.2d 307 (Tex. 1983).

3. *Id.* at 308.

4. *Id.* at 309.

5. *Id.* at 311 (emphasis added).

6. *Id.*

7. The discussion that was presented in the introduction to chapter 3 of a liability claim based on a police officer's failure to detain a drinking driver is a good illustration of a setting in which these same concerns arise.

8. On the subject of tort liability for false imprisonment, see PROSSER & KEETON, LAW OF TORTS, at 47-54.

9. N.H. REV. STAT. ANN. § 507-F:7(III) (Supp. 1989).

10. *See* PROSSER & KEETON, LAW OF TORTS, at 141-42.

11. *See, e.g.,* Tarasoff v. Regents of the University of California, 17 Cal.3d 425, 551 P.2d 334, 131 Cal. Rptr. 14 (1976).

12. 96 N.J. 538, 476 A.2d 1219 (1984).

13. *Id.* at 559, 476 A.2d at 1228.

14. The tort liability implications of this situation are analyzed in Bowe, *"May I Offer You Something To Drink From the Beverage Cart?": A Close Look at the Potential Liability for Airlines Serving Alcohol,* 54 J. AIR L. & COMM. 1013 (1989).

# PART TWO

# The Economics of Compensating Drinking-Driver Traffic-Accident Victims

In part 1, I first identified and then critically analyzed a number of the principal measures by which contemporary tort law attempts to shift the costs of drinking-driver traffic accidents away from the victims of those accidents. In part 2, I will explore in a more theoretical manner the way in which the legal system examines and then exercises its options in deciding which parties should bear the costs. A number of fairly sophisticated ideas must be considered here that form part of an important body of scholarship known generally as the "law and economics" movement.[1] The last few years have seen the publication of two impressive and comprehensive analyses of tort law from scholars who view tort law from the law and economics perspective. One was jointly authored by federal appellate judge Richard A. Posner and University of Chicago professor William Landes,[2] and the other was written by Harvard University professor Steven Shavell.[3] Each of these works offers the reader a quite detailed and highly sophisticated analysis of the economic consequences of particular tort rules, theories, and doctrines, and each provides as well some carefully articulated expressions of opinion about a more desirable direction in which that law should develop.

One of the hallmarks of much of the recent scholarly work in law and economics is the significant extent to which its leading authors rely on mathematical models and proofs to explain and support their ideas. However insightful or provocative those ideas might be, though, it is unfortunately too often true that the highly technical method of their presentation is likely to keep them from being accessible to all but the relatively few legal scholars and public policy decision makers who have a solid grounding in the mathematical branches of economics.[4] Whether one agrees or disagrees with these ideas, if they are actually going to play the important role they attempt to play in affecting both the content and the outcome of a public policy inquiry that includes the participation of people who lack that specialized training, then the ideas have to be stripped of the technical jargon in which they are frequently presented and to be rescued from the appeal to the more obscurantist impulses of the movement insider. At least a working familiarity with the most fundamental of those ideas can be presented in an easily accessible fashion that does not require any formal training in economics, and I will do so here. Readers desiring to pursue further study in the more technical literature on these topics should consult the sources cited in the chapter endnotes.

The exploration of accident cost allocation that I undertake in part 2 has both a general and a specific purpose. Any sort of informed judgment about or appreciation of contemporary tort law in general requires at least some consideration of the basic ideas of the law and economics movement. Tort scholarship and judicial resolutions of tort law questions are increasingly being grounded in or explained on the basis of economic principles. More specifically, an introduction to the basic ideas of the law and economics movement can produce a better-informed evaluation of the performance of tort law in the context of the adequate compensation of victims of drinking-driver accidents. This study can aid both in the determination of when tort remedies work well and in the identification of alternatives that should be put into place when those remedies are found to be deficient. Accordingly, the basic law-and-economics ideas relating to an analysis of liability rules will be introduced in chapter 9. These ideas will then be used in chapter 10 to evaluate the full range of existing tort law remedies that were surveyed in part 1 of the book. Chapter 11 concludes part 2 with a consideration of the economic rationales relevant to the innovative victim compensation fund I propose for victims of drinking-driver accidents. My proposal for this reform measure, which I describe in the last two parts of this book, will be financed by the levying of an additional tax on alcoholic beverages.

## NOTES

1. The basic text of the law and economics movement for legal practitioners is a work entitled ECONOMIC ANALYSIS OF LAW (3d ed. 1986), by

Judge Richard A. Posner, who formerly was a University of Chicago law school professor. A valuable introductory text is AN INTRODUCTION TO LAW AND ECONOMICS (2d ed. 1989), by Stanford University professor A. Mitchell Polinsky.

2. W. LANDES & R. POSNER, THE ECONOMIC STRUCTURE OF TORT LAW (1987).

3. S. SHAVELL, ECONOMIC ANALYSIS OF ACCIDENT LAW (1987).

4. One could contrast, in this respect, such work as that done by Yale law school dean Guido Calabresi and Harvard law school professor Frank Michelman with the recent books by Landes and Posner and by Shavell. In a book entitled THE COSTS OF ACCIDENTS: A LEGAL AND ECONOMIC ANALYSIS (1970), and in such important articles as Calabresi & Melamed, *Property Rules, Liability Rules, and Inalienability: One View of the Cathedral*, 85 HARV. L. REV. 1089 (1972), and Calabresi & Hirschoff, *Toward a Test for Strict Liability in Torts*, 81 YALE L. J. 1055 (1972), Dean Calabresi offers his economic insights about tort law in a presentation that combines clear and forceful prose with interesting and accessible illustrations. Professor Michelman has demonstrated with a similar insight how that sort of economic analysis can be brought to bear on different kinds of problems so that it is useful in specific policy analyses. *See* Michelman, *Pollution as a Tort: A Non-Accidental Perspective on Calabresi's COSTS*, 80 YALE L. J. 647 (1971). In the Landes and Posner book, the mathematical approach to economic analysis is thoroughly integrated into the text. Professor Shavell makes a largely successful attempt in his book to restrict the more technical mathematical discussion to the appendices that he attaches to each of his chapters.

# 9

## A Tale of Two Economists: Coase, Pigou, and the Analysis of Liability Rules

Perhaps the easiest way to understand the basic principles that underlie the economic analysis of an imposition of accident costs on particular parties or activities is to view them as though they involved a hypothetical contest between the ideas associated with two economists. The older of our putative combatants is Arthur Pigou, a British economist who published the first edition of his important work, *The Economics of Welfare*, in 1920.[1] Forty years later, the other economist with whose work it is necessary to become familiar, an American named Ronald Coase, published his seminal article entitled "The Problem of Social Cost."[2]

The differences between the ideas of these two economists are substantial and important. At the heart of the debate is the question of whether and how the legal system should construct rules to promote an efficient allocation of society's resources to activities that result in harm to others. Those who engage in activities create two different kinds of costs, social costs and private costs. Social costs, which cover the full range of the resources that are used in carrying on an activity, are defined, as the name suggests, as what it costs society for the activity to proceed. For purposes of this discussion, the most important social cost of an activity is the cost of the harm that is inflicted on others, which will be termed here "accident costs." Private costs, on the other hand, are the costs that the person engaging in the activity must pay, or, to put the idea in economists' language, the costs that the actor must internalize or take into account.

Four significant points about social and private costs are vital to this discussion. First, the social costs of an activity can be different from the private costs. Second, if the social costs of an activity are higher than its private costs, the activity may be using more resources than would be the case if the private costs were closer to the social costs. If the level of private costs is limited, then the person paying them may be able to engage in more of the activity than would be the case if a higher level of costs had to be internalized. Third, one of the reasons that social costs can diverge from private costs is that the accident costs associated with an activity are not made part of the private costs that must be internalized by the actor. Finally, if it is considered to be desirable from the standpoint of achieving efficiency for the private costs of an activity to reflect as closely as possible its social costs, then the accident costs of the activity should be internalized by those who carry on the activity.

The Pigou-Coase dispute centers on the implications of these four points, and more particularly on the need to identify what costs are properly associated with which activities. Pigou is often credited with advocating the government intervention position, according to which it is desirable to impose a legal requirement that an activity should pay a sum of money that raises its private costs so that they come closer to the social costs. One way of accomplishing this result, although it was not a method that was stressed by Pigou himself, is to require the actor to compensate others for the harm that is inflicted upon them by the activity. The idea is that a rule requiring compensation for injuries stemming from the activity will force the actor to make decisions about the activity, such as the general level of the activity to be carried on and the specific ways in which to conduct the activity, based on a private cost estimate that includes the accident costs involving those injuries (which represent a portion of the activity's social costs). Pigou himself is more directly associated with a position that advocated the imposition of taxes on activities if that would make the private costs better reflect the cost of the harm that the activities cause to others.

A good deal of Ronald Coase's influential study of the legal system's identification of the nature of, and the response to, the problem of social costs is prompted by his dissatisfaction with the assumptions that underlie Pigou's position favoring legal intervention in order to impose a greater share of social costs on those whose activities are thought to cause adverse effects on others. The fundamental nature of the Coasean approach will be explained in detail below. For purposes of this book, however, and in order to follow the rationale behind my reform proposal, the disagreement between Pigou and Coase will be artificially narrowed to a single point of contention. In grossly oversimplified but nevertheless not misleading terms, the conflict turns on the extent to which imposing a tax on an injury-producing activity is an appropriate way to achieve an efficient allocation of society's limited resources in a way that also promotes the safety of those who engage in that activity and those who are affected by it.

We can start the exploration of the economic analysis of legal rules by examining a premise that initially may seem counterintuitive, but which can be shown, through the consideration of a simple illustration, to be true. In a world in which there are no transaction costs (or difficulties in reaching agreement), economists (beginning with Coase) will tell us, whatever assignment of legal responsibility for accident losses is made by the legal system, it will not adversely affect the ability of the affected actors to achieve an efficient allocation of resources to their activities.[3] Under those transaction cost-free conditions, therefore, the tort law question that involves deciding what is an accident cost of which activity[4] is not a matter that is likely to be of serious concern. That general idea of the irrelevance, for efficiency purposes, of the assignment of legal rights in a setting in which there are no transaction costs, is referred to by economic analysts of law as the "Coase theorem."[5] This theorem is important to the issue of how the legal system ought to treat the costs of traffic accidents caused by drinking drivers. Although the theoretical work of Coase followed that of Pigou, and to a great extent rejected Pigou's work,[6] Coase's work plays such a central role in contemporary tort law scholarship that the best way to proceed is to begin with an explanation and an illustration of the Coase theorem, and then to see how the inherent limitations of Coasean analysis leave a substantial window of opportunity for the introduction of a Pigovian solution to the social cost problems associated with drinking-driver traffic accidents.

The nature of the Coase theorem and its implications for tort law can be understood and appreciated if we begin with the consideration of a very simple situation. Suppose that you and I are next-door neighbors. On a certain Saturday in November, I have plans to invite a group of my friends over for a cookout in my backyard. You have plans for that same day to burn a pile of leaves in your backyard. If you follow the course of action you have planned, then the smoke from your fire will necessarily disrupt my plans, given the way the wind is blowing and the timing of my party.

The first point that needs to be appreciated is that this fact pattern actually does present an economic question. While you and I may be inclined to think that what we have is a problem about the timing of your leaf burning and my party, or perhaps even a problem about the thoughtfulness of people who have to live next to each other, an economist would say that what we have is a problem that involves the allocation of a scarce resource. The nature of that resource can be described in various ways; the description we can use for purposes of this discussion is that the resource is the air in my backyard. I want that air to be suitable for the activity that I have planned, which is for my guests to be able to sit around and talk, to barbecue some steaks and chicken, and to spend a pleasant afternoon outdoors. You want to use that air as a place where the smoke from your leaf fire can blow. Our plans thus present inconsistent demands for the use of that resource — one person's use precludes the other person's use. It is precisely that sort of situation that can be dealt with by economic analysis.

The next thing an economist would tell us about our problem is that there is some optimal allocation of this scarce resource that could be determined. All that means is that each of us values our competing and inconsistent uses of our property in particular ways, and that one of us probably places a higher value on that use than the other one does. An efficient solution to our potential conflict would allow the person who places the higher value on the activity to get to make use of the resource.[7] Suppose, for example, that you could just as easily burn your leaves on Friday or Sunday as you could on this Saturday when I wish to have a party in my backyard, and that this Saturday is the only day when I am likely to be able to get together with these particular guests at my home. Common sense would indicate that, at least on the set of facts that has been presented, I would value my use of the scarce resource more than you do, at least in part because my use is constrained by time and the limited opportunities to duplicate the activity in ways that yours is not.

A world of no transaction costs — the operating assumption that is necessary for a consideration of the core of the Coase theorem — is one in which there are no barriers to negotiation between the affected parties, so that they can arrive at the efficient resolution of their conflict. Such a world can be imagined without much difficulty in this example. Suppose that, on Wednesday evening, I notice that you and your children are raking your yard and piling your leaves near our common property line. We have been friendly neighbors who have maintained good social relations over the years. Seeing what you're doing, and remembering that you have burned your leaves in previous autumns, it occurs to me to mention to you that I'm planning a party for Saturday, and you agree to postpone the burning of the leaves until Sunday. In this fashion, we have arrived at the economically efficient solution.[8] The resource that is subject to inconsistent demands will be put to the use that has the higher value attached to it.

It is important to notice the factors that were necessary for us to be able to reach this efficient result. First, we had to have knowledge about the existence of the potential conflict. Second, we had to be able to communicate with each other about our respective positions. Third, we needed to be able to identify which use would be more important to the one who valued it more highly. And fourth, we had to have a sufficiently good relationship that this discussion produced the desirable result.

Coase himself never assumed that transactions were cost-free in the real world. As he put it:

> "In order to carry out a market transaction it is necessary to discover who it is that one wishes to deal with, to inform people that one wishes to deal and on what terms, to conduct negotiations leading up to a bargain, to draw up the contract, to undertake the inspection needed to make sure that the terms of the contract are being observed, and so on. These operations are often extremely costly, sufficiently costly at any rate to prevent many transactions that would be carried out in a world in which the pricing system worked without cost."[9]

A world in which transaction costs do exist even in this uncomplicated setting of our leaf-burning hypothetical can be depicted simply by changing one or more of those factors that made the solution achievable. Suppose, for example, that you light your fire just before my party gets under way, and that you then leave home and can't be reached. Or suppose that, if I realize that there might be this potential conflict between our plans, you don't know whether there will be another good day for leaf burning and I don't know whether I could get my group of friends together just as easily on another day. Finally, suppose that we have a prickly enough relationship that you would deliberately decide to burn your leaves at a time when it would cause me the most annoyance and inconvenience. Each of those conditions, or some combination of them, could very well prevent us from arriving at the efficient solution to our problem. Each of those conditions, which act as barriers to negotiating an efficient solution to a problem, is an example of what an economist means by transaction costs.

This simple hypothetical only involves two people in the potential conflict. Perhaps the most compelling illustration of transaction costs is the situation in which an increase in the number of actors adds complications to the attempt to negotiate an efficient solution. Suppose that there were a number of people in a neighborhood who might burn leaves at a particular time when the smoke from those fires could disrupt my plans. Or suppose that the smoke from your fire could drift across many lawns, each of which was being used for an activity that might be disrupted by the smoke. Adding more parties to the potential conflict increases the difficulty of identifying and then striking a bargain with each of the people who have to agree to a particular solution. A general rule of thumb, then, might be phrased in the form of a statement that an increase in the number of actors will produce an increase in the transaction costs of reaching an efficient solution to a resource-use conflict.

So far in this discussion of our conflicting uses of the scarce resource, we have ignored the role that might be played by legal rules. We can now introduce that additional factor and trace its impact on our conduct. We will do so by considering first the situation in which there are no transaction costs, and then turn to a consideration of the same fact pattern in the presence of transaction costs. There are two different legal rules that need to be considered: first, the legal right will be given to me to be free from smoke pollution from fires that have been set on neighboring land, and second, the legal right will be given to you to set a fire on your land regardless of the fact that the smoke from that fire will affect the surrounding property.

Suppose initially that the state in which we live has a judicial precedent that establishes a rule of the law of nuisance that entitles anyone who is adversely affected by an invasion of smoke from a neighbor's land to collect damages for the harm that results from the invasion and to obtain an injunction against any future invasions. This legal rule would at first glance appear to settle the question of who gets to use the scarce resource—I have a legal right to exclude your smoke from my land and to collect damages for the harm that is caused on those occasions on which smoke does come onto my property. But in fact, upon reflection, it should be apparent that while this rule is one more factor that needs to be taken into account, it does not by itself necessarily determine the outcome.

Consider first the conceptually less difficult situation in which I have the legal right described above, and there are no transaction costs. In order for me not to exercise my legal right, I might insist on receiving something from you. I could ask, for example, that in exchange for my letting you burn your leaves on this day, you will (in this increasingly oppressive suburban hypothetical) let me borrow your bass boat for a fishing trip in the spring. Economists would describe this nonpejoratively as a "bribe" from you so that I will not exercise my legal right to be free from the smoke from your fire. Almost by definition, given the facts that have been presented here, the resolution of our conflicting plans in this situation will be efficient. If I take the bribe, that is very good evidence that you place a higher value on burning leaves than I did on having my outdoor party, as long as I receive the additional payment from you. We are both better off after the transaction. I have more than I had before, and you were able to obtain the opportunity to do what you wanted at a price that you were willing to pay. If, on the other hand, I were to refuse to take the bribe, that would demonstrate that I placed a higher value on that resource than you did. The price you were willing to pay was not enough to induce me to give up my legal right. So at least in the situation where there are no transaction costs, the assignment of the legal right to me will not interfere with our arriving at an efficient outcome: if you value the resource more highly than I do, there will be some mutually agreeable price at which you will buy from me the right that the legal system has given to me.

The less intuitively obvious part of the Coase theorem is that it holds up even when we reverse the assignment of the legal right, as long as we continue to maintain the assumption that there are no transaction costs. Suppose now that instead of my having the right to be free from smoke, you have the legal right to burn your leaves without regard to the effects that the smoke will cause. It may appear at first as if that means that I will have to suffer your disruption of my plans even if I place a higher value on my activity than you place on yours. But in fact, under the conditions of this first pair of hypotheticals in which there are no transaction costs, if I value the resource more highly than you do, there is some price that I can offer and that you will accept that allows me to purchase the exercise of that legal right from you. Again, virtually by definition, in the absence of transaction costs, the solution that we arrive at is efficient, as demonstrated by the result of our negotiation. If you allow me to bribe you, I have valued the resource more highly than you did; conversely, if I am unable to bribe you, then the value that I placed on the resource was lower than yours.

The more interesting question—because it is much more reflective of the real world in which people have conflicts over scarce resources than the assumption that underlies the Coase theorem—asks what happens to the proposition about the irrelevance of the assignment of legal rights when we do introduce transaction costs into the hypothetical. The effect can be seen by a relatively slight modification of our initial hypothetical. Take the situation in which we do not get along very well, and you decide that disrupting my plans is an attractive option, even though you could just as easily burn your leaves on another day. We will begin again with the legal right being assigned to me, and we will further assume that, all else being equal, I value the freedom from smoke more highly than you value the burning of the leaves on that day. The question to ask is whether that means I will be able to enjoy my legal right to be free from smoke, which would allow us to achieve the more efficient resolution of our competing interests.[10]

The fact that the legal system has given me a right to be free from the interference caused by your smoke is obviously relevant to what you do, but that assignment of the legal right to me is not necessarily going to be dispositive. What effect the legal rule will actually have in this situation is a product of at least two different considerations: first, the nature and timing of the legal enforcement of the right that I have, and second, the value that you place on the disruption of my plans. As set out earlier, the legal right that has been given to me is the right to be free from interference with the use and enjoyment of my land. Interference of that sort is thus something that I am entitled to prevent, and I am also entitled to be compensated for the harm that I suffer if an interference does occur. As a practical matter, the enforcement of the legal right by the first kind of entitlement, which is to prevent the harm from occurring, depends on an ability to identify in advance the potential for interference and then to obtain judicial action in the form of an injunction against your burning the leaves in such a way that it interferes with my plans. Furthermore, because I am the person who is required to initiate the judicial proceedings to obtain an injunction, preventing the harm has to be sufficiently valuable for me to incur that expense in the form of time and money. It is much more likely that those conditions would be satisfied in a case of a continuing and substantial interference with the use and enjoyment of my land than in the one-time and relatively minor disruption that is presented in this hypothetical. Accordingly, the more probable means of my enforcing the right that I have been given by the legal system is by using the entitlement to compensation for the harm that I suffer after it has occurred. In that remedial setting, it is still necessary for me to initiate the legal proceedings, but now the remedial focus is retrospective rather than prospective. Instead of stopping you from interfering, I can only get an award of monetary damages for the interference that has already occurred.

The nature and timing of the legal enforcement of my right to be free from smoke are directly related to the decision making that you go through about your course of conduct. While it may be true that your activity creates a social cost that exceeds its benefit to you (and in this version of the hypothetical it is also true that your activity is also contrary to the legal system's assignment of rights) the most important factor in your decision making may very well be the question of what is likely to happen to you if you proceed with your burning. That question replaces an inquiry into what this activity costs me or what it costs the society at large with an assessment of what this activity actually costs *you*.

The effect of that shift in focus is readily apparent in the simple hypothetical that has been presented here. If I am unlikely to try to obtain an injunction before you burn your leaves, then the real risk that you face as a result of burning the leaves is a potential lawsuit for damages for the invasion of my legal right. One factor in determining the extent of that risk is the amount of monetary damages to which I might be entitled, but that is clearly not the only, and may not even be the primary, factor that goes into the evaluation of the potential consequences to you if you violate my legal right. It is going to be at least as important for you to know how likely it is that I will take the trouble to sue you, and then to assess what sort of recovery I am likely to obtain if I am successful in the lawsuit if I do bring one. When the amount of your exposure to the risk of an obligation to pay damages to me is discounted by the improbability of your actually having to pay those damages, then the actual legal cost to you may be significantly *less* than the benefit that you receive from causing me this inconvenience. In this situation, then, the assignment of the legal right to me may complicate the decision making process that a person in your position would undertake, but it does *not* ultimately produce the result that has been identified as the more efficient use of the resource that we both cannot use simultaneously.

The consideration of this hypothetical has so far proceeded from the assumption that the legal right was given to me rather than to you. If that assumption is reversed, so that the legal system now gives you a right to burn your leaves irrespective of the effect that the smoke will have on surrounding property, then the decision-making process is even easier to follow. In this situation, the grant of the legal right to you means that if I am to prevail upon you to postpone your leaf burning, I have to do so on extralegal grounds. (Extralegal, but not illegal. If I resort to self-help, ranging from the use of a water hose to an Uzi automatic weapon, the legal system is committed to bringing a variety of civil and criminal sanctions to bear on me.)[11] It is particularly the case in this setting, in which the person who has been given the legal right must be persuaded not to exercise that right, that transaction costs are most likely to produce an inefficient result. If ignorance about the existence or the nature of the potential conflict or a history of ill-will, for example, get in the way of our negotiating a solution, then you will burn your leaves. If there is some price at which I could persuade you to postpone your burning, but I don't have the financial resources to pay that price, then again you will burn your leaves.

The hypothetical about our inconsistent plans for a Saturday afternoon could be spun out into further variations, but enough information has been presented by now for the essence of the Coase theorem to be illustrated. If there are no barriers to our negotiation, then we will arrive at an efficient solution, regardless of how the legal system assigns the right to use the limited resource. When barriers to negotiation are introduced, however, we may or may not arrive at an efficient solution. In either situation, though, the introduction of a legal right that has been given to one or the other of us will not necessarily affect the outcome. Absent transaction costs, we will arrive at the efficient outcome regardless of which of us has been given the legal right. With transaction costs present, even the assignment of the legal right to the person who can make the more efficient use of the resource will not assure that the efficient decision will be reached.

The discussion that has been presented so far suggests a natural next step, and it is one that has been recommended since the beginning of the law-and-economics movement. If we are able to achieve the efficient outcome in the absence of transaction costs, and if we may be prevented from doing so when there are transaction costs, then perhaps we should attempt to assign legal rights in a way that brings the outcome of conflicts closest to the operating conditions of the Coase theorem. In other words, we should recognize or assign legal rights in such a way that the adverse effects of transaction costs can be minimized.[12] A reconsideration of the leaf-burning hypothetical can illustrate how this rule of assigning rights would work.

In one of the variations of our situation that was raised earlier, you had a desire to cause me inconvenience, and therefore you deliberately chose to burn your leaves at a time when I wanted to hold the party in my backyard. That purpose of causing harm was identified as a transaction cost, because it gets in the way of our identifying the efficient use of the resource and negotiating a course of conduct that achieves the efficient solution to our conflict. If that intent to cause me harm is considered to be too extreme an assumption, the hypothetical could be changed so that your decision to burn leaves is completely indifferent to any consequences that the smoke may have on others. Both of these possibilities could be described in another way, as presenting a situation in which the costs of your leaf burning are externalized. What that means is simply that the benefits of your activity are realized by you, while the costs of that activity are suffered by me.

Consider first the version of the hypothetical under circumstances in which the legal system gives the relevant right to you. As was mentioned before, the decision for you to forego the burning of the leaves has to be reached through measures that are taken and arguments that are made outside of the legal system. Your decision to burn has no legal costs to you. Furthermore, if you decide to give up the exercise of your right, it will be at a price that will be determined solely by you.

Now change the situation so that the legal right is given to me rather than to you. It is certainly still true that you may decide to burn your leaves and thereby invade my now legally protected interest in being free from the interference that is caused by the smoke from your fire. Your decision to do so, however, is now one that does have legal costs attached to it. Furthermore, if you act in a way that invades my right, you can be forced to pay me damages for the harm that was caused—a retrospective purchase of my right—but the price for that purchase/invasion of my right will be set by the courts, not set solely by either one of us.

When the legal regimes with their alternative legal rules are compared, the differences that those rules make in the recognition of who has the legal right can be seen to have an impact on the consideration that goes into the decision to burn. In the first scenario, your possession of the legal right to burn allows you to ignore entirely the social cost of the burning. All of those costs are going to be imposed on those who are affected by the smoke. In the alternative situation, my possession of the legal right forces you to take the social costs of your activity into account. You may still burn, but you have to consider whether I will sue you, whether I will succeed in that lawsuit, and how much I might recover if I do win.

The decision to give the legal right to me rather than to you can produce at least some incentive for you to avoid the interference, by forcing you to internalize some of the social costs of your activity. Some of the social costs will be internalized by you, but not necessarily all of them. We have already seen that the relevant factor in your decision making is likely to be not what your activity costs *society* but rather what your activity costs *you*. The next question to be considered, then, is whether the situation can be improved so that the people who engage in behavior that poses risks to others will be forced to face some internalization of the accident costs of the people who are injured when those risks are realized.

It is at this point in the discussion that it is useful to bring in the other of our representative economists, Arthur Pigou. Pigou, like Coase, published a great deal during a long career. His work is varied, and just as is the case with Coase, any attempt to connect him with a single and simplified idea does a gross injustice to the complexity and sophistication of his work. Coase has criticized Pigou's lack of clarity in the exposition of his ideas: "Not being clear, it was never clearly wrong. Curiously enough, this obscurity in the source has not prevented the emergence of a fairly well-defined oral tradition. What economists think they learn from Pigou, and what they tell their students, which I term the Pigovian tradition, is reasonably clear."[13] It is ironic that the same observation might be made about Coase's own work. There is no "Coase theorem" as such in Coase's seminal article.[14] While there is at least some substantial degree of agreement about the content at the center of Coase's idea, one need not listen to many law-and-economics analyses to conclude that a good deal of flexibility and fuzziness can be found at the edges of the theorem.

Nevertheless, for purposes of this book, it is helpful to be able to attach one person's name to the critical idea at the core of the answer to the question that was just asked about internalization of social costs. A response in the Pigovian tradition to the situation in which the accident-cost portion of the social costs of an activity are externalized by the person who engages in the activity would be to structure the legal rules regarding injury compensation so that those costs are imposed on the person who causes them. To the extent that the compensation rules of tort law are inadequate to accomplish this result, however, society does have an additional means of forcing the actor to internalize social costs. A tax can be imposed on an activity so that the private cost to the actor better reflects the social costs of that activity.

Pigou identified the type of externalities that have been discussed here as services and disservices to persons other than those who are engaged in the same activity.[15] The divergence between private net products (or private costs) and social net products (or social costs) can be eliminated, in the case of disservices to other persons, through governmental intervention in the form of taxes that are imposed on those who engage in the activity. The very first illustration that Pigou gave in favor of the tax strategy of intervention involves alcoholic beverages. According to Pigou, "The private net product of any unit of investment is unduly large relatively to the social net product in the business of producing and distributing alcoholic drinks. Consequently, in nearly all countries, special taxes are placed on these businesses."[16] No further explanation is given of the reasoning that underlies this conclusion. In a sense, the remaining two chapters of part 2 of this book provide the details that flesh out Pigou's statement about the taxation of the production and distribution of alcoholic beverages, doing so as part of a more narrowly focused project of identifying such taxation as an appropriate method of allocating the accident losses of victims of drinking drivers.

Even acknowledging that the preceding discussion has picked out only a couple of ideas and has stripped them to the bone in order to set the stage for an examination of how they might have an impact on the drinking-driver accident problem, it is easy to imagine the reader being less than overwhelmed by either the insight or the originality of what has been said so far. The portion of the conclusion that can be constructed from the Pigovian tradition that is of interest here can be derived from the following line of reasoning. People usually act in ways that are likely to produce net benefits to them. If the cost of an activity is raised, then they are less likely to be inclined to act in that way. If the private cost of an activity to the actor who is actually being forced to compensate accident victims is less than the true accident cost of the activity, then the private cost of acting in that way can be increased by imposing a tax on the activity. Therefore, a tax on the activity that is imposed in addition to an obligation to compensate victims could produce more cost internalization and perhaps have a greater deterrent effect than would either measure if adopted alone.

This progression of ideas seems at least obvious, if not trite. And yet some of the key components of that sequence of thought are quite controversial within the law-and-economics movement. For example, one of the major points that Coase thought needed to be corrected in the Pigovian analysis of legal intervention in the competing uses of resources is the assumption that one party causes harm to another. According to Coase, it is just as plausible to view many situations as involving a reciprocal causation of harm of each party to the other rather than as a unilateral infliction of harm by one party on the other.[17] That idea of reciprocal harm is easily illustrated in our hypothetical about leaf burning. Coase would charge the Pigovian analysts with leaping too quickly to characterize the situation as one in which you were causing harm to me by burning your leaves. The alternative characterization that Coase might offer is that we are causing reciprocal interference with each other. If you burn the leaves, it is true that you have caused me to suffer inconvenience and annoyance. However, it is also true that you have been forced to take my presence into account in ways that would not be necessary if you did not have to live next-door to me.

There are obvious limits to the rational appeal of the reciprocal-cause notion of Coase. To evaluate the strength of the reciprocity concept in a particular instance, we would want to know such things as the time dimension of the competing uses and the assignment of legal rights at the time that the different uses began. For example, we would probably react differently to someone who built a housing subdivision next to a cattle feedlot than to someone who opened a cattle feedlot next to a subdivision.[18] But in an important sense those considerations involve the weight that we are willing to give to the reciprocity claim, and they do not implicate the underlying validity of the claim itself. Coase's idea can be stated more generally as a recognition that conflicts in the use of resources can arise in different ways, and that the legal system's response to a conflict should be based on a careful inquiry into the nature of the conflict rather than on a facile assumption that either the more active participant or the most recent to have acted has been the exclusive agent in producing the harm.

The general sketch of accident cost allocation by the assignment of rights within the legal system, even when it is painted in such broad strokes as it has been here, does have considerable significance for the public policy exploration of additional and alternative measures to deal with the social problem of adequately compensating the victims of drinking-driver traffic accidents. The impact of law-and-economics reasoning on the structure of contemporary legal responses to such accidents is the subject of the next chapter.

### NOTES

1. *See* A. PIGOU, THE ECONOMICS OF WELFARE (4th ed. 1932).

2. *See* Coase, *The Problem of Social Cost,* 3 J. L. & ECON. 1 (1960). This article has spawned an enormous body of literature, a great deal of which appears in two journals published at the University of Chicago, the *Journal of Law and Economics* and the *Journal of Legal Studies.* One of the better supplements to the Coase article is Regan, *The Problem of Social Cost Revisited,* 15 J. L. & ECON. 427 (1972).

3. Any discussion of the economic analysis of law will require the reader to understand some definitions of recurring key terms. To avoid technical jargon, definitions will be interjected into the discussion as the terms are first used in a significant way. For example, the terms "transaction costs"

and "efficient allocation of resources" are explained in more detail as they appear in the discussion below. In the case of controversial definitions, the competing considerations will be indicated either in the text or in the notes.

4. *See* CALABRESI, COSTS OF ACCIDENTS, at 133.

5. The Landes and Posner text articulates the theorem in the following terms: "[T]he efficiency with which resources will be employed is unaffected by the initial assignment of rights, provided that transaction costs are zero." LANDES & POSNER, ECONOMIC STRUCTURE, at 31.

6. *See generally* Coase, *Social Cost,* at 28-42.

7. Various definitions of efficiency could be offered in place of the simple statement used in the text. A utility-maximization approach would conclude that a particular solution to the problem is efficient if it produces the greatest overall utility. A wealth-maximization approach substitutes wealth for utility as the relevant maximization factor for determining which of the two competing activities should be conducted. An approach that employs Pareto criteria would say that an efficient solution is one in which at least one person is better off and no one is put in a worse position. A Kaldor-Hicks approach treats a solution as efficient when the gains to the person who is made better off are sufficiently high that the person whose position is made worse could be compensated from those gains. *See* LANDES & POSNER, ECONOMIC STRUCTURE, at 16-17.

8. Note that the technical definition of efficiency employing Pareto criteria is satisfied in this situation. Because at least one person (me) is made better off, and no one else is made worse off, the decision for you to postpone your activity is Pareto-superior to the alternative decision.

9. Coase, *Social Cost,* at 15.

10. A word of explanation is in order about the assumptions being made in this last set of hypotheticals. Your wish to cause me injury is being treated in the text as a transaction cost because it acts as a barrier to our negotiating a solution to our conflict. That characterization is qualitatively different from treating that desire to cause injury as something that is simply included in the calculation of how highly you value the leaf burning. Under these circumstances, the occurrence of your leaf burning at the time of my party would be inefficient under Pareto criteria. The burning of the leaves is a Pareto-inferior solution to our conflict, because, while it does make you better off, I am left in a worse position.

Perhaps another way to view your desire to cause me harm is to see it as an external cost of your activity. You receive all the benefit of going ahead with the leaf burning (disposing of your pile of leaves plus having the pleasure of disrupting my plans), but the burden of that activity is imposed entirely on me, and I receive no benefit at all.

11. Of course, the economically rational wielder of an Uzi trying to prevent smoke from disrupting his barbecue plans (if that is not too apparently oxymoronic an image) would determine what legal sanctions might be imposed on him, then would discount those sanctions by the improbability of their actually being imposed, and finally would weigh that anticipated

cost of his activity against the benefit that he derived from the use of the weapon. It is probably worth noting that this is *not* a parody of law-and-economics reasoning. *See, e.g.,* R. POSNER, ECONOMIC ANALYSIS OF LAW 205-18 (3d ed. 1986).

12.  Dean Calabresi refers to this as a cheapest-cost-avoider rule of strict liability. According to this rule, liability should be imposed on the party who can both make a calculation of the costs and benefits of a particular activity and act on the basis of that cost-benefit analysis.

13.  Coase, *Social Cost,* at 39.

14.  Henry Manne, who is the chief proselytizer of the right wing of the law-and-economics movement, refers to the fact that "[t]here is no internal evidence in Coase's article that he thought he was developing anything that would become universally known as the 'Coase theorem.' " H. MANNE, THE ECONOMICS OF LEGAL RELATIONSHIPS: READINGS IN THE THEORY OF PROPERTY RIGHTS 123 (1975).

15.  PIGOU, WELFARE, at 183.

16.  *Id.* at 192.

17.  *See* Coase, *Social Cost,* at 2.

18.  *See* Spur Indus., Inc. v. Del E. Webb Dev. Co., 108 Ariz. 178, 494 P.2d 700 (1972).

# 10

## Allocating Accident Costs to Particular Activities

To what extent do the assumptions that underlie the competing Coasean and Pigovian theories of law and economics set forth in the preceding chapter actually obtain in the context of drinking-driver accidents? To develop an answer let us begin by considering three questions about the nature of drinking-driver traffic accidents and then proceed to a specific analysis of the various legal rules that are currently used or could be invoked to compensate the accident victims. The first question is whether drinking-driver traffic accidents involve significant transaction costs. The second question is whether the harm done to the participants was caused unilaterally or whether it was reciprocal. Third, we must ask whether the costs of drinking-driver accidents are externalized in significant ways. An affirmative answer to the first question and a negative answer to the second would indicate that the core conditions of the Coase theorem do not obtain in the drinking-driver accident setting. An affirmative answer to the third question would suggest that we must then ask what set of legal rules is most likely to lead the parties at fault to internalize the accident costs in order to create an incentive for a more acceptable level of drinking driver accidents.

The Coase theorem holds that the way legal rights are assigned to parties in a dispute is irrelevant in terms of ensuring an efficient result if there are no transaction costs. But it is obvious that drinking-driver traffic accidents involve significant transaction costs. Injurers and victims involved in traffic accidents in general rarely have the ability to identify each other prior to the accident or a chance to arrive at a negotiated solution to the conflict between the parties. For the most part, accidents occur as isolated events, and the identity of the participants is the result of coincidence and chance. Driving in a certain manner can create a risk of harm; who happens to be on the other end of a collision when that risk of harm is actually realized is largely a matter of bad luck. Opportunities for accident victims to negotiate their way out of potential injury are obviously limited. Furthermore, the opportunity to purchase greater safety for oneself can be restricted as well by a combination of the limited portion of a person's (or a nation's) wealth that can be spent on safety measures and the limited availability of feasible and effective safety measures.

There are exceptions to the general rule, of course. For example, injurers and victims on occasion can identify each other in advance of an accident, and in some cases victims forego reasonable opportunities to reduce the risk posed by drinking and driving. A passenger who chooses to ride with an intoxicated driver is a good illustration. Other victims contribute to their injuries by their own misconduct, such as drinking and driving themselves. Perhaps both drivers in a two-car collision were alcohol-impaired, or perhaps the passenger of a drinking driver furnished alcohol to the driver.

Cases such as these, in which the transaction costs are reduced, can serve as a basis for a legal rule that either restricts or eliminates altogether a victim's right to recover tort compensation. They would also support such legal rules as the one that prohibits recovery by a person who voluntarily assumes the known risk that is created by the defendant's conduct or recovery by a person who fails to use reasonable care and contributes to the risk posed by the drinking driver. The reasoning behind these rules also forms an important part of the justification for the approach I have taken in structuring my proposal for a victim compensation fund. I exclude claims brought by persons who were at fault in the accident and derivative claims.

Much of the appeal of the Coase theorem, as well as its rejection of the Pigovian tradition that favors governmental intervention to impose social costs on certain actors, depends on being able to characterize the parties involved in a dispute as causing reciprocal harm to each other, which leads us to the second question that must be addressed. Stretching the Coasean idea of reciprocity, one can draw a flawed parallel between the ordinary traffic-accident case and the hypothetical of the adjoining landowners who have a potential conflict involving the smoke from the burning leaves. Assume that your car crosses the median of the highway and strikes my car, injuring me. One might say that although it is true that you caused me to suffer harm, I also caused you harm by being in your way when you lost control of your car, so that you ran into me rather than being able to swerve harmlessly across my lane. That view of reciprocity can ultimately be reduced to the unhelpful realization that simply by existing, we place mutual demands and constraints on each other.

The more meaningful sense of reciprocity that Coase refers to in his work is easier to identify in a situation such as the leaf-burning hypothetical. In that situation, the rights and the interferences that were at issue all turned on the ownership or the use of property. What I can do with my property is dependent in large part on what you can do with your property. If I can restrict or intrude upon your desired use because of what I want to do, then it is meaningful to say that I have caused you to suffer a harm of sorts. When we shift from the realm of property rights,[1] however, and begin to focus on wrongful conduct that inflicts physical and personal injury on another person, the reciprocity of the Coase theorem starts to break down.

Although too encompassing a notion of reciprocity can create a faulty parallel between the ordinary traffic accident situation and the nuisance that is associated with smoke from a neighbor's fire, it would be wrong to suggest that the concept of reciprocity is completely foreign to the routine traffic-accident setting. There is an important sense in which traffic accidents can legitimately be viewed as involving reciprocal risks: travelers on a highway each pose a certain level of risk to other travelers.[2] A car's tire may unexpectedly blow out, for example, or a steering system may suddenly fail, sending a car into the path of another car and producing a collision in which the occupants of both vehicles are injured. Because that sort of incident can happen essentially to anyone, and because it can happen without there being any negligence at all on the part of the operator or the owner of the vehicle, it is not unrealistic to see that kind of occurrence as a reciprocal risk that each of us poses for the other drivers who are on the road when we drive. That is not to say that the accident victim in that situation is denied any recovery; rather it is only to state that the appropriate place to look for recovery is not the other driver. Even though the vehicle owner or operator may not have been at fault in an accident of this sort, the manufacturer may be held liable for putting a defective automobile or tire on the market, knowing that drivers have only very limited opportunities to detect dangerously defective conditions in the vehicles and their component parts. The significant point, however, is that the level of risk that the drivers who are using ordinary care pose to each other is roughly the same in this situation, and therefore the risks that they pose to each other could be called reciprocal.

The drinking driver, however, can introduce a risk that is of a different kind than the ordinary risk posed by driving. Driving while alcohol-impaired poses a higher degree of risk than the ordinary one simply posed by driving. When this nonreciprocal risk flowing from alcohol impairment is introduced into the picture and a traffic accident actually occurs as a result of that risk, the reciprocity assumption of the Coase theorem no longer obtains in as convincing a manner as it does in the property rights hypothetical. In this situation, then, it is correct to speak of the drinking driver as inflicting harm on the victim. It is also worth noting that this sort of reciprocity analysis provides an additional rationale for refusing to allow one alcohol-impaired driver to recover damages from another alcohol-impaired driver. While these drivers pose a different risk and a higher degree of risk than nondrinking drivers do, the risks that they pose to each other are of the same type and of the same degree. Thus two drinking drivers actually do pose reciprocal risks to each other.

The third question that needs to be asked about the general applicability of law-and-economics reasoning to drinking-driver traffic accidents concerns the extent to which the costs of those accidents are externalized to the victims of the accidents rather than internalized by the persons who cause those accidents. The relevant focus here is on the cost of the harm inflicted on innocent victims. To the extent that the legal system fails to shift the costs of those accident injuries away from the victims, whether because of the nature of the legal rules or because of the practical limitations on full recovery of damages awarded by those rules, some externalization of these accident costs will occur. The relevant question then becomes which, if any, of the activities that helped cause the drinking-driver traffic accident are most likely to escape any significant measure of cost internalization.

In the real world, in which negotiations between injurers and victims are at least costly and often impossible, and in which certain kinds of conduct produce a risk of harm that exceeds the background risks that actors routinely and reciprocally impose on each other, attaching accident costs to an appropriate activity can be a complex, troublesome, and frequently controversial task. The simplest of scenarios for drinking-driver traffic accidents can illustrate the difficulties that can arise.

Consider once again a typical fact pattern. A car driven by a drinking driver collides with another car in which a family is traveling. The family members suffer serious physical, financial, and emotional harm as a result of the accident. The costs of the victims' injuries might be attributed to any one of the following activities:

1. the simple operation of the drinking driver's automobile;
2. the drinking driver's operation of an automobile while alcohol-impaired;
3. the operation of the victims' automobile;

4. living in a crowded and dangerous society;

5. the consumption of alcoholic beverages as part of activities performed in carrying out an employment relationship;

6. the selling of alcoholic beverages as part of a commercial transaction;

7. the serving of alcoholic beverages as part of a social function; and

8. the manufacture and wholesale distribution of alcoholic beverages.

Even a superficial consideration of these eight options reveals that they will produce different outcomes in terms of whether the victims' losses should be shifted away from the victims rather than left on them, and if so, to whom they ought to be shifted.

Under options one and two, the accident losses are considered to be a cost of the operation of the drinking driver's vehicle. The only difference is whether the appropriate risk is attached to driving in general or to driving while alcohol-impaired. The second choice has more of an intuitive appeal, as it appears to correspond more closely to a common-sense notion that it is the drinking driver's alcohol-impaired condition that increases the risk posed to others on the highway. For purposes of understanding how the allocation of accident loss actually works, however, the first option is included because it is solidly grounded in how automobile liability insurance is now used for spreading accident losses. Furthermore, as I will demonstrate, the second option can lead to a conclusion that has a dramatically adverse consequence for the accident victims.

Option three presents another instance in which the accident losses of the victims are treated as part of the cost of driving. In this case, however, the risk attaches to the operation of the automobile in which the victims are riding. In the absence of an effective means of obtaining full compensation from a third party, the legal system in effect treats the victims' losses in this way. There is little practical difference in outcome between option three and option four, which views traffic accidents as simply one of many risks of serious injury that come with living in a technologically complex society.

Options five, six, seven, and eight shift the focus from the act of driving vehicles to the intoxicating beverages involved in the accident. Under these options, the predominant risk factor revolves around alcoholic beverages. Options five, six, and seven single out as the key event the consumption of an alcoholic beverage by someone who then drives. The differences among these three options reflect the fact that the drinking driver could have been singly or simultaneously occupying several roles—acting as an employee of one defendant, a commercial patron of another, or a social guest of a third defendant. Option five treats the victims' accident losses as a cost of the business of the person who employs the drinking driver, while options six and seven, respectively, treat them as part of the cost of providing alcohol to a customer and to a guest. Option eight is currently ignored as a possibility, but I will use it as the foundation for my compensation reform proposal.

In deciding what accident losses should be a cost of what activities, the following factors should be taken into consideration: (1) the impact that a particular decision will have on accident deterrence; (2) the ability of a party to bear the accident costs to be imposed on that party; and (3) whether a particular allocation of accident costs will distort market forces or produce artificial market stimuli that adversely affect decisions about production and consumption. Rather than attempt to provide an exhaustive economic analysis in light of these three important factors, the following discussion will highlight the main features of each option in order to give a sense of their economic pros and cons.

## Option 1. A Cost of Operating the Drinking Driver's Vehicle

The first option for allocating drinking-driver accident costs considers the victim's losses to be a general cost of driving by the driver who happened to be drinking on a particular occasion. Contemporary American tort law restricts the use of this option to cases of negligence, that is, cases in which the operation of the drinking driver's vehicle failed to comply with the standard of care that would be used by a reasonable person under the circumstances. The law of negligence, as described in chapter 2, contains the basic doctrinal framework that a court would use if it were to exercise Option 1. Assuming that the legal elements of the breach of a duty and causation can be established in a particular case, and assuming further that there are no applicable affirmative defenses that will reduce or bar a victim's recovery of damages, our fault-based tort system provides a readily available technique—a negligence claim—for allocating accident costs under this Option 1.

The deterrent effect of treating accident losses as a cost of the negligent operation of a vehicle is difficult to determine. What difference does having a negligence liability rule make in terms of reducing the level of negligent driving? The answer depends on what portion of the negligent driving that does not occur in a jurisdiction that has the rule would occur under a legal system that did not have the rule. It is that difference that represents the deterrent effect of a negligence rule of liability.

One way to assess the deterrent effect of potential liability for negligent driving might be to compare accident data from a jurisdiction that has adopted a system of no-fault automobile or accident insurance (a system without the rule) with data from a jurisdiction that has retained a negligence liability rule.[3] Unfortunately, the data do not permit a reliable conclusion to be drawn. In the first place, there are variables of time, geography, and driving patterns that would be difficult to reduce to some common factor. Perhaps even more important is the fact that every no-fault automobile insurance scheme permits victims of more serious accidents to assert common-law negligence claims. This residual negligence claim makes it impossible to say that drivers in no-fault states are totally unaffected by their exposure to liability for negligent driving.

In light of these difficulties, one might very well ask whether a negligence liability rule is likely to play much of a role in affecting the behavior of drivers. A highly skeptical view of the deterrent effect of tort law in general is offered in a recent book by Professor Stephen Sugarman.[4] Professor Sugarman bases his skepticism on such factors as the public's lack of knowledge of the content of legal rules, public ignorance of which particular instances of conduct those rules are likely to prohibit, the inability or unwillingness of some people to conform to those rules, and the common perception that the risk of being held liable is relatively small.[5] Those factors undoubtedly are important, but the relevant question here is whether at least *some* deterrent effect can be attributed to a liability rule.

To some extent, it makes sense to assume that the threat of liability might at least minimally deter negligent driving. Tort law, however, is only one of many influences on drivers' behavior, and it may very well not be the most significant one. What is likely to be the single most important factor is the risk of harm to the drivers themselves. Professor Sugarman also identifies market forces, moral inhibitions, and direct regulation as other factors besides tort law that can affect a driver's behavior.[6]

In considering the first option for allocating drinking-driver accident losses, it is important to recognize that the legal rules of our fault-based tort system do not exist in isolation. The dominant feature of this system is the ubiquitous presence of automobile liability insurance, which could produce significant effects in three ways. First, liability insurance may reduce the deterrent potential of a negligence liability rule. Second, it almost certainly does increase the ability of negligent drivers who are insured to bear the costs of accidents. Last, by spreading accident losses among a broad base of policyholders, liability insurance externalizes some of the accident costs for which drivers are held liable.

Is the presence of liability insurance likely to reduce the deterrent effect of potential tort liability? Implicit in this question is a concern that reduced deterrence might lead to an increase in negligent behavior and thus to an increase in the overall level of accident costs. There is room for a good deal of skepticism about such an effect, even despite the potential development of a "moral hazard" problem, in which the availability of insurance leads to an increased occurrence of the events covered by the insurance. Examples of the moral hazard phenomenon are easy to find, such as the unsuccessful business owner who conveniently suffers a fire that provides insurance proceeds at just the right time to enable the owner to avoid bankruptcy. It is almost always the case, however, that the insured event poses no significant risk of physical harm to the person who stands to benefit from the insurance proceeds. Even in the case of life insurance, the policy proceeds go to the beneficiary of the person who commits suicide, while the homicidal beneficiary acts in a way that places the insured, not the beneficiary, at risk. In any event, it is at least partly in response to the moral hazard problem that life insurance policies routinely exclude suicide of the policyholder as a covered event, at least within a year or two of the issuance of the policy, and that courts typically treat the murderer of the insured as someone who is prohibited from receiving the proceeds of the policy.

Leaving those cases aside, however, the temptation to profit from the availability of insurance is in general frequently tempered by a recognition of the threat of physical injury to oneself or to others. In the fire example, it is probably accurate to say that many business arsons occur at night when the premises are deserted, rather than at a time when the fire would create a substantial risk of harm to the owner or to employees and customers of the business. In the context of automobile liability insurance, however, given the fact that the driver and the passengers of a carelessly driven vehicle are themselves just as much at risk as anyone else within the vehicle's range of destructive power, it is unlikely that the presence of liability insurance reduces in any appreciable way the incentive to drive with reasonable care.

Nevertheless, liability insurance may reduce the monetary expenses that a driver incurs as a result of causing harm to others. Instead of internalizing the entire liability cost in the event of an accident, the insured driver will only have internalized the cost of the liability insurance premiums. Here too, though, the inclination to attribute an increase in accidents to the ability of insured drivers to avoid internalizing accident costs needs to be tempered by an understanding of other factors. First, the driver's insurance policy limits are likely to be exhausted by the most serious accident claims, and the claims in excess of policy limits represent the potential liability cost to the insured personally for negligent driving. Second, insured drivers who invoke their policy benefits may face higher future premiums and possibly even cancellation of their insurance. Thus automobile liability insurance may not significantly undermine the deterrent effect of legal liability in this setting.

If accident costs do exceed policy limits, a significant portion of the costs of the driver's negligence may be externalized to the accident victims. Insurance policy limits can be quickly exhausted in multiple-victim or serious injury accidents, leaving the victims with a claim on the driver's unprotected assets. The substantial legal protection given to the assets of judgment debtors may leave the typical drinking-driver defendant "judgment proof," because many of them are likely not to have any substantial assets beyond insurance. As a result, the driver will actually bear none of the additional losses that the accident victims suffered, regardless of the legal judgment declaring the damages the driver may owe to the victims.

A case of a judgment-proof defendant driver is a clear example of accident cost externalization. The victims' losses will in fact not be imposed on the negligent driver. Different types of externalization are possible. Some of the unrecovered damages will be costs that are left on the accident victims. Other portions of the accident costs might be shifted to additional defendants under a theory of vicarious liability or some other fault-based option for allocating drinking-driver accident costs.

The liability insurance policy itself is a device that externalizes accident costs for the driver who is held liable for the harm suffered by the victims of the accident. The private cost that the driver actually must internalize is not the amount of the tort judgment or settlement that the insurer is obligated to indemnify but rather only the amount of the insurance premium that the insured had paid in order to obtain that coverage. The sums paid to the accident victims out of the liability insurance fund that indemnifies the driver will be spread among the insurance policyholders who are in the same rate-making class as the driver. The insurance premiums of those policyholders will reflect the accident-liability loss experience of all the members of that class, including those who are held liable as drinking drivers.

It is important to note that this externalization of the drinking driver's accident liability costs is partially offset through the loss-spreading mechanism of liability insurance. Just as any particular insured driver's accident liability costs will be spread over a wider class of policyholders, so too will the losses of all the other policyholders in a rate-making class be spread over the other members that class, including this particular driver. Thus a certain degree of socialization of accident losses is already built into the liability insurance mechanism. Under existing insurance practices, the covered accident losses of individual policyholders are externalized to others who are within the same insurance rate-making class, while the individual policyholder who is held liable for a particular accident loss is forced to internalize at least a fraction of the accident losses for which the other class members are legally responsible.

The concept of spreading accident costs over a broad class of persons is important in countering objections to other cost allocation decisions that involve a socialization of drinking-driver accident costs over a different class of people, some of whom, it will be argued, do not drive while they are adversely affected by alcohol. Even in this clearest and simplest case of the first option, in which the victims' accident loses are assigned to someone other than the victims themselves, there will be an imperfect match between accident loss or risk-of-loss creation and accident loss internalization. Furthermore, the match that does take place will not reflect the extent to which the wider class of cost-bearers engages in the same culpable conduct as the defendant who actually caused a particular accident. It is instead a product of a less discriminating accident risk characterization that is shared by broadly defined classes of insurance policyholders who are treated identically for rate-making purposes by liability insurers. As a result of the accident cost externalization provided by automobile liability insurance, some portion of the costs that are caused by insured drinking drivers will be spread to people who share with drinking drivers the general characteristics of the members of particular rate-making classes. Every policyholder therefore bears some of the costs of the accident losses that are caused by the drinking drivers who are in the same rate-making class.

### Option 2. A Cost of Driving while Impaired by Alcohol

As was mentioned in the introduction to this chapter, there is a good deal of similarity in the effects of allocating the victims' accident costs under Option 1 and Option 2. Each of these options places the accident costs initially on the same person, the drinking driver. The same loss-shifting and loss-spreading possibilities and limitations that are provided by the driver's liability insurance in connection with Option 1 are also present in Option 2 as it is currently practiced. The conceptual difference between the two options turns on how the accident-producing activity of the drinking driver is characterized. Option 1 treats the accident costs of the victims as a cost of the drinking driver's negligent operation of a motor vehicle, however that negligence might be defined, while the second option focuses more narrowly on the driver's alcohol impairment. This difference tends to be fairly innocuous under contemporary tort law. Nevertheless, the different characterization of the driver's conduct that is offered in Option 2 is worth noting because of the significant effect that it could have on the decision of how to structure both the legal rules and the insurance practices that are applied to drinking-driver accidents.

If the losses of accident victims are treated as a cost of the negligent operation of the drinking driver's automobile, then the portion of those losses that are covered by the driver's automobile liability insurance will be spread over a base of other vehicle operators and insurance policyholders. All the policyholders who are in the same rate-making class as the drinking driver will have to bear a share of the accident losses caused by this driver and all the other drinking drivers in the class. The accident loss is spread across all members of the class whether or not any individual policyholder in that rate-making class drinks and drives. Option 2, however, characterizes the accident losses as a cost of drinking and driving rather than just driving (or driving negligently). It creates a basis, at least in principle, for setting up a different method for distributing the loss that would more precisely discriminate among policyholders according to whether they all engage in the same accident-causing activity. The rate-making classes could be structured so as to divide those drivers who drink from those who do not drink. Within the category of those who drink, further distinctions could be drawn between those who drink and drive and those who drink but do not drive after drinking. Because the relevant rate-making classification that would take this factor into account would be based on the practices of drivers rather than of the owners of the vehicles that are covered by the insurance policies, the distinctions that are contemplated by these additional categories would have to be based on a determination of the driving patterns of all those who could be deemed "insureds" under the standard insurance policy omnibus clause (see chapter 3).

There is a limit on the practicability of structuring insurance rate-making classes in a way that reflects the alcohol-related habits of those who are covered by the insurance policies. At some point in this classification process, the effort to introduce greater precision in rate-making will involve a greater expense than it is worth. Making additional refinements in identifying more narrowly drawn classes of policyholders will require more research effort than is currently demanded in automobile insurance underwriting. These refinements will also require lines to be drawn on subjective and changeable factors involving alcohol use and driving habits rather than on objective and more easily verifiable matters such as age and driving experience. Insurance premiums that are charged under this sort of rate-making scheme would arguably depend on whether any driver in the household drinks alcoholic beverages or whether anyone drives after drinking. How the accuracy of answers to questions such as those could be monitored by insurers is difficult to determine. The answer might never be known until an alcohol-related accident occurred. This discussion is therefore intended to provide an illustration, not necessarily to advocate a change in the rate-making classification system for automobile liability insurance. This example further illustrates the difficulty of matching, with any great degree of accuracy, the allocation of specific accident costs and the various activities that are involved in producing those accidents.

The discussion of Option 2 does suggest two possible lines of reform. First, a rate-making differential in automobile liability insurance premiums might justifiably be introduced for nondrinking households. Such a differential would reduce the externalization of the costs of drinking-driver accidents. Nondrinkers would be excluded from the rate-making population base that includes drinkers, just as nonsmokers are often put in a different health insurance rate-making class than are smokers. Nevertheless, the match between drinking-driver accident costs and the activity of drinking and driving would still be imperfect under this reform measure because some nondrinking drivers would come from households that contain drinkers and thus be forced to pay the higher rates. Furthermore, a likely consequence of this change in underwriting practices would be to drive up the cost of insurance for drinkers. In the long run this increase might produce an overall decrease in the size of the insurance fund available to compensate accident victims. With higher rates, drinkers might purchase less optional liability coverage above the minimum limits required by state law. In fact, more drivers might opt out or be priced out of the liability insurance market entirely. Thus, a seriously injured victim of a drinking driver might be left with having to pay an even greater portion of the accident costs.

One of the advantages of the broad-brushed insurance rate-making classification schemes that are currently used is that they spread losses over a group of people who do not pose precisely the same type and magnitude of risk of loss, thus making it possible or profitable for the insurance industry to underwrite the risks that are associated with specific subgroups within the class. This practice of risk-socialization through liability insurance is a useful mechanism for increasing the size of the insurance asset pool that accident victims are able to tap into. If that advantage must be sacrificed in order to obtain greater precision in defining rate-making classes, then the potential diminished ability of victims to satisfy judgments obtained against high-risk policyholders is a factor that needs to be taken into account.

The second possible reform is to exclude the activity of driving while alcohol-impaired from coverage entirely. The rationale for this reform could be that liability insurers are underwriting the normal or background risks associated with the operation of vehicles; the conduct of the drinking driver lies so far outside the scope of normal risk creation, it ought to be excluded from coverage. This reform is directly supported by provisions in some no-fault insurance statutes that authorize insurers to exclude first-party claims by their own policyholders for losses that are derived from accidents that occur when the policyholder was driving while intoxicated.[7] Indirect support could come from state statutes prohibiting the payment of punitive damages out of liability insurance funds and from statutes mandating that policies exclude from coverage the results of intentional wrongdoing by an insured. Drinking and driving, it might be argued, is an activity that is sufficiently analogous to intentional wrongdoing that the person who engages in that activity ought not to be able to use liability insurance to spread the accident costs. Those accident losses instead ought to be imposed in such a way that their full impact is felt by the drinking driver, according to this argument, in order to obtain to the fullest extent the social benefit of whatever deterrent effect might follow from an increase in the private cost that a drinking driver faces for engaging in that activity.

Excluding drinking-driver accidents from the scope of automobile liability insurance coverage is, on balance, a reform idea that requires too high a price for the benefits that might be obtained. However attractive the argument for excluding drinking-driver accident losses from coverage might seem, the obvious, and almost certainly unacceptable, effect would be to remove the most likely, and perhaps the only effective, source from which a significant number of accident victims could be compensated. If a drinking driver's conduct is not covered by automobile liability insurance, then the accident victim will frequently be left with a virtually unenforceable legal right to be compensated for the harm caused by that driver. That effect would in turn increase the pressure on courts and on legislatures to identify other more financially responsible actors and activities to which the accident losses of the victims could be allocated. As drinking drivers become less likely to be able to compensate their accident victims, legislation or common-law rulings would probably extend the scope of liability to parties in addition to the drinking drivers.

In what might seem to be a logical variant of the idea that liability insurance coverage should be denied to drinking drivers, Blue Cross and Blue Shield of Maryland has instituted a rule that denies medical insurance benefits for injuries that are suffered by repeat-offender drinking drivers. The exclusion is only supposed to come into effect upon a policyholder's second conviction for driving under the influence of alcohol, and the company has said that it will continue to make payments for medical expenses until the time of the conviction. After the conviction, the company will attempt to recover any payments from the policyholder.[8] As Professor Jacobs aptly points out, "taking this strategy to the limits of its logic might suggest denying medical care itself!"[9]

### Option 3. A Cost of Operating the Vehicle in Which the Victim Was Riding

Rather than treating the accident losses of the victims of drinking drivers as a cost of an activity engaged in by the drinking drivers, the third cost allocation option would treat those losses instead as a cost of the operation of the victims' own vehicles. The rationale for adopting this option is not complicated. One of the risks of driving is that the driver could be involved in a collision or in another type of accident in which serious harm occurs. Such accidents can happen in a variety of ways, whether through the fault of the driver of the victim's car, through some mechanical defect either in that car or in another vehicle, through the fault of some other driver, or even through the operation of some natural force that involves no fault on anyone's part. Under the view of accident cost allocation that supports the use of Option 3, the fortuity of a traffic accident being caused by a drinking driver would not change the underlying assumption that driving on a highway is a risky enterprise that has attached to it not only the easily identifiable costs of operating an automobile such as loan payments and fuel costs, but also accident costs.

Anyone who has lived in a state that has adopted no-fault automobile insurance is well aware that this third option for allocating accident costs is neither a fanciful idea nor a purely theoretical one. It is instead arguably a rational solution to the difficulties that are encountered in using a fault-based tort litigation system to shift and spread the costs of traffic accidents.[10] Rather than submit the most common type of accident claim to the expense and the delay of a lawsuit, the no-fault insurance alternative treats it as an insurance matter, to be compensated from the injured party's own insurer.[11] No-fault insurance premiums are therefore supposed to be calculated in theory on a first-party claims basis, with the insurer determining its risk exposure by asking how much of the covered harm the insured is likely to *suffer* during the period the policy is in effect. Liability insurance, on the other hand, covers claims that are made against the insured on a third-party basis, which requires the insurer to ask how much of the covered harm the insured is likely to *cause* and be held liable for during the same period. The divergence that exists between the theory of no-fault automobile insurance schemes and the practice that is actually followed in states with some version of no-fault automobile insurance reveals the more significant adverse consequences of relying exclusively on Option 3 and treating drinking-driver accident victims' losses as a cost of the operation of their vehicles.

The nearly universally accurate assessment that can be made about no-fault automobile insurance as it has been implemented in this country is that in practice the no-fault theory has fallen a good distance short of its promise. Rather than treat all traffic accident losses as matters that are to be compensated by a driver's own first-party no-fault insurer, most of the states that have adopted a no-fault plan use it as an exclusive remedy only at the lowest level of accident losses.[12] When injury costs rise above a threshold set by the governing no-fault statute, the victim is entitled to sue the driver under a common-law negligence theory of liability. The lower the threshold is set, the higher will be the number of traffic accidents that lead to tort litigation. Furthermore, if the statutory threshold is not amended periodically to reflect both the general rate of inflation and increases in the amount of damages the local tort system is generally awarding, the no-fault insurance system might end up with a diminishing percentage of traffic accidents within its exclusive grasp. And because the no-fault insurance policyholders may also be involved in accidents in which other people

suffer injuries whose costs go over the threshold, each insurance policyholder also needs to carry ordinary automobile liability insurance.
The costs of insurance under a no-fault scheme in which the threshold
is set too low can predictably exceed the costs of liability insurance
in a state without a no-fault system. When the threshold is low, insurers
must charge higher premiums to pay for losses that are covered by
the no-fault system as well losses that take an accident case out of
that system and into the tort system.

The experience of states with no-fault schemes suggests that our
society is fairly strongly reluctant to treat any but the most minor
accident losses as a cost of operation of a person's own vehicle. Another
sign of this reluctance is the controversy over how high to set the
threshold for accident loss that would allow the victim to maintain a
tort claim. This no-fault cost-allocation option requires an accident
victim to internalize accident costs in full, at least as an initial matter,
while allowing drivers who are at fault in causing the accidents to
externalize the costs. In general it would seem that our society accepts
the no-fault system's way of treating accident costs only at the lower
levels of harm. Its acceptability in principle undoubtedly comes from
a sense that the cost to the legal system of handling smaller accident
claims exceeds the benefits. The acceptability of using the tort system
for accident claims above a certain magnitude may reflect a sentiment
that there is a societal benefit in making a fault determination first
and then shifting of accident losses to the person at fault.

### Option 4. A Cost of Living in a Crowded and Complex Society

Option 4 is an extension of the approach that was taken in Option
3, which treats the losses suffered by victims of drinking-driver traffic
accidents as a cost of operating the vehicle in which they were riding
at the time. Whereas Option 3 treats driving in general as a risky
enterprise, Option 4 deems such accident losses to be a normal cost
of living in today's complex society.

The rationale for Option 3 was that not much significance should
be attached to the fortuity that a particular traffic accident is caused
by a drinking driver. Under Option 4, the risky enterprise is not
driving, but simply living. Simply conducting the activities of a normal
life in a society that presents many encounters with other people and
many occasions for harm to occur is a risky enterprise. Furthermore,
some harm results from self-created risks and natural causes as well.
With as many opportunities to suffer harm as we face every day,

Option 4 would assert, no undue significance should be attached to the fact that an injury occurred in a traffic accident or the fact that it involved a drinking driver.

Having initially chosen in Option 4 to treat accident costs as a general cost of living, a society would still need to decide whether those costs should be left to the private methods of loss spreading that are available to the individual victims or whether instead those losses should be broadly socialized through a governmental mechanism. This country probably comes closest to using the first approach for those losses that are not shifted away from the victims through the operation of tort liability rules. For much of the population, the risks of large medical expenses and interrupted income flow are spread over a broader population base through the purchase of health, disability, and life insurance. Indeed, because of the delay that an accident victim normally encounters in obtaining the compensation that is available through the tort litigation system, these individual or group insurance policies are frequently the first line of loss-spreading protection on which the average individual must rely.

New Zealand has come closest to adoption of the second approach of a broader socialization of accident costs.[13] As is true of the general experience in this country under no-fault automobile insurance, however, this sort of comprehensive accident compensation scheme is characterized by a relatively low level of benefits provided to injured claimants, at least for benefits provided directly through the accident compensation plan. This relatively low level of benefits from the plan does not necessarily mean that an accident victim will be disadvantaged by being denied the opportunity to pursue larger amounts of recovery through a tort claim against the person who caused the injury. That disadvantage is comparatively less in a society in which medical care is provided at little or no cost and in which the financial dislocation that results from accident-related unemployment is relatively well cushioned. Accident losses in that society can place less strain on an accident compensation plan than would occur in a society such as ours, in which the normal provision of medical services and income protection depends on a private insurance market that presents significant problems of availability and affordability.

A comprehensive accident compensation plan that was enacted to implement Option 4 could be financed through taxes that were calculated according to the general level of risk that the taxpayer posed to others. The closer that the tax rate approximated the accident risk that was created by the taxpayer, there would be less externalization of the accident costs that are associated with the activities that are conducted by the taxpayer. As with the liability insurance modifications that were sketched out in connection with Option 2, however, achieving any sort of precision in this process is likely to be extremely expensive, given the fact that all activities that pose a risk of harm should be included in the taxpaying base that is used to support this kind of universal compensation plan.

### Option 5. A Cost of the Employment Enterprise of the Drinking Driver

In cases in which a drinking driver is acting within the scope of employment at the time of an accident that causes injuries to other people, the tort system may impose the losses that were suffered by those victims on the driver's employer through a vicarious liability doctrine.[14] The economic consequences of that sort of accident loss allocation decision involve some significant differences from those attached to Options 1-4.

The first difference worth noting is in the deterrent effect that might be expected from implementing Option 5. Vicarious liability imposes accident costs on a party who was not at fault and who did not personally cause the accident. As a result, any deterrent effect in terms of reducing accidents will almost certainly involve indirect action on the part of the employer. Economic analysts of legal rules have identified the imposition of vicarious liability on an employer, for example, as a way to increase the level of care exercised by employees who lack sufficient assets to satisfy tort judgments on their own. The prospect of receiving sanctions from the employer could provide a greater incentive for the judgment-proof employee to exercise reasonable care than that created by the largely empty threat of tort liability.[15]

The most socially beneficial course of action on the part of an employer who faces a prospect of being held vicariously liable would be to select more responsible employees and to train and instruct them to avoid drinking and driving. Taking steps along these lines may at least lower the frequency with which employment-related drinking-driver accidents take place. But an equally effective way for an employer to escape vicarious liability is to structure its enterprise to avoid meeting the prerequisites for the imposition of liability in case such a claim is brought when an accident actually does occur. One option would be to arrange its relationships with employees in such a way that those who perform tasks for the employer are classified as independent contractors rather than as servants for whose wrongdoing the employer is normally held liable. Another option would be for an employer to arrange its business practices in a way that keeps the drinking and driving of the employee more strictly confined to the personal conduct of the employee rather than allowing it to be considered part of the employment enterprise. These two options may be effective means of reducing the tort liability of employers, but they are unlikely to produce any beneficial effect in reducing the frequency of drinking-driver accidents. Furthermore, there may be some net societal loss as a result of the employer's expenditure of time and energy on the task of avoiding vicarious liability, when those resources might be better spent in carrying out the duties of the enterprise itself or perhaps even in addressing more directly the accident problem that is associated with the enterprise.

The second major difference that comes into play with the choice of Option 5 concerns the loss-bearing capacity of the defendant upon whom the accident losses are being placed. As an employee for whose conduct the employer can be held vicariously liable, the drinking driver will normally be engaged in some activity that furthers the business purpose of the employer. The employer's business often provides an opportunity to pass on or to spread the costs of the accidents that are shifted to the employer that is not available to individual drivers, who are considered as the loss bearers under Options 1-4. If the employer is engaged in a business that provides a service or a product to another segment of the population, then the price charged for it can be adjusted to reflect the accident costs or, more likely, the costs of insuring against liability for them. Employers may be put at a competitive disadvantage as a result of passing on these accident costs to their consumers. If those disadvantages are significant enough, an employer may be subjected to market pressure to reduce the scope of its vicarious liability. As mentioned above, however, that pressure will not necessarily cause the employer to engage in efforts to reduce the frequency of drinking-driver accidents.

The passing on of accident costs to the consumers who pay for the vicariously liable employer's activity is a third new feature of this fifth cost allocation option. Each of the previous options involved some degree of externalization of the accident costs away from the activity that was most directly responsible for the accident, which is assumed to be the conduct of the drinking driver. With this fifth option, accident costs are externalized to a population that is only indirectly related to the accident by virtue of its consumption of the goods or services provided by the vicariously liable employer. This effect can be defended, however, with a fairly strong argument. Passing accident costs along to consumers may raise prices enough to affect consumer demand adversely. If that is the case, then the level of production will fall, and with it, the frequency of the accidents associated with it. Of course, a number of assumptions in this economic argument may simply not be borne out in a particular instance in the real world. Nevertheless, this fifth option, more than the previously discussed options, introduces in a more striking fashion the effect that accident cost allocation decisions can have on the price and the demand for a product. That effect may in turn produce an indirect effect on the frequency of the underlying activity associated with the accident losses.

Tort liability rules involve decisions about the allocation of accident costs and the distribution of risks. A significant feature of the vicarious liability rules that are applied in contemporary American tort law is that they introduce a specific type of risk distribution that is related to the possibility that a person whose wrongful conduct has caused harm will lack sufficient resources with which to compensate for that harm. In the standard employment-related vicarious liability cases, the three relevant actors are an accident victim, a negligent employee, and an employer who has not been negligent. If the negligent employee were able to satisfy a tort judgment for the costs of the victim's injuries the victim would be largely indifferent to the potential vicarious liability of the employer. It is when the employee is for all practical purposes judgment-proof that the vicarious liability rules become significant vehicles for risk distribution.[16]

The significant risk that is distributed by the vicarious liability option is the risk that the negligent employee will be financially unable to compensate for the harm that has been caused by the employee. In the absence of a rule imposing vicarious liability on the employer, that risk lies with the accident victim. When vicarious liability is introduced, the employer is put in the position of having to compensate the victim, and it is then the employer rather than the victim who possesses a legal but practically worthless right to obtain compensation. Specifically, the employer becomes entitled to complete indemnification from the negligent employee up to the amount of the damages that had to be paid to the victim.

An important way to view the question of whether to choose this fifth option of imposing of vicarious liability, then, is to see it as asking whether the risk that a negligent employee may be judgment-proof is better left on the accident victim or whether it should be shifted to the employer. By and large, the doctrinal devices currently used to determine whether vicarious liability is properly imposed in a particular traffic accident case, such as the control and the benefit tests to decide whether a negligent employee was acting within the scope of employment, can resolve this particular risk distribution issue in an economically satisfactory manner.[17] When an employee is acting within the scope of employment (under the control of an employer or is acting for the benefit of an employer), the risk that the employee will be financially unable to pay damages is more appropriately placed on the employer (who is unable as a practical matter to enforce the legal right to obtain indemnity from the employee) than on the victim (who is unable as a practical matter to get the employee to satisfy a tort judgment that is obtainable against the employee).

*Option 6. A Cost of a Commercial Transaction Involving the Furnishing of Alcohol to the Drinking Driver*

Tort liability under a dram shop act or under a common-law dispenser liability theory will have the effect of allocating some of the costs of drinking-driver traffic accidents to the activity of serving or selling alcoholic beverages to the person who drinks and drives. This sixth loss allocation option shares some features in common with the preceding five options.

As long as the liability that is imposed on commercial dispensers is based on fault rather than a strict liability theory, allocating accident losses to dispensers might deter the conduct that leads to those accidents. A dispenser who exercises reasonable care to avoid serving or selling alcoholic beverages to patrons who are under the legal drinking age or who are already intoxicated can escape liability in most of the states that have recognized a commercial dispenser liability theory. Avoiding high premiums for liquor liability insurance is an incentive to reduce a dispenser's liability exposure by developing and following safer practices in the service and the sale of alcohol.[18] These practices may in turn reduce the frequency of drinking-driver accidents. Commercial dispensers who adopt responsible service practices that control the provision of alcohol to their patrons may help keep a greater number of drinking drivers off the highway or at least reduce the degree to which they are alcohol-impaired.

To the extent that accidents continue to occur as a result of irresponsible conduct by commercial dispensers, it generally makes sense for commercial dispensers to bear the loss and for the cost of those accidents to be externalized to their customers under this sixth cost allocation option. A commercial dispenser is, by definition, engaged in an enterprise that has a customer base across which the accident costs or the relevant liability insurance costs can be spread. Additionally, the accident-cost externalization that does take place as a result of the dispenser passing on the accident costs to its customers means that the costs are ultimately being spread among a population of consumers of alcoholic beverages in commercial transactions that can lead to dispenser liability.

Aside from the class of drinking drivers themselves, this group of people may be one of the most appropriate segments of the population to whom the costs of drinking-driver traffic accidents can be imposed. A number of hypotheses, to the extent that they are accurate, support this conclusion. For example, younger drivers who purchase alcoholic beverages at convenience stores may be more responsive to price increases than other consumers. And drinkers who are served alcohol at commercial establishments may have a higher propensity to drink and drive than the rest of the drinking population at large. Shifting the accident losses of the victims of drinking drivers to commercial dispensers who then pass on the cost to their patrons may force the portion of the drinking population that creates most of the drinking-driver accident risk to bear some of the costs of those accidents in the price that they pay for their alcoholic beverages.

Another important factor ought to be taken into account when assessing the economic consequences of treating accident-victim losses as a cost of a commercial sale or service of alcohol. Tort liability is almost always imposed on a commercial dispenser of alcohol on the basis of unlawful conduct as defined by statutes or regulations that operate independently of whether the dispenser's conduct leads to a drinking-driver traffic accident. Prohibitions on the sale or service of alcohol to minors and to persons who are already intoxicated reflect societal judgments about the standard of behavior that is appropriate for commercial dispensers. Dispensing alcohol to people in those categories is deemed to be wrong regardless of whether the patron drives after drinking or not. The cost of enforcing those prohibitions can be so high, however, that in practice enforcement of the regulations falls far short of the goal. The fact that enforcement is not perfect should not be surprising, though. An awfully high number of firms are licensed to sell and to serve alcoholic beverages compared to the very few inspectors available to enforce the regulations. Furthermore, the enforcement of these regulations may be fairly low on the list of priorities for criminal law enforcement agencies.

A commercial dispenser may rationally conclude that the cost of sanctions, discounted to reflect the improbability of a violation being detected, is not a sufficient deterrent to justify taking steps to avoid liability, especially when those steps would otherwise not be profitable. In that case, imposing tort liability on commercial dispensers for wrongfully serving drinking drivers can raise the cost of noncompliance. It also provides an incentive for victims to fill some of the gap in enforcement left by the official law enforcement structure as they attempt to prove their tort claim. Finally, the tort damages themselves serve in effect as an additional sanction on the unlawful behavior of the commercial dispenser. An accident cost-allocation decision that includes Option 6 can therefore effectively supplement or reinforce the legal prohibition of certain conduct by commercial dispensers of alcohol.

### Option 7. A Cost of Hosting a Social Function at Which the Drinking Driver Is Served Alcohol

The tort liability theories that impose liability on social hosts are a means of at least partially implementing the accident cost allocation scheme behind Option 7. There is a good deal of tension among the various strands of the economic analysis of this option for allocating accident loss. The basic conflict is between the goal of deterring accidents and the disruption in forcing social hosts who might be held liable to bear the costs of these accidents. One might expect that Option 7 would do a better job of meeting the goal of marginal deterrence than just about any of the other options that have been surveyed, but the limited opportunities of the class of social hosts to spread the loss may make this a markedly inferior option for shifting accident losses away from drinking-driver accident victims to other parties.

The major innovation that Option 7 introduces into the loss allocation picture is its addition of a new class of people, social hosts, who might be held liable for the accident losses of the victims of drinking drivers. In the typical social-host situation, the conduct of the new potential defendants is directly related to the service of alcohol to a guest who is visiting and can be expected to have to travel, most often by automobile. The potential liability of a social host to the victims of a guest who causes an accident after a social occasion may have more of a deterrent effect on behavior than any of the other loss allocation options that have been considered.

Without the prospect of liability, the decision of whether and how to serve alcoholic beverages to social guests can easily be seen as a matter solely of the price of alcohol and the desired tone of the occasion. Within those constraints, how much a guest chooses to consume is thus a matter of the guest's own responsibility. Once a host is made aware of the possibility that the conditions of alcohol service could provide a basis for liability to victims of a guest who drinks and drives, an important new factor must be included in the host's decision-making process. A class of people who formerly may have been indifferent and fairly oblivious to the social consequences of their behavior may face an eye-opening realization of those consequences in the wake of a decision that recognizes social-host liability.

It is not necessary to rely just on intuition to support that premise. The speed and the vehemence with which state legislatures have typically rejected a court's adoption of a social-host liability theory provides very strong evidence that this is a loss allocation decision that has immediate and dramatic effects on the potential new defendants. It is possible that the legislative response to judicially imposed social host liability is simply a cheap political maneuver that has no real drive behind it. However, given the number of state legislatures that have acted to narrow or to eliminate social host liability, one might conclude that there is genuine popular concern over the prospect of a social host being held liable to the victims of a drinking-driver guest and that this is a sufficiently significant departure from the status quo that the effects of such liability would actually be felt with some considerable impact.

The legislative response thus far in most of the states that have flirted with social host liability suggests that this is literally, as well as figuratively, an accident cost allocation decision that "hits home." The beneficial deterrent effect that social host liability might have in reducing the frequency of drinking-driver traffic accidents involving social guests might be offset by the new rule's drastic effect on the population that would be exposed to the risk of liability. A social host's homeowner's insurance may or may not cover the losses connected with the new liability. Because most of the drinking-driver accidents caused by guests occur off the premises of the host, they may fall outside the scope of the harms that are covered by the typical policy. If they are covered by a policy, the most predictable effect of recognizing social host liability would be a fairly substantial increase in premiums.

In addition, Option 7 differs from Options 5 and 6 with respect to the ability of the party held liable to pass on the cost to other parties — either liability costs or insurance costs. Employers of those who drink and drive while acting within the scope of their employment and commercial dispensers of alcohol to customers who drink and drive will usually have a broader consumer base across which to spread the costs relating to their liability. Social hosts, on the other hand, will typically not have any significant loss-spreading ability beyond homeowner's liability insurance. If the adoption of a theory of social host tort liability raises premiums significantly, homeowner's insurance will be less affordable and perhaps, then, less available, further hampering the ability of social hosts to spread the costs associated with their new liability. Furthermore, should the homeowner's insurance industry suddenly be faced with liability claims against their social host policyholders, the industry would probably respond by writing exclusions into the policies it sells in the future.

## Option 8. The Ignored Option: A Cost of Manufacturing and Distributing Alcoholic Beverages

The eighth and final option for allocating the accident costs of the victims of drinking drivers adopts a focus that has largely been ignored in the legal schemes of contemporary tort law and compensation for injury. Under this option, more attention will be given to the role played by those who are responsible for making available the alcoholic beverages that drinking drivers consume. While the commercial dispenser and social host theories of tort liability that underlie Options 6 and 7 treat drinking-driver accident losses as a cost of the activity that directly placed the alcoholic beverages in the hand of the drinking driver, this eighth option shifts some of the responsibility for those losses farther up the chain of distribution of alcoholic beverages. The next chapter presents arguments in support of a compensation system that includes a mechanism for attaching the drinking-driver accident costs to the segments of the alcohol industry that have control over the beverages before they are made available for retail sale or service to the ultimate consumer. A preliminary look at some objections that are likely to be raised in terms of an economic analysis of such a cost-allocation decision will also be presented in this concluding chapter of part 2.

### NOTES

1. Economists use the term property rights in a variety of ways. The meaning of the term as it is used in this text includes rights that involve the possession, use, and enjoyment of land.

2. This discussion of reciprocal risks draws on the work of George Fletcher in which he attempts to develop a unified theory of tort liability from the notion of reciprocity. *See* Fletcher, *Fairness and Utility in Tort Theory*, 85 HARV. L. REV. 537 (1972).

3. *See, e.g.,* Brown, *Deterrence in Tort and No-Fault: The New Zealand Experience,* 73 CALIF. L. REV. 976 (1985).

4. S. SUGARMAN, DOING AWAY WITH PERSONAL INJURY LAW: NEW COMPENSATION MECHANISMS FOR VICTIMS, CONSUMERS, AND BUSINESS (1989).

5. *Id.* at 6-12.

6. *Id.* at 4-6.

7. *See, e.g.,* N.Y. INS. LAW § 5103(b)(2) (McKinney 1985).

8. Duke, *Blue Cross Stops Paying Repeat Drunk Drivers' Bills,* Washington Post, Jan. 6, 1990, at B3, col. 1.

9. JACOBS, DRUNK DRIVING, at 133.

10. *See generally* R. KEETON & J. O'CONNELL, BASIC PROTECTION FOR THE TRAFFIC VICTIM: A BLUEPRINT FOR REFORMING AUTOMOBILE INSURANCE (1965).

11. The most accessible account for the general reader of the nature and the operation of a no-fault automobile insurance scheme is R. KEETON & J. O'CONNELL, AFTER CARS CRASH: THE NEED FOR LEGAL AND INSURANCE REFORM (1967).

12. Some no-fault statutes provide for fairly extensive benefits. *See, e.g.,* MICH. COMP. LAWS ANN. § 500.3107 (West 1989 & Supp. 1990).

13. *See* G. PALMER, COMPENSATION FOR INCAPACITY: A STUDY OF LAW AND SOCIAL CHANGE IN NEW ZEALAND AND AUSTRALIA (1979); Brown, *Deterrence in Tort and No-Fault: The New Zealand Experience,* 73 CALIF. L. REV. 976 (1985); Gaskins, *Tort Reform in the Welfare State: The New Zealand Accident Compensation Act,* 18 OSGOODE HALL L. J. 238 (1980).

14. Although the discussion of Option 5 presented in the text focuses only on the allocation of the accident costs to the employer of the drinking driver, the basic points about accident deterrence and accident cost externalization are equally applicable to the other categories of parties upon whom vicarious liability may be imposed.

15. *See* SHAVELL, ECONOMIC ANALYSIS, at 170-75; LANDES & POSNER, ECONOMIC STRUCTURE, at 121.

16. *See* Sykes, *The Economics of Vicarious Liability,* 93 YALE L. J. 1231 (1984).

17. *See id.* at 1268-69.

18. *See* 2 MOSHER, LIQUOR LIABILITY LAW, at Appendix B. The Model Alcoholic Beverage Retail Licensee Liability Act presented in Appendix B has been adopted in part in a handful of states. The central feature of the model act is the recognition of a dispenser's use of responsible business practices as a defense to a claim asserted against a commercial dispenser. The commentary to the act states that the drafters hope that the adoption of the act with this defense will reduce the cost of liability insurance to those who implement these practices.

# 11

## The Case for an Alcohol Tax
## to Finance Compensation

An analysis of the different consequences for accident prevention and loss allocation attached to the various tort liability rules that have been presented thus far might make use of the elaborate mathematical economic analytical models employed by such scholars as Richard Posner, William Landes, and Steven Shavell. Indeed, Harold Votey, a professor of economics at the University of California at Santa Barbara, has contributed a sophisticated version of such an analysis to a recently published study of the drinking-driver problem.[1] Such studies are useful in arriving at a deeper understanding of the economic consequences of legal rules and for developing an additional dimension to the arguments that might be made for and against particular rules.

In the drinking-driver context, however, we already know, with a substantial degree of certainty, one all-important fact about the relationship between legal rules and accident costs: our legal system's current civil and criminal liability rules have produced an unsatisfactory state of affairs from a public policy perspective. The various techniques now used to impose legal sanctions on the drinking driver and to assign legal responsibility for the costs of drinking-driver accidents, in conjunction with a variety of other social control factors, have only had limited success in reducing the frequency of drinking-driver traffic accidents and the severity of the losses that victims suffer no lower than their current levels. If this level of losses attributable to drinking-driver accidents is socially unacceptable, despite all that is being done under the present legal regime, then clearly there is room for an attempt to implement additional measures beyond those that have been adopted thus far. A compensation fund should be established for the accident victims of drinking drivers, financed by a special tax on alcoholic beverages. A broad outline of this measure follows, and it demonstrates how the proposed new tax can be justified under the economic analysis used in the preceding two chapters of part 2.

The best starting point for understanding the rationale for this reform proposal is to look at a recurrent theme in the public-policy examination of the drinking-driver problem in contemporary society. Much of the literature on alcohol in general and on the drinking-driver problem in particular asserts that the public costs or the social costs of alcohol are inadequately represented in the price that the consumer pays for alcoholic beverages. The discussions that have been presented so far in this book demonstrate that there is ample reason to conclude that the underpricing of alcoholic beverages is not alleviated by contemporary tort law. Employing some or all of the current options for assigning legal responsibility for drinking-driver accident losses falls well short of effectively remedying that inadequacy by attempting to attach those losses to the activity of drinking drivers. Even when potential tort liability to accident victims is factored into the calculation of what it costs the drinking driver to drink and drive and cause traffic accidents, a substantial part of this portion of the social cost of alcohol is not reflected in the price the alcohol consumer pays.

The obvious next step for public policymakers who are faced with this discrepancy between private costs and social costs is to address the inadequacy directly through the taxation system, rather than being limited to operating only indirectly through the tort liability system.[2] Accordingly, a growing body of literature in the public policy and the social science fields proposes that the excise tax on alcohol be raised so that the price the consumer must pay for alcohol is increased to come more into line with the social cost of alcohol. In 1989 some of these academic studies were translated into a call for a statewide initiative in California to impose what is in effect a five-cent-per-drink tax on alcohol to help fund institutional efforts to meet the social costs of alcohol in terms of emergency room care, mental health programs, and law enforcement efforts.[3] Although that initiative was defeated in the 1990 election, the idea is one that is likely to surface again.[4]

Alcoholic beverages are currently subject to both federal and state excise taxes. Prior to 1991, the federal excise tax rate was $12.50 per gallon of 100-proof distilled spirits (spirits with an alcohol content of 50 percent) or gallon of wine with an alcohol content greater than 24 percent. Wine with a lower alcohol content was taxed on a sliding scale, from 17 cents per gallon up to 14 percent alcohol, 67 cents per gallon up to 21 percent alcohol, and $2.25 per gallon up to 24 percent alcohol. Beer was subject to a federal excise tax of $9 per barrel of thirty-one gallons, with smaller brewers paying only $7 per barrel on their first sixty thousand barrels of production.[5] During the Reagan and Bush administrations, pressure to raise the excise tax on alcoholic beverages was regularly exerted as a way to reduce the budget deficit rather than as a way to earmark funds to ameliorate the social costs of alcohol. That pressure was successful in producing increases in the federal excise tax rates as part of the Omnibus Budget Reconciliation Act of 1990. Under that statute, the basic rate on distilled spirits was raised from $12.50 to $13.50. Wine was subjected to a proportionally higher rate of increase, particularly at the lower levels of alcohol content. The rate in the lowest alcohol content category went from 17 cents to $1.07, with the higher categories raised from 67 cents and $2.25 to $1.57 and $3.15, respectively. The tax rate on beer was doubled form $9 to $18.[6]

States also typically vary the excise tax rate according to the type of alcoholic beverage. Virginia provides a good illustration of a state in which the basic excise tax on alcohol is assessed in two different categories, reflecting the fact that Virginia has a system of government stores for the sale of alcoholic beverages other than beer and most wines. For beverages sold through government stores, the excise tax, as fixed by state statute, is 40 cents on each liter of wine, 4 percent of the price charged for vermouth and wine produced by farm wineries, and 20 percent of the price charged for other alcoholic beverages.[7] Beer and other fermented beverages that are not sold through government stores are subject to an excise tax, when sold in barrels, at the rate of $7.95 per thirty-one gallons. For beer and beverages sold in bottles, the rate varies according to the size of the bottle, from 2 cents per bottle (7 oz. or less), to 2.65 cents per bottle (12 oz. or less but over 7 oz.), to 2.22 mills per ounce per bottle (more than 12 oz.).[8] Massachusetts is a good example of a state without government stores that permits the sale of alcoholic beverages in private stores. Under its excise tax system beer and other malt beverages are taxed at a rate of $3.30 a barrel, distilled spirits at a rate of $4.05 per proof gallon, and wine at a rate that ranges from 3 cents to $1.10 per gallon according to the alcohol content of the wine.[9] These examples illustrate that the variations in tax rates can address a variety of matters, including sales packaging, the size of the business selling alcohol, and the type of beverage being taxed.

A group of researchers from the University of Michigan and other institutions recently reported in the *Journal of the American Medical Association* on a study of the relationship between tax rates and the cost of alcohol. They concluded that the federal and state excise taxes on alcohol fail to cover the external costs of heavy drinking (defined as alcohol consumption in excess of two drinks per day) by somewhere between 15 and 63 cents per ounce of alcohol above those first two drinks, depending on various assumptions.[10]

The Surgeon General's Workshop on Drunk Driving similarly concluded that the social costs of alcohol needed to be reflected more fully in the price of alcoholic beverages both by restructuring and by increasing the rate of excise taxes. The workshop offered a three-part recommendation regarding changes in the way that excise taxes are imposed on alcohol: first, equalize the tax rate according to the ethanol content of alcoholic beverages (this would require a substantial increase in beer and wine taxes); second, adjust the tax rates to account for past inflation (which had led to an effective decrease in the rates over the last forty years); and third, index future tax rates to a price index so that annual adjustments for inflation can be made.[11] Those changes in alcohol taxes, it was estimated, could eliminate between 8,400 and 11,000 fatalities a year.[12]

The proposal at the heart of this book begins with the proposition that a tax increase on alcoholic beverages should be imposed at the state level. The resulting funds should not be used to add to the state's general revenues. Instead, the new alcohol tax should be used to finance the operation of a compensation fund that makes up for the tort system's shortcomings in adequately compensating the victims of drinking drivers. The benefit of such a fund would begin to be felt at the point at which a state's tort liability rules begin to leave accident victims undercompensated. The remainder of this chapter presents the arguments for linking the proposal for an excise tax increase on alcoholic beverages to a fund that will supplement the injury-compensation function that the legal system now performs.[13]

My proposal for the creation of a compensation fund for alcohol-related accident victims brings together two components—an alcoholic beverage tax and a new method for compensating injuries—in one reform effort. Raising the price of alcohol by identifying some of the costs of drinking-driver accident injuries as a business cost of the alcohol industry creates an opportunity to achieve two major aims. First, the compensatory aspects of this accident cost-allocation proposal respond to some of the more compelling rationales for reforming the way the legal system currently treats the victims of drinking-driver accidents to reduce the extent to which more seriously injured victims are forced to bear their own losses. Second, the new tax proposed to finance the victim compensation system will force the alcohol industry to internalize those accident costs to a much greater extent than is currently the case. That internalization can create the basis for achieving a higher level of efficiency in our society's use of resources in the production and consumption of alcoholic beverages. The initial effect of the new tax on alcohol would be an increase in the price of alcohol so that it more accurately reflects the social costs of alcohol. That price increase can in turn be justified by its two further effects: it will reduce the impact of accident victims' losses and it will allocate accident costs more efficiently than the current system of underpricing alcohol compared to its social costs.

The key feature of the victim compensation system I propose is its injury-compensation function accomplished through a tax increase. It is not primarily a tax increase measure that has an incidental compensatory function. One of the strongest arguments that can be made in favor of imposing some of these accident costs on the alcohol industry focuses on the fact that so many of the victims of drinking drivers are innocent bystanders. A surprisingly large number of drinking-driver traffic accident cases examined in part 1 of this book fall into the pattern of a drinking driver striking an automobile containing the members of a family, often killing or seriously injuring one or more of them. Forcing innocent victims to cope with the financial consequences of a catastrophic accident while they are coping with the emotional trauma of experiencing a family member's injury or death is an insult that our society ought to avoid. To the extent that current tort remedies fall short of fully compensating the victims of drinking drivers, the search for another entity to bear the accident costs becomes that much more compelling.

An objection might well be raised at this point whether a victim undercompensation problem really does exist. Empirical research on the point is admittedly necessary, but it is important to understand precisely what needs to be measured. Each state presents a unique combination of legal and practical factors that affect the manner and the degree to which accident victims are compensated for their injuries. As a result of the disparate experiences among the states, each state should be studied individually. Within each state, the critical measurement is the extent to which the victims of drinking-driver accidents are forced to bear their own losses, that is, what amount of accident costs are *not* shifted away from the victims of those losses. The fewer the options there are for loss-shifting in a particular state, the more likely it is that an undercompensation problem exists. In any event, each state that considers adopting the reform proposed here will have to determine, in at least a rough way, how effectively accident costs are shifted away from victims in that state, given the legal rules that affect the recovery of compensation and the practical experience in assessing damages and collecting them under those legal rules.

The second general argument for allocating the costs of drinking-driver accidents to the alcohol industry is based on an allocative efficiency rationale. The new tax that would fund the system will increase the price of alcoholic beverages to better reflect more of the social cost of alcohol. Because externalized costs are unlikely to be reflected in the price of a product, they are also unlikely to be taken into account by consumers. As a result, to the extent that the level of consumption is driven by price or is responsive to price, it will not reflect the accident costs that are attributable to the product. If the costs of accidents involving drinking drivers are imposed on the parts of the alcohol industry that are currently able to avoid them, then the price of the product is likely to increase, and at least some decrease in consumption is likely to follow.

The superiority of a tax-financed compensation system in allocating costs efficiently compared with the variety of tort remedies currently available is even stronger when one compares cost internalization in the products liability context and the drinking driver context. One argument for imposing strict liability on the product manufacturer for a defective product was to avoid the inefficiency of having to rely on a series of indemnity or breach-of-warranty actions to shift accident losses up the chain of distribution and ultimately to the product manufacturer.[14] The prospect of an accident victim imposing tort liability on a commercial dispenser or a social host—the closest equivalents to the product retailer in the products liability context—is uneven at best. Even when some route to imposing that liability on dispensers of alcohol is made available within a jurisdiction, it is not at all clear that the dispenser can establish a basis for indemnity from the dispenser's manufacturer or distributor, given the absence of contractual provisions to that effect and the arguably nondefective nature of the alcoholic beverage product being marketed. As a result, to the extent that the price of alcohol does reflect drinking-driver traffic-accident costs under present legal rules, it is likely only to reflect that portion of the total costs that is imposed on the commercial dispenser. In effect, commercial dispensers constitute the only level of the alcohol industry that faces the realistic prospect of having to internalize drinking-driver accident costs (through statutory or common-law dram shop liability).

The imposition of a new tax on alcohol to finance a victim compensation fund would almost certainly produce a price increase for alcoholic beverages. As the distributors who pay the tax passed the increase on as part of the price charged to commercial dispensers, so too would the dispensers pass it on to the ultimate purchasers and consumers. This consequence of the alcohol industry's internalization of some of the costs of drinking-driver traffic accidents would then provide the basis for alcohol consumers to make purchase decisions in a way that more fully reflects the social costs associated with the use of the product.[15]

Some alcohol consumers are likely to respond to the price increase by decreasing their consumption, although the degree to which the demand for alcoholic beverages will respond to the price increase is a matter of some uncertainty. To the extent that a decreased demand for alcoholic beverages lowers the level of overall consumption, some reduction in the frequency of drinking-driver accidents may also occur. Both of these assumptions are quite controversial, but the allocative efficiency rationale that supports the tax increase on alcohol will remain valid regardless of the accuracy of the assumptions. Even if the internalization of these accident costs by the alcohol industry is followed neither by a marked decline in the overall level of alcoholic beverage consumption nor by a reduction in the frequency with which drinking-driver accidents occur, a market in alcoholic beverages that is freed of the distortions caused by the externalization of the social costs of those beverages is more likely to be able to arrive at efficient levels of production and consumption than one in which significant portions of the social costs are externalized. From the standpoint of pure allocative efficiency, then, the increase in the price of alcohol that would result from the adoption of a tax-financed compensation system proposal would be beneficial.

As mentioned above, the price elasticity of alcoholic beverages can be difficult to determine with precision because elasticity can vary as well according to the type of alcoholic beverage at issue. The significant point is that a tax-financed compensation fund can be justified equally effectively whether the demand for alcohol is price elastic or price inelastic. Suppose that the demand for alcoholic beverages is highly price elastic. If the demand for alcohol drops significantly as a result of the price increase that follows the imposition of the new tax, then the chances are improved that there might be a corresponding decrease in the number of drinking-driver traffic accidents. If that is the consequence of the imposition of the tax, then society would be better off as its citizens incur fewer drinking-driver accident losses.

If, on the other hand, that assumption is reversed, so that the demand for alcohol is relatively unresponsive to price increases, then the in-elasticity of alcoholic beverages will simply result in a larger pool of funds being generated by the new tax. Although the level of accidents may not decrease, the tax on alcohol would generate funds that would be used to compensate the victims of the drinking-driver accidents that do occur.

My proposed compensation fund for victims of drinking-driver ac-cidents could probably be justified most easily if it could be expected to produce a decrease in the number of drinking-driver accidents. The likelihood of that kind of result is frequently debated by social science researchers who study the relationship between alcohol con-sumption and accidents, but there really is no way to be sure how significant a decrease in accidents, if any, would be attributable to a particular reform measure such as a tax increase. Current estimates that might be constructed would depend on an extrapolation from incomplete data and on the use of models that contain highly con-troversial assumptions. If the acceptability of the compensation fund proposal rested exclusively on a prediction about the accident-reduc-tion effects of the proposed alcohol tax increase, the public policy debate about the proposal would have to assess the validity and the plausibility of those sorts of studies. The primary purpose of the tax increase, however, is not simply to raise the price of alcohol but to generate a level of funding large enough to make the victim com-pensation fund work. If effective, the fund might result in reduction in overall accident costs—a different, but no less valuable, effect than the desired reduction in the number of accidents following a price increase for alcoholic beverages.

The legal scholar who has given the most careful thought to an understanding of the types of accident costs is Guido Calabresi, dean of Yale law school. In *The Costs of Accidents,* Dean Calabresi identified a number of types of accident cost reduction. The first, which he called "primary" accident cost reduction, is an attempt to reduce the number and the severity of accidents.[16] A reform proposal that actually reduced the frequency of drinking-driver traffic accidents would fit into this category. The second type of accident cost reduction concerns the "secondary costs" of accidents, which are the societal costs that result from how we allocate the primary costs of accidents.[17] Secondary accident costs are, in a sense, the indirect costs of accidents. In con-sidering them, we must ask whether accident losses are shifted away from accident victims or left on those victims. To the extent that the losses that are allowed to remain with the victims have a disruptive effect that could be avoided by shifting the losses to other parties, then there is potential room for achieving a reduction in the indirect or secondary costs of accidents.

For example, suppose that the victims of a drinking-driver accident in a particular state are the members of the Bloom family (whom the reader encountered in the introductions to chapters 1-4). Suppose further that only a minimal amount of compensation is available to the surviving family members under the governing state tort law. We could easily identify many of the primary costs of the accident, such as the victims' medical expenses and the lost income attributable to the accident. Other primary costs would be more difficult to quantify, such as the pain and suffering of the survivors, but these are no less real.

Secondary costs are the adverse effects that follow from a failure to make an effective, rather than just a theoretical, shift of the burden of the primary accident costs away from the victims. It is plausible to assume that a substantial decline in the financial position of the surviving members of the Bloom family could mean, for example, that the children's educational opportunities are diminished. If the children's primary accident losses are not fully compensated from other sources, then those lost opportunities are secondary cost effects of the accident. The later additional ramifications of an accident that result from the way in which we do or do not shift accident losses away from the victims have secondary cost effects. An accident victim who quickly exhausted all the compensation that was available from tort defendants and other private sources and then had to draw on public assistance programs could provide another illustration of how secondary accident costs can occur. The proposal for a victim compensation fund developed in the remainder of this book provides a means of reducing the secondary costs of drinking-driver accidents, and it can effectively carry out that function regardless whether it reduces actual primary accident costs.

The adoption of a reform proposal structured along the lines suggested here will result in a redistribution of wealth from the population that purchases alcoholic beverages to the population that is injured in drinking-driver traffic accidents. The tax used to finance the victim compensation fund will be paid indirectly by all purchasers of alcohol, whether they drink and drive or not. For those drinkers who do not drink and drive, the tax represents a transfer of money from them to the people who are entitled to recover from the fund, even though they have arguably done absolutely nothing to contribute to the plight of the accident victims. This argument provides a potentially powerful basis for objecting to the reform proposal, especially its alcohol-tax component. Two questions about this redistributive effect need to be addressed in order to determine the actual strength of this potential objection. First, in a technical economic sense, is an accident compensation system an appropriate way to effectuate any redistribution? Second, and more importantly, is it sound public policy to adopt a compensation system that has this particular kind of redistributive effect?

The more technical question can be answered fairly easily. Although traditional tort law rules and remedies that shift losses from victims to injurers can be justified in theory on both compensatory and allocative efficiency grounds, contemporary law-and-economics scholarship tends to question the redistributive effectiveness of tort liability rules. That skepticism about redistribution has the potential to undercut one of the supporting rationales for the victim compensation system I propose, but a careful consideration of this issue reveals that the objection actually turns out to provide additional support for the proposed compensation system.

In their book on the economic analysis of tort law, Professor Landes and Judge Posner suggest that the way to understand the redistributive effect of a liability rule is to analogize it to an excise tax on the activity to which liability is attached.[18] They then go on to suggest that the analogy is of "no obvious application to tort law" because such "taxes are poorly suited for achieving 'equitable' wealth redistributions *unless the activity taxed is in the nature of a luxury good.*"[19] Because alcoholic beverages are precisely that kind of commodity, the excise tax analogy is apt. The analogy partly justifies imposing some responsibility for the drinking-driver accident losses upon the makers and the distributors of alcoholic beverages who would otherwise effectively escape any liability under the traditional tort system.

That response may be satisfactory as far as the imposition of accident costs on alcohol distributors is concerned. The logical expectation is that the taxes that the distributors will have to pay under this reform proposal will be passed on, perhaps in their entirety, to the purchasers of the beverages that are taxed. The more significant issue, therefore, is whether the redistribution from the class of alcoholic beverage purchasers (or "drinkers") to the class of people injured in drinking-driver traffic accidents (or "victims") can be justified.

Those who might object to the redistribution that takes place under this proposal are likely to argue that the more appropriate redistribution should be from drinking drivers to victims, not from drinkers to victims. The problem is that the likelihood of drinking drivers being able to provide full compensation to the victims of the more serious accidents they cause is fairly low. At the very least, the likelihood is low enough that some proportion of the losses is bound to be left on the accident victims themselves. The question, therefore, is not whether it is better to impose accident losses on drinking drivers or on accident victims, but whether it is better to impose accident losses on victims or on other people to whom the losses can be shifted, and more specifically in this case, to drinkers.

The decision to approve or to tolerate the redistributive effects that will occur between drinkers and victims if this proposal is adopted can be defended in a number of ways. First, the amount of redistribution that will occur is likely to be so small that the average individual drinker would not be affected very much at all. (Chapter 13 will illustrate the level of price increase that can be attributed to the adoption of the tax that would be used to finance this compensation system.) It should be noted as well that there is likely to be at least some overlap between the categories of drinkers and victims. Some of the people who are innocent victims of particular drinking-driver traffic accidents are likely to be purchasers of alcoholic beverages on other occasions. That subcategory of drinkers can thus receive a substantial benefit, in the form of the availability of compensation from the proposed fund, for the relatively minor contribution that they have been forced to make by paying a higher price for the alcohol they purchase.

Second, to the extent that the new tax subjects an individual drinker to a substantial, rather than a minimal, impact, an argument can be made that this impact is a beneficial effect rather than merely an incidental and generally adverse consequence that has to be tolerated. The federal government's study of alcohol consumption patterns over the last decade reveals data that generally help to support the proposal to finance victim compensation by a tax on alcohol. The agencies that are charged with monitoring the relationship between alcohol and health report an uneven pattern of alcoholic beverage consumption within the population of drinkers. While two-thirds of the adult population of this country drinks alcoholic beverages, 10 percent of the drinkers account for half of all the alcoholic beverage consumption.[20] This statistic means that of the total amount of the new tax that will be paid by drinkers, half of the tax will be paid by (and thus half of the redistributive effects will be felt by), only 10 percent of the drinking population. In other words, 90 percent of the drinking population will end up bearing only 50 percent of the new tax burden. A further bit of data strengthens the case in favor of the proposal even further. Social scientists who study alcohol-related accidents report that a particular subclass of the drinking population, which they have labelled "problem drinkers," accounts for a significant share of the most serious drinking-driver traffic accidents.[21] To the extent that heavy drinkers are more likely to be involved in alcohol-related traffic accidents than the more infrequent consumers of alcohol, then a tax that increases the individual drinker's share of the redistributive effect according to the volume of that drinker's consumption seems to be operating in the right sort of way.

The proposal will nevertheless still impose on some proportion of the drinking population an obligation to pay a tax that takes money away from them and gives it to accident victims whose injuries were caused by other parties. The third rationale in favor of this redistributive effect draws on an analysis of the externalization of accident costs. Even the best option for allocating accident losses so as to avoid redistribution—which is to impose accident losses on drinking drivers— involves a significant measure of cost externalization by the drinking drivers. Automobile liability insurance spreads accident costs across an insurance rate-making base that encompasses a wide variety of drivers, typically according to such categories as age range, gender, driving pattern and history, and primary location of the insured vehicle. Thus some portion of insurance premiums already redistributes some of the costs of drinking-driver accident to drivers who do not drink and those who drink but do not drive while alcohol-impaired.

This last observation about how automobile liability insurance externalizes drinking-driver accident costs suggests that we must refine the question about redistributive effects and ask whether it is more appropriate to redistribute wealth from drivers to victims or from drinkers to victims. The answer to that question may depend on how comfortable one is with the assumption that there are more drinkers who drive than there are drivers who drink. If the former is more likely to be true, then the victim compensation fund proposal seems to be taking a step in the right direction.

NOTES

1. *See* Votey, *The Economic Perspective on Controlling the Drunken Driver,* in Laurence et al., Social Control, at 270.

2. This step is discussed at some length in A. PIGOU, A STUDY IN PUBLIC FINANCE (3d rev. ed. 1952).

3. *See* Asimov, *Initiative for Big Alcohol Tax Increase,* San Francisco Chronicle, Dec. 30, 1989, at A6; Jones, *Coalition Seeks 5-Cent Tax on Alcohol Drinks,* Los Angeles Times, Dec. 30, 1989, § B, at 4, col. 5. The initiative effort was met by an alcohol-industry counterproposal for a tax increase that would be used for budget-deficit reduction. Ellis, *Assembly Puts Alcohol Industry's Tax Hike on Ballot,* Los Angeles Times, June 29, 1990, § A, at 36, col. 3.

4. *Final California Election Returns,* Los Angeles Times, Nov. 8, 1990, § A, at 26, col. 1.

5. FEDERAL EXCISE TAXES para. 191,690 (Prentice-Hall Supp. 1989).

6. Pub. L. No. 101-508, § 11201 (1990).

7. VA. CODE § 4-22.1 (1988).

8. *Id.* at § 4-128.

9. MASS. GEN. LAWS ANN. ch. 138, § 21 (West Supp. 1990).

10. Manning, Keeler, Newhouse, Sloss & Wasserman, *The Taxes of Sin: Do Smokers and Drinkers Pay Their Way?,* 261 J.A.M.A. 1604 (March 17, 1989). The study was completed before the increase in federal excise taxes.

11. SURGEON GENERAL'S WORKSHOP ON DRUNK DRIVING, PROCEEDINGS 18-19 (1989).

12. Phelps, *Estimating Effects of Increased Federal Excise Tax on Alcoholic Beverages, id.,* at 25.

13. A highly technical discussion of the tax/compensation combination can be found in Polinsky, *Controlling Externalities and Protecting Entitlements: Property Rights, Liability Rules, and Tax-Subsidy Approaches,* 8 J. LEGAL STUD. 1 (1979).

14. *See* Greenman v. Yuba Power Products, Inc., 59 Cal. 2d 57, 63-64, 27 Cal. Rptr. 697, 701, 377 P.2d 897, 901 (1963); Escola v. Coca Cola Bottling Co. of Fresno, 24 Cal. 2d 453, 464, 150 P.2d 436, 442 (1949) (Traynor, J., concurring) ("retailer cannot bear the burden of this warranty, [so courts] allow him to recoup any losses by means of warranty . . . attending the wholesaler's or manufacturer's sale to him. . . . Such a procedure . . . is needlessly circuitous and engenders wasteful litigation").

15. For an extended discussion of the way in which a theory of strict liability in tort can act as a substitute for perfect consumer information about the risks that are associated with products, see A. POLINSKY, AN INTRODUCTION TO LAW AND ECONOMICS 97-106 (2d ed. 1989). Much of that discussion is directly applicable in the context of consumers underestimating the social costs of alcoholic beverages.

16. CALABRESI, COSTS OF ACCIDENTS, at 26.

17. *Id.* at 27. The third category, or tertiary cost reduction, looks at the cost of accomplishing the first two types of cost reduction, and thus in effect acts as a side constraint on primary and secondary cost-reduction efforts. Chapter 13 of this book deals with these economic constraints.

18. LANDES & POSNER, ECONOMIC STRUCTURE, at 18.

19. *Id.* at 18-19 (emphasis added).

20. NATIONAL INSTITUTE ON ALCOHOL ABUSE AND ALCOHOLISM, REPORT ON ALCOHOLISM AND HEALTH (1987).

21. *See* Fell & Nash, *The Nature of the Alcohol Problem in U.S. Fatal Crashes,* 16 HEALTH ED. Q. 335 (1989). These researchers do report a decrease in the percentage of drinking drivers who have blood alcohol concentrations at very high levels (.20 percent or higher), but their estimate is that still around 20 percent of fatal crashes involve drivers with these high levels of alcohol impairment.

# PART THREE

---

# The Design and Administration of a Victim Compensation Fund

An accident victim who has been injured by a drinking driver may, at first glance, appear to have available a fairly impressive array of tort claims that can be used individually or collectively to produce a recovery of monetary damages that will provide full compensation to the victim. Among the potential defendants who have been identified in part 1 as parties to whom the accident losses may be shifted are the drinking driver, a person who is vicariously liable for harms caused by the drinking driver, and a person who served alcohol to the drinking driver, whether in a commercial transaction or on a social occasion. Nevertheless, as should be apparent from part 1's survey of some of these representative tort claims, the tort system may very well leave an injured party with a realistic prospect of only recovering an amount substantially less than the total amount of monetary damages that would fully compensate the victim for all of the accident-related losses. In light of the shortcomings of the current patchwork scheme of tort actions available to victims of drinking-driver traffic accidents, one can begin to outline a set of goals for an optimum compensation system.

One goal was described and explained in chapter 11, which brought part 2 to a close. A compensation system for the victims of drinking drivers should attach the social costs of alcohol, in particular the costs of drinking-driver traffic accidents, to the enterprises that receive the benefit of the public's alcohol consumption and are at least in some way responsible for the injuries caused by drinking and driving. Imposing those costs on manufacturers and distributors who do not presently internalize them under the current methods of allocating accident costs will thus expand the range of accident cost-bearers to include the alcohol industry as a whole.

Two other goals will be addressed in part 3. First, the compensation fund should provide a level of compensation that more closely reflects the losses that were actually suffered by the injured parties who are entitled to compensation. The goal should therefore be to avoid both the inadequate compensation of serious injuries and the overcompensation of lesser harms. Chapter 12 describes how the compensation fund I propose will attempt to set appropriate levels of compensation.

Second, the proposal should be structured in such a way that it is possible to operate the accident compensation system with a minimum of waste and duplication. The goal here is to attempt to control the administrative costs and tertiary costs of accidents. Tertiary costs are the costs of administering a system that is concerned both with reducing accident costs and with allocating the costs of the accidents that do occur. Dean Calabresi refers to tertiary cost reduction as an efficiency goal.[1] In effect, he asks whether the administrative costs of the legal system's efforts to reduce the frequency and severity of accidents and to shift accident costs away from victims outweigh the benefits. Chapter 13 will discuss how the compensation system can address this problem.

In developing a reform proposal, it is necessary to be sensitive to yet another goal: the necessity of political and social compromise. A new compensation system must have enough political acceptability that at least some of its elements can supplement or replace the existing legal framework. Chapter 14, which opens part 4, will specifically address this issue, but the need to generate political support lies behind some of the provisions of the new system that are set out here in part 3. The victim compensation fund I propose comes closer than the current tort system does to striking a proper balance among the various goals for an optimum compensation system. In chapter 15, I will set forth model legislation and commentary that can be used to set up the fund. Part 4 will conclude with a more general discussion of the nature and the utility of tort law remedies in general, based on issues raised by my critique of the way the current tort law system undercompensates victims of drinking-driver accidents.

## NOTE

1. *See* CALABRESI, COSTS OF ACCIDENTS, at 28.

# 12

---

# Setting Appropriate Levels
# of Compensation

Drafting a proposal to reform the current tort law system of injury compensation presents an opportunity to introduce a greater measure of rationality and precision into the way the level of compensation to be provided is determined. Critics of tort law frequently argue that the tort litigation system does a fairly poor job of matching both the ability of an accident victim to obtain a legal remedy and the size of the monetary awards provided to the victim with any objectively determined measure of the victim's losses.[1]

In large part, of course, the controversy over the amount of compensation that the tort system provides arises from the admitted difficulty of agreeing on any objective measure of loss. Awards of damages that contemplate providing compensation to a victim at the present time for elements of accident loss that will occur in the future almost necessarily involve a considerable degree of uncertainty both about how to determine the nature of that loss and how to express that loss in monetary terms when an award of tort damages for future losses must be reduced to present value. Even for losses that have already been suffered by the accident victim, there can be substantial disagreement about how most accurately to put a value on the harm that was suffered when it is translated into an award of monetary damages to the victim. In many cases, then, controversy can surround the issue of how well the legal system goes about the quantification task in assessing the amount of monetary damages that a tort plaintiff is entitled to recover.

Sometimes, however, the complaints that are voiced about the tort system's inaccuracy in determining the level of compensable damages have a motivation that extends beyond questioning the competence of judges and juries to make those quantification determinations in particular cases. Objections to the way in which the tort system compensates for harm can expand beyond questioning either damages methodology or institutional competence to assert some variation of the following substantive proposition: tort liability ought to be limited to providing compensation only for those out-of-pocket monetary losses that are not otherwise protected through private or public sources of payments such as medical insurance or worker's compensation benefits that are available to the victim apart from any liability that is contemplated within the tort system.

That broad proposition about limiting the damages that can be awarded in tort cases combines two distinct ideas. The first is that no award of damages should be made to compensate an accident victim for nonpecuniary or noneconomic losses, such as pain and suffering or emotional distress. Instead, according to this criticism of tort law, legal compensation ought to be limited to a replacement or a reimbursement of the out-of-pocket losses that were actually suffered by the injured person as a result of the defendant's culpable conduct. A more modest version of this first idea would permit at least some recovery of damages for noneconomic losses but would cap the permissible award at a certain arbitrarily selected level. The second idea embedded in the proposition is that the amount of damages awarded should be reduced by any amount that the injured person has already been paid from a source other than one of the liable parties. The technical term for this source is a "collateral source." One common example of a collateral source is the payment of an accident victim's medical expenses by the victim's own health insurer.

These two ideas for limiting the recovery of damages that are obtainable in tort litigation are not matters of idle speculation. The Reagan administration's Tort Policy Working Group recommended in 1986 that, among other reforms, limits should be imposed on the recovery of noneconomic damages and that tort awards should be reduced to reflect payments the plaintiff received from collateral sources.[2] The following year, a follow-up report of the working group identified fifteen states in which the legislature had implemented some version of one or the other of those recommendations just during the 1986 legislative session.[3] In assessing the competing arguments about the way that the tort system evaluates and then compensates for accident losses, it is necessary to differentiate these sorts of substantive reform measures from the questions about loss calculation methodology and competence that were raised earlier.

Even if one accepts the legitimacy of open-ended or uncapped compensation for noneconomic losses that were actually suffered by accident victims, one might object to the degree of inaccuracy that the tort system tolerates in the way compensable damages are determined. The logic of Winston Churchill's famous statement about democracy — that it is "the worst form of government except all those other forms that have been tried"[4] — does not apply to the flaws in the tort system's approach to measuring damages. The inaccuracy of the system's approach probably cannot be excused on the basis that there is no better way to execute the details of the task. Reform legislation can be a vehicle for experimenting with different techniques of injury compensation, not only for the specific problems addressed by the legislation but also for the sake of seeing what lessons might be learned with regard to the broader question of injury compensation in general.

## The Undercompensation Problem in Modern Tort Law

As we have seen, the current legal system can be faulted for failing to provide full compensation for the victims of drinking-driver traffic accidents. In some instances, that failure is the practical result of the defendant's lack of financial resources (the judgment-proof defendant). In other instances, the failure can be traced to the decision to restrict the range of parties who can be held liable. These two types of failure to provide full compensation are obviously closely related. If the potentially liable parties are also financially unable to satisfy a tort judgment, then the adverse consequences to the undercompensated plaintiffs can be alleviated by expanding the range of liability to include other parties. Similarly, to the extent that liable parties do have sufficient assets, there may be less pressure on courts and legislatures to recognize or create new theories of tort liability that encompass parties who are more tenuously connected to the accident. Recall the image used in part 1 of concentric circles of tort liability expanding outward from the drinking driver. How far out from the center a particular jurisdiction chooses to extend the scope of tort liability may be more responsive to the issue of adequately compensating accident victims than to any other factor.

Undercompensation involves both practical and legal barriers to full and fair recovery. One sort of undercompensation focuses on whether the plaintiff has a realistic chance of actually collecting the amount of compensation that has been awarded. The focus here, however, will be on the inadequacy of the amount of damages awarded.

One extremely significant factor behind inadequate awards is the prevailing practice in American tort law to exclude any possibility of the plaintiff recovering attorney's fees from the defendant. Under the "American rule" regarding litigation costs and expenses, the parties must usually pay their own attorney's fees.[5] As a result of this rule, part of the plaintiff's damage award must be used to pay attorney's fees and litigation expenses. A successful plaintiff must incur these expenses to obtain compensation but without being able to recover them as part of the damages awarded. In determining the degree to which an accident victim has actually been compensated for an injury, therefore, one needs to determine the costs of obtaining relief that the plaintiff was forced to incur, and then to subtract that cost from the amount of damages awarded to that plaintiff. The resulting figure is the net recovery to the plaintiff. It is that net-recovery figure, rather than the amount of damages awarded in the judgment, that represents the money that is actually available to the plaintiff for injury compensation.

Suppose, for example, that a tort plaintiff asserts a claim that seeks to recover damages for medical expenses and lost wages that amount to $25,000. Suppose as well that the amount of the attorney's fees that are owed by this plaintiff are to be determined on the basis of a contingent fee arrangement in which the plaintiff's attorney will receive one-third of the recovery after the litigation expenses have been deducted. If we assume that those expenses were $4,000, so that the attorney's fee is one-third of $21,000, then the net recovery to the plaintiff is $14,000, not the $25,000 that was awarded to the plaintiff. While these figures by themselves do not necessarily mean that the plaintiff has been undercompensated, they do at least demonstrate that the size of the judgment the plaintiff is able to win is an inadequate basis for determining the degree to which the tort system has actually provided full compensation. The larger the gap between the amount that was awarded to the plaintiff and the plaintiff's net recovery, the more severe the potential undercompensation can be.

An accident victim who has incurred expenses for such elements of damages as hospitalization, medical expenses, and lost wages may still be able to recover at least enough money to cover those expenses even if a substantial part of the tort judgment awarded to the victim has had to be used to pay the costs of obtaining that recovery. The availability of an award of damages for elements of recovery other than pecuniary or economic losses is frequently claimed to make up for the harsh effect of the American rule on attorney's fees. A recovery of damages for nonpecuniary losses can bridge the gap between the amount that is purportedly awarded as compensation and the net recovery to the plaintiff. Damages for nonpecuniary loss can be awarded under the heading of a recovery for pain and suffering or as an award of punitive damages when a defendant's conduct has been particularly culpable. These sorts of damages create funds that may allow the plaintiff to pay attorney's fees and litigation expenses without having to divert any funds awarded for out-of-pocket expenses to this purpose.

The impact of the introduction of an award of damages for pain and suffering can be illustrated in terms of the hypothetical that was just described. Suppose that in this revised hypothetical, the economic losses of the plaintiff were still $25,000, but now the plaintiff also receives $18,000 in damages for pain and suffering. Assuming that the plaintiff has still incurred litigation expenses that amount to $4,000, we now have attorney's fees of $13,000, or one-third of $39,000 (25,000 + 18,000 − 4,000). The net recovery to the plaintiff is $26,000, which is a greater sum than the $25,000 in economic loss that the plaintiff has suffered as a result of the accident.

Covering attorney's fees in this way may not be a satisfactory strategy if a feasible alternative is available. It may very well be true that nonpecuniary damage awards are actually used by plaintiffs to pay attorney's fees and litigation expenses. It may also be true that judges and juries who set the amount of damages are sufficiently aware of that practice that they build a "fudge factor" into a high percentage of tort awards so that plaintiffs' out-of-pocket losses are covered by their net recoveries. Nevertheless, because this practice involves a substantial reliance on what appears to be a subterfuge, one might well conclude that it should be avoided.

For one thing, nonpecuniary damage awards for losses such as pain and suffering are made in order to provide compensation for an actual injury that was suffered by the plaintiff. Nonpecuniary losses are no less real than pecuniary ones. Forcing the plaintiff to use such awards to pay for the cost of obtaining a recovery can act to undercut the legitimacy or urgency of damage claims for pain and suffering. Furthermore, if public awareness of this subterfuge were to grow, then the true role of nonpecuniary damage awards—to compensate the plaintiff for actual harm—could become less important. That development, in turn could lessen the popular understanding of how an accident disrupts the life of the victim and the variety of injuries for which the legal system can and should provide some redress.

Ironically, the use of nonpecuniary damage awards to provide plaintiffs with the funds to finance a tort recovery can skew the system so that, rather than bringing otherwise inadequate awards more into line with the plaintiff's actual losses, they instead seem to overcompensate the plaintiff. The kinds of complaints that critics sometimes express about runaway juries and the breakdown of any responsible constraints on the award of tort damages are probably much more frequently prompted by six- or seven-figure awards for nonpecuniary losses than they are by even very large awards for actual pecuniary losses or out-of-pocket expenses.

An alternative victim compensation system may be able to provide a forthright response to the actual loss that is suffered in accidents and avoid having to use certain parts of damage awards as surrogates for other purposes. If the physical pain that is suffered in an accident is thought to be a legitimately compensable item of loss, then an accident victim who proves that such pain was in fact suffered should be entitled to obtain compensation for that element of harm without having to use that portion of a tort judgment to pay attorney's fees and other litigation expenses. The compensation fund for victims of drinking-driver accidents that I propose would supplement existing state tort remedies, and it might allow more flexibility in determining damages awards and a greater opportunity to reach compromise than what is now possible under existing rules and doctrines. For example, to counter the fear that awards for items of loss such as actual pain could vastly exceed any practical ability of a compensation fund to provide payment, authority should be given to the agency that administers the compensation fund to adopt a schedule of payments for those elements. Scheduled payments are not a new device. They are currently employed in many workers' compensation schemes, where they are frequently justified as part of a trade-off in which compensation levels are kept within a certain range to control the financial pressure on the system.

The demonstrable difficulty of hitting the target of accurate compensation for injury when one is aiming at false targets suggests that a schedule of payments should also be adopted regarding attorney's fees and expenses. The legislation creating the victim compensation fund should include a provision that allows the award to earmark a portion of the compensation funds for the payment of the legitimate and reasonable expenses the accident victim incurred in obtaining a recovery. The design of such a provision for attorney's fees and litigation expenses must take into account two different scenarios by which an accident victim might attempt to obtain compensation from the victim compensation fund.

In the first scenario, the accident victim hires an attorney who proceeds to litigate the tort liability of whichever parties may be legally responsible for the harm the victim suffered, according to the law of the state in which the accident occurred. This standard process of obtaining compensation would result in the determination of a sum of money that is ostensibly to be paid to the plaintiff. As we have seen, however, all that the judgment establishes is that the defendant owes a debt to the plaintiff. The figure that is relevant for determining whether the accident victim has really been fully compensated is the amount of money that the plaintiff is actually able to collect from the defendant. That collectible amount may be a substantially lower than the amount of damages to which the judgment says the plaintiff is entitled. In addition, the plaintiff's legal costs will still have to be deducted from that collectible amount, as well as the fees the plaintiff owes the attorney. If that plaintiff were then to turn to the victim compensation fund for further payment, the agency administering the fund should at least be aware of the compensation that the plaintiff has already received. In calculating the amount of injury compensation that the plaintiff has been awarded under this tort litigation scenario, some recognition of this deduction of costs and fees must be made.

A different compensation scenario involves an accident victim who resorts to the compensation fund not as a supplement to the initial tort litigation but as an alternative to it. Under a scenario of this sort, the compensation-fund claimant would still likely need a lawyer to navigate the recovery process. However desirable a "lawyer-free" compensation system might seem to be in the abstract, the simple fact is that many people will need professional representation if they are going to understand their legal rights and fully enforce them. If a claimant does retain counsel to aid in pursuing relief from the compensation fund, then the compensation fund system should provide, as part of the compensation given to the claimant, a sum that is specifically earmarked for attorney's fees. A provision to this effect is contained in the federal National Childhood Vaccine Injury Act, which sets up a compensation system that is roughly analogous to the one I am proposing here. The vaccine injury legislation requires an award of compensation to include an amount to cover "reasonable" attorneys' fees and other costs that are incurred in the proceedings to obtain compensation.[6]

The process of recovery through administrative compensation systems is typically less complex than tort litigation, and administrative claims are usually less complex than tort claims. Because it is frequently easier to provide legal representation under the administrative system, awards for attorney's fees should be capped at a certain level, either as a percentage of the award or at a specific dollar amount, or by using some combination of the two. The legislation creating the California Crime Victim Restitution Fund provides a good example. It allows attorney's fees to be granted but caps the compensation for those fees at the lesser of 10 percent of the sum awarded to the claimant or five-hundred dollars.[7]

A state legislature that creates a victim compensation fund for the victims of drinking-driver traffic accidents could grant the head of the agency that is to administer the fund the authority to issue a fee schedule to govern the compensation of plaintiffs for attorneys' fees under the system. As long as fees are set at reasonable levels, a fee schedule can lend predictability and stability to the payment of attorney's fees by the fund.

### The Problem of Overcompensating the Victim

Accuracy in setting damage awards is improved by substituting an express award to cover the plaintiff's expenses incurred in obtaining a recovery, including attorney's fees, for the hit-or-miss methods by which juries might otherwise attempt to provide adequate levels of compensation. Nevertheless, the adoption of that reform by itself may not necessarily make compensation under a tort litigation scheme of recovery substantially more accurate. Reform measures must address the problem of overcompensating a claimant in excess of actual loss as well as the problem of undercompensating the claimant. In deciding what elements of a recovery are to be considered excessive, some fairly controversial choices must be made. Nevertheless, one of the goals of the victim compensation system I propose to deal with drinking-driver accidents is to provide supplementary compensation that more accurately reflects the losses that are actually attributable to drinking-driver accidents. While the details may be subject to substantial differences of opinion, some measure of agreement on the outline of an acceptable scheme may be easier to achieve.

The most likely cause of a perception that an accident victim has been overcompensated is an award of damages that duplicate items of loss that have already been paid to (or for) the victim by a collateral source (that is, a source other than the defendant from whom the tort recovery is obtained). Under the collateral source rule used in the common-law calculation of tort damages, the defendant remains liable for any losses for which the plaintiff has already been reimbursed by a collateral source (including both payments received by the plaintiff and payments made to others for the plaintiff's losses).[8] The collateral source payments are not credited to the tort defendant. As a result of the operation of this rule, a tort plaintiff may recover from a defendant a sum that represents losses that have actually already been shifted by the plaintiff to a source other than the plaintiff or the defendant.

An example will illustrate both the nature of the collateral source rule and the way in which its operation can create an appearance of providing overcompensation. Suppose that an accident victim is hospitalized for two days as a result of an accident, incurs medical expenses both for treatment that is received immediately after the accident and for follow-up care, and misses two weeks of work. That victim may have health insurance that pays all or nearly all of the hospital and medical expenses and an employment sick leave policy that pays all or nearly all of the victim's wages for the days of work that were missed. If the victim sues the person who caused the accident, that defendant could be held liable to pay damages for the medical and hospital expenses and the lost wages of the plaintiff, even though the plaintiff personally has not actually had to pay for those items of loss. At first glance, the plaintiff might appear to be getting a double recovery, first, from the health insurer and the employer, and second, from the defendant who is now held liable to compensate the plaintiff for the same items of loss.

The recent rash of proposals for a general reform of tort law have commonly called for collateral source payments to be excluded from a defendant's tort liability. Under this sort of proposal, the defendant does not have to bear any of the plaintiff's losses that have been paid by a collateral source. Such a proposal would raise significant problems if it were to have the effect of abolishing completely or automatically all tort liability for accident losses that were covered by a collateral source payment. In the first place, it is important to recognize that the collateral source rule does not inevitably produce a double recovery that appears to overcompensate the accident victim. In some circumstances, the payment that the plaintiff has received from the collateral source may be subject to a subrogation agreement. Under an agreement of this sort, the collateral source must be reimbursed out of any tort judgment that the plaintiff recovers from a defendant. While this sequence of payments from two different sources for the same element of harm may very well produce an undesirable situation that ought to be corrected, it is unrealistic to characterize a situation of this sort as presenting a problem of overcompensation. Two of the worst features of this system of payment and subrogation are the expense and the delay it causes. In effect, the tort litigation system is used as a means for transferring funds between the liability insurers of drinking drivers who are held liable to accident victims and the first-party insurers or other collateral sources who pay for the harm to the accident victims and who have retained a right of subrogation to the damages that the plaintiff is able to obtain in tort litigation. Enforcement of the subrogation right that is retained by the collateral source eliminates any potential double recovery because the plaintiff must pay back a portion of the damages recovered to reimburse the collateral source. Nevertheless, the potential social cost of this method of preventing a double recovery may be higher than it is worth.

In other circumstances in which an accident victim has received payments from collateral sources, the plaintiff's losses may be so inadequately valued under the tort system, either because of a legal rule[9] or as a matter of fact-finding in the plaintiff's particular case, that an apparent double recovery seems justified. In some cases, allowing the plaintiff to enjoy duplicate payments for the same item of loss from a defendant and from an unsubrogated collateral source is the only practical means of approaching complete compensation. In situations such as these, a blanket rejection of the collateral source rule in litigation would be more likely to result in the undercompensation of accident victims rather than just the elimination of overcompensation.

In some cases, however, ignoring collateral source payments for a plaintiff's losses seems to result in an unjustified double recovery. Consider, for example, the person who is injured in a traffic accident and misses two days of work as a result. Tort law traditionally treats lost wages as one of the out-of-pocket losses for which compensation from a defendant is readily available. Now suppose that the injured person's employer pays those lost wages in full as part of its sick-leave policy. In a jurisdiction that follows the traditional tort rule, this payment will not be taken into account in computing the damages for which the tort defendant will be liable.

The argument in favor of permitting what appears to be a double recovery even in this situation is not frivolous, however. Had the plaintiff not been injured in the traffic accident, those days of sick leave would have been available for another purpose, either for use in the event of an illness or as a de facto additional vacation period. Accordingly, it can accurately be said that the defendant's conduct has deprived the plaintiff of a benefit that would otherwise have been available had the accident not taken place. Furthermore, an economist would tell us that the employer's sick-leave policy is not a "free" benefit that is provided to the plaintiff. Instead, the plaintiff's total package of wages and benefits reflects a calculation of the cost to the employer of providing these wages even on days when the employer's enterprise is not being served by the employee.[10] In the simplest of terms, if an employee is provided with a benefit such as a paid sick-leave program, then the employee is ultimately paying for that benefit in the form of a reduction in wages or other possible benefits that are not received.

This relatively simple example illustrates the complexity of evaluating a collateral source rule either on the basis of trying to correct for an overcompensation of accident victims or on the basis of trying to cure an undercompensation problem. Determining the effects of different treatment for each separate element of harm for which an injured person might receive payment from a collateral source would be a daunting task. Even then, the rough approximations and the reliance on what is, or is thought to be, generally the case might lead to miscalculations or erroneous conclusions in the individual case.

A first-party health insurance policy is a typical example of a collateral source, and so is an employee-benefit package. But some accident costs may also be covered by social insurance plans, such as disability payments under the Social Security Administration. It is also necessary to decide whether to distinguish between public and private sources when considering how to handle collateral source payments.

Should accident losses covered by collateral sources be brought within the scope of the proposed victim compensation plan? Should an accident victim be given an opportunity to receive compensation from the fund for items of loss that are covered by payments from collateral sources? Although fairly strong competing arguments can be made, a negative answer seems, on balance, to be best.

A cost-allocation analysis in this context might suggest that the collateral source rule should be retained. A decision to compensate a claimant for a loss already paid through a collateral source would increase the extent to which the victim's accident losses are treated as a cost attributable specifically to the drinking-driver accident in which the victim was injured. If an accident victim is allowed to obtain compensation from the fund, the losses that have been paid by the collateral sources would be identified more precisely as part of the cost of the drinking-driver accident.

To exclude a claimant from recovering compensation from the fund for specific drinking-driver accident losses covered by public or private collateral sources would be to treat those losses as though they were indistinguishable from any other sort of loss, whether or not that loss was based on culpable conduct of another person and whether or not some additional avenue to obtaining compensation was available. The primary financial impact of the accident loss would be felt by the collateral source, not by the compensation fund, and that impact would not be directed toward the parties who ultimately bear the burden of financing the compensation fund.

In effect, then, if the new victim compensation system rejected the collateral source rule, drinking-driver accidents would be treated as if they were simply one among a variety of loss-producing events that a society or an individual must accommodate. When collateral source payments are used to reduce the amount of compensation that the accident victim is entitled to seek from the compensation fund, then the specific losses at issue are treated as a cost of the activity that gave rise to the obligation of the collateral source to pay for those losses. Instead of being attributed to the cost of drinking and driving, the accident losses would become a cost of citizenship (social insurance programs) or a cost of employment (employee-benefit programs) or a cost of being a member of an insurance rate-making pool (private insurance programs). If the payments that are received from benefit or protection programs of this sort are not going to be treated in the way the tort system treats payments from collateral sources, then some portion of the losses from drinking-driver accidents will be externalized, as they are shifted away from the parties whose alcohol-related activities caused the accidents.

The argument in favor of retaining the collateral source rule in the case of drinking-driver traffic accidents undoubtedly has some merit. For a number of reasons, however, the argument ought not to be compelling when it comes to designing a new accident victim compensation system along the lines proposed in this book. One of the facts that needs to be kept uppermost when evaluating the performance of tort law (and a specific proposal for reform) is that the individual goals of a victim compensation system do not exist in isolation. Conflicts between the demands placed on a system may have to be reconciled in a way that interferes with the fullest attainment of any particular goal. Furthermore, the relief offered by the compensation system proposed here is primarily intended to supplement existing remedies under state tort law systems rather than to displace the tort system at the outset. For that reason, the system does not necessarily have to be bound by the existing rules within tort law for determining damages. If a state currently adheres to a collateral source rule in its calculation of damages in tort litigation, the state should be permitted to continue to receive whatever benefits are thought to result from the retention of the rule in the litigation context. Tort defendants would thus be subjected to as full an internalization of the accident losses that they cause as the existing tort law permits.

Under a victim compensation system that supplements the existing tort law regime, collateral source payments should not be duplicated by the compensation fund. The new system should follow the example set by the National Childhood Vaccine Injury Act. Under this federal no-fault statute, no payment can be made from the compensation fund for injuries or expenses that are compensable from other sources. This prohibition includes payments that have been made or can be expected to be made from a state compensation program, a federal or state health benefits program, an insurance policy, or a prepaid health service provider.[11] The collateral sources themselves are thereby required to be the primary loss bearers for the injuries for which they have an obligation to pay the victim.

There are a number of reasons why the victim compensation fund should not be allowed to duplicate collateral source payments. The most important reason is a simple matter of finances. Particularly in the early stages of the new system's operation, a good deal of uncertainty will exist about how large the demand for compensation will be. Furthermore, only a limited amount of funds will be available to finance and to operate the new system. In light of the uncertainty about the number and the size of the claims that will be made, sound public policy would seem to dictate that the best use of the limited compensation dollars available would be to provide compensation only for uncompensated losses.

Treating collateral source payments this way should complement the proposed treatment of payments for damages received from tort defendants. The optimum structure of the new victim compensation system would treat the compensation fund as a source of supplementary compensation that fills the gap left by the inadequacy of other available means of obtaining compensation. In determining what amount of payment a claimant is entitled to receive from the fund, there is no compelling reason to distinguish between the losses that have been paid from collateral sources and the losses that have been paid through a settlement of the plaintiff's tort case or in satisfying a tort judgment. Both payments should be treated as matters that reduce the amount of the claim that can be made on the victim compensation fund.

The enabling legislation that adopts the compensation fund proposal should therefore refuse to incorporate the prevailing tort rule that refuses to subtract collateral source payments when setting the amount of compensation to which an accident victim is entitled. Instead, the payment from the fund ought to be reduced by the amount of any payment or other consideration the claimant has received from any source, whether a collateral source or a tort defendant, for the same items of loss for which the claimant is seeking compensation from the fund. This includes collateral source payments from both public and private sources. By not distinguishing between public and private sources, inequalities based on one's ability to afford private insurance will not be perpetuated.[12]

A final issue that needs to be addressed is the matter of subrogation. The basic question is whether some provision ought to be made to reflect the fact that collateral source payments will be deducted from the compensation that an accident victim is entitled to receive from the victim compensation fund. The apparently obvious answer is that the question of subrogation is unlikely to arise because the victim will not receive any payment from the fund to which the right of subrogation could attach. Nevertheless, to avoid any potential problems or uncertainty, the enabling legislation ought to make clear that no right of subrogation should be allowed from the compensation that is made from the victim compensation fund. Payments from the fund should go exclusively to accident victims. They should not be used to reimburse insurance companies and other sources for payments that those sources have made.

### Setting the Threshold for Obtaining Compensation from the Victim Compensation Fund

As has been the case with many new compensation systems, the adoption of a compensation fund in the context of drinking-driver traffic accidents requires a decision to be made about whether to create a threshold for obtaining compensation from the fund. In what manner and at what level the threshold requirements ought to be constructed depend primarily on the how the system is primarily intended to function. No-fault automobile insurance plans, for example, are largely designed to remove relatively minor and fairly routine claims from the tort litigation system. The typical threshold in these plans is defined as a certain level of injury below which the exclusive source of compensation is the no-fault system. Until that threshold is crossed, an accident victim cannot assert a tort claim. Once the threshold has been crossed, however, the victim is permitted to enter the tort litigation system and seek whatever remedies are otherwise available under state tort law.

The decision to construct a compensation system such as a no-fault automobile insurance plan with a threshold that must be crossed before an injured party is permitted to *leave* the system means that the system typically operates to compensate accident victims only up to a certain level of injury. In the less serious accidents, in which the exclusivity of the no-fault system keeps an injured party out of the tort litigation system, the compensation is paid by that party's own no-fault insurer, at least up to the policy limits that have been selected and paid for by the insured. As the policy limits are exceeded and the no-fault threshold is crossed, the natural tendency would be for the accident victim to rely more heavily on whatever ability the tort liability rules create for the shifting of losses to other parties. As a result, the upper limit on the potential demand that might be placed on the no-fault portion of the insurance fund would predictably be substantially lower than an amount that would provide full compensation to the more seriously injured accident victims.

The no-fault-insurance sort of injury compensation system has a functional counterpart in systems such as those that compensate victims of violent crimes. A common feature of systems of that sort is a cap on the size of the award that can be made to a person who is entitled to recover from the compensation fund, regardless of the fact that a particular claimant's losses may exceed that cap. California, for example, sets a limit of $23,000 on the total award that can be made to a person who applies for assistance under its crime victims' restitution fund.[13]

In no-fault insurance and the crime victim restitution fund, the threshold for remaining exclusively in the no-fault system and the cap on the amount of recovery permitted from the restitution fund both act as an effective determinant of the upper limit on the payment that will have to be made, respectively, by the no-fault insurer or by the victim restitution fund to any particular claimant. That sort of knowledge increases the ability to predict the magnitude of the financial drain that claims covered by the system are likely to place on the system. Adopting a threshold of this sort therefore could make it easier to determine the level either of the insurance premiums that need to be charged or of the legislative funding that would be required to operate the system.

A significant characteristic of both of the systems that have just been described is that they operate as a compensation source of first resort for a person who is injured in an automobile accident or who is a victim of a violent crime. That role is expressly mandated by the exclusivity provisions of no-fault automobile insurance statutes, which keep the less seriously injured claimant out of the tort litigation system. That role of first resort, and frequently the only resort, is more a practical result of crime victim compensation systems than the result of a legal requirement. The tort law of every state contains legal theories that are available to crime victims and that would suffice to establish the tort liability of the criminal defendant for the victim's injuries. The law of liability for intentional torts follows much of the criminal law in its definitions of the kinds of tortious behavior that result in a person being held liable and in the specific types of harms for which a tort remedy is available.[14] In the relatively infrequent case of a known assailant who possesses the financial resources to provide compensation to the victim, the assertion of intentional tort claims against the criminal can be an effective method of redressing the harm that was done to the victim. In the much more likely situation in which an assailant either is unknown or is unable to satisfy any tort judgment that might be obtained by the victim, the restitution fund may very well present the victim's only realistic chance of receiving any compensation.

The drinking-driver traffic accident presents quite a different scenario from the one that has just been sketched, however, and that difference should be reflected in the design of the threshold for compensation under the new system. In the typical alcohol-related traffic accident, it is likely that the accident victim already has a realistic possibility of obtaining at least some compensation from the existing tort law remedies and insurance mechanisms that are in place. The more seriously injured victims are unlikely to receive full compensation for their injuries, however. In a state with a no-fault insurance system, an injured party's own no-fault insurer will be contractually obligated to provide injury compensation at least up to a certain level. In a fault state, the prevalence of automobile liability insurance makes it likely that at least a minimum amount of funds will be available from most tort defendants to compensate the victims. Furthermore, in both fault and no-fault states, accident victims themselves are likely to be able to draw on some collateral sources that will reduce or spread the financial impact of such accident losses as medical expenses or a temporary interruption in the flow of income. The result is that the alcohol-related accident victim compensation system can be designed so that it will operate as a compensation source of last resort rather than first resort for the victims.

The difference between the two approaches to setting a threshold is illustrated in figure 12-1. The figure is constructed in this way. First, identify each claim that could be made for compensation from a particular system over a given period of time. Second, determine the amount of losses for which compensation might be sought in each of those claims. Third, illustrate the size of each claim as a bar that rises the appropriate distance above a horizontal axis. It is likely that

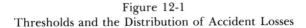

Figure 12-1
Thresholds and the Distribution of Accident Losses

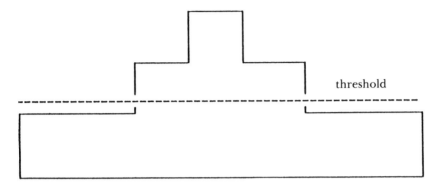

threshold

Distribution of Compensation Claims by Size of Claim. Threshold line depicts size of claim above or below which the compensation system operates.

there will be more smaller claims than large claims, so the total distribution of losses for which compensation might be sought can be arranged in the shape of a rough pyramidal structure.

If the compensation system is set up so that it acts as the compensation source of first resort, then the major expenditure of compensation dollars will be made for losses at or near the base of the pyramid in figure 12-1, leaving less money available for the more seriously injured claimants. Systems such as the automobile no-fault insurance scheme target accident losses below the dotted line that bisects the pyramid. If, on the other hand, the existing range of tort remedies and insurance coverage provides some degree of confidence that the losses at or near the base of the pyramid are largely already being covered, then the compensation system could be set up so that the limited pool of funds available for compensation is directed at the losses lying at the upper levels of the pyramid.

Because of the nature of the undercompensation problem for victims of drinking drivers, a more desirable way to structure the fund's threshold is to establish the threshold requirements as a barrier that must be crossed *before* the claimant is entitled to obtain compensation from the new system, in other words, to reserve compensation dollars for the losses that occupy the area above the line that bisects the pyramid. The rationale is that the accident victim compensation fund is best conceived as a way to supplement other existing measures when they fail to provide full compensation to the victims. Accordingly, entry into the compensation fund system can legitimately and feasibly be conditioned on a showing by a claimant that the existing remedies available to the victim have failed, or are likely to fail, to provide full compensation to the victim.

The threshold for entering the victim compensation system might be defined in various ways. In setting a threshold, the initial decision is whether to opt for a quantitative definition, such as losses that exceed a certain dollar amount, or a qualitative definition, such as the victim's death or permanent disability or disfigurement. In the drinking-driver accident context, it probably makes the most sense to use a quantitative factor such as losses that can be proven to exceed a certain amount. Although an alternative or supplementary qualitative definition could be selected, accidents defined in such a way are likely to be picked up by a threshold that is defined in purely quantitative terms. The use of a quantitative definition would require the claimant to come forward with at least a preliminary showing of the value of the accident losses that are eligible for compensation from the fund as a threshold matter.

Precisely how high the threshold is set depends on the purpose that the compensation system is intended to serve and on the problem it is trying to correct. The major purpose of the fund proposed here is to respond to the need of those who are inadequately compensated by the existing tort and insurance remedies. The threshold could therefore logically be set at a certain dollar value of *uncompensated losses* that have been suffered by the claimant in an alcohol-related traffic accident. There is no single figure that leaps out as the obvious choice for that threshold amount. The specific injury compensation experience that exists within a particular state will have a significant impact on whether the threshold is set high or low.

The fundamental reason that the threshold is structured as a barrier to entry into the compensation system does, however, offer some initial guidance in setting the amount of the uncompensated injuries that have to be proven in order to be entitled to compensation from the fund. The basic rationale for structuring the system as a supplement to existing remedies is that those existing remedies are adequate to deal with most of the smaller accidents that occur. If that is true, then the threshold for obtaining entry into the new compensation system could be set at the amount that is considered to be typically available to compensate victims. That amount would normally be the minimum liability insurance limits that are required within a state that retains a fault system, or the required first-party insurance protection in a no-fault state. For purposes of the discussion in the remainder of this book, and for the draft of the model legislation that is presented in chapter 15, that amount will be assumed to be $10,000. It needs to be emphasized, however, that this figure is nothing more than a plausible working hypothesis. Each state legislature should adopt a specific threshold figure that reflects its state's own experience and estimate of the size of the uncompensated loss problem.

Thus far we have decided that in order to enter the compensation system a claimant must prove to have suffered uncompensated losses greater than $10,000. How the threshold is satisfied is the second matter that needs to be addressed. That determination involves two distinct issues: how to calculate uncompensated losses and what elements of harm should be compensable under the new system.

The resolution of the first issue, how to calculate uncompensated losses, follows naturally from our previous assumptions. The purpose of the compensation fund is to step in when the other tort and insurance mechanisms have failed to provide full compensation to the victim. Accordingly, a claimant under the fund should first be required to subtract from the estimate of compensable losses that the claimant suffered any compensation the claimant has already received or is likely to receive in the future. Payments that must be deducted would include payments received from a collateral source and payments on behalf of a tort defendant who has been found liable to the claimant. Besides reflecting these deductions, the threshold estimate of uncompensated losses should take into account the amount of attorney's fees and litigation expenses the claimant incurred in obtaining a tort judgment against a defendant. When deducting any payments received from a tort defendant, therefore, the sum that is subtracted should be the net recovery to the plaintiff (recall the discussion early in this chapter).

The threshold calculation should proceed in accordance with the following formula:

$$U = L - Cl - (T - F),$$

where $U$ stands for the uncompensated losses that determine whether the threshold has been satisfied so that the claimant may enter the system, $L$ stands for the estimate of the total compensable losses, as defined below, that have been suffered by the claimant,

$Cl$ stands for any payments for those losses that have been made by a collateral source,

*T* stands for any amount that has been recovered for those losses from a tort defendant who is held liable or who has entered into a settlement,

and *F* stands for the attorney's fees and litigation expenses that were incurred by the claimant in obtaining the tort recovery.

The threshold for a claimant's entitlement to recovery from the alcohol-related accident victim compensation fund can therefore be expressed in brief form as follows: if *U* is greater than $10,000, then the threshold requirement has been satisfied. In simple terms, if the estimate of total compensable losses minus payments made from collateral sources minus tort recovery from defendant (minus attorney's fees and litigation expenses in obtaining that recovery) equals more than $10,000, then the threshold for recovery from the compensation fund has been satisfied.

Later, in chapter 15, I will illustrate how the compensation fund operates with a series of hypothetical cases. A couple of hypotheticals here will illustrate how the threshold requirement set out here should be calculated.

Assume first that Claimant 1 has estimated compensable losses of $50,000. The claimant has already received medical insurance payments of $12,000 and $3,000 in continued salary payments over the period in which the claimant was unable to return to work. Although the accident occurred in a state that has a fault system, Claimant 1 has no reasonable prospect of recovering a judgment against any tort defendant other than the drinking driver who caused the accident, and that driver carries the minimum liability insurance policy coverage of $10,000 that is required in that state. Rather than litigate the issue of the drinking driver's liability, the insurance carrier has agreed to settle for the policy limits. Claimant 1's attorney receives 25 percent of that settlement as a fee, leaving a net tort recovery of $7,500. Plugging this information into the threshold formula, we see that Claimant 1 has crossed the threshold. The compensable losses of $50,000 minus the collateral source payments of $12,000 and $3,000 minus the net tort recovery of $7,500 produces an uncompensated loss figure of $27,500. Claimant 1 would therefore be entitled to proceed with a claim for compensation from the fund.

Claimant 2 has suffered an estimated compensable loss of $20,000. Of that loss, $8,000 has already been paid by the group medical insurance policy that is part of Claimant 2's employment benefit package, and another $2,000 will be paid for future physical therapy. In addition, the claimant's disability insurance pays 80 percent of the wages the claimant would have received but for the accident, which will amount to $2,500 by the time the claimant returns to work. Finally, although fault is in dispute in the accident, the drinking driver's liability insurer has agreed to settle for $5,000, of which the claimant's attorney will retain $2,000 as a fee. Under the formula, Claimant 2 fails to cross the threshold. Compensable losses of $20,000, minus collateral payments of $8,000 and $2,000 and $2,500, minus a net tort recovery of $3,000, results in a calculation of uncompensated losses of $4,500. Claimant 2 would therefore not be entitled to compensation from the fund.

Now that the question of how to calculate the amount of uncompensated loss has been answered, we turn to the question of what elements of harm should be compensable under the fund. The basic options are either to allow a claim for any injuries that were suffered in the accident or to specify those elements of harm for which claims from the compensation fund will be available. The former option seems to be most appropriate in the case of compensation systems that act either as the exclusive source of compensation or as a first resort. In the supplemental or last resort compensation situation, which exists here, it would be preferable for the enabling legislation to specify the elements of harm for which compensation is available. My proposed fund would specify the following four categories of compensable harm: (1) medical expenses, (2) loss of income, (3) physical pain, and (4) economic loss to survivors of a victim who is killed.

Given the purpose of the proposal, the fund at least ought to compensate for medical expenses. Included within this general category would be such items as hospital and physician expenses, medication, rehabilitation, and therapy. The fund should also cover another major category of pecuniary loss—the victim's loss of income from being unable to work after the accident.

What of nonpecuniary losses? In fault states, the tort system frequently allows their recovery, but no-fault insurance schemes typically refuse to compensate for such nonpecuniary items of loss as pain and suffering. In my proposal for an alcohol-related accident victim compensation fund, I adopt an intermediate position that includes a payment for physical pain as an element of compensable loss. This position is controversial in at least two respects, that it goes too far and that it does not go far enough.

Some critics will object that pain is too subjective a phenomenon to be suited for compensation from this kind of tax-based system. A related objection is that allowing for compensation of pain might quickly exhaust the fund. A compromise might be either to place a cap on payments for physical pain or to create a schedule for such payments. The National Childhood Vaccine Injury Act, unlike most no-fault plans that have been proposed or adopted in the United States, includes pain and suffering and emotional distress among the elements of injury for which compensation is available but caps the award at $250,000.[15] Another possibility would be to establish a grid system in which pain compensation was calculated according to more objective factors such as the nature of the physical injuries that were received in the accident and the medical evaluation of the existence and the severity of the pain that an accident victim has suffered.

Setting limits on compensation for pain is a way to respond to criticism that pain should not be included as a compensable loss. But limiting compensation could also raise criticism. I include physical pain among the compensable harms for this system because it is acknowledged to be a real consequence of the accident victim's injury. If that is so, a critic could argue, then mental anguish should be included within the scope of the compensation system as well.

No reasonable person would deny the reality of the emotional distress suffered by someone who is involved in a serious traffic accident, such as fear for one's own safety or for the safety of one's companions. Accident victims may also experience uncertainty about the seriousness of their own injuries or the injuries of others. Another reaction is the anguish of witnessing the injury or death of a family member or a companion as a result of the accident. A critic may therefore legitimately ask why physical pain is compensable from the fund but these other types of suffering are not.

The justification for this limitation admittedly may be less than completely satisfying. In part, the justification rests on a recognition that there are limits on the demands that a new compensation system can feasibly hope to meet. Lines have to be drawn somewhere, compromises have to be made, and this is simply one of those instances. Unlimited recovery for pain and suffering may raise the cost of a compensation system beyond the level at which it is likely to be supportable. A compromise position such as the one I propose is a practical alternative to eliminating pain and suffering entirely from the scope of the compensation system. Furthermore, constructing the sort of physical pain compensation schedule that was suggested earlier might be less arbitrary than attempting to provide some set schedule of recovery for a victim's mental anguish. Finally, because my compensation fund proposal does offer at least some compensation for pain, it is arguably more favorable to claimants than systems such as worker's compensation or automobile no-fault insurance, which typically exclude any recovery for pain and suffering. It would thus be inaccurate to characterize this part of the proposal as a measure that is insensitive to the nonpecuniary losses of accident victims.

The last type of compensable harm under the victim compensation fund is the death of the victim in an alcohol-related traffic accident. The wrongful death statutes that have been enacted in each state allow the courts to hold the person who wrongfully caused that victim's death liable for some measure of tort damages to the survivors of the decedent. That sort of legal remedy is obviously not very meaningful when the defendant is financially unable to satisfy a tort judgment. Accordingly, the victim compensation fund should make some provision for dealing with inadequate compensation in death cases. Here too, however, just as with the previous element of damages, some compromise may well be called for with respect both to the kinds of death claims that are within the scope of the fund and to the nature of the recovery that is available from the compensation fund.

The otherwise uncompensated or undercompensated accident fatalities that are most likely to produce a severe economic dislocation to the survivors of the decedent are those in which the decedent has left a surviving spouse and minor dependent children. The victim compensation fund I propose here limits death claims to those that are made by or on behalf of a survivor who falls into one of these categories. Similarly, the measure of recovery that I propose for those survivors is limited to the economic loss to the survivors. Finally, it should be made clear that the general rejection of a collateral source rule from the operation of the victim compensation fund applies to this element of accident loss just as much as to the others. As a result, the calculation of the economic loss to survivors should subtract any life insurance or pension fund proceeds that have been or that will be paid to those survivors.

Nothing in this part of the proposal should be interpreted as a suggestion that the deaths of accident victims who do not leave these particular categories of survivors are any less traumatic than are those that are selected for inclusion within the scope of the victim compensation fund. Nor should anyone take this proposal to mean that the only loss, or even the primary loss, that survivors suffer is financial. The fundamental point once again is that choices have to be made about what elements of loss can effectively be compensated from a finite source of funds, and where the limited dollars that are available for compensation can be put to the most effective use. The answer to those questions in this particular context suggests the desirability of using the victim compensation fund payments to reduce the negative financial impact that is caused by the accident-related death of a spouse or of a parent of a minor dependent child.

A compensation system that contains a threshold defined in terms of a dollar value of the losses suffered in an accident raises a legitimate concern about whether it creates an incentive for a claimant to inflate the estimate of loss in order to cross the threshold.[16] While the fear of inflation is not unjustified, it presents a substantially less serious problem in the context of an alcohol-related accident victim compensation fund than it does in the context of the typical automobile no-fault insurance scheme.

In a no-fault scheme, an accident victim may see that there is an advantage to increasing the amount of the expenses that are attributable to the accident in order to cross the threshold. The obvious benefit of crossing the threshold lies in the availability of a tort claim against another driver. When the gain from a tort claim includes the prospect of recovery of damages for a major item of loss, such as pain and suffering, that is excluded from the no-fault scheme, running up medical expenses and employing other methods for inflating the size of the accident loss would appear to be a rational means of buying a ticket in what Professor Jeffrey O'Connell has called the "lawsuit lottery."[17] Increasing the size of the loss that is attributable to an accident may be the best way for an accident victim in a no-fault jurisdiction to open up the possibility of a substantial tort recovery of damages for the nonpecuniary losses that are not available under the no-fault scheme.

In the victim compensation fund proposal offered here, the critical figure that must be calculated consists of the uncompensated losses that are compensable under the new system. As the preceding subsection has shown, those losses are limited to the four categories of harm that have been identified. Is there an incentive to inflate the estimate or the evidence of accident losses in a compensation system that is structured in this way?

The proposal, as it has been set out so far, does appear to create an incentive to inflate the estimate of accident losses. An accident victim who suffers $9,000 in uncompensated losses would be able to recover nothing from the compensation fund, while a similar victim who suffers $11,000 would be able to pursue a claim for $11,000 in compensation from the fund unless some other provision was included to deal with the problem. A claimant who is faced with the prospect of recovering nothing may very well decide it is best to try to raise the level of uncompensated losses so that the threshold is crossed.

Going from $9,000 to $11,000, as in this example, would produce a fairly high return on the investment that is made in increasing the amount of the loss.

The fact that the victim compensation fund threshold concentrates on uncompensated compensable losses may somewhat alleviate the incentive to inflate accident losses. Unlike the accident victim in a no-fault insurance state, a compensation fund claimant would not be able to open up the possibility of an unlimited recovery by crossing the threshold. Instead, recovery from the fund is limited to losses within four categories of compensable loss that have not been paid and will not likely be paid from other sources. The need to show that the losses are otherwise uncompensated will complicate the task of inflating losses. The fund claimant must show not only that a loss is attributable to the accident but also that any other coverage of that loss falls short of the total by at least the threshold amount.

A common method of crossing the threshold from the exclusivity of no-fault insurance to the potentially unlimited recovery of a tort judgment is to incur additional medical expenses. In the tort system, with its collateral source rule, a plaintiff would be able to recover damages from a defendant even if the additional expenses were covered by a first-party health insurance policy, so there is little disincentive to inflate those expenses. The proposed threshold for the victim compensation fund creates less of an incentive to exaggerate or to inflate losses. In the illustration that was just given, for example, incurring an additional $2,000 in medical expenses would not be to the claimant's advantage if those expenses were also covered by medical insurance, because the claimant's uncompensated loss would still be $9,000. Finally, the claimant will have to demonstrate that the losses for which compensation is claimed actually were suffered and that those losses are legitimately valued at the amount at which the claimant estimated them.

It cannot be denied, however, that some advantage is to be gained by successfully inflating the size of the uncompensated losses covered by the fund. In the case in which the uncompensated losses were $9,000 absent the inflation, the fund would pay nothing to the claimant. Nevertheless, even if the inflation attempt were successful, the fund would not have to be liable for the full amount of the covered losses the claimant proved. Instead, the incentive to inflate the size of the losses could be reduced by cutting down on the gain that a claimant could be expected to receive from the inflation attempt.

One method of accomplishing this result would be to treat the loss threshold as if it were also a loss-deductible provision of the system.

The claimant who was able to inflate the estimated uncompensated covered loss from $9,000 to $11,000 would thereby become entitled only to $1,000 in compensation from the fund. Limiting the claimant's gain in this way could diminish the incentive to inflate the threshold estimate of losses. But there are other reasons for structuring the threshold provision so that it operates as a loss-deductible provision, as we shall see.

The uncompensated loss threshold for a claimant's entry into the alcohol-related accident victim compensation fund could be constructed in such a way that it would operate with an effect that resembles two cost-sharing devices that are commonly included in insurance compensation schemes. Those devices are loss deductibles and coinsurance requirements. This proposal opts for treating the $10,000 threshold limit as an uncompensated deductible loss.

A loss deductible provision in an insurance policy typically requires an insurer to pay for a covered loss only if that loss is above the specified amount of the deductible. In a routine case, the insured is obligated to pay the first increment of the cost of the loss that was suffered in the insured event while the insurer must pay the rest of the cost, up to any policy limits that may apply. A coinsurance provision differs from a deductible provision by extending the insured's loss-paying obligation to include a specified proportion of the total covered loss rather than just the first increment of the loss. Under a deductible requirement in a standard first-party insurance coverage provision covering automobile collisions, for example, an insured could be required to pay the first $250 of a covered loss. A coinsurance provision in a similar policy could require the insured to absorb 20 percent of the total expenses that were generated by the loss. From the standpoint of the impact of the financial demands that these two types of provisions place on the insured, deductibles are favorable to the insured for large losses, while coinsurance is better for smaller losses.

The effect of both of these provisions is to make the insured bear some of the loss in every case. Part of the rationale for a provision of this sort is that it gives the insured a direct financial incentive to avoid losses, or at least to avoid filing claims on smaller covered losses. The uncompensated loss threshold could have the same effect in some alcohol-related accident cases, if the threshold were treated as a loss-sharing device rather than simply as a loss threshold that, once crossed, entitled the claimant to a payment from the fund for all of the covered losses.

The proposed compensation fund threshold is designed in large part to keep smaller claims out of the victim compensation fund system, thus reserving funds for the more seriously injured accident victims. It can, however, also be made to serve a loss-sharing function between the fund and the victim by designing the fund so that the claimant who crosses the threshold is only entitled to compensation for losses above the first $10,000 of uncompensated covered losses.

In this way the fund would benefit from a reduced demand on fund assets, in keeping with the rationale for having an uncompensated loss threshold provision in the first place. A loss-sharing provision might also have some effect in reducing the incentive to inflate losses, although that is not necessarily going to be true. A loss-sharing provision may actually end up increasing rather than decreasing the inflationary incentive as claimants attempt to reduce the size of the loss that they are ostensibly forced to share as a result of this type of provision.

A compensation entitlement limitation that effectively introduces an uncompensated loss deductible provision of $10,000 would require the accident victim to absorb the first $10,000 of uncompensated accident losses in every case. While it is probably true that some combination of tort remedies and first-party insurance payments are available to shift the first $10,000 of the accident loss away from most victims, a deductible requirement that is built into the compensation fund would require some loss sharing by all victims, whether they had some other source of compensation or not. This part of the proposal makes it more likely that compensation fund payments are reserved for those accident victims who are most seriously injured and undercompensated. A loss-deductible provision should tend to deter claims from being filed for less serious accidents. This would reduce the pressure on the fund to become the compensation source of first resort for victims injured in alcohol-related accidents that are difficult to establish as a basis for a tort claim.

The deductible provision will also avoid the undesirable effect of appearing to reward those accident victims who have no other source of compensation while penalizing those who have some other source. Consider, for example, three accident victims who have suffered identical losses of $15,000. The maximum claim on the compensation system with a $10,000 uncompensated loss deductible provision would be $5,000, regardless of whether any or all of the remaining $10,000 was covered by any other source. Conversely, no accident victim would be subjected to an uncompensated accident loss of more than $10,000 regardless of the existence of other sources of accident loss compensation. A victim in this example who has no other source of compensation would, it is true, end up with compensation for only one-third of the accident loss. That effect needs to be kept in perspective, however, by considering the other possibilities that could be presented with the other two victims. A victim who received any compensation from another source up to $5,000 would be entitled to recover from the fund, but only to the extent that the uncompensated loss exceeded $10,000. A victim who received some other compensation that amounted to $5,000 or more would not be eligible to receive any compensation from the fund.

The accident victims in this illustration are affected by a provision of the victim compensation fund that treats the uncompensated loss threshold as a deductible. Suppose, on the other hand, that the uncompensated loss threshold were to operate differently, so that there was no loss-sharing effect. If the first accident victim again had no other source of compensation for the accident loss, the uncompensated losses of the victim would be greater than the threshold amount to allow the claimant to obtain entry into the compensation system. Unlike the loss deductible treatment that is included in the fund proposal that was just described, however, the result of this claimant's crossing the threshold is that the victim would be entitled to compensation from the fund for the full $15,000 of uncompensated loss.

Now consider the effect that this alternative treatment of the threshold would have on a victim who is able to obtain some compensation or payment for losses that were suffered in an identical accident. A claimant who was able to draw on some other source of payment for covered losses, such as medical and disability insurance, would be precluded from any recovery from the fund as long as the other source paid more than $5,000. The effect would be that the accident victims who were more able to spread the costs of the losses that they suffer would be less likely to shift any of those losses to the victim compensation fund.

It is, of course, possible that this effect might be considered desirable. Accident victims who have no other source of compensation may be among the most truly disadvantaged citizens of our society. Requiring them to bear any of the loss that is attributable to an accident may have a disproportionately adverse effect on their lives and welfare. On balance, however, it would seem to be preferable that the entitlement to compensation from the fund should be constructed in such a way that a similar loss-sharing effect is imposed on all accident victims who are otherwise eligible for compensation, regardless of whether they have other sources of payment for the covered losses.

The initial major significance of the fund threshold, then, is that it serves to identify those who are most seriously injured and under-compensated. Once those victims have been identified, the fund is designed to step in to provide payment of the otherwise uncompensated losses that are covered by the fund. However, the obligation to pay for those losses extends only above the first $10,000 of uncompensated compensable losses. As a result, no victim of an alcohol-related accident who is entitled to be compensated from the fund should ever have to bear without compensation more than $10,000 of accident losses that fall into the four categories of harm that are covered by this proposed compensation system.

## NOTES

1. The classic study of the relationship between accident losses and the level of compensation that is provided by the tort system was performed by researchers from the University of Michigan more than a quarter-century ago. *See* A. CONARD, J. MORGAN, R. PRATT, C. VOLTZ & R. BOMBAUGH, AUTOMOBILE ACCIDENT COST AND PAYMENT: STUDIES IN THE ECONOMICS OF INJURY REPARATION (1964). Subsequent studies have been performed by the United States Department of Transportation. *See, e.g.,* AUTOMOBILE INSURANCE AND COMPENSATION STUDY: MOTOR VEHICLE CRASH LOSSES AND THEIR COMPENSATION IN THE UNITED STATES (1971). *See also* O'Connell & Barker, *Compensation for Injury and Illness: An Update of the Conard-Morgan Tabulations,* 47 OHIO ST. L. J. 913 (1986).

2. TORT POLICY WORKING GROUP, REPORT OF THE TORT POLICY WORKING GROUP ON THE CAUSES, EXTENT, AND POLICY IMPLICATIONS IN THE CURRENT CRISIS IN INSURANCE AVAILABILITY AND AFFORDABILITY (1986). The Working Group consisted of personnel drawn from a variety of federal agencies charged with some responsibility for activities affected by the imposition of tort liability. The political agenda of this study of tort law was marked by hostility to the expansion of tort liability that had occurred over the previous two decades.

3. *Id.,* AN UPDATE ON THE LIABILITY CRISIS (1987).

4. "No one pretends that democracy is perfect or all-wise. Indeed, it has been said that democracy is the worst form of Government except all those other forms that have been tried from time to time." W. CHURCHILL, Speech to House of Commons (Nov. 11, 1947).

5. *See* RESTATEMENT (SECOND) OF TORTS § 914 (1979).

6. 42 U.S.C. § 300aa-15(e)(1).

7. CAL. GOV'T CODE § 13965(d) (West Supp. 1990).

8. The collateral source rule is explained in D. DOBBS, HANDBOOK OF THE LAW OF REMEDIES 185-86 (1973). A careful analysis of the rule is offered

in Fleming, *The Collateral Source Rule and Loss Allocation*, 54 CALIF. L. REV. 1478 (1966).

9. The American rule that generally prohibits a recovery of attorney's fees, which was discussed in the first section of this chapter, is probably the best example of this phenomenon.

10. *See, e.g.*, LANDES & POSNER, ECONOMIC STRUCTURE, at 252.

11. 42 U.S.C. § 300aa-15(g).

12. *See* HUTCHINSON, DWELLING ON THE THRESHOLD, at 219-20.

13. CAL. GOV'T CODE § 13965(a)(5) (West Supp. 1990).

14. The intentional torts that are most closely linked to criminal activity that produces personal injury to the victim are thoroughly discussed in PROSSER & KEETON, LAW OF TORTS, at 33-54.

15. 42 U.S.C. § 300aa-15(a)(4).

16. *See, e.g.*, O'Connell, *Must Health and Disability Insurance Subsidize Wasteful Injury Suits?*, 41 RUTGERS L. REV. 1055 (1989).

17. J. O'CONNELL, THE LAWSUIT LOTTERY: ONLY THE LAWYERS WIN (1979).

# 13

## Financing and Operating the Compensation System

The remedies available to victims of drinking-driver traffic accidents under the current tort litigation system are seriously deficient. The tort system, as it currently operates, allows manufacturers and distributors of alcoholic beverages to avoid most of the accident costs associated with their products. When the tort system does provide compensation to injured victims, it frequently does so in ways that greatly risk undercompensating or overcompensating the victims. It is possible to design an administrative structure that is more effective than the current tort system in channeling more complete compensation to the most seriously injured and undercompensated victims of drinking drivers and in imposing a greater portion of the accident costs on the alcohol industry.

Injury-compensation dollars tend to be worth less to the injured person the longer that payment is delayed and the greater the cost of processing the claim before those dollars have arrived. The tort system's method of compensating accident victims seems calculated to produce an award that is worth far less than would be acceptable under a system that prized speed and efficiency of compensation, particularly when prompt compensation would improve an accident victim's chances of receiving effective rehabilitation treatment.[1]

At the opposite end of the spectrum, in terms of delay and expense, lies an administrative compensation scheme featuring routinely prompt payment once the appropriate prerequisites have been satisfied. Social Security Administration schemes, at least in the ideal, are a good example of this sort of system,[2] as are workers' compensation systems. The administrative alternative to tort compensation is not without its drawbacks, however. What is gained in speed and in cheaper claim processing costs may be offset by decreases in precision and care and in the attention given to the unique factors of a particular case. A further cost is the administrative insensitivity that results from placing the individual problems presented by specific cases within a narrow bureaucratic context. Even within an administrative compensation system, the benefits of processing claims in a nonjudicial setting can easily be lost if the decision-making process that is used by the relevant agencies is modeled too closely after the adversarial trial system.[3]

Removing accident claims in drinking-driver cases from the tort system entirely and relegating them either to a purely private insurance scheme or to a governmental compensation vehicle is a step that is unlikely to prove attractive or beneficial to the various interests affected. The alternative proposal that I offer here draws on the experience of other compensation plans to create a compensation fund that will at least provide the more seriously injured victims of drinking-driver accidents payment for some of their uncompensated losses. In this chapter I will describe how the compensation fund will be financed and how the compensation claims system will operate. In chapter 14, I will further explain the political constraints on designing a compensation fund, and then in chapter 15 I will present a comprehensive model statute to establish the compensation fund I envision.

## Financing the Compensation Fund System

The first practical concern in creating a new injury-compensation fund is determining the source and the amount of the financing needed to operate the system. This determination depends more than anything else on an evaluation within each state of the extent to which existing tort remedies and insurance resources are likely to leave the target population undercompensated. As an initial step, then, a state legislature should develop as clear a picture as possible of the compensation that drinking-driver accident victims actually receive under current legal rules and loss-distribution practices.

This is not an easy task. It will be necessary to estimate the compensation that is *not* provided for victims of accidents that involve intoxicated or alcohol-impaired drivers. Furthermore, because the compensation fund proposal expands the scope of what is considered to be an alcohol-related accident for purposes of compensation from the fund, an estimate will have to be made as well of the number of accidents that would fall under the scope of the fund. Legislative expertise, combined with a sensitivity to local experience and a willingness to act in the face of uncertainty, should provide a sufficient understanding of the magnitude of the problem to avoid paralysis in responding to it.

If a legislature decides to put the victim compensation fund into operation, considerable care must be given to the design of the tax assessment and collection process. In order to work with any success at all, the tax on alcoholic beverages that is intended to finance the victim compensation system should involve a relatively uncomplicated way of identifying both who should pay the new tax and how much is owed.

To ensure that the system's administrative costs do not outweigh the value of the system, the timing of the tax's assessment and collection should occur in conjunction with, rather than in isolation from, the routine business operations of the alcohol industry. One of the major objectives of this compensation system is to shift some portion of drinking-driver accident losses to the upper reaches of the alcohol industry, so their routine business transactions should be targeted. Furthermore, because the parties engaged in those transactions are already subject to state and federal excise taxes on alcoholic beverages, a fairly complete record of relevant sales is available, as well as a clearly identifiable event to which the collection of the new taxes can be tied.

I propose that the alcohol-related accident victim compensation fund be financed by a tax assessed at the level of the last wholesale distribution of alcoholic beverages prior to the goods passing into the hands of the retailers who will be responsible for the sale or service of the alcohol to the ultimate consumer. Wholesalers will pass the costs of the new tax on to commercial dispensers, who will then pass them on to consumers. Such a tax should effectively reach all alcoholic beverage consumers approximately equally, whether through higher prices for alcoholic drinks served by a commercial dispenser or higher prices for alcoholic beverages purchased directly from a retail seller.

The justification for levying the tax on the last wholesale distributor is based on an attempt to make collection of the tax easier and a wish to promote an appropriate degree of localization of the tax. Obviously, the number of wholesalers who do business within a state is much lower than the number of retailers and commercial service establishments. Attaching the obligation to pay the tax at the wholesale level will reduce the record-keeping and accounting burden on industry members and on the state agency charged with the responsibility for collecting the tax.

If this rationale of administrative convenience is extended too far, however, it could lead to a decision to assess the tax at the point of import or at the point of initial distribution from the domestic brewer or distiller. If a tax of this sort were imposed as a federal rather than a state matter, then this decision would be both defensible and sensible.

But because the tax is a state matter in this proposal, it makes more sense to tie the tax to an in-state event. Such a conclusion is not logically necessary, however. A liquor distiller could, for example, keep track of the volume and the type of distribution that is made to firms located within a particular state and then be responsible for paying a tax based on that distribution. On the other hand, wholesaler taxation, though not logically compelled, has the advantage of localizing the tax within the state that adopted the proposal based on its benefits to accident victims and the rationale of allocative efficiency. Taxing wholesalers involves a minimal degree of administrative inconvenience compared to attaching the tax at the manufacturing or importing stages of distribution. If a wholesaler were to move operations out of a state that adopted this victim compensation system, the tax obligation could simply shift to the occurrence of the first transaction that takes place within the state.

The next step in implementing the tax-supported victim compensation fund is to calculate the tax to be assessed on alcoholic beverages. First a basic taxing unit must be chosen. I propose that the tax be levied on a uniform basis according to the alcohol content of the beverage being taxed. The easiest way to structure the tax would be to set it at a certain amount per ounce of ethanol (or ethyl alcohol) contained in the beverage.

Some examples of the size and volume of common alcoholic beverage sales containers can show the general effects that a tax constructed in this way can have on the price of alcohol to the consumer who purchases from a retailer. Alcohol consumers who purchase drinks from a commercial dispenser would face similar increases, because the dispenser will have paid a price for the alcohol that reflects precisely the same rate of taxation.

Assume a tax rate for these illustrations of one cent per ounce of ethanol contained in a beverage. The first illustration involves a beer that is 4.5 percent ethanol, which is roughly the alcohol content of a common domestic beer. Some of the higher quality beers are around 5 percent, while others, particularly the light beers, have alcohol contents between 3.5 and 4 percent. If the beer in this example is sold in the usual manner, in a six-pack of twelve-ounce cans, then each six-pack contains a total of 72 ounces of beer, with 4.5 percent of those 72 ounces consisting of the ethanol that is subject to the tax. Those figures mean that for each cent at which ethanol content is taxed, a six-pack of this average beer would be subject to an additional compensation fund tax of 3.24 cents. A tax of four cents per ounce of ethanol, would raise the price of a six-pack by only thirteen cents. Considering that the current federal excise tax on a six-pack of beer is only 32 cents, this increase is not a very dramatic price to pay for the benefits to be gained by setting up the compensation fund.

Distilled spirits, if not sold in liters or fractions of liters, are frequently sold in bottles that contain one-fifth of a gallon (which is why a bottle of whiskey or other distilled spirits is called a "fifth"). For a second example of the price effect of the new tax, consider a whiskey that is 80 proof, a common proof value for an average whiskey. The alcohol content of a beverage is one-half of the proof of the beverage. Accordingly, an 80-proof whiskey has an ethanol content of 40 percent. There are 128 ounces in a gallon and 25.6 ounces in a bottle that holds a fifth of a gallon, with 40 percent of those ounces being ethanol. The resulting calculation therefore shows that each one cent of tax on an ounce of ethanol would result in a compensation fund tax of 10.24 cents per fifth of 80-proof distilled spirits.

Similar calculations can be made for wine. Consider a wine sold in bottles that hold three-quarters of a liter (or 750 milliliters), or 25.2 ounces. If the wine has an alcohol content of twelve percent, then that bottle of wine would be subject to a compensation fund tax of 3.02 cents.

Each one cent of the tax that is levied on alcoholic beverages would therefore be translated into a proportional tax increase as follows:

Beer (six-pack of 12 oz. containers)—3.24 cents
Whiskey (80-proof fifth)—10.24 cents
Wine (750 ml. bottle)—3.02 cents

The actual consumer price increase would probably be slightly higher than this calculation indicates, assuming that firms will pass the costs of their internal administrative process to pay the tax on to consumers. It should be noted, however, that the cost of complying with the taxation requirements of this compensation fund proposal would be fixed at a particular level, regardless of the level of the tax rate adopted. As the tax rate increases, therefore, the proportional share of a price increase that reflects compliance costs should decrease.

The size of the tax increase that a consumer would face as a result of adopting the new tax on alcohol are not very large compared to the other federal and state excise taxes on alcohol. Nor do they seem very significant when they are compared to the costs of production and distribution that are already factored into the price of alcoholic beverages. In fact, one might be concerned that the new tax is unlikely to produce much revenue with which to finance the compensation fund. Representative consumption figures for each of the fifty states should dispel that concern, however.

The National Institute on Alcohol Abuse and Alcoholism reported the "apparent alcohol consumption" of beer, wine, and spirits in 1987 in the fifty states.[4] The results are labeled "apparent" because they are based on assumptions about the average ethanol content of the beverages whose sales were monitored.[5] The first four columns of table 13-1 are derived from that report, and they list consumption in thousands of gallons of alcoholic beverages and ethanol. Based on those consumption figures, the final column shows the revenue that would be produced in each state by each one cent per ounce of ethanol the new tax levied on that volume of consumption. Based on these figures, the application of a tax on a multiple of each ounce of ethanol sold would result in significant revenues (see table 13-1). Of course, estimates of the exact amount of tax revenue that would result would have to take into account future consumption of alcohol based on the responsiveness of consumer demand for alcohol to price increases and a host of other behavioral factors as well. Nevertheless, it is apparent that substantial sums of money can be raised for accident victim compensation by relatively small tax increases on alcoholic beverages. Remember that the revenue figure in table 13-1 for each state can be generated by a tax increase of only a little over three cents for the average six-pack of beer or bottle of wine, and a little over ten cents for the average bottle of distilled spirits.

As the size of the demand that is likely to be made on the victim compensation fund in a particular state becomes clearer during the legislative hearing process as the legislature considers a proposal of this type, then the amount of tax revenue needed to meet that demand can be estimated. The initial tax rate per ounce of ethanol contained in an alcoholic beverage can then be made by dividing the estimated demand by a figure that roughly corresponds to the expected revenue listed in table 13-1.

Take, for example, the state of Illinois. At 1987 levels of consumption, just under $100 million in tax revenue could be generated for the compensation fund by a tax of 3 cents per ounce of ethanol (see table 13-1). That tax would only raise the price of a six-pack of beer or a bottle of wine by around ten cents. Similarly, if the legislature of Virginia were to determine that the compensation fund should be provided with $75 million per year, a tax on 1987 levels of consumption of only 5 cents per ounce of ethanol would be sufficient.

State alcohol-beverage-control agencies already compile records on the manufacture, import, and sale of alcoholic beverages for purposes of the excise taxes that they are responsible for collecting. Thus, the additional administrative burden of compiling substantial amounts of completely new data should not prove to be a drawback of financing the compensation system with an additional tax on alcohol. The consumption figures that the National Institute on Alcohol and Alcoholism generated in its 1987 study were derived from actual sales figures or by extrapolation from the excise tax experience within each of the states. Alcoholic beverages are products that are already subject to a good deal of information gathering, so the new tax to finance the accident victim compensation fund should have a minimal impact as far as the burden of tax data collection is concerned.

In trying to estimate this burden, it may be helpful to distinguish between the two basic types of state regulation of the distribution of alcoholic beverages that are used in this country.[6] In a "control" state, an agency of the state itself engages in the retail sale of at least some alcoholic beverages, usually distilled spirits, that are marketed for consumption outside the premises on which they are sold. In a "license" state, a state agency issues licenses for private firms to sell alcoholic beverages to consumers. Even control states issue licenses, such as licenses for sales that involve consumption on the premises and licenses for the retail sale of beverages sold outside the "state store" system. The critical difference between the two types of regulation thus turns on whether or not the state is itself a retail seller of alcoholic beverages.

The difference between control states and license states will have some effect on the ease with which the new tax for financing the compensation fund can be collected. In license states, wholesale distributors will be required to record the types and the amounts of alcoholic beverages they distribute for retail sale within the state. Then they will have to calculate their tax liability based on the ethanol content of those beverages. The new tax may require the distributors to determine what is the ethanol content of the beverages they distribute, but the other information that is required should already be a matter of record under the existing excise tax system. Payments from distributors to the appropriate state agency could then be made at regular intervals, such as the end of each quarter or of each month. It would be even easier to levy the new tax in control states, where retail sales to the public are made predominantly or exclusively through state-owned stores. With the distribution system controlled by a state agency, the tax can easily be levied on a distributor at the point in

Table 13-1
1987 Consumption Levels and Potential Tax Revenue by State

| State | Total Gallons Consumed[a] | | | Total Gallons Ethanol[a] | Expected Tax Revenue[a] |
|---|---|---|---|---|---|
| | Beer | Wine | Spirits | | |
| AL | 78,730 | 4,571 | 4,803 | 6,121 | $ 7,834,880 |
| AK | 14,041 | 1,605 | 1,208 | 1,339 | 1,713,920 |
| AZ | 98,739 | 9,557 | 5,546 | 7,972 | 10,204,160 |
| AR | 45,262 | 1,548 | 2,420 | 3,238 | 4,144,640 |
| CA | 662,484 | 125,764 | 49,516 | 66,535 | 85,164,800 |
| CO | 83,022 | 8,941 | 5,875 | 7,322 | 9,372,160 |
| CT | 67,603 | 10,695 | 7,183 | 7,383 | 9,450,240 |
| DE | 16,691 | 1,711 | 1,537 | 1,608 | 2,058,240 |
| FL | 332,631 | 32,128 | 24,895 | 29,419 | 37,656,320 |
| GA | 132,740 | 10,166 | 11,971 | 12,241 | 15,668,480 |
| HI | 29,852 | 2,661 | 1,587 | 2,344 | 3,000,320 |
| ID | 21,972 | 2,219 | 1,061 | 1,714 | 2,193,920 |
| IL | 288,792 | 27,637 | 19,489 | 24,629 | 31,525,120 |
| IN | 121,685 | 7,624 | 7,150 | 9,419 | 12,056,320 |
| IA | 65,507 | 3,699 | 3,171 | 4,738 | 6,064,640 |
| KS | 48,926 | 2,481 | 2,671 | 3,628 | 4,643,840 |
| KY | 67,736 | 3,155 | 4,297 | 5,234 | 6,699,520 |
| LA | 103,346 | 6,348 | 6,218 | 8,044 | 10,296,320 |
| ME | 26,872 | 2,783 | 2,113 | 2,443 | 3,127,040 |
| MD | 105,649 | 10,791 | 9,534 | 10,093 | 12,919,040 |
| MA | 138,965 | 19,189 | 13,255 | 14,216 | 18,196,480 |
| MI | 215,038 | 18,944 | 15,204 | 18,415 | 23,571,200 |
| MN | 98,593 | 8,256 | 7,689 | 8,685 | 11,116,800 |
| MS | 56,609 | 1,455 | 3,217 | 4,067 | 5,205,760 |
| MO | 123,762 | 8,682 | 7,164 | 9,655 | 12,358,400 |
| MT | 22,017 | 1,624 | 1,178 | 1,688 | 2,160,640 |
| NE | 39,155 | 2,162 | 2,011 | 2,873 | 3,677,440 |
| NV | 36,850 | 5,292 | 4,118 | 4,046 | 5,178,880 |
| NH | 36,631 | 3,302 | 4,118 | 3,779 | 4,837,120 |
| NJ | 164,728 | 26,171 | 15,388 | 17,159 | 21,963,520 |
| NM | 41,494 | 3,128 | 1,863 | 3,042 | 3,893,760 |
| NY | 370,987 | 53,585 | 31,814 | 36,778 | 47,075,840 |
| NC | 127,989 | 11,174 | 8,965 | 10,913 | 13,968,640 |
| ND | 15,634 | 817 | 1,110 | 1,269 | 1,624,320 |
| OH | 258,237 | 15,795 | 12,292 | 18,747 | 23,996,160 |

Table 13-1 (Continued)
1987 Consumption Levels and Potential Tax Revenue by State

| State | Total Gallons Consumed[a] | | | Total Gallons Ethanol[a] | Expected Tax Revenue[a] |
|---|---|---|---|---|---|
| | Beer | Wine | Spirits | | |
| OK | 59,591 | 2,975 | 3,539 | 4,531 | 5,799,680 |
| OR | 61,539 | 8,925 | 3,814 | 5,500 | 7,040,000 |
| PA | 299,912 | 15,352 | 14,607 | 21,524 | 27,550,720 |
| RI | 25,221 | 3,242 | 1,858 | 2,322 | 2,972,160 |
| SC | 80,644 | 5,699 | 5,791 | 6,762 | 8,655,360 |
| SD | 15,215 | 829 | 1,063 | 1,232 | 1,576,960 |
| TN | 101,866 | 4,600 | 5,876 | 7,610 | 9,740,800 |
| TX | 461,986 | 28,992 | 19,066 | 32,423 | 41,501,440 |
| UT | 21,850 | 1,366 | 1,407 | 1,742 | 2,229,760 |
| VT | 15,229 | 1,970 | 1,055 | 1,376 | 1,761,280 |
| VA | 148,506 | 9,497 | 8,233 | 11,316 | 14,484,480 |
| WA | 99,376 | 15,647 | 6,978 | 9,379 | 12,005,120 |
| WV | 37,683 | 1,525 | 1,508 | 2,517 | 3,221,760 |
| WI | 151,475 | 10,516 | 9,066 | 11,926 | 15,265,280 |
| WY | 12,020 | 698 | 780 | 954 | 1,221,120 |

*Note:* The consumption data are drawn from the National Institute on Alcohol Abuse and Alcoholism, *Surveillance Report No. 13: Apparent Per Capita Alcohol Consumption, National, State and Regional Trends, 1977-87* (1989), Table 2, 16-17.

[a] In thousands of gallons.

[b] Based on a tax of one cent per ounce of ethanol.

the chain of distribution at which the beverages first come under the agency's control.

Adopting a new administrative program also requires a look at what administrative mechanisms will be needed to implement the program and what the start-up costs of the program will be. If the prices of alcoholic beverages sold through state-owned stores in a control state currently generate a profit for the state, perhaps a portion of that profit could be used to fund the start-up costs of the new compensation fund system. The basic tax rate could be based, then, on an estimate of the on-going expenses of administering the claims system. If retail sales operate outside of a state store system, so that the state has no opportunity to make a profit from the sale of alcohol, then the basic tax rate could be set to cover both the start-up costs of the fund and its on-going expenses. Another way to finance the fund's start-up costs would be to build an additional charge into the license fee that states require distributors of alcoholic beverages to pay for the privilege of dealing in such products. Yet a third option, which I have adopted for the model statute presented in chapter 15, is to plan for a delay between the date the tax is first collected and the date on which the claims process will actually start to run (that is, the date on which the occurrence of an alcohol-related accident will entitle an accident victim to be compensated from the fund). If the new tax is collected quarterly, for example, and the implementation of the claims process is postponed for as long as a year, then the state would have on hand at least two or three quarterly receipts of revenue prior to the first obligation of the compensation fund to make payments to eligible accident victims.

The current excise tax structure for alcoholic beverages at both the federal and state levels assesses taxes against different categories of alcoholic beverages at different rates of taxation. Should the new tax on alcohol used to finance the victim compensation fund attempt to equalize these rates by raising the tax on beer and wine to equal the tax on distilled spirits? A move toward equalizing these taxes on alcohol is likely to be highly controversial to the segments of the industry that are currently taxed at a low rate. Furthermore, it would have a dramatically different effect on the price that consumers would pay for alcoholic beverages. Thus it would be best to resist any suggestion that a measure to equalize alcohol taxes overall be linked to the implementation of the compensation fund. Nor is this an instance in which some compromise needs to be made in the proposed structure of the compensation fund. There is no reason either in principle or as a matter of policy why the new tax could not simply be calculated in a manner that preserves the existing federal and state tax rate differentials among the various categories of alcoholic beverages.

Given the purpose of this new tax, however, it is very important that the tax be based not simply on the volume of the beverage but on the alcohol content of the beverage as well. Ideally, to meet the goal of cost internalization to the fullest extent, the price of alcohol consumed by drinking drivers should reflect the accident costs associated with that consumption, while alcohol consumers who do not drink and drive should pay a price that does not include that particular social cost of alcohol. Unfortunately, that price differential is impossible to impose, at least at anything that even remotely resembles a reasonable level of cost.

The next best alternative is to identify the intoxicating agent in alcoholic beverages as the appropriate determinant of the amount of tax that will be assessed. In that way, the tax that is levied on a particular beverage will bear some rough correlation to the beverage's potential to produce alcohol impairment. Further refinement of the tax rate would not seem to be feasible or cost effective, at least during the initial consideration of a compensation fund proposal of this sort. The proposal's uniform tax rate according to ethanol content of the alcoholic beverage being taxed is considerably more manageable than attempting to apportion tax rates according to the involvement of a particular beverage or brand name, or a particular alcohol manufacturer or distributor, with drinking-driver accidents. The difficulty of apportioning liability in products liability cases and other tort suits demonstrates the problems that such specific assignments of legal responsibility would cause. Sound legal precedent exists for the kind of rough accident-loss apportionment scheme incorporated into the tax-based financing structure I propose here.

One of the key features of current tort liability rules is the need to establish a causal link between the defendant's conduct and the injury to the plaintiff. A tort plaintiff is normally required to prove that the defendant's conduct was a cause in fact of the injury for which compensation is sought. In the routine tort case, this requirement does not pose much of a problem for the plaintiff. However, there are some recurrent situations in which even minimal causal evidence is difficult or impossible for a plaintiff to produce. Suppose, for example, that the plaintiff was a passenger who was riding in a car that was involved in a three-vehicle collision. Car A, which was traveling north, crossed the center line of the highway and struck Car B, which was traveling south. Car C then hit the rear of Car B. The plaintiff was a passenger in Car B, and she suffered serious physical injuries. When she sues the driver of Car A, she is met with the allegation that her proof of a causal connection between that defendant's conduct and her injury is purely speculative, on the reasoning that the injury could just as well have come about exclusively from the second collision by Car C as from the first collision with Car A. The standard tort law response today, as we have seen, would be to treat all of the contributing causes as causes in fact of an indivisible injury to the plaintiff. The system would then let the individual defendants who are treated in that way sort out among themselves how the damages for the injury to the plaintiff should be apportioned.

The causation proof problems in this first example are matters of assigning specific responsibility for particular items of harm in a situation in which there is uncertainty about what actually happened. Those problems are resolvable, albeit not without some controversy, because there is at least an agreement that each of the parties who is potentially liable to the plaintiff was involved in *some* way in the incident in which the plaintiff was injured. Other cases involving multiple possible causes can present more difficult conceptual problems. Consider the plaintiff who develops cancer as a result of her mother's ingestion of the drug DES, which was prescribed prior to 1970 to prevent miscarriage, during the time she was pregnant with the plaintiff. Hundreds of firms manufactured and sold DES during the relevant years in a form that was indistinguishable from any other firm's product. The "DES daughters" who sue to recover compensation for their DES-related injuries today seldom have persuasive evidence about the identity of the pharmaceutical firm that manufactured the particular doses of DES that were taken by their mothers as long ago as two decades prior to the first appearance of their medical problems. Identifying which of the many possible manufacturers of the drug actually made the specific quantity of DES that caused the injury to the plaintiff has proven to be an insurmountable hurdle to compensation in virtually all of the DES cases that have been filed.

The response of the more liberal courts has been to fashion some sort of innovative causal doctrine that allows the plaintiff to proceed against one or more DES manufacturers despite the absence of any evidence that a particular manufacturer made the DES that was taken by her mother.[7] An important part of these new doctrines is the courts' decision that the liability of the DES manufacturers who are sued should be apportioned according to the percentage of sales that the manufacturers made either nationally or in the relevant geographic market at the time in which the plaintiff's mother received DES.

The justification for a decision along these lines rests on two general ideas. First, each of the manufacturers was engaged in precisely the same risk-creating conduct. Second, it is a matter of fortuity that the plaintiff's mother purchased one manufacturer's DES rather than another's. Combining these ideas, it is apparent that each manufacturer contributed to a general risk of injury to the daughters of DES consumers. The share of that risk for any manufacturer of the identical versions of the drug is that manufacturer's market share. When a plaintiff can prove that she has suffered harm as a result of her mother taking DES, a rough sense of justice supports holding manufacturers liable for the approximate share of the risk of harm that they created.

It is just that sort of general apportionment concept that underlies the tax structure I have adopted in my compensation fund proposal for victims of drinking drivers. The alcoholic beverages distributed by the wholesalers who are subject to the new alcohol tax that will finance the fund all create some risk of contributing to a traffic accident caused by alcohol-impaired driving. A tax structure based on the ethanol content of alcoholic beverages serves just as well as any other to reflect both the market share that the individual beverage and its distributors have in the taxing jurisdiction and the general share of the risk of an alcohol-related accident that is attributable to the beverage and its distributor. Given that the dual purposes of the tax are to compensate alcohol-related accident victims and to do so from a fund that associates drinking-driver accident losses more closely with the alcohol industry, the tax structure proposed here is optimal, at least in the introductory stage of the compensation fund operation. In chapter 14, I will briefly describe a proposal for a statutory provision for a post-enactment reallocation of the tax burden that would be based on actual experience with the operation of the fund, following the development of more precise and reliable information.

## *Processing Compensation Claims*

How claims are processed will have the greatest impact on the administrative costs of adopting a new system of compensation. The compensation fund system proposed here is designed to complement, rather than completely replace, the remedies provided by the existing tort system in a state. With the system viewed in that way, establishing a proper relationship between tort claims and compensation fund claims requires a good deal of care. At least an equal degree of care is required to maintain whatever advantages can be derived from using an administrative rather than a litigation system for processing claims for injury compensation.

A state that is considering putting a new compensation scheme into effect has two basic choices in deciding how to administer the program. The first is to create a new state agency charged with the specific and exclusive task of administering the new system. The alternative is to authorize appropriate existing state administrative agencies to operate the new system. Obviously, each option has its pros and cons that must be evaluated. A new agency can bring a fresh perspective to the problem that is addressed by the creation of the compensation system. However, a new agency will also need time to develop experience and a level of expertise in the routine functioning of the program.

Which option a state selects will depend in large part on the degree of confidence that the state legislature has in identifying existing agencies capable of administering the new program. Essentially, the system's operation involves three tasks. First, information about the distribution of alcoholic beverages within a state needs to be collected. Second, the tax that is used to finance the compensation system needs to be collected. Third, the claims for payment of compensation from the fund need to be administered. Rather than create a new agency that would then be required to develop expertise in all three areas, the legislature could keep administrative costs at an acceptable level by assigning each task to the respective state agencies with the greatest experience in performing that task in other contexts. Under this approach, the state's alcohol beverage control agency would be given the primary responsibility for collecting the necessary information about alcohol distribution. Employing this agency has the considerable advantage of drawing on the expertise about the alcohol industry that has been built up over the operating lifetime of the agency. The responsibility for the assessment and collection of the new alcohol tax could be given to the state agency currently responsible for collecting the revenues of the state's excise tax on alcoholic beverages. Depending on a state's practice, that agency may be the state department of taxation or it may be the alcoholic beverage control department.[8] Finally, the authority to process compensation fund claims could be given to the agency that has developed the most experience in that type of activity. Each state has some agency responsible for administering its existing compensation or benefit systems, such as workers' compensation plans or public welfare programs. Some activities called for under this proposal will likely be outside the previous experience of an existing agency, such as asserting a tort claim in exercise of the agency's subrogation rights. Nevertheless, although an agency may have to acquire new talents and draw on different skills in order to perform some of its additional responsibilities, at least an existing agency can build on the considerable store of knowledge and expertise in claims processing with which it starts.

If a state does decide to parcel out the various responsibilities that are involved in administering the compensation fund system among some of the existing parts of its administrative agency structure, it is essential that their activities be coordinated. To that end, an office of victim compensation fund administrator should be created. This administrator should be given the ultimate responsibility and accountability for the implementation of the legislation creating the new compensation fund. Administrative regulations required by the enabling legislation should be issued by the administrator. If they are issued by the separate agencies, they should at least be subject to the approval of the administrator. Coordination of the efforts within and among the different agencies involved in the taxing and claims-processing functions would be the major on-going task of the administrator. If a state were to opt instead for the creation of a new state agency that was given sole responsibility for all of the aspects of administering the victim compensation fund, then the head of that state agency would assume the responsibilities of the fund administrator.

The initial determination that the claims processing agency must make is whether a claimant is eligible for compensation from the victim compensation fund. Recall that under this proposal the claimant must cross a threshold for entry into the system (chapter 12). The claimant must prove to the satisfaction of the agency that administers the fund (this agency will be referred to simply as "the agency" or "the fund" in the remainder of this chapter) that the uncompensated losses the claimant suffered (which must qualify as one of the types of loss covered by the fund) have exceeded the threshold amount, which is set at $10,000 in this working model of the proposal. In addition, the claimant must show that the claim is based on a covered event. In the case of this proposal, that means that the claim must arise from an "alcohol-related accident."

The definition of the covered event, or what constitutes an "alcohol-related accident," and the kind of proof that will be required to establish that a specific claim arises from a covered event, will obviously play a significant role in establishing the sweep of the compensation system's operation and its effectiveness at addressing the problems that led to its creation. The twin goals of the system—the compensation of accident victims of drinking drivers and the internalization of drinking-driver traffic-accident costs by the alcohol industry—can most reliably be achieved by initially specifying a wide scope of claims that qualify for compensation. The scope of claims covered by the fund should encompass as wide a group of accidents relating to the drinking-driver traffic-accident problem as is reasonably possible. Accordingly, the covered event that triggers entitlement to compensation under the fund should be specified in general terms as a traffic accident in which the consumption of alcohol has impaired the performance of a driver in a manner that contributed to the accident. The question then becomes how a claimant proves that the accident that caused the claimant's uncompensated injuries was an alcohol-related accident.

One objective in setting up the compensation fund should be to keep to a minimum both the range of discretion that the agency has in determining whether this prerequisite has been proven and the time and expense that must be devoted to its resolution. To this end, the legislation that adopts the compensation system proposal should provide that any judicial or administrative finding of the driver's alcohol impairment establishes that the claimant's injuries were suffered in an accident that brings the claim within the scope of the compensation fund. There are three likely circumstances in which such a finding would be made. First, the driver's alcohol-impaired condition may have been proven earlier as part of a successful tort claim. Second, the driver may have received, as a result of the accident, a criminal conviction for driving while intoxicated or driving under the influence, which provides an even more credible indication of the driver's alcohol impairment. Third, a state agency may have revoked or suspended the driver's license of the impaired driver as a result of the accident. In that case, the claimant could use the administrative determination that the driver was driving while intoxicated or driving under the influence as presumptive proof of the driver's impairment. Presented with one of these findings, the fund should accept the earlier official determination that the accident resulted from the alcohol impairment of the driver who caused the accident. An exception might be recognized for a situation in which the agency decision maker is clearly convinced that the claimant was not injured as a result of an alcohol-related traffic accident as defined in the fund's enabling legislation. When deciding whether to invoke the exception, however, the agency needs to keep in mind the remedial function of the legislation that it is administering.

Some fund claimants, however, will be unable to obtain this sort of evidence to establish the driver's alcohol impairment through the findings just described. If the claimant does not have the required official finding of a driver's alcohol impairment to offer to the fund, then the burden of production of evidence on this eligibility issue ought to rest on the claimant. In light of the purposes of the new compensation system, however, that burden should be relatively light. A claimant should be required merely to produce credible evidence that satisfies the agency decision maker that the accident in which the claimant was injured was at least to some degree a result of the alcohol-impaired condition of a driver who was involved in that accident.

The standard proposed here for proving that an alcohol-related accident occurred so that a claimant can enter the compensation fund system contemplates a relationship between the harm to the victim and the driver's consumption of alcohol that might most accurately be described as a "causal linkage." Described by Dean Guido Calabresi and subsequently developed in the course of John Borgo's insightful discussion of causation in the law of torts, the term "causal linkage" identifies a looser relationship between two events than is entailed by notions of necessary causes or sufficient causes.[9] In the context of the victim compensation fund proposal, the causal linkage between a driver's alcohol consumption and a traffic accident that is sufficient to characterize the accident as alcohol-related should be established on a weaker causal showing than that required in establishing the driver's civil liability or criminal responsibility. Thus alcohol impairment under the fund could be acceptably defined as follows: the impairment of a person's mental or physical faculties as a result of the consumption of alcoholic beverages so as to diminish that person's ability to think and act in a manner in which a person in full possession of his or her faculties, and exercising the care of a reasonable person, would act under the same or similar circumstances.[10]

An alcohol-related accident for purposes of the victim compensation fund ought to be defined more liberally than would be the case in tort or criminal litigation. Yet this more liberal determination should not be allowed to prejudice the driver in other contexts. Its effect should be limited to helping claimants satisfy the fund's eligibility requirement. To ensure that the compensation fund's liberal definition of alcohol impairment does not produce adverse consequences for a driver in another setting, the fund's enabling legislation should explicitly provide that a finding of alcohol impairment by a fund decision maker shall have no effect in any other proceeding.

The enabling legislation for the alcohol-related accident victim compensation fund should contain three provisions specifying how a claimant may prove that the driver's operation of a motor vehicle was alcohol-impaired and that the alcohol impairment contributed to the accident that injured the claimant. Under the first method, a claimant may prove impairment by providing evidence that one of the official determinations of alcohol impairment described earlier was properly made, such as proof that a driver has been convicted of a drinking-and-driving offense as a result of the driver's alcohol-impaired condition at the time of the accident.

Under the second method, a claimant may offer evidence that the driver's blood alcohol concentration, or BAC, was at a level sufficient to indicate alcohol impairment. In keeping with the remedial nature of the compensation fund system, and in recognition that this determination is being made purely for purposes of deciding a claimant's eligibility for compensation, the BAC levels can be set substantially lower than the levels used for imposing criminal sanctions. In fact, a variation of the Surgeon General's suggested allowable BAC levels could be used: .04 percent for adults and .00 percent for minors. Under the compensation system proposed here, a claimant would be able to prove a driver's alcohol impairment upon showing that an adult driver's BAC was .04 percent or higher or that a minor driver's BAC was .01 percent or higher. The latter BAC standard is admittedly less stringent than the Surgeon General's standard of .00 percent for minors, which is based on the fact that any alcohol consumption by a minor is likely to be unlawful. But the fund's standard rests on another assumption — that there is a sufficiently good chance that the alcohol consumption adversely affected the driver's operation of a vehicle so that the accident that injured the claimant is a covered event under the fund.

The third method of establishing a driver's impairment is to prove that the driver has been designated as alcohol impaired by a law enforcement officer who was present at the scene of the accident and who had a sufficient opportunity to observe the driver and to form a professional judgment that the consumption of alcohol by the driver adversely affected the driver's ability to operate the vehicle in a safe manner. Again, it is important to recognize that this determination is being made only for purposes of establishing that a particular accident is a covered event for purposes of making a claim for compensation from the fund. This third way to establish alcohol impairment relies on the ability of law enforcement personnel to make rough judgments about a driver's alcohol consumption and about the effects of that consumption. Social science evidence about the difficulty of estimating the more precise and higher levels of impairment that are involved in drinking-and-driving criminal offenses would therefore not undermine the use of this method by a compensation fund claimant.

While these types of evidence will frequently be available to accident victims, some claimants will undoubtedly fail to obtain the findings or designations described above to prove the driver's alcohol impairment and thus gain entry into the compensation system. In such a case, the claimant ought to be entitled to offer any proof that is relevant to the issue of whether the claimant's injuries were caused by an alcohol-related accident as defined by the fund's enabling legislation.

Assuming that a claimant is able to meet the preliminary requirement of proving that the accident was alcohol-related, the next step is for the agency decision maker to determine whether the claimant has any losses that qualify for compensation under the fund's rules. (Recall that claims are allowed for four types of uncompensated accident losses and that a $10,000 threshold must be crossed as well. Those covered losses are medical expenses, lost income, physical pain, and economic loss to a surviving spouse or minor children.) What evidence should the agency rely on and what procedures should it follow to determine not only that the threshold has been crossed but also the amount of loss to be paid out by the fund?

This administrative determination, more than any other part of the claims process, will require the agency to engage in a significant amount of fact-finding. In structuring that fact-finding process, the legislature that is adopting the compensation fund proposal ought to keep two objectives in mind. First, to the extent that it is possible to do so, the compensation fund claimant should be permitted to present to the fund decision maker the results of whatever reliable fact-finding has already been accomplished in another forum. Second, and again to the extent that it is possible, the fact-finding process should avoid the adversarial nature of the tort litigation process.

The agency's consideration of the issue of the amount of the losses that a compensation fund claimant has suffered should take advantage of prior fact-finding in accordance with the following operating principles. First, any person who otherwise qualifies for compensation under the terms of the compensation fund should be entitled to present to the agency decision maker a tort judgment that has been obtained against a tortfeasor who has been held liable for the same injuries for which the claimant is seeking compensation from the fund. As long as that judgment has not been satisfied to an extent that brings the compensation fund claim below the applicable threshold figure of uncompensated losses, then the presentation of the judgment ought to act as prima facie evidence of accident losses in the amount that is contained in the tort judgment. Some agency fact-finding may still be required, however, if the tort judgment simply enters an undifferentiated sum of damages that were awarded in a general verdict. In that case, the fund would have to refine that award of damages in order to identify how the losses fall into the four categories of harm that are compensable from the fund.

Perhaps the compensation fund claimant has an uncollected tort judgment. In this case the agency may postpone its consideration of the claims until the claimant has demonstrated that the judgment cannot be satisfied or that the uncompensated losses that remain after satisfaction of the judgment are still large enough to cross the threshold for compensation from the fund. As an alternative, the agency could decide to make a payment to the claimant for the losses that are covered by the compensation fund system. In that event, the fund should then be subrogated to the rights of the claimant as a judgment creditor to seek the satisfaction of the tort judgment up to the amount of the payments that were made from the fund.

This first scenario, in which a compensation fund claimant first obtains a tort judgment before filing a claim with the fund, may not occur as frequently as a second scenario in which an accident victim first files a claim for payment from the fund. Given the delay that is associated with the litigation process, a victim's attorney may advise in favor of filing a claim with the fund either as an alternative to litigation or as a matter that proceeds simultaneously with tort litigation. This second situation is somewhat more complicated. First, as always, the agency should make an initial evaluation of the claim to determine whether the claimant's uncompensated losses exceed the fund's threshold. If the losses do not exceed the threshold, then the claim should be rejected on that basis. If the threshold has been crossed, however, then the agency should next focus on the tort remedies that may be available to the claimant. If the agency concludes either that no tort claim exists or that the prospect of recovery is so slim that the claimant would still be substantially undercompensated and have uncompensated losses that exceed the fund's threshold, then the agency should simply proceed with the remainder of the administrative fact-finding process.

If a tort claim is available to the claimant that is likely to result in adequate compensation for the claimant, then the agency has two courses of action. First, the agency could direct the claimant to pursue the tort claim, leaving open the possibility that a subsequent claim may be available if the claimant is left with uncompensated losses that exceed the fund's threshold. Second, the agency could compensate the claimant and then have the agency become subrogated to the rights of the claimant against the person who might be held liable in tort to the claimant, up to the amount of any payment that has been made from the fund. The first option should probably be restricted to those situations in which the agency is reasonably satisfied that the tort remedies that are actually available to the claimant are at least sufficient to provide as complete a level of compensation as would be available from the fund.

Each of the claims scenarios envisions the agency having some occasion to assert a tort claim against a person who might be liable for the claimant's losses for which the fund compensated the claimant. The same role is also envisioned for the agency administering the National Childhood Vaccine Injury Act. That legislation provides that the trust fund paying compensation shall be subrogated to the rights of the person to whom compensation is paid, up to the amount of the payments.[11]

If the fund is to act as a tort litigant, then it obviously needs to include in its personnel attorneys who are competent to represent the fund when it is subrogated to the rights of the claimant and bring an action against potential tort defendants. Using government agency staff attorneys is likely to be less expensive than using privately re-tained attorneys. Staff attorneys are paid a regular salary rather than contingent fees. Thus any tort recovery made by the fund should produce a higher percentage of recovery above expenses and legal fees involved.

The damages the fund thus recovers represent an additional source of financing for the fund beyond the revenues generated by the tax on alcoholic beverages that constitutes the principal source of the fund's budget. Whether the agency pursues a tort claim would depend on the result of a cost-benefit analysis of that course of action. If the cost to the agency is greater than the size of the recovery discounted by the improbability of its being recovered, then it would be rational economic behavior for the agency to assert the rights that it would receive through subrogation. The fund's enabling legislation should also include a provision whereby the agency that steps into the role of a tort litigant asserting the rights of a claimant is entitled to an additional award of damages from the tort defendant to reimburse the fund for the costs of administering the claim paid by the fund and for the costs of maintaining the tort suit that resulted in the establishment of the defendant's liability for the losses paid by the fund.

The basic purpose of permitting the victim compensation fund to be subrogated to the rights of the claimant is to make the availability of the fund as neutral a factor as possible in the decisions of accident victims about whether to assert preexisting tort rights. The object is neither to encourage nor to discourage tort litigation by the struc-turing of the compensation fund in a particular way. Litigation would be encouraged, for example, by a requirement that a compensation fund claimant exhaust all possible tort remedies before applying to the fund for compensation. Litigation would also be encouraged by decision-making procedures that gives a significant advantage to a claimant who has already been able to establish a tort defendant's liability for the losses for which payment from the fund was being sought. Insofar as possible, the procedure proposed for processing claims should not encourage tort litigation in these ways.

Perhaps the more controversial working assumption underlying the subrogation role that is given to the fund is the rationale that the compensation fund should be set up in such a way that it does not discourage tort litigation. After all, many of the compensation systems that have been adopted or proposed have exclusivity provisions that are justified in part by reference to their ability to reduce the work load of courts and to eliminate or minimize the delay and the expense associated with the litigation system. Over the course of his career, Professor Jeffrey O'Connell has been the torts scholar who has done the most sophisticated work on channeling injury compensation claims out of the tort litigation system. Professor O'Connell's proposals over the last decade have tended to offer nonlitigation options to potential parties to a tort lawsuit, with some trade-off of costs and benefits extracted as the price for taking the alternative. In his most recent work, he has addressed more directly the coordination of a tort scheme and a compensation system to reduce the extent to which victims who choose a nonlitigation alternative or are forced to resort to one give up much of the compensation they might have received in a tort lawsuit.[12] As always, these latest proposals are thought-provoking and deserve careful consideration by any state legislature that begins to pursue a tort reform strategy.

My decision to design this compensation fund proposal so as not to discourage tort litigation by accident victims rests on two grounds. First, the fund is designed to be a supplemental remedial measure that picks up the injury-compensation task when the existing tort litigation and insurance systems fail to provide complete compensation to the more seriously injured victims of drinking drivers. The intent of this proposal is to accomplish two goals: to compensate those victims more completely and to make the alcohol industry internalize accident costs without necessarily changing the way that current mechanisms provide for victim compensation and cost internalization. Given the supplemental role of the compensation fund, then, there is less reason to discourage accident victims from pursuing whatever remedies they now have under the tort law rules that govern their legal rights.

Second, the proposed compensation fund does not compensate claimants for some types of harm for which damages may be available under the governing rules of tort law. The principle examples are punitive damages and damages for emotional distress and other non-pecuniary losses distinct from physical pain. Because in some situations even a very seriously injured accident victim might be much better off by pursuing a state's tort remedies, the compensation fund proposal is structured in such a way that it does not interfere with or reduce those advantages to the victim who chooses to become a tort litigant.

Any claimant who chooses to pursue both remedies, however, should be prevented from obtaining duplicate payments for the same items of loss. This goal could be accomplished by modifying the collateral source rule in any tort litigation that is pursued by a claimant who has received or who will receive a payment from the compensation fund. That claimant's tort recovery should be reduced by the amount of payment the claimant is entitled to receive from the compensation fund. When most of an accident victim's losses fall into the categories of harm for which payment is available from the compensation fund, the advantage to the claimant in using the tort system in addition to the fund would be fairly small, particularly when the tort defendant has limited assets with which to satisfy a tort judgment. A provision to this effect may alleviate some of the legitimate concern that has been expressed by Professor O'Connell that compensation system payments from outside the tort system are used to subsidize tort litigation.[13]

Another important administrative detail that needs to be addressed in the accident victim compensation fund proposal is how to structure payments from the fund. Two categories of losses need to be treated differently: past losses and future losses.

The first category, past losses, is comprised of compensable losses the claimant has already suffered at the time that compensation is sought from the fund. These would include such items as medical and hospital expenses and lost wages incurred up until the time the claim is determined. For these past losses, the claimant should be given a lump-sum payment from the compensation fund. Included in this payment as well should be the attorney's fees and expenses to which the claimant is entitled and reimbursement for any payments the claimant has made to alleviate physical pain. These latter payments presumably would be made pursuant to administrative rule-making that establishes a fee schedule or other method of determining the size of the payments to be made for these elements of compensable accident loss.

The more problematic category of accident losses are those that will occur in the future as a result of the harm the victim suffered in the drinking-driver accident. In the tort system, the general rule is first to identify the total amount of losses expected to occur in the future and then to calculate the present value of that figure. The objective in reducing an award for future losses to its present value is to avoid giving the successful tort plaintiff any economic windfall from the accident. The award is therefore supposed to be tailored so that after the plaintiff invests the money and draws on both the principal and interest over the period of time in which the future losses are expected to occur, a zero balance will be left. It is unrealistic, however, to suggest that a reduction to present value is anything more than a theoretical concept, especially in light of the routine practice of allowing lay juries to make these calculations, often after the jurors have been presented with conflicting evidence from expert witnesses who have been hired by the two sides in the tort litigation.

In providing for future losses in the victim compensation fund proposal, it is not necessary to mimic the details of the tort litigation system that could be handled more rationally in another way. Fortunately, alternatives exist, and the proposal follows some recent developments that move away from a present award of money to compensate an accident victim for future losses. The proposal's most important provision for future losses is that they should be paid periodically as they occur rather than in a lump-sum payment awarded when the claimant's entitlement to compensation is initially determined.

Periodic payment of losses as they occur has a number of advantages over lump-sum payment. For one thing, periodic payments come closer to matching what the accident victim's financial situation would have been if there had been no accident. When a person's regular stream of income is interrupted as a result of an accident, for example, the best use of compensation fund payments is to allow that flow to resume rather than to pay all of the future income at one time.

Periodic payments also reduce the risk of erroneously assessing the nature of the victim's future losses and the appropriate dollar value to attach to them. Sometimes a portion of estimated future medical expenses end ups proving to be unnecessary. Conversely, a present estimate of future medical expenses may be too low. Periodic payments allow the agency to tailor payments to a victim's actual losses rather than to some projection of what those losses will be. Furthermore, paying future losses periodically lessens the financial demand on the agency by preserving current funds. The agency could even take advantage of the delayed obligation to make payments by investing a sum of money that would provide a sufficient return so that those payments could be made at a lower cost in the long term than the fund would face if it had to make the payment immediately and in a lump sum.

Periodic payments do pose one potential disadvantage that must be avoided as much as possible. The fund's administrative costs could be driven up significantly if periodic payments required continued extensive fact-finding about future losses as they occur. The agency ought not to be put in the position of having to conduct recurrent hearings on the existence and the value of future losses. A preferable policy is to give the administrator the authority to issue regulations to deal with this problem. First, the agency should be able to make an initial determination of a schedule of payments that will be made in the future, provided that there is a sufficient degree of certainty about the nature and the value of those losses. Second, any agency monitoring of claimants who are receiving periodic payments for future losses, as well as the consideration of any requests for modification of awards to reflect changes in the circumstances of claimants, should be kept as streamlined as possible. The goal should be to prevent the fund from having to engage in an expensive redetermination of claims. This goal can be accomplished in part by designing standard reporting forms and by conditioning the receipt of payments on an efficient method of furnishing information about a claimant's continuing need to receive payments.

Any proposal for a compensation system that involves administrative determinations of eligibility and amounts to be paid out in individual cases must also address the issue of judicial review of agency decisions. The paramount principle that should guide both the drafting and the interpretation of the legislative provision on judicial review for the alcohol-related accident victim compensation fund is clear. To the maximum extent that is consistent with fairness and due process, decisions that are reached with regard to individual claims by the agency that administers the fund should not be subject to a court appeal. One of the more serious ways in which the fund's potential success could be destroyed would be by turning the claims process into an occasion for a new and more peripheral layer of litigation arising out of drinking-driver accidents. The tertiary costs of dealing with accident losses would multiply unacceptably if the existing level of potential tort litigation and the administration of the new victim compensation fund were then to be followed by litigation about the manner in which the compensation fund reached its decisions and about the correctness of those decisions on the merits. Therefore, the enabling legislation should include a provision that the decisions of the agency on individual claims for compensation should not be subject to review in any judicial proceeding, but rather that those decisions should be within the exclusive jurisdiction of the agency.

A provision that precludes judicial review of individual claims decisions should raise no serious constitutional objections. A hallmark of the alcohol-related accident victim compensation fund proposal is that it takes nothing away from an accident victim who resorts to the fund for compensation. All of the tort remedies that a victim had before the adoption of the fund proposal would still be available after its adoption. Because the claimant is not forced to give up a previously recognized right the necessity for judicial review of agency determinations is significantly reduced, if not eliminated. If the legislature that adopts the compensation fund proposal nevertheless decides that judicial review ought to be available, the scope of that review should be narrowly circumscribed so that courts are precluded from extensively redetermining claims.

Judicial review of broader questions about the administration of the compensation fund should be made available. There might be legitimate concern about programmatic failures on the part of the agency that administers the fund's claims process. However, the standing to challenge the manner in which the agency is carrying out its functions should be restricted. Standing could either be limited to a small group of potential challengers, such as the state attorney general, or it could be limited to a narrowly defined range of issues. The latter option would allow financially interested persons, such as members of the alcohol industry subject to the tax that finances the compensation fund, to obtain judicial review of how the agency is interpreting and applying its legislative mandate, without opening up the potential for litigation about the merits of individual cases.

To create a meaningful opportunity to obtain judicial review of the fund's administrative methods and mode of operation, the fund should be required to publish reports at least annually that describe both its taxing and claims processing activities. In addition, the fund's enabling legislation could allow interested persons to petition the agency for a rule-making proceeding to correct perceived flaws in its interpretation or application of its mandate. Judicial review of the result of the agency's action on that petition could then be sought in an appellate court, where it would proceed as a matter of reviewing the rule-making record rather than as a matter that involved a de novo determination by the court. Assuming the agency develops experience and expertise, courts should show a substantial degree of deference to the agency's interpretation and application of the enabling legislation that created it.

Even if agency decisions on individual claims are not subject to judicial review, they should not be allowed to go completely unchecked in any other forum. A preferable alternative to judicial review, however, is to establish an appellate procedure within the agency itself, in the form of an agency appeal board. The administrative appeals process should be conducted as speedily and simply as possible while still maintaining a measure of control over the agency's initial decision-making level. The decisions of the agency appeals board with respect to individual claims for compensation should be final and not subject to judicial review.

The interstate contacts that are present in a number of drinking-driver traffic accidents could present administrative problems for the compensation fund that should be addressed at the time the fund is created rather than left for courts to decide when faced with choice-of-law issues in the event of litigation. The interstate complications have two aspects. One is the dilemma that occurs when there are differences in the state in which the accident occurred, the state in which the alcoholic beverages were purchased or consumed, and the state of residence of the people involved in the accident. Unless all the states involved have adopted a victim compensation system along the particular lines I propose here, difficult issues can arise regarding the extent to which the benefits of the compensation system should be available to those who do not share the burdens.

The second aspect of the interstate problem concerns the uneven imposition of the tax burden that occurs when neighboring states with compensation systems adopt different tax rates and when some states adopt the system but others nearby do not. The special compensation fund tax imposed on alcoholic beverages that are sold in one state can obviously have the effect of raising the prices of those beverages above the price that is charged in another state. In areas close to state borders, sellers of alcoholic beverages will suffer a competitive dis-advantage by the special tax as purchasers travel out of state to buy alcoholic beverages at a lower price.

Looking at these two aspects of the problem together helps make its solution clearer, or at least the general principle that should guide it. To the maximum extent possible, the benefits of the compensation fund should be coextensive with the burdens imposed by the fund. No system that hopes to keep administrative costs under control will be able to achieve a perfect match between the system's benefits and the burdens. The choices that need to be made concern which instances of mismatch are acceptable and which are to be avoided.

The simplest solution to the problem is a provision that limits eligibility for compensation from the victim compensation fund to those claimants who are injured as a result of accidents that occur within the state that has adopted the fund proposal. This provision will admittedly exclude some of the people who have to bear the burden of the compensation system from the opportunity to share the benefits. For example, residents of a state that has adopted the proposal will be unable to assert a claim if they are injured in a neighboring state that does not have a system. To add to the problem, they may also have purchased alcoholic beverages in their home state at prices that reflect the special tax that finances the fund. Conversely, this proposed provision may allow victims who have not had to share the burdens of the compensation fund to enjoy the benefits. Consider, for example, the victim who was injured by a drinking driver who consumed alcoholic beverages purchased out of state. Or perhaps the accident victim is simply not a resident of the state that has adopted the compensation system.

Nevertheless, solutions directed at particular mismatch problems such as the ones just described could easily cause more difficulty than they are worth. Limiting the fund to claims by residents of the state that has adopted the proposal, for example, would probably create an impermissible distinction that could be challenged as a violation of the federal constitution. Similarly, the scope of the fund could be limited to accidents involving the consumption of alcoholic beverages that were purchased within state, but the additional fact-finding burden imposed by this provision would probably exceed any gain in precision. The general in-state accident exclusivity provision that is part of this proposal does give the bulk of the benefits of the compensation fund system most of the time to the people who bear the major share of the burden of supporting the compensation fund. In practical terms, that is probably the most that can feasibly be accomplished in attempting to deal with interstate complications.

### NOTES

1. *See* KEETON & O'CONNELL, BASIC PROTECTION, at 28-34.

2. The basic structure of the Social Security benefit scheme is outlined in M. BERNSTEIN & J. BERNSTEIN, SOCIAL SECURITY: THE SYSTEM THAT WORKS (1988).

3. Two of the prominent scholars who address the operation of the administrative agency machinery with clarity and insight are Professors Jerry Mashaw and Peter Schuck, both of whom are on the faculty of the Yale Law School. *See, e.g.,* J. MASHAW, BUREAUCRATIC JUSTICE: MANAGING SOCIAL SECURITY DISABILITY CLAIMS (1983); P. SCHUCK, SUING GOVERNMENT: CITIZEN REMEDIES FOR OFFICIAL WRONGS 123-46 (1983).

4. NATIONAL INSTITUTE ON ALCOHOL ABUSE AND ALCOHOLISM, SURVEILLANCE REPORT NO. 13: APPARENT PER CAPITA ALCOHOL CONSUMP-

TION, NATIONAL, STATE, AND REGIONAL TRENDS, 1977-1987 16-17 (1989) (table 2).

5. The NIAAA study used the following coefficients to determine the ethanol content of different alcoholic beverages: .045 for beer, .129 for wine, and .414 for distilled spirits. *Id.* at 2. Those figures roughly correspond to the assumptions that were used in the illustrative calculations of the new tax presented earlier.

6. *See* 2 MOSHER, LIQUOR LIABILITY LAW § 21.02[2].

7. The path-breaking case was a decision of the Supreme Court of California, in Sindell v. Abbott Laboratories, 26 Cal.3d 588, 607 P.2d 924, 163 Cal.Rptr. 132 (1980), *cert. denied*, 449 U.S. 912 (1980). Equally significant is the Wisconsin decision in Collins v. Eli Lilly Co., 116 Wis.2d 166, 342 N.W.2d 37 (1984), *cert. denied*, 469 U.S. 826 (1984).

8. Virginia, for example, recently shifted the responsibility for the collection of the state excise tax on beer and malt beverages from the state tax department to the alcoholic beverage control department. If a state were to keep those agency functions separate for other purposes, then the legislation creating the compensation fund should probably maintain the same general division of responsibility with regard to the collection of the tax that is used to finance the compensation fund.

9. *See* Calabresi, *Concerning Cause and the Law of Torts: An Essay for Harry Kalven, Jr.,* 43 U. CHI. L. REV. 69 (1975); Borgo, *Causal Paradigms in Tort Law,* 8 J. LEGAL STUD. 419 (1979).

10. This definition is a modified, and somewhat weaker, version of the definition of intoxication used in the dram shop act of New Hampshire, N. H. REV. STAT. ANN. § 507-F:1(IV) (Supp. 1989).

11. 42 U.S.C. § 300aa-17(a).

12. In addition to the many works by Professor O'Connell that have already been cited, see also O'Connell, *A Draft Bill to Allow Choice Between No-Fault and Fault-Based Auto Insurance,* 27 HARV. J. LEGIS. 143 (1990); O'Connell, Brown & Vennell, *Reforming New Zealand's Reform: Accident Compensation Revisited,* N. Z. L. J. 399 (Nov. 1989); O'Connell, *Balanced Proposals for Product Liability Reform,* 48 OHIO ST. L. J. 317 (1987); O'Connell & Joost, *Giving Motorists a Choice Between Fault and No-Fault Insurance,* 72 VA. L. REV. 61 (1986).

13. O'Connell, *Must Health and Disability Insurance Subsidize Wasteful Injury Suits?,* 41 RUTGERS L. REV. 1055 (1989).

# PART FOUR

# A Social Solution to a Social Problem: The Compensation Fund for the Victims of Drinking Drivers

The work of Dean Guido Calabresi on accident costs makes it clear that diverse alternatives exist for alleviating the adverse consequences of accidents. Behavior can be modified so that fewer accidents occur, or the accident environment can be changed so that victims' injuries will be less serious. These are two types of primary cost avoidance. Yet even if those measures fail to bring the overall costs of accidents down to acceptable levels, the financial impact of accident costs on the victims can be eased by shifting them away from the victims and spreading them so that they are borne in much smaller increments by a broader segment of the population. The legal system may have only incidental effects on the primary costs of drinking-driver traffic accidents, but it can and should do more to avoid the secondary accident costs that those accidents impose on the victims.

This final part of *John Barleycorn Must Pay* ties together the ideas that were put forward in the preceding chapters. Chapter 14 singles out and makes more explicit the rationales for some of the most controversial features of the proposal that are likely to prove most important in building a coalition of general supporters of this proposal. Chapter 15 begins by presenting a draft of a model statute that a state legislature could use to enact the proposal and concludes with a series of hypothetical cases that illustrate the operation of the victim compensation fund. This statutory draft should be taken as a preliminary or tentative sketch of the kind of legislative provisions that could be put together to accomplish the goals behind this proposal and to implement the policy choices outlined earlier.

Chapter 16, the final chapter, then explores the applicability of the proposal and the ideas that inspire it to other contexts. A victim compensation fund could be used, for example, to help people injured by dangerous products or people who are exposed to risks of harm posed by dangerous activities. The chapter concludes with a brief apologia for the contemporary tort litigation system. It proceeds from a recognition that, although reform is needed, the operation of modern tort law still achieves a great deal of good. There is a continuing need for a strong and healthy tort liability system, but at the same time there should be a constant examination of particular social problems to determine whether the tort system can be supplemented or superseded in specific ways in order to attack the problem more effectively.

# 14

## Gaining Support for the Compensation Fund Proposal

The details of an improved plan for compensating the seriously injured accident victims of drinking drivers may be much easier to identify than to implement. Even the best injury compensation system that legal scholars could devise is likely to remain a matter of little more than academic interest if its provisions are so out of touch with the pragmatic and political considerations of contemporary society that the system has no reasonable chance of attracting legislative, judicial, or popular support. This is not to say that scholarship describing the best system, even if it is currently thought to be impractical, is a futile exercise. The contours of what is considered possible are only sufficiently expanded when we have before us a vision of what would be most desirable. In this way, a view of what is desirable can stretch our conception of what is possible. Nevertheless, legal scholars who enter the arena of public policy-making can borrow from their colleagues in economics the concept of the "second best" solution to a problem and offer proposals tailored to reflect, rather than ignore, the realities of the larger social and political context in which these complicated issues of accident loss allocation and risk reduction arise. While second-best proposals may admittedly contain compromises that detract from the purity of their adherence to particular theories or from the completeness of their attainment of certain goals, scholarly involvement in the policy-making endeavor can produce an increase in both the number and the scope of the options that are given serious consideration.[1]

This first chapter of part 4 approaches the drinking-driver accident-victim compensation problem in its broader political context. In that setting, one needs to realize above all that public policymakers are presented with inconsistent demands for an increasingly limited supply of funds with which to attack a myriad of serious social problems. Furthermore, an equally significant limit on the amount of public and official time and energy that can be devoted to addressing any one problem also acts as a constraint on the ability to implement sweeping reform efforts. In the Coasean world of no transaction costs good things appear to happen automatically. In our world, however, difficult choices have to be made, and a more confining sense of reality has to be accommodated.

### Microreform, Policy Wars, and Unified Theories

In public policy-making and in scholarship, we live in an age of cosmic efforts. The last three decades have given us wars against poverty, inflation, and drugs. Ironically, the major real armed conflict that was fought before the 1990s was never formally declared as such. It might appear to the causal observer as if, prior to the war in the Persian Gulf, the only "war casualties" we were prepared to acknowledge were the credibility and the support-generating capacity of the officials who issue these grandiose pronouncements about social problems.[2]

The scholarship of tort law displays an ample basis for expressing a similar concern about the size and the sweep of some of the major efforts that are being undertaken. In what is perhaps an attempt to match the significance of the theoretical physicists' search for a "theory of everything," our most influential tort scholars of the last quarter-century have devoted a good deal of their energy to producing and then defending unified theories of liability or injury compensation. Among the most noteworthy of these efforts have been the causal reductionist theory of the early work of Richard Epstein,[3] the reliance on property rights and market transactions to allocate some risks in the later work of Epstein,[4] the law-and-economics approach of Richard Posner and William Landes, as well as that of Steven Shavell and others,[5] the no-fault alternatives advocated by Jeffrey O'Connell,[6] and the risk-reciprocity focus offered by George Fletcher.[7]

The proposal for an alcohol-related accident victim compensation fund that I offer in this book does not depend on a call for a war against drunk driving, and I do not claim for it the ability to serve as a model suitable for universal application to injury compensation problems. Indeed, in the concluding chapter of this book I point out the factors that limit the proposal's general applicability. One fundamental question that undoubtedly will arise about the enterprise I have undertaken in *John Barleycorn Must Pay* is whether it makes sense to take such a small bite at the injury compensation problem as the one I propose here. Rather than tinker with the existing system, one might ask, wouldn't it be better simply to implement a comprehensive accident compensation plan along the lines of the New Zealand system?

Wouldn't it be more productive to concentrate our efforts, as Professor Sugarman provocatively suggests in the title of his recent book, on doing away with personal injury law altogether?[8]

Two rationales might be offered to support a negative answer to that question, one relating to feasibility and the other to desirability. In the first place, in a political climate in which the most recent presidential campaign demonstrated that even "the 'L' word" carries an air of opprobrium, it is unlikely that such a "socialist" measure would attract enough support for it to be enacted. Furthermore, even if widespread enthusiasm for the adoption of that sort of comprehensive program could be generated, it might not be as desirable as the kind of narrowly targeted proposal presented here. The alcohol-related accident victim compensation fund that I propose here differs from a comprehensive accident or injury compensation system in terms of the relationship between accident costs and particular activities. The New Zealand system, for example, treats all accident costs as a cost of citizenship in a complex and technologically sophisticated society (see chapter 10). The cost of accident compensation in a system like that is, in a sense, as socialized or as universalized as the general risk of accidental injury to the population, whatever the source. The proposal offered here treats the costs of drinking-driver traffic accidents more particularly—and for the first time in an effective manner— as a cost of an activity carried on for profit that creates or enhances risks to third parties who are not engaged in that activity. Rather than treating these accident costs as reciprocally imposed on and by all citizens, the proposal treats them as attributable in part to a specific enterprise, the manufacture and distribution of alcoholic beverages, that currently is able to avoid almost all of the impact of those costs.

The new compensation system offered in this book would change little of the existing tort law in a state that was to adopt it. It is designed to complement, rather than replace, existing tort remedies for a number of reasons. Perhaps the most important one is the recognition that a state's existing tort law rules and doctrines, embodied in judicial decisions and in statutes, represent earlier policy choices. While we can criticize those choices when they produce an incomplete solution or an inconsistent pattern of legal rights and practical responsibilities, nevertheless we must remember that each state's complex system of common-law rules and statutory provisions was developed in order to obtain specific benefits or to impose particular adverse consequences on risky behavior. It is at least presumptuous for a reformer to construct a proposal that throws aside all previous law-making efforts in the expectation that the only benefits and consequences worth having are those that belong to the proposal.

That point is particularly relevant in the case of drinking-driver accidents, about which we actually know very little. We now experience what is probably an unacceptably high level of drinking-driver traffic accidents in spite of the range of criminal penalties and tort liability rules now in place. Social scientists can venture predictions about what would happen to the level of accidents if parts of that complex set of rules and sanctions were removed, but it seems foolhardy to do so. Why run the risk of reducing whatever deterrent effect existing rules and sanctions have on drinking and driving when a reform proposal can be put into place that does not tamper with existing law?[9]

A second reason to layer the accident victim compensation fund on top of the existing framework of rights and remedies is to avoid possible constitutional challenges to the proposal. As I mentioned earlier, the proposed system takes nothing away from the victims of drinking-driver accidents as a condition for receiving the benefits available under the new system. Furthermore, those affected by the new tax burden imposed by the system are not likely to be any worse off than they would be otherwise; taxes on such items as alcohol and tobacco are obvious sources of revenue for governments seeking to balance their budgets. The very first trial balloon that President Bush sent up after he reneged on his campaign pledge not to raise taxes included a substantial increase in the federal excise taxes on alcohol.[10] As noted in chapter 11, increases in the federal excise taxes on alcohol were included as part of the revenue-raising measures in the 1990 budget reconciliation legislation. The advantage of the compensation fund tax is that it is specifically earmarked to deal with a particular social problem. Should the magnitude of the problem decrease over time, the tax burden could be reduced.

A third reason not to abandon the existing system is the diversity of tort law rules in different jurisdictions. For this reason, the compensation fund is designed to be adopted at the state level rather than the federal level. A federal reform proposal would require a good deal of state-specific tailoring that could substantially stall its adoption. The system I propose here has the virtue of being applicable to any state, regardless of the way each state now imposes tort liability for drinking-driver accidents, or regulates the sale and service of alcoholic beverages, or structures its excise taxes on alcoholic beverages. In a significant sense, then, one proposal fits all.

*Developing Support for Legislative Action on*
*the Victim Compensation Fund Proposal*

Successful legislative reform efforts frequently depend on the mobilization of a constituency that is either large enough or committed enough to overcome the normal legislative inertia that can so easily stall reform efforts. The drinking-driver problem in general may already have a high enough visibility in contemporary society that a widespread interest exists in doing *something* about the problem. The key is determining what should be done and then developing a reform coalition that will get people who share a more diffuse sense that some reform is necessary to support a particular reform effort.

The British novelist Ian McEwan wrote a marvelous line in one of his most recent books: "The art of bad government was to sever the line between public policy and intimate feeling, the instinct for what was right."[11] There is a good deal of truth in this ironic statement. Given the ubiquity of the drinking-driver problem and the way that its effects touch so many people, there may be an opportunity here for *good* government to shape a public policy response in such a way that it is more in keeping with McEwan's "intimate feeling" and it taps into and builds on "the instinct for what [is] right."

Support for the proposed alcohol-related accident victim compensation fund is most likely to come from those now involved in reform efforts, such as supporters of such organizations as MADD and SADD. The proposal should prove especially appealing because of its concern with what happens to the victims of drinking-driver traffic accidents. Because many of the most active participants in the public debate about drunk driving have themselves been victims of such accidents in one way or another, a reform proposal that takes their perspective as its own should strike a responsive chord in them.

The people who are currently mobilized in the effort to reduce the scope of the drinking-driver problem in this country would compose a formidable constituency if they were to support the accident victim compensation fund proposed here. But another substantial segment of the population might support it as well. Perhaps surprisingly, that additional potential constituency is composed of those engaged in the retail sale of alcoholic beverages and those who serve alcohol as part of a commercial transaction or a social occasion.

As we have seen, commercial dispensers of alcohol and social hosts can be held liable for drinking-driver accident losses under a variety of legal theories (chapters 4, 6, and 7). One of the more compelling arguments for extending the scope of tort liability to include these parties is that the innocent victim of a drinking-driver accident would otherwise be left without effective relief. The victim compensation fund proposed here responds to precisely that same argument, and it addresses just that same concern about the inadequacy of existing tort remedies. Thus, adopting the proposal could very well relieve some of the pressure on judicial and legislative policymakers to extend the scope of tort liability. Those parties in the path of this expanding scope of tort liability could become supporters of the proposal. Similarly, in the face of expanding liability, the insurance industry lobby might be interested in supporting the proposal in order to deflect the risk of a sudden increased demand on insurance assets. The proposal's potential supporters would include not only commercial dispensers of alcohol but also average people who serve alcohol on social occasions. The trade associations that represent commercial retailers and commercial servers, as well as insurers of both commercial and social dispensers, could thus become valuable members of the constituency mobilized in support of the victim compensation fund proposal.

One way to build a legislative coalition is to stretch a legislative proposal beyond its original concept to address concerns that are on the agendas of other legislators. Doing so poses a considerable risk, however, if the additional provisions that are tacked on to the original reform proposal carry with them enough negative baggage to move the focus of the public policy debate away from the original problem the proposal addresses or the specific solution it offers. If the risk is worth it in the case of the victim compensation fund legislation, or if expanding the proposed legislation becomes necessary, the tax used to finance the fund could be used to accomplish other goals desired by legislators and thus gain their support.

For example, the current policy debates about the high social costs of alcohol and tobacco products, particularly to younger consumers, periodically include some expressions of support for regulating or even banning tobacco and alcohol advertising. The proposal could allow the tax rate to be adjustable so that it could be used to discourage the advertising of alcoholic beverages. The amount of tax assessed could be tied, for example, to an amount of money that is spent on advertising the product. The more money spent on advertising for a beverage, the higher the tax on that beverage would be.

An effort along those lines would unquestionably raise considerably more difficulties than simply promoting the victim compensation fund itself. Among the more troublesome issues would be determining what advertising counted against which taxable product and dealing with constitutional claims that a tax that varied according to the exercise of free speech rights in a commercial setting violated the First Amendment. One of the fund proposal's advantages is that it tries to keep the administrative burden of assessing and collecting the tax as low as possible. Tampering with that simplicity and uniformity could easily undercut the attractiveness of the proposal.

It is easier to build support for proposed legislation that involves a substantial change from the status quo if it can be given a catchy title, or at least an easily pronounceable acronym. The names of legislative sponsors often serve this purpose, as in the case of the Gramm-Rudman legislation to reduce the federal deficit or the Taft-Hartley labor relations legislation of a few decades ago. And as some recent federal legislation makes clear, the working titles that are given to statutes can even be misleading, as long as they mislead in politically popular directions. Some illustrative statutory titles are the Paperwork Reduction Act of 1980,[12] the Deficit Reduction Act of 1984, and the Tax Equity and Fiscal Responsibility Act of 1982.

Failing that sort of attention-grabbing official title, a popular name or nickname can convey to the public both the nature and the importance of the proposed legislation. In the face of a comprehensive official title, one is left with the hope that unofficial but fairly standard ways of referring to the legislation will capture the public's attention and elicit an initial favorable response. Thus it might be good to find a less technical name for the "Alcohol-Related Accident Victim Compensation Fund" legislation proposed here.

The author of a newspaper article a few years ago proposed a general Alcohol Indemnity Fund,[13] which would cover much more of the societal costs of alcohol than the fund I propose. A notable feature of that newspaper proposal was its author's richly evocative labeling of the indemnity fund as an Alcohol Superfund. That sort of designation would likely attach to the proposal some of the favorable public response to the federal environmental superfund.

Actually, the official title of the environmental superfund legislation is "The Comprehensive Environmental Response, Compensation and Liability Act of 1980."[14] Although some environmental lawyers use the acronym CERCLA to refer to the legislation, by far the most popular name for the act is simply Superfund. It is also probably true that many people associate the term "Superfund" with a generally positive step to do something about an environmental problem, without having much, if any, sense of what the problem is or how exactly the legislation will deal with it. It is easier to pass reform legislation when its general thrust has captured popular approval in the face of concentrated opposition than it is when a reform campaign is never able to tap into a vein of popular sentiment for the proposal.

Early in the public policy discussion of a proposal of the sort that has been put forward here, proponents would be well advised to seize the opportunity to present the essential thrust of the proposal in as positive and as simple a fashion as possible. With shorthand references such as the "Drunk-Driver Victim Fund," proponents may be able to gain a larger sympathetic audience both among members of the public and in the legislative circles where action must be taken.

Some of the current concern with alcohol-related health and safety problems may spring from a more comprehensive neoprohibitionist, or temperance-revival, sentiment.[15] One sign of this phenomenon is the change in the names of some of the public awareness and lobbying groups in the movement. The first generation of such groups labeled themselves in ways that indicated that they were "against drunk driving" (e.g., MADD) or "against driving drunk" (e.g., SADD). Recent advertising and public awareness campaigns indicate a partial shift in focus to being "against drugs and alcohol" (e.g., Students Against Drugs and Alcohol).

It may be that a more careful exploration of the policy of these latest groups would reveal that they are not prohibitionist in the way that their names seem to suggest. For a younger audience, any alcohol consumption is legally prohibited; thus a message targeted to this audience that is against all alcohol use makes as much sense as a message against all drug use. For older audiences, however, a distinction should be drawn between prohibited substances and lawful substances. While it is true that alcohol is a drug, it is not the case that every use of alcohol constitutes abuse, nor does every use necessarily pose an unacceptable risk of harm to the consumer or to others. For the sake of sending a clear message, then, the problem being addressed should be put in as narrow a set of terms as is feasible.

To avoid any misunderstanding, it should be noted that the focus of the proposal set forth in this book is on a reallocation of the losses suffered by the victims of traffic accidents in which alcohol has played a part. The resolution of that issue and the acceptability of the proposal do not turn on any particular moral attitude toward the production of alcohol or its use. The title of this book plays on "John Barleycorn Must Die,"[16] which was the title song of an album by the rock group

Traffic, and which in turn can be traced to an English folk song. The reader should make no mistake, however, about the thrust of the proposal that is presented in this book. The aim is for "John Barleycorn" to *pay*, not to die.

### Excluding Drinking Drivers from Obtaining the Benefits of the Compensation Fund

Arguably the most controversial aspect of the current movement in tort law that seeks to impose liability on commercial dispensers and social hosts involves the potential for drinking drivers injured in an accident to receive compensation from an alcohol dispenser for those injuries. This result can be supported by a plausible legal argument on the issue of causation: the part that the drinking driver played in causing the accident did not supersede the alcohol dispenser's causal contribution; rather, the two are concurrent, and therefore the drinking driver should be permitted at least some recovery. This argument is more likely to be persuasive in a jurisdiction that routinely treats a tort plaintiff's own negligent conduct as a matter that reduces the plaintiff's recovery but does not bar it entirely. A case can even be made for the proposition that because minors who are drinking drivers are particularly vulnerable to the effects of alcoholic beverages, the people who wrongfully serve alcohol to them are more responsible for their injuries than the drinking driver is.

Those arguments have a sufficient level of plausibility that a court or a legislature would have some basis for refusing to exclude recovery by a drinking driver. Nevertheless, allowing drinking drivers to shift their own accident losses to another party strikes many courts and legislatures as fundamentally inconsistent with the aspirations and the goals of a predominantly fault-based tort system.[17] Therefore, it might be wise to avoid the appearance of rewarding drinking drivers for their own wrongdoing by allowing them to receive compensation from the victim compensation fund.

For these and other reasons that will be explained, the alcohol-related accident victim compensation fund proposal is structured to exclude from eligibility for payment from the compensation fund any claims that are made by, or that are made on behalf of, or that are derived from, a drinking driver whose alcohol impairment contributed to the occurrence of the accident. At a minimum, this provision bars drinking drivers from any claim for compensation from the fund. In addition, it excludes claims brought on behalf of the drinking driver, such as claims by parents of minor drinking drivers. Finally, claims derived from the injury to a drinking driver are excluded from the fund, such as a claim brought by a surviving spouse or child for death benefits after the drinking driver has been killed in the accident.

The policy choice to exclude drinking driver claims from the compensation fund is just that — a policy choice.[18] No state legislature is logically compelled to make this exclusion. It may be that the consensus in a particular state is that an exception should be made for minor drinking drivers, for example. Nevertheless, several legitimate reasons exist for preferring a policy that excludes all drinking drivers.

First, it is wrong to drive while impaired by alcohol. Seldom, if ever, will this conduct create a justified risk to the driver and to others unfortunate enough to encounter that driver. In this respect, this conduct is distinguishable from other kinds of negligent or unreasonable conduct by an accident victim that contributes to the risk of harm to that victim. Ordinary determinations of contributory negligence in traffic accident cases often require fairly close judgment calls about how a person acted in a split second of time under harrowing circumstances.[19] Drinking and driving is different; it involves a deliberate and voluntary decision to engage in socially unacceptable conduct. When people act in that way and are then injured in an accident partially caused by their alcohol impairment, it would seem that the legal system is justified in refusing to devote some of its limited resources to the task of compensating them for those injuries.

True emergency situations in which the decision to drive while impaired by alcohol is justified or excused will be rare. To take them into account, however, I have included in the model enabling legislation a provision that allows claims to be brought by drinking drivers who were acting in an emergency. The definition of an emergency should be very narrowly drawn, though, and the burden should be placed on the fund claimant to establish that the emergency conditions were satisfied. Emergencies should be restricted to those situations in which the driver faced a clear danger to life or safety that arose after the driver's ability to operate a motor vehicle was already impaired by the consumption of alcohol, and that presented the driver with no other reasonable alternative to driving while alcohol-impaired.

Another reason to exclude drinking-driver claims from the compensation fund relates to the issue of deterrence. In the great sweep of things, perhaps it is true that one's decision to drink and drive is as little influenced by the prospect of being denied an opportunity to recover damages for one's own injuries as it is by the prospect of being held liable for injuries to others. Nevertheless, that uncertainty does not necessarily mean that policymakers should be neutral on the issue of including or excluding drinking-driver claims. In the first place, no one knows with any degree of precision what factors determine the behavior of those who drink and drive versus those who do not or how significant any of these factors are. It would seem wise, then, not to remove any deterrent effect that the current legal system has on drinking and driving, however small it may be. Similarly, there is something to be said for having society send consistent messages on drinking and driving to its members. Excluding drinking-driver claims from the compensation fund would support, rather than undercut, the strong message of social and official disapproval of drinking and driving.

The exclusion of claims by the survivors of drinking drivers who are killed in traffic accidents may strike some readers as particularly harsh. After all, they too are among the innocent victims. Viewed in that regard, they may appear to be just the kind of accident victims who should be brought within the scope of the compensation fund. In fact, when the family members of a drinking driver are themselves injured in an alcohol-related accident, they would be entitled to compensation from the fund for their own losses. It may be that, on balance, compensation fund claims by survivors of drinking drivers are thought to be more appropriately included in rather than excluded from the fund.

Admittedly, the exclusion provision I propose in the model legislation for the fund is based on a worst-case scenario that others may find less troubling. Suppose, for instance, that an individual who decides to commit suicide stages the death as part of an alcohol-related traffic accident to open up a claim for payment of the economic loss to the surviving spouse and minor dependent children from the fund. The details of the fund proposal, including the exclusion provision that is at issue, have been constructed so that, to the maximum feasible extent, they produce a positive effect on behavior. Although it is possible to draft an exclusion provision narrowly targeted at a specific concern such as this, it is probably best to keep to a more widely sweeping provision instead. It is doubtful that a narrower type of provision could be applied at acceptable levels of accuracy or administrative cost. Nevertheless, the exclusion provision can be modified without doing serious damage to the rest of the compensation fund proposal.

## Anticipating the Objections of the Alcohol Industry

At the heart of the victim compensation proposal is a new tax that would be imposed on firms in the alcoholic beverage industry. The tax's effects on industry sales may be fairly minimal or more drastic, depending on the rate of taxation set by the state and the price elasticity of the demand for alcohol. It is undoubtedly true, however, that at least some marginal consumers will be priced out of the market and that a somewhat greater percentage of consumers will decrease their consumption.

That result is not necessarily an unfortunate and undesirable result of adopting the compensation fund proposal. Many scholars and public health officials think that a decrease in the consumption of alcohol unequivocally provides a social benefit. In fact, it may be one of the proposal's stronger selling points. That reaction, however, is unlikely to be shared by the alcohol industry. Depending on how consumers react to the price increase spurred by the new tax, sales may decrease so dramatically that the industry decides to make cutbacks and layoffs.

My first response is that my proposal is extremely unlikely to bring about this sort of result. Substantial sums of money can be raised by relatively small rates of taxation, and the amount of money needed to finance the system may not be all that large, particularly in states that already have taken aggressive measures to shift and to spread the accident losses of victims of drinking drivers. Nevertheless, even a relatively small risk of economic disruption raises the prospect of substantial industry opposition to the proposal.

In its most blunt terms, the question the industry is likely to ask is, "What's in it for us?" The remote possibility does exist, of course, that the alcohol industry will see the victim compensation fund as a socially responsible way to deal with an important part of the drinking-driver problem. The alcohol industry as a whole has not seemed as totally devoid of a social conscience as the tobacco industry has or the asbestos industry[20] or such individual firms as the A. H. Robins Company, which marketed the Dalkon Shield intrauterine device in virtually complete disregard of women's health and safety.[21] Still, it is a lot easier to devote corporate resources to an advertising campaign about "the right thing to do" when the "right thing" happens to be eating oatmeal, the corporation's product.

It is possible that the compensation fund proposal does offer one advantage to the alcohol industry—a relatively lower increase in the taxes on alcohol. I mentioned earlier my belief that a tax increase on alcoholic beverages sometime in the future is likely as a result of pressure from two sources. The first pressure comes from those who are concerned about the adverse public health consequences of alcohol consumption. Increased taxes are seen by many as an effective way of reducing demand. The second source of pressure comes from officials seeking to reduce budget deficits without having to call for a general tax increase. It is reasonable to predict that alcohol tax increases in response to these two pressures would be substantially greater than a tax increase to finance the victim compensation fund. The tax rate for the compensation fund tax on alcohol need be no higher than is necessary to finance the fund. In addition, enacting the compensation fund tax could lessen the pressure for other types of alcohol tax increases by preempting those increases. A further tax increase might garner less revenues because of a decrease in demand. The alcohol industry could oppose a further alcohol tax increase with an argument along the lines of "we gave at the office." In effect, the industry would be able to say, "We gave at the compensation fund."

This may appear to be a relatively weak reason for the alcohol industry to support the victim compensation fund proposal, but keep in mind that relatively little weight need be given to it. The ultimate response to industry objections is, of course, that the purpose of the proposal is to do something for society, not the industry. If the social benefits from this proposal are achievable only at an unavoidable and generally acceptable cost to the industry, the bottom-line response must be, "So be it."

One of the major goals of the accident victim compensation fund is to shift more of the victims' losses from drinking-driver accidents to the alcohol industry. In principle, the agency that administers the compensation fund is to act not as an adversary of the claimant but rather as an administrative adjudicator of the eligibility of the claimant for payment from the fund. Thus a direct relationship exists between the level of compensation paid to victims and the level of the demand for financing the fund through the tax imposed on the distributors of alcoholic beverages.

That relationship between the compensation levels and the tax requirements means that, while the fund and the claimant do not have an adversarial relationship, one party will be adversely affected by the fund's decisions—the alcohol industry. The greater the total amount of claims approved by the fund is, the higher the tax rate needs to be. The higher the tax rate is, the more demand will decrease, and the lower will be the profits from making and distributing alcoholic beverages. If the true adversary of the claimant is the alcohol industry, then, one might speculate that the industry should be allowed in some fashion to resist claims.

That argument might have some superficial appeal, but it is actually not only incorrect but bad policy as well. In the first place, the apparent adversarial relationship between the industry and claimants in no way entails a right to representation in a claim determination. A simple illustration will support that conclusion. Suppose that the disability claimants who appear before the Social Security Administration put such a drain on available funds that pressure begins to build for an increase in the social security withholding tax, or FICA contribution. That state of affairs would not give a taxpayer a right to contest someone else's disability claim in order to relieve the pressure for a tax increase. A person's status as a taxpayer for a program that provides benefits to others does not create any sort of right to contest individual awards that are made in administrative adjudications of claims to those benefits. The position of the alcohol industry is similar; the industry is a taxpayer for the victim compensation fund. Taxpayers have no legally protectable interest at stake that would give them the right to contest individual claims.

Allowing the alcohol industry to appear before the agency would produce almost exactly the wrong climate in which to determine an individual's entitlement to compensation. Making the administrative process adversarial would undercut the advantages it offers over litigation in terms of cost reduction and efficiency. If the agency decision-making process were to become more adversarial and include trial-type hearings, then those advantages are likely to be lost, and probably with relatively little increase in the fairness or accuracy of decisions.

Another feature of the victim compensation fund that might draw political fire from the alcohol industry is the decision to impose an equal rate of taxation on all segments of the alcohol industry by tying the tax rate to the ethanol content of the beverage taxed. Different alcoholic beverages may have different rates of involvement in traffic accidents. If this is true, then a more equitable taxing system would take pains to set the tax rate for a particular class of alcoholic beverage so that it reflected its relative share in causing drinking-driver traffic accidents.

While the rate of involvement may very well differ across classes of beverages, this contention is difficult, if not impossible, to prove. One of the more striking themes that comes through in the scholarly literature on drinking-driver accidents is the significant extent to which policymakers are acting without a solid grounding in data about the extent of the problem and about the effects of different solutions that have been attempted.[22] Choosing to apply the tax uniformly to all alcoholic beverages based on ethanol content recognizes the need to adopt *some* starting point if a reform effort is to get underway.

In the face of this uncertainty, and in order to accommodate the possibility of a differential impact according to type of alcoholic beverage, the proposal should provide that the agency that administers the fund establish a suitable information base and act on it at reasonable intervals. The agency should be required to collect as much data as it possibly can on the type of alcoholic beverages consumed by drinking drivers. The agency could then periodically correlate that data on consumption with information on the frequency and the severity of injuries from all alcohol-related traffic accidents.

The most reliable comprehensive information on alcohol-related accidents comes from the accident reports made by law enforcement officers who are often the first to arrive at an accident scene. These officers could be required to file a report for the compensation fund that addresses a number of specific questions about the role that alcohol played in the accident. Ideally, the report would cover the following items: the amount of alcoholic beverages consumed by each person involved in the accident, the time at which the consumption occurred, the location where the beverages were purchased and consumed and the circumstances surrounding these activities, the type of beverages consumed and their brand names, the grounds on which the officer's suspicion of alcohol involvement was based, and the results of any tests for alcohol impairment that were performed. The compensation fund administrator could develop a convenient reporting form that enables the information to be recorded in a simple and brief format so that the reporting requirement will not unduly burden law enforcement personnel.

Unfortunately, much of the information that must be collected is likely to incriminate the drinking driver asked to provide it. Indeed, this fact may explain why the greatest amount of information regarding alcohol consumption and traffic accidents has been assembled in connection with fatal accidents, whose victims are obviously unable to object to tests that determine the level of alcohol in their blood. The problem of incrimination might be addressed in either of two ways: first, after compelled disclosure, the information given by the driver could then be made privileged; second, the information gathered at the scene of the accident could be supplemented by additional information from further legal or administrative proceedings arising out of the accident. Although the second option would leave informational gaps and entail extra administrative work, it is still probably preferable to the first option. Under the first option, the drinking driver may not understand the terms under which the information is being sought, or else the driver may not trust the privilege enough to provide accurate information. Finally, it is perhaps unrealistic to expect law enforcement officers to perform the dual duties of completing an initial criminal investigation while at the same time recording privileged information for submission to the compensation fund.

An intermediate approach would assign someone from the fund to conduct a follow-up inquiry with the drinking driver. The results would be treated as privileged and kept separate from the criminal prosecutorial process. Such a solution would add considerably to the cost of administering the fund, however. At a minimum, a legislature considering this intermediate option ought to be sure that the marginal increase in information hoped for is worth the additional time and expense of gathering it.

After as much relevant data as possible is obtained, either the legislature or the compensation fund administrator could use it to recalculate the tax assessment based on the relationship between particular kinds of alcohol and drinking-driver accident injuries. As more complete information becomes available, policy choices can be adjusted, as was done in the case of asbestos claims in the 1980s. Members of the asbestos industry entered into an agreement to evaluate compensation claims for asbestos-related injuries and pay them. It was called the Wellington Agreement, named after Harry Wellington, the former Yale law school dean who was influential in its implementation. The participating asbestos producers and their insurers agreed to establish a claims fund and set initial percentages of responsibility for contributing to the fund.[23] However, the agreement also provided for the collection of detailed information about the claims that were filed and called for the allocation percentages to be adjusted one year after the claims facility had opened and then at three-year intervals thereafter.[24]

A similar provision could be built into the enabling legislation for the alcohol-related accident victim compensation fund, with two caveats. First, the intervals at which the tax rate is to be redetermined should be carefully set in order to avoid too much uncertainty about tax liability and anticipated revenues. Second, any readjustment of a tax rate should be based on clear evidence of a significant difference in the accident involvement of different alcoholic beverages. The uniform tax rate based on ethanol content should be retained unless it is possible to conclude with a reasonable degree of certainty that the tax burden is being distributed incorrectly.

## NOTES

1. The phenomenon described in the text is nicely illustrated in the exchange between Richard Epstein and Jeffrey O'Connell about the Virginia Birth-Related Neurological Injury Compensation Act that was enacted in 1987. *See* Epstein, *Market and Regulatory Approaches to Medical Malpractice: The Virginia Obstetrical No-Fault Statute*, 74 VA. L. REV. 1451 (1988); O'Connell, *Pragmatic Constraints on Market Approaches: A Response to Professor Epstein*, 74 VA. L. REV. 1475 (1988).

2. Professor Jacobs suggests that the size of the drinking-driver problem is not immune from the tendency to exaggerate in order to attract attention to the problem and to evoke support for the investment in reform. JACOBS, DRUNK DRIVING, at 27-29.

3. Epstein, *A Theory of Strict Liability*, 2 J. LEGAL STUD. 151 (1973); Epstein, *Defenses and Subsequent Pleas in a System of Strict Liability*, 3 J. LEGAL STUD. 165 (1974); Epstein, *Intentional Harms*, 4 J. LEGAL STUD. 391 (1975); Epstein, *Nuisance Law: Corrective Justice and Its Utilitarian Constraints*, 8 J. LEGAL STUD. 49 (1979).

4. R. EPSTEIN, TAKINGS: PRIVATE PROPERTY AND THE POWER OF EMINENT DOMAIN (1985); Epstein, *Medical Malpractice: The Case for Contract*, 1976 AM. B. FOUND. RES. J. 87; Epstein, *Market and Regulatory Approaches to Medical Malpractice: The Virginia Obstetrical No-Fault Statute*, 74 VA. L. REV. 1451 (1988).

5. LANDES & POSNER, ECONOMIC STRUCTURE; SHAVELL, ECONOMIC ANALYSIS.

6. *See, e.g.,* J. O'CONNELL & C. KELLY, THE BLAME GAME: INJURIES, INSURANCE, AND INJUSTICE (1987); J. O'CONNELL, THE LAWSUIT LOTTERY: ONLY THE LAWYERS WIN (1979).

7. Fletcher, *Fairness and Utility in Tort Theory*, 85 HARV. L. REV. 537 (1972).

8. SUGARMAN, DOING AWAY WITH PERSONAL INJURY LAW.

9. A similar attitude is expressed in Snortum, *Deterrence of Alcohol-Impaired Driving: An Effect in Search of a Cause*, in LAURENCE et al., SOCIAL CONTROL, at 219: "Social scientists can readily identify with the wish to hold out for the highest standards of evidence and to pronounce, in concert with the great scientific skeptics, that the case is 'not proved.' But scientific effort is a two-edged sword and lives are at stake. Can we pronounce, with equal confidence, that the enormous investment in countermeasures, during the past five years in the United States and the past fifty years in Norway, is *irrelevant* to current levels of compliance?"

10. *See* Meecham, *Higher Alcohol Taxes Would Be Hard to Swallow, Merchants Say*, Washington Post, August 14, 1990, at B5.

11. I. MCEWAN, THE CHILD IN TIME 3 (1987).

12. 44 U.S.C. §§ 3501-3512.

13. *See* Ognibene, *An Alcohol Superfund: Let Boozers Pay for the Misery They Create*, The Washington Post, Sept. 28, 1986, sec. C (Outlook), at 1.

14. 42 U.S.C. §§ 9601-9675.

15. *See, e.g.,* Barron, *The Teen Drug of Choice: Alcohol,* New York Times, August 7, 1988, sec. 4A (Education Life), at 41, 42 (discussion of replacement of "responsible use" educational strategy with "a hard line . . . discouraging the use of alcohol entirely"). *See also* Bernstein, *New DWI Proposals: Prohibition Reincarnated,* NATION'S RESTAURANT NEWS, Nov. 17, 1986, at 9.

16. Island Records, Ltd. (1970).

17. *See, e.g.,* Bertelmann v. Taas Assoc., 735 P.2d 930 (Haw. 1987) (no common-law commercial dispenser liability action will be recognized when it is based on fatal injuries to the intoxicated driver).

18. One might object that there is no principled basis for drawing this distinction. At one level, that objection might be conceded to be accurate and yet not be treated as compelling a different outcome. The jurisprudential work of the legal philosopher Ronald Dworkin contains a good deal of writing that distinguishes principle and policy and that argues that a response to policy arguments is legitimately within the prerogative of legislative decision makers. *See generally* R. DWORKIN, LAW'S EMPIRE (1986); R. DWORKIN, A MATTER OF PRINCIPLE (1985); R. DWORKIN, TAKING RIGHTS SERIOUSLY (1977).

19. Dissatisfaction with the ability to make such determinations has led to a number of proposals for a reform of the contributory and comparative negligence rules that operate in routine tort litigation. A recent proposal that is driven in large part by the unrealistically precise calculations that comparative fault schemes appear to require is found in Little, *Eliminating the Fallacies of Comparative Negligence and Proportional Liability,* 41 ALA. L. REV. 13 (1989).

20. *See* P. BRODEUR, OUTRAGEOUS MISCONDUCT: THE ASBESTOS INDUSTRY ON TRIAL (1985).

21. *See* S. ENGELMAYER & R. WAGMAN, LORD'S JUSTICE (1985); M. MINTZ, AT ANY COST: CORPORATE GREED, WOMEN, AND THE DALKON SHIELD (1985); S. PERRY & J. DAWSON, NIGHTMARE: WOMEN AND THE DALKON SHIELD (1985).

22. The inadequacy of the data about drinking and driving is discussed in Gusfield, *The Control of Drinking-Driving in the United States: A Period in Transition?,* in LAURENCE et al., SOCIAL CONTROL, at 109.

23. ASBESTOS CLAIMS FACILITY, AGREEMENT CONCERNING ASBESTOS-RELATED CLAIMS 18-19 (1985).

24. *Id.* at 20-22.

# 15

## The Compensation Fund
## Legislation and Operation

This chapter offers a comprehensive view of how the proposed alcohol-related accident victim compensation fund will operate. I first present both a draft of a model statute that could be used to create the victim compensation fund and a section-by-section commentary on the statutory language that might also be of use. The chief virtue of the model legislation is that it provides a fairly well directed focus for a policy debate about the drinking-driver problem as it affects its victims and about the strengths and weaknesses of specific solutions to the accident-victim compensation problem. I then present a number of hypothetical drinking-driver traffic accidents and track how they would be treated under the terms of the proposed compensation fund.

### A Model Statute Creating an Alcohol-Related
### Accident Victim Compensation Fund

The first half of this chapter reduces the principal features of the victim compensation fund proposal to the language of a model statute. A state legislature could use this statute to set up an alcohol-related accident victim compensation fund that would create an opportunity for fuller compensation of victims of drinking drivers and at the same time shift more of the costs of drinking-driver traffic accidents to the alcoholic beverage industry. The commentary that is provided for the statutory sections is minimal, because in a real sense the first fourteen chapters of *John Barleycorn Must Pay* have been the commentary to this model statute. The purpose of the commentary is to provide simple and direct statements about the legislative purpose that is reflected in the model statute's choice of language. A state legislature will, of course, expand upon the commentary provided here in order to reflect its own policy choices. The statements of legislative purpose that it provides can play an important role at three major times: first, during the policy debate both outside and within the legislature about whether to adopt a plan and what type of plan to adopt; second, at the time of the fund's implementation and during its continuing administration; and third, when judicial decision makers are called upon to interpret statutory provisions.

*Section 1. TITLE.*
   *This Act shall be known as the Alcohol-Related Accident Victim Compensation Act (the "Act").*

*Section 2. ALCOHOL-RELATED ACCIDENT VICTIM COMPENSATION FUND.*

   *a. Creation of Fund.*
*There shall be created in this state a fund known as the Alcohol-Related Accident Victim Compensation Fund (the "Fund").*

   *b. Compensation Fund Administrator.*
*The position of Alcohol-Related Accident Victim Compensation Fund Administrator (the "Administrator") shall be created. The Administrator shall assist in the establishment of whatever procedures and in the performance of whatever duties are necessary to implement the Act, and shall have a continuing responsibility to monitor and to coordinate the activities of the administrative agencies that are responsible for the operation of the Fund in order to achieve the purposes of the Act. Sufficient staff shall be appointed by the Administrator to carry out the functions of the office.*

   *c. Funding.*
*All alcoholic beverages that are to be sold to ultimate consumers within this state shall be subject to a tax which shall be paid into the Fund. For purposes of the Act, the term "alcoholic beverages" shall include distilled spirits, beer and other malt beverages, and wine.*

   *d. Assessment.*
*The tax that is required by section 2c of the Act shall be levied at a uniform rate according to the alcohol content of the alcoholic beverages that are being taxed. The basic rate shall be _____ cents per ounce of ethyl alcohol or ethanol that is contained in the beverage. The obligation to pay the tax shall be determined and the tax shall be paid upon the occasion of the last wholesale distribution of the alcoholic beverage that is subject to the tax that occurs within this state prior to retail sale.*

   *e. Collection and Disbursement.*
*The collection of the tax that is required by the Act shall be performed by the [state agency that is responsible for the collection of alcohol excise taxes or by*

*the new agency created to administer the Fund], pursuant to regulations promulgated by the Administrator. The administration of claims and the payment of compensation from the Fund shall be performed by the [state agency that is responsible for administering claims for compensation under the state regulatory scheme that most closely resembles the operation of the Fund or by the new agency created to administer the Fund], pursuant to regulations promulgated by the Administrator. The Administrator shall have authority to issue any regulations regarding the assessment and the collection of the tax and the processing of claims for compensation that are required in order to implement the provisions of the Act.*

## Commentary on Section 2

Section 2 of the Act contains the two basic changes that must be made in state government in order to carry out the purposes of the legislation. First, an administrative structure must be created to implement the compensation function of the Act, and second, the source of the financing for the Victim Compensation Fund must be designed.

In Subsection b, a simple reference is made to a Fund Administrator who will have the principal responsibility for carrying out the tasks required in this and subsequent sections of the Act. The language of this subsection is neutral with respect to the other administrative structural decisions that must be made to accomplish the taxing and claims processing functions required under the Act. The Administrator can thus be the head of a new administrative agency that is charged with the specific and exclusive task of operating the Fund, or the Administrator can operate more as a coordinator and a facilitator of the authority and the responsibility that will be delegated to other agencies that currently perform functions similar to the ones required by the Act. In either event, the Act should make clear that the ultimate responsibility and accountability for the successful operation of the Fund rests with the Administrator. Whatever authority over other agency functions is necessary for meeting that responsibility should be delegated to the Administrator. The Act is silent with respect to the terms of the appointment, method of confirmation, rank, salary, etc., of the Administrator. Such details can be best determined by considering how this new office fits within the context of the state's general administrative structure.

Subsection c specifies that the tax applies to all alcoholic beverages that will be sold to ultimate consumers within the state. The definition of alcoholic beverages that is used in the Act should be phrased so that it is consistent with any definition that is used in the alcoholic beverage control legislation of the state adopting the Act.

Subsection d both sets the rate and locates the obligation to pay the tax created in the preceding subsection. The tax rate is uniform on all alcoholic beverages according to the ethanol content of the beverages. The precise rate of tax that is chosen will be determined by the legislature based on a consideration of the magnitude of the undercompensation problem that is identified in the state adopting the Act and an estimate of the extent of the impact on consumer demand that the legislature concludes is a desirable or acceptable consequence of the new tax.

The tax is to be paid by the last wholesaler who has control over the beverages within the state adopting the Act. In a control state, that will be the distributor who sells the alcoholic beverages to the agency that operates the state stores. In a license state, and for beverages that are sold by licensees in a control state, that will be the wholesaler that sells to retailers or to commercial dispensers. The responsibility for keeping adequate records from which the volume and the ethanol content of beverages can be determined is imposed on the distributor who must pay the tax.

Subsection e allows the state legislature to exercise its option regarding the designation of the appropriate administrative agency or agencies to carry out the Fund's functions. The model legislation contemplates the delegation of the taxing and claims processing functions to existing state agencies, but a new agency could be created to perform either or both of those functions. This subsection also specifies that the Fund Administrator is responsible for issuing the regulations that govern those functions, and it grants the Administrator the authority to issue any necessary regulations.

*Section 3. CLAIMS FOR COMPENSATION.*

   *a. Entitlement to Compensation.*
*Any person who has been injured in an alcohol-related traffic accident occurring in this state in which the alcohol impairment of a driver contributed to the occurrence of the accident shall be entitled to compensation from the Fund, provided that:*

      *(i) the claim is not made by, nor made on behalf of, nor derivative from an injury to, an alcohol-impaired driver; and*
      *(ii) the claim threshold prerequisite of Section 3c of the Act has been satisfied.*
*Notwithstanding the proviso of subsection (i), payment may be made from the*

*Fund in a situation in which a claimant proves by clear and convincing evidence that a driver who was alcohol-impaired was driving in an emergency situation. For purposes of the Act, an "emergency situation" shall be defined as a situation in which a driver acted to avoid a threat to life or safety that arose after the driver's ability to operate a motor vehicle was already impaired by the consumption of alcohol and that presented the driver with no other reasonable alternative to driving while alcohol-impaired.*

*b. Proof and Presumption of Alcohol Impairment.*
*"Alcohol impairment" shall be defined for purposes of the Act as an impairment of a person's mental or physical faculties as a result of alcoholic beverage consumption so as to diminish that person's ability to think and act in a manner in which a person in full possession of his or her faculties and exercising the care of a reasonable person would act under the same or similar circumstances. For purposes of determining eligibility for compensation from the Fund, the alcohol impairment of a driver shall be found to have existed at the time of an accident and to have contributed to the occurrence of a traffic accident involving that driver whenever:*

*(i) the claimant provides evidence of an official finding from which the alcohol impairment of a driver can reasonably be inferred, including but not limited to a finding that:*

*(a) the driver has been convicted of an alcohol-related driving offense in connection with the accident out of which the claim for compensation arises, or*

*(b) the driver has been held civilly liable for harm caused in that accident as a result of the alcohol-impaired operation of a vehicle, or*

*(c) the driver has had his or her legal right to drive subjected to administrative or other sanction as a result of an alcohol-related driving offense related to that accident; or*

*(ii) the driver has been proven to have operated the vehicle with a blood alcohol concentration of .04 percent or higher, if the driver is an adult, or with a blood alcohol concentration of .01 percent or higher, if the driver is a minor; or*

*(iii) the driver has been designated as alcohol-impaired by a law enforcement officer who was present at the scene of the accident out of which the claim for compensation arises.*

*Nothing in this section shall preclude the ability of a claimant to prove by any other relevant evidence that the accident in which the claimant was injured was a result of the alcohol impairment of a driver who was involved in the accident. No finding of alcohol impairment that is made under subsections (ii) or (iii) of this section shall be used as evidence in any other forum or for any purpose other than determining the entitlement of a claimant to compensation from the Fund.*

  *c. Threshold for Compensation Fund Claim.*
*In order for a claimant to be entitled to obtain compensation from the Fund, the claimant must establish that the claim requests compensation for otherwise uncompensated personal injuries and economic losses, of the type for which compensation is available under Section 4b of the Act, that exceed the value of $10,000.*

  *d. Calculation of Uncompensated Injuries.*
*In calculating whether the uncompensated personal injuries and economic losses of the claimant exceed $10,000 for purposes of determining the claimant's entitlement to compensation from the Fund, the estimate of the total amount of the losses that are compensable under Section 4b that have been or that will be suffered by the claimant as a result of the accident giving rise to the claim shall be reduced by:*

  *(i) any tort recovery, whether obtained by settlement or in satisfaction of a judgment, that the claimant has been paid for losses that were incurred in the accident out of which the claim arises, provided that the amount of that tort recovery shall be reduced by an amount that is equivalent to the litigation expenses and the reasonable attorney's fees that were incurred in obtaining the recovery; and*

  *(ii) any payment that has been or that will be received by the claimant or paid on behalf of the claimant from a collateral source for an item of loss for which the claimant is otherwise entitled to compensation from the Fund. For purposes of the Act, a collateral source shall be defined as any provider of a payment or other benefit to compensate a claimant for an accident loss, who provides such payment or benefit for a reason other than an actual or a potential legal responsibility for the harm that was inflicted by a tortfeasor.*

## Commentary on Section 3

Section 3 contains the statutory provisions according to which eligibility for compensation from the Fund will be determined. Those provisions establish two basic prerequisites: the claimant must be injured in an alcohol-related accident and the claimant must have uncompensated accident losses of the types covered by the Fund that exceed a certain value (such as the $10,000 limit used here).

Subsection a accomplishes a number of preliminary tasks related to the definition of eligibility. First, it defines the scope of compensation from the Fund as injuries that are received in alcohol-related traffic accidents that occur in the state adopting the Act. Second, it defines the class of alcohol-related traffic accidents that are deemed to be within the scope of the Act as those in which a driver was alcohol-impaired and in which the alcohol-impairment of the driver contributed to the occurrence of the accident. Third, it excludes compensation fund claims that are made by, on behalf of, or derived from, an alcohol-impaired driver. Fourth, it creates an exception to that exclusion, in the narrowly drafted definition of an emergency situation that is intended to identify and make allowance for the infrequent situation in which the only reasonable method of preserving life or safety is to drive while impaired by alcohol consumption. Finally, it contains a cross-reference to the other major threshold element, that a claimant must prove a certain level of uncompensated losses, which is the subject of Subsection c.

Subsection b defines alcohol impairment and establishes a number of routes by which a claimant can prove that a driver was alcohol-impaired and that the driver's alcohol impairment contributed to the occurrence of the traffic accident in which the claimant was injured. The definition of alcohol impairment that is used in Subsection b is modeled on the New Hampshire dram shop act, New Hampshire Revised Statutes Annotated § 507-F:1(IV) (Supp. 1989), which defines "intoxication" in similar terms.

Subsection b identifies three methods by which a compensation fund claimant can establish the operative facts for designating the accident as alcohol-related for purposes of the Act. First, the claimant may produce an official finding that supports those facts. Three different types of findings that establish that the accident was alcohol-related are listed in the Act: a criminal conviction, a civil judgment, and the suspension or revocation of a driver's license. Second, the claimant may establish the driver's blood alcohol concentration at the level specified in the Act. Third, the claimant may establish that a law enforcement officer present at the scene of the accident has designated the driver as alcohol-impaired. To prove this fact the claimant could use an official citation for an alcohol-related driving offense or a report made to the Fund under the provisions of Section 7 of the Act. A claimant who is not able to establish the statutory prerequisite in one of these ways may nevertheless offer other relevant evidence regarding the operative facts of an alcohol-related accident.

The conclusions that are reached under Subsection b are to be used only for purposes of determining entitlement to compensation from the Fund. Evidence of an alcohol-impairment finding that is made either as a result of the BAC level referred to in Subsection b(ii) or as a result of a law enforcement officer's opinion under subsection b(iii) shall not be admitted in any other forum for any other purpose. The presumptions are established in the Act to carry out the purposes of the Act and should not have any adverse consequences for drivers in other settings.

Subsection c adopts an uncompensated loss threshold of $10,000 for a claimant's entry into the compensation fund system. The fundamental rationale for establishing such a threshold is that the Fund exists as a compensation source of last resort for the more seriously injured and undercompensated victims of alcohol-related accidents. The normal presence of a variety of tort remedies and insurance coverages for obtaining compensation for lower levels of accident loss justifies setting the threshold in terms of a certain amount of loss that the claimant must bear before compensation from the Fund becomes available. A legislature adopting the Act is free to set the threshold higher or lower.

Subsection d explains how to calculate the amount of uncompensated losses in order to determine eligibility for compensation from the Fund. This subsection requires certain amounts to be deducted from the claimant's estimated amount of compensable accident losses. The claimant must deduct any payments that have been made or that will be made for those elements of loss either from collateral sources or from parties who are or who might be liable under the governing rules of tort law.

*Section 4. APPLICATION FOR COMPENSATION.*

*a. Submission of Claims.*
*The Administrator shall issue regulations specifying the procedures that are to be followed for submitting applications for compensation from the Fund and for processing applications.*

*b. Elements of Accident Loss Compensated by the Fund.*
*A claimant who has otherwise satisfied the requirements for obtaining compensation under the terms of the Act shall be entitled to payment of uncompensated losses that exceed the value of $10,000. Payment shall be made in the form of a lump-sum amount as compensation for the following items of loss, to the extent that such losses have not been and will not be paid by either of the methods described in Section 3d of the Act:*

*(i) medical expenses and rehabilitation costs, including special education requirements, that have already been incurred by the claimant;*

*(ii) loss of income that has already been incurred by the claimant and that is attributable to the accident for which the claim is being made;*

*(iii) physical pain that has been suffered as a result of the injuries that were received in the accident;*

*(iv) in the case of a claim by a surviving spouse or a surviving minor dependent child of a person who died as a result of an accident that meets the conditions of the Act, the economic loss to the claimant that is attributable to the death of the decedent; and*

*(v) attorney's fees and expenses that were incurred in the process of establishing an entitlement to compensation from the Fund.*

For the payment of compensation for items that are listed in subsections *(iii)*, *(iv)*, and *(v)*, the amount of compensation that is payable to a claimant may be limited according to a schedule of compensation that is contained in a regulation issued by the Administrator.

*c. Future Loss Compensated by the Fund Periodically.*
A claimant who is otherwise entitled to compensation from the Fund and who establishes the substantial likelihood of suffering future loss as a result of the accident for which the claim is asserted shall be entitled to recover compensation for future losses that satisfy subsections *(i)* through *(iv)* of Section *4b* of the Act. Payment from the Fund for these elements of accident loss shall be made periodically as the losses or expenses are incurred, provided that an initial agency determination of a claimant's entitlement to compensation from the Fund may establish a schedule of future payments to be fulfilled upon proof that the items of loss for which compensation is to be awarded have actually been incurred. The Administrator shall issue regulations providing a method by which a claimant may establish an entitlement to continuing compensation.

*d. Administrative Appeals and Judicial Review of Claims Decisions.*
A determination regarding a claimant's entitlement to compensation from the Fund shall be subject to an appeal within the Fund to an Appeals Board that is created by regulations issued by the Administrator. Such appeal must be filed within sixty days of the notice to the claimant of the determination. Decisions of the Appeals Board shall be final, and there shall be no judicial review of the decisions of the Appeals Board in any judicial forum.

*e. Rule-making Petitions and Judicial Review of Fund Regulations.*
Any person who is interested in or who is adversely affected by the performance of the Fund in the interpretation and application of the provisions of the Act may petition the Administrator for the issuance of a regulation regarding such interpretation or application. Judicial review of the result of the agency consideration of any such petition for rule making shall be obtainable only in the *[appellate court that is typically given jurisdiction over administrative agency decisions within the state that adopts the Act]*. When reviewing regulations that have been issued by the Fund Administrator, including the

*decision not to issue a regulation in response to a petition that has been filed under this section, the Court shall give deference to the Administrator's interpretation of the Act, and it shall set aside a regulation only if it is arbitrary and capricious.*

## Commentary on Section 4

Section 4 of the Act contains the provisions regarding the administration of the Fund's claims process. Included are a general authorization for the Administrator to issue necessary regulations and some specific provisions dealing with concerns that are unique or especially significant to the operation of the Fund.

Subsection a grants the Fund Administrator authority to adopt regulations that will govern the submission of claims for compensation and the processing of those claims. The model legislation that is offered here contemplates that the adoption of regulations by the Administrator will be governed by the state's Administrative Procedure Act, unless the legislature specifies otherwise.

Subsection b lists the elements of accident loss for which claims for compensation from the Fund may be submitted. Payments may be made for covered losses in excess of $10,000 of uncompensated loss. The uncompensated loss threshold thus serves also as a loss deductible provision for the Fund. The abrogation of the collateral source rule and the elimination of an entitlement to recover for elements of harm for which the claimant has already received payment, which were made part of the calculation of the Fund threshold in Section 3d of the Act, are carried over to the determination of the amount of compensation that is payable from the Fund. The elements of loss for which compensation may be claimed are: (1) medical expenses, which should be broadly construed to include such items as hospital costs, doctor's bills, medication, and rehabilitation; (2) loss of income of the claimant; (3) physical pain; (4) economic loss to a surviving spouse or a surviving minor dependent child of a person who is killed in, or dies as a result of, an alcohol-related accident; and (5) attorney's fees and the expenses of obtaining compensation from the Fund. The amount that is payable for the last three elements of accident loss may be scheduled or capped according to regulations issued by the Administrator.

Subsections b and c together specify the two major elements of the method of payment of claims from the Fund that the Administrator must adopt. Losses that have occurred in the past will be paid in a lump-sum to the claimant. Losses that will occur in the future may only be paid periodically as they occur. The Fund may, however, make a determination of the losses that are expected to occur and issue a schedule of payments from the Fund to compensate for those losses. The Administrator is given authority to issue regulations dealing with the proof of eligibility for continuing payment of compensation from the Fund, but such regulations should create as little of a burden on the claimant as is necessary to accomplish their purpose. The intent should be to avoid requiring a full-scale redetermination of entitlement to compensation unless circumstances have changed in such a way that the award of compensation that was made in the past no longer reflects the losses suffered by the claimant.

Many of the details of the operation of the Fund and of the relationship between the Fund and the courts will be covered by the Administrative Procedure Act of the state that adopts the Act. Subsections d and e are examples of matters that are important enough to be singled out for special treatment in the enabling legislation for the Fund.

Subsection d provides that a determination regarding a claimant's entitlement to compensation from the Fund shall be reviewable only by an Appeals Board set up by regulations issued by the Administrator. Decisions on individual claims for compensation are precluded from judicial review.

Subsection e establishes a method of obtaining an agency consideration and subsequent judicial review of the Fund's administrative policy decisions, which includes decisions about the interpretation and the application of the Act's provisions. Although judicial review is precluded for decisions on individual claims, the more generally applicable administrative decisions of the Fund should be subject to some judicial control. This subsection contemplates a two-step procedure for obtaining judicial review. First, a person who wishes to challenge the way that the Fund is carrying out its tasks under the Act may file a petition for rule making with the Administrator requesting the adoption of a regulation. Second, after the Administrator acts on that petition, including a denial of the request, judicial review of that decision may be sought in the appellate court that normally has jurisdiction over such administrative agency decision making. The standard of review is specified in order to make clear that the court should give a significant degree of deference to the agency charged with the principal responsibility of administering the Act.

*Section 5. SUBROGATION.*

*a. Fund Subrogated to Rights of Accident Victim.*
*The Fund shall be subrogated to the legal right of any claimant to obtain*

*compensation for accident losses to the extent of any payments that have been or will be made from the Fund to the claimant for those losses.*

*b. Enforcement of Fund Subrogation Rights.*
*The Fund may assert its right of subrogation either in a separate action filed by the Fund or by intervening in a tort action arising out of the same traffic accident that is the basis of the claim for compensation from the Fund filed against a person against whom the claimant has a legal right to seek compensation for accident losses for which payment has been or will be made from the Fund.*

*c. No Subrogation Rights for Collateral Source Payments.*
*No person who makes a payment to a claimant of a sum which is treated under Section 3d(ii) or Section 4b of the Act as an amount that reduces the entitlement of a claimant to compensation from the Fund shall be entitled to assert any right of subrogation or other right to recover any payment that the claimant receives from the Fund as compensation for harm arising out of the accident for which the payment was made.*

### Commentary on Section 5

This section of the Act identifies the subrogation rights of the Fund and the methods of asserting those rights. Essentially, the Fund is subrogated to the right of a claimant to recover tort compensation for accident losses for which payments have been or will be received from the Fund. Subsection a grants that right of subrogation, while Subsection b allows that right to be asserted independently or by intervention. Subsection c simply states clearly what is probably already true as a practical matter, which is that no person who makes a payment that is treated as a collateral source payment that reduces the claimant's entitlement to compensation from the Fund shall have any right to recover from the claimant as a result of payments that are made from the Fund.

### Section 6. RELATIONSHIP TO EXISTING LAW.

*a. General Principle.*
*Nothing in this Act shall create, abolish, expand, limit, or affect in any way the civil or criminal liability of any person, except in the manner prescribed in section 6b of this Act.*

*b. Exceptions.*
*The payment of compensation to a claimant from the Fund shall have the following effects on the litigation of tort claims to recover damages for injuries*

*arising out of the accident for which compensation was or will be paid from the Fund:*

    *(i) in any tort action that is brought by a victim of an alcohol-impaired driver for the recovery of damages for injuries for which compensation has been received from the Fund under the provisions of the Act, the party from whom recovery is sought shall be entitled to a reduction in liability corresponding to the compensation that has been or will be received from the Fund; and*

    *(ii) in any tort action that is brought by the Fund under Section 5a of the Act against an alcohol-impaired driver or any other person who may be liable for the injuries caused to a claimant by an alcohol-impaired driver, the liability of that driver or other person, if otherwise established, shall include:*

    *(a) any amount that has been or will be paid from the Fund to the claimant,*

    *(b) a sum that represents the administrative expense of providing the compensation from the Fund to the claimant, and*

    *(c) the attorney's fees and litigation expenses that are incurred by the Fund in litigating the tort claim against the driver or the other person who is legally responsible for the injuries that were caused by the driver.*

## Commentary on Section 6

Section 6 first states a general principle and then carves out two exceptions to that principle. The principle that is stated in Subsection a is that the adoption of the Act has no effect on the existing civil or criminal liability of any person who is involved in an accident that becomes the subject of a claim for compensation from the Fund.

The exceptions deal with the situations in which a person can be held liable in tort litigation to pay damages for the injuries suffered by a claimant who is entitled to compensation from the Fund. In the first situation, the tort plaintiff is the claimant who has already established an entitlement to compensation from the Fund. In that tort litigation, the defendant should receive a reduction in liability that corresponds to the plaintiff's receipt of compensation from the Fund. In the second situation, the tort plaintiff is the Fund asserting its right of subrogation under Section 5 of the Act. In that tort litigation, the Fund is entitled to recover from the tort defendant any amount that it has paid or will pay to the claimant, as well as the administrative and litigation expenses incurred in compensating the claimant and in establishing the tort liability of the defendant. To that extent, then, this subsection represents a modification of the American rule that requires litigants to pay their own attorney's fees and litigation expenses.

*Section 7. ALCOHOL-RELATED ACCIDENT INFORMATION.*

*a. Reporting Requirement.*
*Pursuant to regulations issued by the Administrator, law enforcement agencies investigating traffic accidents shall collect and report to the Administrator information about the role of alcoholic beverages in any traffic accident in which personal injury was sustained.*

*b. Information to be Reported.*
*The information that is required to be reported by Section 7a shall, whenever feasible, include:*

*(i) the amount of alcoholic beverage consumption by each person who was involved as a driver in the accident;*

*(ii) the time at which such consumption occurred;*

*(iii) the location and the circumstances under which purchase or consumption (or both) occurred;*

*(iv) the type and the brand name of the beverages that were consumed;*

*(v) the grounds on which the officer's suspicion of a driver's alcohol impairment was based; and*

*(vi) the results of any tests for alcohol impairment that were performed.*

*c. Manner of Reporting Information.*
*The Administrator shall issue to all of the state's law enforcement agencies that are charged with the responsibility of investigating traffic accidents a questionnaire that will enable the information that is required to be reported under the Act to be communicated in a standard format and with a minimum of inconvenience to the law enforcement personnel conducting accident investigations.*

*d. Recalculation of Tax Rate.*
*As a result of the information that is collected by the Administrator under this section of the Act, the [legislature or the Administrator] may recalculate the tax rate that is imposed under Section 2 of the Act. This recalculation shall take place no earlier than three years after the implementation of the Act and no more frequently than at three-year intervals thereafter. No recalculation shall depart from the uniform rate of taxation that is based on the ethanol content of the beverages being taxed unless the [legislature or Administrator] is clearly convinced that the uniform rate significantly fails to reflect the involvement of different types of alcoholic beverages in alcohol-related traffic accidents.*

*Commentary on Section 7*

Section 7 recognizes and attempts to provide at least a partial solution to one of the more glaring difficulties in trying to understand the drinking-driver problem, which is the lack of comprehensive and reliable information about the nature and the extent of the relationship between traffic accidents and the consumption of alcoholic beverages. Subsection a places a demand on law enforcement officials to collect and report to the Administrator information about the role that alcohol consumption plays in accidents that involve personal injury, with Subsection b specifying the minimum information that should be collected. Subsection c charges the Administrator with the responsibility for developing an efficient and convenient questionnaire law enforcement officers can use to collect and record the required information. The collection of this information will necessarily be subject to whatever constraints flow from a drinking driver's right against self-incrimination.

Subsection d provides for the recalculation of the tax rate for alcoholic beverages. This recalculation may raise or lower the rate to reflect the demands for compensation that are actually placed on the Fund. In addition, if the agency administering the Fund is clearly convinced that the uniform rate of taxation based on ethanol content does not reflect how the involvement of alcoholic beverages in drinking-driver traffic accidents differs according to type of beverage, the rate structure of the tax may also be recalculated. In order to reduce the administrative burden of recalculation, the Act specifies time intervals between recalculations. The legislature adopting the Act must choose whether it will make recalculations itself or delegate that authority to the Administrator.

*Section 8. IMPLEMENTATION.*

*a. Regulations.*
*Within six months after appointment to the position, the Administrator shall promulgate the regulations that are required by the Act.*

*b. Claims.*
*Applications for compensation under the Act may be filed only for injuries that arise out of traffic accidents that occur no earlier than one year after the effective date of the Act.*

*c. Collection of Tax.*
*The obligation to pay the tax that is required by Section 2 of the Act shall commence in the fiscal quarter that begins immediately following the effective date of the Act.*

## Commentary on Section 8

The implementation provisions of Section 8 are designed to facilitate the Fund's establishment and its financial integrity. Subsection b postpones the availability of claims for compensation from the Fund to allow extra time for claims procedures to be adopted and for the tax used to finance the Fund to be collected. Subsection c specifies that the collection of the tax shall begin soon after the adoption of the Act. As a result of the delays that are built into these latter subsections, the Fund should begin its operation in a sound financial position and with an administrative structure that is capable of carrying out the responsibilities imposed by the Act.

## The Operation of the Alcohol-Related Accident Victim Compensation Fund

The running Bloom family hypothetical featured in the early chapters of this book portrayed various situations in which the current tort system fails to provide adequate or complete compensation for the more seriously injured victims of drinking-driver accidents. In this final section of chapter 15, the operation of the proposed compensation system will be demonstrated initially by considering once again the Bloom family's plight. This time, however, we will be looking at the compensation picture in a state that has chosen to supplement its range of currently available tort remedies with an alcohol-related accident victim compensation fund that was developed along the lines I have proposed.

Recall that the Bloom family — Alan, Molly, and their two children, Billy and Sally — were driving home from the beach when their car was struck by an automobile operated by a drinking driver named Tommy Smith. Alan was killed, and each of the surviving family members suffered serious physical injuries. Billy has a permanent learning disability as a result of head injuries that were suffered in the accident, while Sally continues to display signs of severe emotional distress that psychologists say is attributable to experiencing the accident, seeing the death of her father, and being trapped inside the wreckage for nearly half an hour.

The driver who struck the Bloom car, Tommy Smith, had been drinking for much of the afternoon before the accident. Blood tests revealed that the level of his blood alcohol concentration had been well above the state statutory standard for driving while intoxicated. Investigations by the Blooms' lawyer revealed that the driver had minimal assets from which any tort judgment could be satisfied. The car that Smith was driving was owned by his brother-in-law, Bill Green, who did have automobile liability insurance, but the policy limits were the minimum required by state law—$10,000 per person/$25,000 per accident. There was some possibility of the lawyer being able to establish that at the time of the accident Smith was acting within the scope of employment for the construction business that employed Green. That raised a fairly complicated legal question, the outcome of which was difficult to predict. Finally, the Blooms could pursue a tort claim against the bar at which Smith was drinking before the accident occurred and a claim against the social host at whose home he was drinking immediately prior to the collision, but these were novel claims for relief that had not previously been allowed in their state. Even if these claims were recognized, however, the Blooms would still face the burden of proving them. The Blooms would have to show that the bartender who served Smith should have known that he was intoxicated at the time of service, and that the social host acted negligently in serving alcohol to Smith. Establishing proof of these elements would be quite difficult, and the alcohol-dispenser defendants would undoubtedly vigorously defend themselves.

In many states, then, the Bloom family would thus find itself with a strong case for receiving a large judgment awarding them compensation from a party with no practical ability to pay them anything approaching the amount of damages to which they were legally entitled. As they expanded the search for greater compensation to include claims against more financially responsible parties, they would be likely to encounter increasing difficulty in establishing liability because these parties were not involved in the accident itself.

Now, consider what happens to the Bloom family in a state whose legislature has adopted a model victim compensation fund along the lines I have proposed. First note, however, that whatever rights or liabilities of the various actors in this drama existed before the compensation fund was established would continue to be in force under my model. Thus any criminal proceeding against the drinking driver would proceed just as it would have before. Similarly, the availability of any civil proceeding by the Blooms against the drinking driver or against other potential tort defendants would be just the same. What has changed is not the pieces of the legal remedy puzzle but rather the way they can be evaluated in light of the supplementary relief provided by the fund. Now when the Bloom family's lawyer looks at the legal landscape, the picture is nowhere near as bleak as it was before the establishment of the fund.

The first thing that the Bloom family lawyer will do is determine that this case satisfies the statutory prerequisites for making a claim for compensation from the fund. The first prerequisite is that the claimant's injury must have been received in an alcohol-related accident, defined as one in which the driver's alcohol impairment contributed to the occurrence of the accident. The second prerequisite is that the amount of the victims' uncompensated losses must be greater than the quantitative threshold set by the statute ($10,000 under the working model of my proposal).

In the case of the Bloom family's accident, the police investigation included a blood test of Tommy Smith, the driver who hit them. Smith's blood alcohol concentration was far above the legal level used to establish intoxication, and the test results were used to convict Smith of driving while intoxicated, among other criminal offenses. To meet the first claim prerequisite, the Blooms' lawyer can take advantage of the statutory provision that an official finding that the drinking driver was legally intoxicated establishes that the driver was alcohol-impaired and that his alcohol impairment contributed to the occurrence of the accident.

As for the second prerequisite, the surviving members of the Bloom family suffered pecuniary losses that are almost certainly high enough to cross the statutory threshold for uncompensated losses, even taking into account possible collateral source payments. The Blooms' lawyer will calculate the Blooms' uncompensated losses by first estimating the total value of the accident losses covered under the fund. These include the Blooms' medical expenses, their physical pain, and the economic loss to them as a result of the death of Alan Bloom. Because the definition of medical expenses should be broadly construed, the lawyer will include the expenses expected to be incurred for Billy's extensive rehabilitation and for the special education that he will need in the future. Sally's injuries included not just her physical injuries but also some psychological harm. While the compensation fund will not make any payment for emotional injury as such, the professional care that Sally needs for her psychological injury does constitute a medical expense for which compensation is available from the fund. The Blooms' physical pain will be reduced to a dollar value according to a grid schedule published by the fund administrator. The economic loss to Alan's surviving spouse and his two minor dependent children is determined by estimating the amount of money that Alan would have earned over his working life and calculating how much of that money would have been available for the support of Molly and for the support of the children while they would have remained dependent on Alan.

These various calculations will enable the lawyer to arrive at an estimate of the Bloom family's covered accident losses. From that figure, the lawyer will subtract the payments that have already been received from collateral sources. In this case, those include health insurance payments and proceeds from the life insurance policy on Alan's life that named Molly as the beneficiary. The lawyer will also subtract any payments received from the drinking driver or any other possible defendant. In this case, the lawyer has decided that the damages the Blooms might be awarded are so far in excess of the ability of the driver and the owner of the other car to pay them that tort litigation is not worth the time and the expense entailed. Because there will be no tort settlements or judgments to satisfy, there is nothing further to subtract from the estimated losses. Another alternative, however, is to try to settle the case with the insurance company that insured the car Smith was driving for the amount defined by the policy's limits, which in this case amounts to $25,000.

Confident that the uncompensated loss threshold has been crossed, the Blooms' lawyer next consults the fund's regulations regarding the claims process. She discovers that the fund has issued guidelines for the evidence that should be submitted to verify a claimant's eligibility and the amount of compensation that may be received. Following agency procedures, the lawyer prepares an application for compensation and files it with the fund. On a form that has been issued by the fund, and in supporting affidavits and attachments, she describes the losses that have been incurred up to the time of filing and the losses that are expected to occur in the future. She also indicates in the appropriate place on the application form that her clients request a hearing before a fund examiner if there should be any dispute as to the items for which compensation is being claimed.

The Bloom application for compensation is received by the fund and referred to a claims examiner. The examiner first verifies the Blooms' eligibility for compensation from the fund. From a review of the record of Smith's criminal conviction and the state trooper's accident report the examiner finds that the alcohol-related accident prerequisite has been satisfied. To determine whether the uncompensated loss threshold has been crossed, the examiner inspects the copies of the records of medical treatment and expenses, insurance documents, and affidavits from treating physicians and a rehabilitation therapist both about past treatment and what can be expected to be needed in the future. This review convinces the examiner that the

Blooms' uncompensated losses that are covered by the compensation fund exceed the $10,000 threshold.

Next, the examiner makes a recommendation about whether to proceed directly with the compensation fund claims payment process or instead to refer the Blooms to the tort system. In light of the serious injuries that were suffered by the Blooms, and considering the limited financial resources of the parties who might be held liable for those injuries, the examiner decides to continue with the payment process within the fund. However, the examiner does refer the application and its supporting documentation to a lawyer who is on the staff of the fund to consider whether the fund should proceed against any or all of those parties. The fund's legal staff decides to contact the insurance company that issued a liability insurance policy to Bill Green, the owner of the vehicle that Smith was driving. Because this is a straightforward case of liability and the policy limits are relatively small, the insurance company ultimately agrees to a settlement for the $25,000 amount of the policy's limits. That money is paid into the budget of the fund when it is received from the insurance company. The Blooms will have already been paid more than that amount from the fund.

Next the examiner takes a careful look at the Blooms' supporting documentation. Based on the evidence in hand, there is some question about the exact nature of Billy's disability, how much its treatment will cost, and how long Billy will require special education. The examiner contacts the Blooms' lawyer and requests that she schedule an appointment with a physician and a rehabilitation expert, both of whom have been selected by the fund. The cost of these examinations is paid directly by the fund to the consultants, and the results of the examinations are made available to the lawyer who represents the Blooms as soon as the reports reach the fund examiner.

With all the information in hand, the fund claims examiner calculates the amount of money to which the Blooms are entitled as a lump-sum payment for the uncompensated losses they have already suffered. The examiner also calculates the losses that they will incur in the future and sets up a payment schedule under which regular payments will be made to cover the expenses as they arise. The examiner then communicates the results to the Blooms' lawyer. The lawyer and Molly Bloom meet to discuss the terms of the award, and Molly agrees to its terms. The appropriate paperwork is completed and signed by the relevant parties, and Molly receives a check for the past losses. At regular intervals she will receive checks to cover the ongoing expenses resulting from the accident. She will also receive a simple form each year to complete and return to the fund that verifies the continuation of the conditions that entitle her and the children to the continuing payments.

At the end of the claims process, the Blooms' lawyer also receives a check from the fund. The check represents the lawyer's fees and the expenses that the lawyer incurred in putting together the information that was used to support the Blooms' claim. The size of the fee is determined by a fee schedule that was contained in a regulation issued by the fund administrator. The fee is directly related to the complexity of the case and the amount of work the lawyer performed rather than simply being a percentage of the total compensation to which the claimants are entitled.

If the award that was initially recommended by the fund examiner had been unsatisfactory to Molly Bloom, her lawyer could have requested a hearing before the examiner to discuss the recommendation. If that hearing failed to produce a satisfactory result, then the lawyer could have appealed the examiner's decision to an appeals board located within the fund. The appeals board is authorized to affirm or to modify the examiner's determination. No judicial review would be allowed of the decision that was reached by the appeals board.

Given the medical and life insurance coverage of the Bloom family at the time of the accident, the initial check that Molly received as a lump-sum payment for past losses was not very large. The greatest satisfaction that Molly has received from the compensation fund process is, without a doubt, the confidence that she will not have to face without assistance the long and expensive efforts to take care of her children and return them to the good health they enjoyed before the accident with a drinking driver devastated their lives.

## The Small Claim and the Fund

The alcohol-related accident victim compensation fund is designed to come into play with the more serious drinking-driver traffic accidents. If the victim's uncompensated losses are under $10,000, then no compensation is available from the fund. The following hypothetical will illustrate a claim that does not meet the threshold requirement.

Suppose that a drinking driver collides with a vehicle driven by Jim. Jim is the only occupant of that vehicle, and he receives some physical injuries in the accident. Jim is taken to the hospital emergency room for treatment and is also admitted overnight for observation. He also is advised by the treating physician to stay home from work for three days following his discharge from the hospital.

Jim's hospital expenses are covered by the Blue Cross policy that he receives as part of his employee benefit package. He also receives full pay for the three days of work that he missed, although that amount of time is deducted from the total leave time that he has accrued. There are no other long-term effects of Jim's injuries, and he returns to work on the fourth day after the accident.

Based on these facts, Jim is not entitled to compensation from the fund. His covered losses were well compensated by his collateral sources, so that he was left either with no uncompensated losses at all or only with uncompensated losses well under $10,000. He thus has not crossed the threshold for entry into the compensation fund system.

It should be noted, however, that if the tort law of Jim's state retains the collateral source rule, he may sue the other driver and recover damages compensating him for elements of harm that have already been paid from collateral sources. That tort suit may also entitle Jim to recover damages for nonpecuniary losses not covered by the fund. If the cost of obtaining the tort remedy is not too high in relation to the potential benefit, then Jim will probably pursue the tort claim, at least to the extent of attempting to get a settlement from the drinking driver's liability insurer. The victim compensation fund is only meant to offer additional relief to the most seriously injured and undercompensated victims of drinking drivers. It does not deprive the less seriously injured victims of any of their preexisting legal rights, nor does it in any way relieve the drinking driver of having to face existing legal responsibilities and sanctions.

### The Accident with Two Intoxicated Drivers

The Bloom family hypothetical was a classic case of a drinking-driver traffic accident with innocent victims. Suppose, however, that an accident involves two drivers who were both alcohol-impaired. In this situation, the terms of the proposed victim compensation fund clearly exclude these drinking drivers from eligibility for compensation. As a result of the exclusion, neither drinking driver could make a claim for the losses suffered in the accident, nor could someone else assert a claim derived from the injuries to the drinking drivers.

If one of the drivers had been killed in the accident, the model legislation I propose for the fund would preclude any claim for compensation by the driver's surviving spouse or children, assuming that they were not themselves injured in the accident. Nevertheless, a legislature might choose, for other policy reasons, to allow a claim for the economic loss to those survivors. As with all other uncompensated losses covered by the fund, the total economic loss in this case minus any life insurance payments to the survivors would have to exceed the $10,000 threshold for eligibility.

### An Accident with No Tort Liability

Harry and Jack are drivers whose cars collide on the highway. Each suffers some physical injuries and damage to his vehicle. The police officer who arrives at the scene of the accident suspects that Harry has been drinking and asks Harry to take a test to determine his blood alcohol concentration. Harry agrees to take the test and registers a BAC level of .07. Under state statute, that level is not high enough to constitute a per se offense, and the officer is not persuaded that she has enough evidence to make a strong case against Harry for driving while under the influence of alcohol. Nevertheless, the test results are noted on an accident report form, as well as the officer's belief that Harry's consumption of alcohol impaired his ability to operate his vehicle and contributed to the occurrence of the accident.

Jack consults a lawyer after the accident. Following a review of Jack's story about what happened and the police officer's accident report, the lawyer advises Jack that he would probably lose a tort claim against Harry. It appears that Jack pulled into an intersection in front of Harry's oncoming car. Although it is fairly easy to establish that Harry was driving negligently, Jack's own operation of his vehicle would probably be considered negligent. In a state with a comparative negligence law that prevents any recovery by a plaintiff whose own negligence is as great as that of the defendant, the prospects of Jack recovering damages from Harry are slim.

The lawyer further advises Jack that he may be eligible to file a claim with the alcohol-related accident victim compensation fund. Given the police officer's report, this accident is presumptively an alcohol-related accident covered by the fund. The focus of the lawyer's investigation then turns to the amount of Jack's uncompensated losses that fall into the four categories of harm covered by the fund.

If Jack's injuries were serious and Jack had few resources with which to pay the costs of his losses, then he might cross the $10,000 uncompensated loss threshold. In that case, Jack would be eligible to collect a payment from the fund for his covered uncompensated losses that exceed $10,000. If the accident was less serious and Jack had other sources besides the fund from which the accident losses could be covered, he would fail to cross the threshold and thus be ineligible for compensation. In either case, however, eligibility depends on Jack's ability to meet the fund's requirements, not on his ability to prove Harry's tort liability.

# 16

## Victim Compensation Funds and the Role of Tort Law

Alcoholic beverages and drinking and driving are similar to other dangerous products and risky activities in their capacity to contribute to the production of injuries to other persons besides immediate consumers or actors. As we have seen, not even the expanded reach of modern products liability theory has been able to accomplish the goal of fully compensating the victims of drinking-driver traffic accidents. The existing network of tort remedies needs to be supplemented with an alcohol-related accident victim compensation fund financed by a new tax on alcoholic beverages. The question that might naturally follow is whether this reform idea can be applied to other types of injury frequently encountered in today's technologically sophisticated and crowded society. The thrust of this inquiry is to determine where else in the universe of decisions about accident cost allocation might we expect a compensation fund supported by a tax on a product or activity to work reasonably well.

The second question that this reform proposal raises has to do with the role of tort litigation as an injury compensation vehicle. Contemporary tort law actually does accomplish in a meaningful way a number of important goals that may go unnoticed in an analysis almost exclusively focused on the system's failure to achieve certain ends. In a real sense, then, these concluding observations complement the earlier discussions of the policy choices behind the proposal for an alcohol-related accident victim compensation fund. Reassessing the value of the present tort system underlines the importance of treating the benefits to be obtained from the fund as a supplement to, rather than as a complete replacement of, the current system of tort remedies available to the accident victims of drinking drivers.

### The Compensation Fund Alternative: Prospects and Limitations

The first task in considering how widely the compensation fund idea might be applied is to identify the features of the drinking-driver traffic-accident problem that make the fund both necessary and feasible. Having done that, one can then see to what extent those same features show up in other contexts involving dangerous products and risky activities. The first feature to note is the existence of an industry that is both lawful and profitable, the alcohol industry, upon which the costs of the new system may be imposed. Such is not the case, for example, with drug-related traffic accidents. Drivers may be just as impaired after using controlled substances such as marijuana or cocaine as they are after drinking bourbon or beer. The distributors of Michelob and Jim Beam, however, can be forced to internalize accident costs in ways that the members of the Medellin drug cartel cannot. However, in the unlikely and equally unwise event that drugs should be legalized and then taxed as alcoholic beverages are now taxed, then some portion of the revenues from the excise tax that would be levied on the newly legal drugs clearly ought to go toward alleviating the victim compensation problem.

Second, numerous compensation options are typically available to the victims of drinking-driver traffic accidents under existing tort law rules and insurance mechanisms. Thus the victim compensation fund need not be treated as the first option for a recovery of accident losses. In this respect, the compensation fund can be distinguished from such social welfare programs as Aid to Families with Dependent Children or the federal food stamp program, in which the funds that are distributed to eligible recipients are frequently the critical factor in assuring the survival of the recipients. The compensation fund can be distinguished on this basis as well from compensation programs that address a need that is largely unfilled by other parts of the legal or social service systems, such as programs to compensate crime victims. As a result, the compensation fund enjoys the comparative luxury of dealing only with the most seriously injured victims who have slipped through the gaps in the current system's coverage, as opposed to acting as the first line of compensation in the routine injury case.

Third, the drinking-driver traffic-accident problem has received attention from the public at large, from public officials, and from scholars and researchers in a variety of disciplines. There is a growing sense in this country that there is no good excuse for drinking and driving, regardless of the acceptability of drinking in general. This convergence of attention offers public policymakers a chance to take advantage of a potentially united front on this particular social cost of alcohol. The contrast with the cigarette industry is striking with respect to this factor. The public policy debate about the social cost of smoking runs headlong into deeply entrenched opinions both for and against the basic practice itself. That sort of conflict, which is muted or nonexistent in the drinking-driver context, makes it difficult to focus on a careful identification of the basic costs of smoking, let alone to sustain any realistic prospect of developing a consensus for a particular reform effort.

Fourth, drinking-driver traffic accidents often feature completely innocent victims. Drinking drivers inflict tremendous losses on victims who were doing little or nothing to expose themselves to such a risk of devastation. Those injured parties who contributed nothing to their losses other than being within the range of the destructive capacity of a drinking driver present an attractive target for public policy-making. As the preceding chapters have shown, a reform program in the drinking-driver accident context can be structured so that it reaches the more seriously injured victims of drinking drivers while excluding drinking drivers who are injured themselves from eligibility.

The tobacco analogy again reveals a marked difference. The primary adverse health effects of smoking are on the smoker. Thus a program that attempted to redistribute the social costs of smoking in a way that also excluded smokers from obtaining the program's benefits would probably be substantially less beneficial than a similar program in the drinking-driver context. As passive or secondary smoking harm becomes better documented, however, the number of identifiably innocent victims of smoking may very well increase to the point that victims of smoking are analogous to the victims of drinking-driver traffic accidents.[1] In that event, taxing the distribution of tobacco products might come to be seen as an appropriate way to finance a victim compensation fund.

The alcohol-related accident victim compensation fund proposed here could also be applied to other types of alcohol-related injuries beyond the context of drinking-driver traffic accidents. Perhaps the closest analogous instance is the drinking-boater accident. The level of harm that can be attributed to the alcohol-impaired operation of recreational watercraft is being increasingly well documented each year.[2] The legal system's response to alcohol-related boating accidents stands in striking contrast to its general approach to drinking-driver traffic accidents: the states and the federal government have only recently been willing to give serious consideration to legislation that prohibits operating a boat while under the influence of alcohol.[3] There is no reason in principle why the alcohol-related accident victim compensation fund proposed here could not be expanded to cover victims of alcohol-related boating accidents.

The circumstances under which the two types of accidents occur are similar enough that the details of the compensation fund system can fairly easily be applied to boating accident victims. In fact, what is perhaps the major difference between the two types of accidents argues in favor of covering alcohol-related boating accidents. Unlike the case with drinking-driver traffic accidents, it is unlikely that the circumstances of the typical boating case would support commercial dispenser liability in its traditional statutory or common law versions. The extent to which victims of alcohol-related boating accidents are able to shift their accident losses to parties other than the drinker may thus be significantly lower than is the case in drinking-driver traffic accidents.

That inability to shift these accident losses to commercial dispensers may be offset by an increased likelihood that the drinking boater has assets that will cover at least some of those losses. Unlike automobiles, which are ubiquitous and distributed across almost all income levels within society, it may be the case that recreational watercraft are typically owned by persons better able to satisfy a tort judgment than the typical traffic accident tort defendant. That phenomenon is also likely to be true in the case of a third category of alcohol-related accidents, those that involve the impaired operation of an airplane.[4]

One general feature of my compensation fund proposal that may offer an increasingly attractive course of action for policymakers is the way it links accident costs and a special tax to pay for those costs. This idea is, of course, not unique to this proposal. That kind of activity-based social-cost-bearing provision is at the heart of the federal environmental superfund legislation,[5] for example, under which the manufacturers of chemicals and other toxic materials are assessed a fee based on their production levels[6] that is used to finance a fund for cleaning up toxic waste sites.

The identification of particular portions of social costs of activities or products and the subsequent attempt to reduce the problems associated with those costs by forcing a greater measure of cost internalization may have some feasibility in other settings. The tobacco industry again serves as a possible candidate for further exploration of the applicability of this general idea. To the extent that policymakers are satisfied about the relationship between smoking and certain health problems, a tax could be assessed on tobacco products to finance both research efforts on those problems and the operation of treatment programs and facilities for those who suffer from those problems. Indeed, the use of such an excise tax to finance some public health efforts surfaces periodically in official and unofficial proposals. Caution needs to be expressed, however, regarding proposals of this sort at a time when both federal and state governments are trying to manage a budget deficit crisis while avoiding income tax increases. Instead of financing new efforts to alleviate the social costs of an activity, these excise taxes or "user fees" could end up being nothing more than a way to fund existing governmental activities.

A health problem that is just starting to receive widespread attention is the risk associated with electromagnetic radiation from power stations and power lines.[7] Tort litigation against power companies will undoubtedly increase in the coming decade as the link between certain types of harm and exposure to this kind of radiation is strengthened.[8] If this problem should prove to involve massive potential injury and low levels of culpability, it may be better to begin now to construct a loss allocation mechanism that adequately compensates radiation victims in a way that imposes the costs of those injuries on electric power consumers, who are the ultimate beneficiaries of the power industry's practices.

The main thrust of the proposed alcohol-related accident victim compensation fund is to compensate victims more fully by associating the costs of drinking-driver traffic accidents more closely with the alcohol industry. One criticism that might be made about this strategy is that it misses the most obvious target, at least after the drinking driver is ruled out for having insufficient assets. Rather than focusing on the alcohol involvement in the drinking-driver accident, the critic might assert, an activity-linked compensation system might better associate these accident costs with the activity of driving.

This extension of the compensation fund proposal undoubtedly has a good deal of merit. In the first place, even the basic term "drinking and driving" suggests that the connection between drinking-driver accidents and *driving* is at least as obvious as the connection between drinking-driver accidents and *drinking*. Furthermore, it is possible to modify the victim compensation fund proposal to select driving as the more appropriate accident cost-bearing activity. The tax used to finance the fund could be imposed on fuel or on motor vehicles rather than on alcoholic beverages. Finally, a tax on fuel or on motor vehicles lends itself more readily to a federal compensation scheme than a tax on alcohol. Considering these factors, then, it might appear that the loss allocation effort of the fund that has been proposed here is misdirected and should be shifted from alcohol to a product that is more closely associated with driving in general.

In the sixteenth chapter of a book that proposes the adoption of a victim compensation fund that is financed by a tax on alcoholic beverages, the reader ought not to expect an abandonment of the basic idea that dominated the fifteen preceding chapters! Nevertheless, the potential criticism is legitimate enough to necessitate some explanation of why a different choice of accident loss allocation was made.

The most significant reason for linking the victim compensation fund to drinking rather than driving is that a great deal of accident costs related to driving in general are already imposed on the people who drive and purchase vehicles. First, automobile insurance currently allocates some drinking-driver traffic-accident losses to policyholders who are not drinkers or who do not drink and drive. Automobile insurance rates vary according to broadly drawn categories, which are based on such items as daily commuting mileage and total annual mileage. These insurance rates rise to reflect increases in these usage categories. Thus the price structure of automobile insurance is roughly parallel to the distribution of the burden of a fuel tax.

Second, automobiles are among the most frequent objects of products liability litigation. A decision to impose liability on a vehicle manufacturer or distributor for a design defect, for example, acts in a way that allocates accident losses to all the purchasers of the category of vehicles to whom the liability costs will be passed on. Not all of these people are in fact involved in such accidents. As a result, the current system of products liability law as it is applied to automobile manufacturers and distributors already involves a good deal of externalization of traffic accident costs to the broader population of vehicle purchasers.

In the final analysis, then, the decision to use the fund to link loss allocation to drinking rather than driving can be defended in two ways. First, the accident costs associated with driving in general are already externalized as they are shifted from drivers (including drinking drivers) involved in accidents to automobile insurance policyholders in general and to vehicle purchasers in general. Second, while the victim compensation system I propose builds on the general principles that underlie much of our current system of accident cost allocation, it seeks to strike out in a new direction in applying them. The hope that underlies this effort is that the combination of a supplemental compensation scheme for the most seriously injured victims of drinking-driver accidents and a tax on alcohol to finance that scheme can produce significant social benefits, even if it admittedly operates only at the margins of the drinking-driver problem.

## The Continuing Need for Tort Liability

In 1960, on a school safety patrol trip to Washington, I was taken to my first major league baseball game, played between the New York Yankees and the Washington Senators. I have since come to recognize as one of the more convincing pieces of evidence for the existence of a benevolent deity the fact that I came away from that game as a Senators fan rather than a Yankees fan. Being a fan was even then obviously the only baseball role I would ever fill. At the age of eleven, I was already a year or two beyond the time when the ability of more than ninety-five percent of those whose task it was to get a ball safely by my bat had exceeded by far my ability to bring bat into contact with ball. The next year, the Senators moved to Minneapolis and were renamed the Twins, and they took my long-distance allegiance along with them.

Being a Minnesota Twins fan has occupied many of my adolescences, but none so happily (at least so far) as during their winning of the World Series in 1987. In that championship year, one of the people who made a real contribution to the team was a reserve infielder named Al Newman. Newman appeared in 110 games that year, playing at three infield positions and in the outfield. He hit .221, with fifteen doubles and five triples, and he had fifteen stolen bases. During the World Series itself, he appeared in four games, playing second base, pinch hitting, and pinch running. He got one hit in five plate appearances, a single in the fourth game, which the Twins lost by five runs.

If I were picking a dream team, I would pick players who hit for a better average than an Al Newman, and hit for more power, and had more stolen bases, and were more dazzling fielders at second base, shortstop, third base, and the outfield. But if I were going into a season in which my team was a possible contender for a division title, I would want an Al Newman on my twenty-five-man roster, because I would know that I could count on him to be a steady performer who contributed in lots of ways, on and off the field. When injuries or fatigue led me to replace one of my starters, I could put Newman into the lineup without fear that my team would be badly hurt by the substitution. Other people hit better than Al Newman in 1987, fielded better than Al Newman in 1987, and stole more bases than Al Newman in 1987. Al Newman has a World Series championship ring from 1987.

The reader might very well ask what Al Newman has got to do with the continuing need for tort liability. Anyone proposing a reform proposal such as the one presented in this book must respond to some of the observations that recent critics of tort law have made.[9] The latest global attack, and one of the more formidable, on contemporary tort law and on alternatives of limited scope, such as the victim compensation fund scheme I propose, is contained in a recent book by Berkeley law professor Stephen D. Sugarman.[10] What Professor Sugarman wants is a substantially restructured society in which the burden of the unequal distribution of life's misfortunes is alleviated. Tort law comes under attack in large measure because it fails to accomplish that goal. It seems to me that at least some of this sort of criticism of the tort law system for what it fails to do is similar to what could be said about Al Newman as a hitter, fielder, and base runner: other people clearly do each of those things better.

Among the criticisms that have been leveled at the tort system are charges such as the following: the prospect of tort liability for injuries that are caused to other people does not eliminate all careless conduct; nor does tort liability fully compensate all those who are injured by the wrongful conduct of other people; nor is tort liability good for manufacturers of products, who are deterred from putting new designs on the market; and the tort litigation system is an imperfect mechanism for fact-finding and for applying legal rules. All of those observations are to some extent accurate, but they are remarkably similar to the observations about Al Newman and the Minnesota Twins in their championship year. Tort law, like Al Newman, needs to be looked at in a way that acknowledges what contribution is actually being made.

The appropriate reference point for an evaluation of tort law is not a world in which there were no accidents or negligent conduct, any more than the appropriate reference for an evaluation of the 1987 Twins or any team member is a team consisting of the best of the American League and National League All-Stars. The legitimate comparison is between a world with tort law as opposed to a world without tort law. The question then becomes whether tort law has any success in accomplishing the various goals within its reach. Accordingly, the right question to ask in assessing injury compensation and injury deterrence is whether we are better off with a legal system that holds people accountable for the injuries they cause when they behave in a tortious manner than we are with a system that does not hold them liable in that way.

Unfortunately, it is virtually impossible to answer this question in any quantitatively satisfactory manner. We don't know what the Minnesota Twins would have done with a different utility infielder in

1987. We also simply do not know what the world would be like today without tort law. The answer depends on how many injuries do *not* occur as a result of our current tort liability rules and the net social gain or loss that would occur if we did *not* shift accident losses from victims as they are shifted now. Instead of comparing the current legal regime to one under which all injuries are avoided, we need to ask ourselves realistically whether we would be better off if people were not held accountable for their conduct the way they are now.

The proper comparison is thus with a world in which we derive none of the benefits of contemporary tort law, not one in which all of the many roles that tort law fills imperfectly were accomplished with absolute precision and perfection. Before acceding too readily to a proposal for "doing away with tort law," we need to be a lot more confident that we can live without the contributions that tort law makes, imperfect and incomplete as it is, to the level of safety and stability that we enjoy in this society.

## NOTES

1. *See, e.g.,* Altman, *The Evidence Mounts on Passive Smoking,* New York Times, May 29, 1990, at C1.

2. *See, e.g.,* Cavanaugh, *Drinking and Boating: A Deadly Combination,* New York Times, June 14, 1987, § 11CN, at 6.

3. *See, e.g., Crackdown on Drunken Boaters,* 107 U.S. NEWS & WORLD REP., July 24, 1989, at 67.

4. *See* Wolk, *Flying While Intoxicated,* BUS. & COMM. AVIATION, August 1986, at 82.

5. The "superfund" legislation is the Comprehensive Environmental Response, Compensation and Liability Act of 1980, 42 U.S.C. §§ 9601-9675.

6. The lists of taxable chemicals and other substances and the tax rates are found in the Internal Revenue Code, 26 U.S.C. § 4661, 4671.

7. *See* P. BRODEUR, CURRENTS OF DEATH: POWER LINES, COMPUTER TERMINALS, AND THE ATTEMPT TO COVER UP THEIR THREAT TO YOUR HEALTH (1990).

8. *See* DeBoskey, *Non-Ionizing Radiation: Hidden Hazards,* TRIAL, August 1990, at 32.

9. *See, e.g.,* P. HUBER, LIABILITY: THE LEGAL REVOLUTION AND ITS CONSEQUENCES (1988).

10. SUGARMAN, DOING AWAY WITH PERSONAL INJURY LAW.

# Index

# Note on the Author

PAUL A. LEBEL is the James Goold Cutler Professor of Law at the College of William and Mary. He received his J.D. with highest honors from the University of Florida in 1977 and began his teaching career at the School of Law of the University of Alabama. He is a member of the Florida Bar and the Virginia State Bar and has written numerous scholarly articles for a wide range of law journals. LeBel's major fields of interest are tort law, constitutional law, products liability jurisprudence, and law and literature.